WANE

D0106074

Maura Murphy was born in Clonmore, County Offaly in 1928. She left Ballybryan National School when she was 14 with 'no qualifications and even fewer prospects'. She worked as a domestic servant in various houses in Dublin until she met and married John Murphy, a soldier stationed at Portobello Barracks. The couple moved to Birmingham, England in 1959 where they reared nine children. They have eleven grandchildren and one great-grandchild.

Maura now lives in Birmingham in the West Midlands.

'A lovely memoir of a roving life, full of dread and great affection'
Kirkus Reviews

'Murphy's skilful storytelling and optimistic spirit give even the grimmest moments of her difficult life story levity' *Publishers Weekly*

'Fearlessly honest . . . her voice is that of a forgotten generation'
Woman's Way

DON'T WAKE ME AT DOYLES

The remarkable memoir of an ordinary Irish woman and her extraordinary life

MAURA MURPHY

headline

Copyright © 2004 Maura Murphy and Macalla Ltd

The right of Maura Murphy to be identified as the Author of
the Work has been asserted by her in accordance with the
Copyright, Designs and Patents Act 1988.

First published in 2004
by HEADLINE BOOK PUBLISHING

First published in paperback in 2005
by HEADLINE BOOK PUBLISHING

5

Apart from any use permitted under UK copyright law, this publication
may only be reproduced, stored, or transmitted, in any form, or by any
means, with prior permission in writing of the publishers or, in the case of
reprographic production, in accordance with the terms of licences issued by
the Copyright Licensing Agency.

Every effort has been made to fulfil requirements with regard to
reproducing copyright material. The author and publisher will be glad
to rectify any omissions at the earliest opportunity.

Cataloguing in Publication Data is available from the British Library

ISBN 0 7553 1305 4

Typeset in Sabon MT by Palimpsest Book Production Limited,
Polmont, Stirlingshire

Printed and bound in Great Britain by
Clays Ltd, St Ives plc

Headline's policy is to use papers that are natural, renewable and
recyclable products and made from wood grown in sustainable forests.
The logging and manufacturing processes are expected to conform to
the environmental regulations of the country of origin.

HEADLINE BOOK PUBLISHING
A division of Hodder Headline
338 Euston Road
London NW1 3BH

www.headline.co.uk
www.hodderheadline.com

To Mammy and Father

Contents

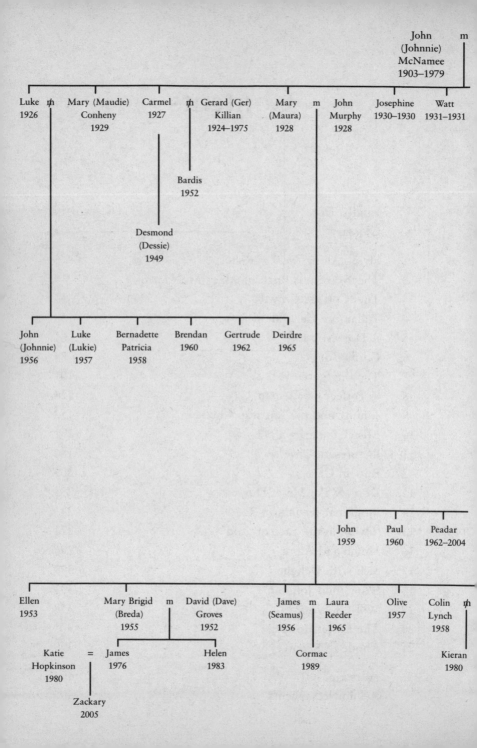

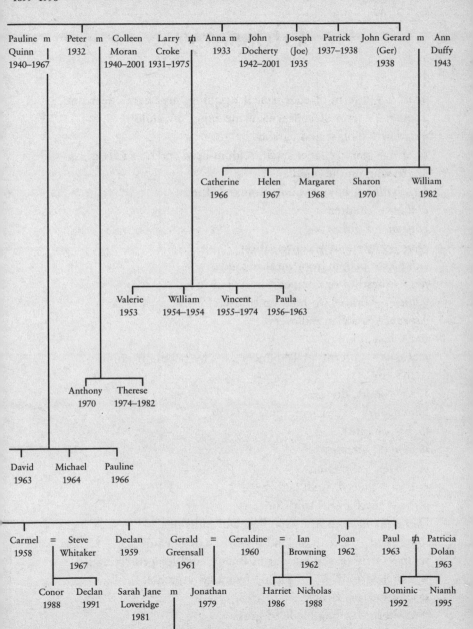

Glossary

acushla – a term of endearment meaning 'my heart's dear one'

alanna – a term of endearment meaning 'my child'

amadán – fool, stupid person

boreen – country lane; small, seldom-used road, usually grass growing up the middle

buachaill – a boy; a young, unmarried man

childer – children

colleen – a girl

craic – entertaining conversation

culchies – people from rural Ireland

feis – a festival or competition of music

galluses – braces (to hold up trousers)

ganseys – woollen pullovers

grá – love; liking

jackeens – a term for Dubliners used by people from outside the city

keeb – short, dry grass

launawaula – sufficient, quite enough

lock – quantity

mairn – a stream

messages – shopping

musha – indeed; well; is that so?

puca – mischievous spirit or fairy

Slán agus Beannacht – Goodbye and Blessings

slang field – a strip of land by a river or stream

scraw – strip of sod cut out of boggy land for protecting a thatched roof; or for pitting fruit and vegetables

stocious – very drunk

thrawneen – strong blade of grass

yoke – indescribable person

ONE

Flying Along the Tar Road

There is something elegant about a line of washing blowing in the wind. It looks so pure and fresh and reminds me of how, as a child, I would stand at the top of Wakley's Hill and see our neighbours' beautiful white linen flapping spectacularly in the distance. Mammy would have loved a line but she had to throw her washing on the hedge to dry, like the gypsies.

Tuesday 15 June 1999 was a good day to do a wash. It was bright and sunny – not too hot – with a cool gentle breeze. I was delighted: by evening, I'd got two loads done. It had turned into a beautiful evening. The crows were taking their last flight home and a settling calm was descending in Rhode. John was inside, preparing for bed, and I was in the garden bringing in the last of the washing, dry and crisp and smelling of summer.

That's when I felt the unfamiliar wheeze below my left collar-bone. I started to cough and, very quickly, my mouth filled up with vile spit. It smelled like detergent and tasted of metal. I felt nauseous. It was overwhelming. I didn't want to swallow, and I couldn't spit it out. I wasn't brought up to spit on the ground. Mammy would have been very cross to see me do that. I held the stinking liquid in my mouth until I got inside. Throwing the clothes down on the kitchen table, I reached for a tissue. My heart was pumping and my head began to pound.

What the hell is this? I thought, seeing the thick clot of blood before me. I panicked, and shouted, 'John!'

I had been happy that morning pegging out John's shirts and listening to the cars racing past the cottage. It seemed that everyone had only minutes to live. Up in the clouds, birds of all kinds were swooping to and fro and, above them, a plane was flying over in the direction of Galway.

I stopped for a moment, as I always do, and glanced up. The sound of a plane has held a fascination for me ever since I was a child during the war: I had been disturbed by the news that a stray German bomb was dropped – apparently by accident – on Dublin, wiping out some of my father's relations. Now when I hear a plane I have to watch it until it disappears over the horizon, safely out of sight.

John, my husband for forty-six years, was in the garden with me that day, sleeves rolled up, cap on head, clipping the conifers. It was usual for the pair of us to finish our morning chores before sitting down to read the daily papers. He liked to scan the *Irish Independent*; I preferred the *Daily Mail*. Reading an English newspaper was my way of keeping in touch with the children. We had lived and worked in England for thirty years, rearing and educating our nine children there, before retiring to Offaly – the county where I was born, and where we had set out on our married life in 1953. It wasn't where we thought we'd end up in old age but we had settled into a comfortable routine, discussing the affairs of the day, eating breakfast and sitting back to do our crosswords. We might even stroll to the village to buy something fresh for lunch.

Rhode is a small village, surrounded by bog land and turf fires, with little more than a church, three pubs, a funeral parlour and a police station. For a big shop, to settle bills or pay into our credit union accounts, we would take the car to Edenderry, our nearest town.

After securing John's shirts on the line, and clearing away the breakfast dishes, I decided it was a perfect day to drive to Edenderry. The six-mile journey was a normal, twice-weekly activity but today it seemed like more of an effort: I was feeling tired. It was an unusual, heavy tiredness that I hadn't experienced before.

As I got into the car, John remarked that I looked pale and asked did I want him to come with me. 'No, I'm fine,' I said, and drove off, calling back to him that I wouldn't be long and to have the kettle on when I came home: I'd bring back something nice for our afternoon tea.

'Oh, and don't forget the pop,' he shouted after me. He had a *grá* for fizzy pop, especially following a date with 'the blonde in the black skirt' in Doyles pub.

The town was choked with traffic, as usual, but I managed to squeeze myself into a space outside the credit union. Edenderry is one, long, narrow road with shops on both sides and The Square at the top. Viewed from above, it looks spookily like an axe.

I've never liked Edenderry but it has always been a central part of my life. Years ago, it had a bakery owned by a family of Quakers. Williams's Bakery specialised in a flat-bottomed loaf with a brown-crusted top that looked like a hat. When I was a child, I would get a whiff of the baking bread wafting out of the ovens as I passed by. The smell would put the hunger in me, especially as I never had the price of a loaf. We were so poor, Mammy often sent me over to the Mulvins of Clonmore to beg a bit of food. Old Mrs Mulvin was a rich farmer's wife and was happy to slip us the scraps off her table.

I always had to walk, barefoot, into Edenderry to pay some bill or other for Mammy. To avoid the gravel roads, I would go through the fields, cross over the *mairn*, into the *slang field*, up over the high bog and on to the tar road by the graveyard. Then it was easy to fly along the smooth tar in my bare feet.

I'd get the odd penny for going and spend it on apples from Edgil's, 'The Bad Bugger'. I never knew why he went by that name but that's what we all called him. No one ever saw him: he was a wealthy Protestant farmer who lived quietly on a large estate behind a big stone wall. An angry red bull stood guard over the apples in his orchard. The Bad Bugger was very well known and his apples were legendary. He would pick his apples in the autumn and pit them – throw them into a deep pit in the ground – and cover them with straw and large sods of turf. This would ripen and preserve them so we had apples all year round. You could always get apples at Edgil's. They were delicious.

Some of my pennies would go on sweets, mainly bullseyes, aniseed balls or sugar sticks, but I never had enough to buy chocolate. If I didn't spend the money on sweets or apples, I preferred to save it up for a packet of marbles or a vanilla wafer from Nolan's ice-cream shop. It would take months for me to save up enough money to buy the wafer but it was always worth it: Nolan's sold the best ice-cream in the town.

The Nolan girls would often be serving behind the counter. They were great Irish step dancers and I often bumped into them at the *feis*, where their father would be selling his wares from a steel coolbox on the front of his famous ice-cream bike.

I ran errands more than anyone in my family: I was so fond of the pennies. I was that mean, I'd walk half a mile for a farthing and further for a ha'penny. I was never afraid of the twelve-mile round trip. There weren't many cars around in those days but plenty of bikes, asses and carts. The townspeople would never speak to you, no more than the Dublin people. But if I bumped into someone I knew from the country, they would shout, 'Morra, Maura!' I liked that.

Father hardly ever went into town. He would have gone in more if he'd had a bank account but poor people didn't have bank accounts in those days: they had nothing to put in them. Father did try to open an account once, in the Bank of Ireland, but he was forbidden: he wasn't a big-noise farmer with money. The arrival of the credit union was a godsend to the working classes.

Twice a year, Father sold a pig or a calf at the Fair Day in The Square. If he got a fair price, he would go into McNally's butchers and return home with the rare treat of a steak for our dinner. I would be waiting, fork at the ready, with my six brothers and sisters at the kitchen table. Mammy would hop the steak on to the pan and then into our drooling mouths.

The Square was, and still is, at the heart of life in Edenderry. Fair Day years ago was held for those rich farmers with their fat bank accounts to sell cattle, pigs, sheep and fowl. The poor usually went in to buy cheap, second-hand clothes from the stalls set up by the Dublin traders.

Fair Day still happens on the first Tuesday of every month but now it's called Market Day and there isn't an animal in sight. You wouldn't get into Edenderry on Market Day but it's a busy town any day of the week.

The Tuesday I went in, for my *messages* and John's pop, it was so busy it took me twenty minutes to park the car. My first stop was the post office to put on my lottery – the most important task of the week. I trudged up the hill to the credit union to pay in a cheque, then walked across the main road to the supermarket and parted with a pound coin to release a trolley. There, I bumped into my sister-in-law, Ann, who was after coming back from an appointment in Mullingar.

'Maura, you look very pale. Are you all right?' she asked, suggesting I go home straightaway and get a rest. I acknowledged her concern but put it out of my head because I had shopping to do.

I picked up what I needed, not forgetting the pop and an apple pie to go with the cup of tea, hauled the trolley over to my car

and packed my *messages* into the boot. I abandoned the trolley:
I thought feck the pound, and headed back home.

Halfway there, I started to feel hot and shivery. Ann's words
were ringing in my ears. I was having trouble focusing and
decided to pull in off the road, right outside Edgil's of all places.

I waited for the queer feeling to pass. There were cars flying
by me but no one stopped to see what was wrong. Normally, in
that part of Ireland, you could expect somebody to stop. Not
that day.

My heart was thumping but I made to move off again. I was
glad to be home: by the time I pulled into the drive, I was feeling
quite sick. John had the kettle hopping on the range and we had
our tea and apple pie. I thought a bit of food might help, and
nothing was going to stand in the way of me and my pie – not
a bit of sickness, anyway.

I brought in the dry clothes and went down for my afternoon
snooze. I had a rest most days but this one seemed more important. I knew I was suffering from more than afternoon fatigue.
I thought I was going to faint. I put it all down to the heat, took
painkillers and fell, exhausted, into bed.

I woke two hours later, refreshed, and put on another wash.
I couldn't waste a good drying day and I still had all the bed
linen to do. John was preparing the dinner – bacon and cabbage
– as he did every day. I didn't always feel like a dinner but, once
it was cooked and put out on a plate in front of me, I would
eat it.

The next hour was spent folding clothes and placing them into
the hot press. The evening wore on in its usual fashion. I pottered
around doing my bits and bobs, waiting for the RTE news at
nine o'clock. John and I always watched the news together,
providing he was in a talking mood. If he wasn't, he would go
to his bed straight after dinner and I would write up my diary.

We had our own bedrooms in the cottage. We'd slept sepa-
rately since 1989. I didn't want to share his bed any more after

what he did to me. My bedroom was just off the hallway, next to the bathroom, and John's was on the other side of the living room, in the old part of the cottage. We joked that I was in the East Wing and he was in the West!

Most nights, I would sit in my chair by the fire, shouting at the television and airing my strong views. John would sit on the couch, doing the same. It was our usual practice to comment and interject along with the politicians and commentators. We were particularly interested in the Peace Process.

'I wonder what Seamus has got to say,' I would mumble. We admired Seamus Mallon: we thought he was an honest person.

'Yeh, he has it right,' John would say. 'He's about the best of them.'

My interest in Irish politics was formed very early; both my parents were staunch Republicans who were actively involved in the 1916–21 War of Independence. When we were children, we would listen to Father singing rebel songs after his supper, then he would regale us with stories of the conflict with England. Mammy used to think she was Madam Markievicz: she was as strong as the Countess and they shared the same ideas and ideals. It was my mammy's dearest wish to see a united Ireland before she died. And it's mine too.

The news that night was all about the Peace Process. It was a frustrating time: both sides had reached an impasse over the formation of a power-sharing Assembly. I thought, how odd to watch politicians refusing to speak to each other or listen to what the other was saying. Even though Sinn Fein was democratically elected, Paisley's crowd, the DUP, wouldn't take part in any discussions with it.

'Ah,' said John, 'the Unionists won't listen to that. Not Jeffrey Donaldson anyway.'

'Donaldson, that little fucker,' I said.

I couldn't stand to look at that fella. Any chance he got he would say *Sinn Fein/IRA*. It used to madden me. Supposing the

Republicans started saying *DUP/UFF.* How would that go down?

Donaldson was challenging Tony Blair that day. 'It has to be no guns – no government for Sinn Fein/IRA,' he was saying. He angered me that much I had to turn off the television.

'That's it then,' I said. John went to the bathroom and I went back outside to bring in my second line of washing.

15 June 1999 had been an ordinary day. A strange wheeze and a tissue full of blood changed all that. 'John!' I shouted. 'Oh my God, come here, come here quick.' We both stared at the sodden tissue.

'Am I goin' to die, John?'

TWO

The Notorious Birth of Mary McNamee

I was born a delicate child with a peculiar shape: one leg was thinner and slightly shorter than the other, and a strange hairless head with squinty little eyes sat on top of an odd, bottle-shaped neck. I was chronically ugly and as cross as a briar.

When word got around Clonmore about the freak that was born to Mary Ann and Johnnie McNamee, a stream of curious neighbours dropped in to see the product of the much-talked-about birth. Mammy didn't mind; she was proud of her infant child and was delighted to show her off.

I came into the world among the turmoil of depression and poverty on the seventh – or sixth – of September 1928. There was never any confusion about the date I was born until I took the time to study a copy of my birth certificate when I retired. It seems that Mammy actually gave birth to me on the hour of midnight on 6 September 1928, and *that* is the date recorded. For some reason I was never told and I've celebrated my birthday on the wrong day all my life.

At least there's no disputing the *place* of my birth. It happened at Brocka, Clonmore, in County Offaly in the heart of the Irish

Midlands. I was the third child of seven born into the McNamee household – fourteen months after my sister Carmel.

I did not thrive in the first year and a half of my life: I was a sick baby, always vomiting, unable to keep down even a drop of water. I was a painfully slow developer. Mammy used to say I was so delicate I wasn't expected to live, and visitors often commented solemnly, 'If that child lives, any child has a chance.'

Mammy took me to see the doctor at Rhode dispensary to see what could be done, even though she didn't have much faith in doctors and none at all in hospitals. She was happier to put her trust in home-grown remedies and in her strong religious beliefs, praying to the Blessed Virgin every night to make me strong. She believed in the power of prayer.

Mammy would call on the help of a local girl called Babby Foy to mind Carmel and my brother Luke, leaving Mammy to nurse me all day long. Our nearest neighbour, Old Katie McNamee, was another of Mammy's little helpers.

Despite Mammy's undivided attention, I seemed to be plagued by bad luck. She often reminded me of the day my cradle caught fire while she was out of the house on an errand. Old Katie had paid us a visit on her way home from Fay's shop at The Harrow. She came into the house carrying a tin of paraffin, which she plonked down in the middle of the floor.

Mammy asked Katie to stay and mind the children while she called on a neighbour for a bucket of milk. Mammy placed Carmel in a large boiling pot – the one used to boil the pig food – and left me dozing in my crib by the fire. Luke was left to toddle where he liked.

Katie, old and slightly forgetful, wandered out of the house before Mammy came back, leaving her can of paraffin behind. Whatever sort of a mischievous child Luke was, he picked up the paraffin and threw it on the fire. Up it went, into a blaze. Mammy sensed something was wrong and booted it back home.

She got as far as Biddy Hickey's Turn when she saw smoke billowing out of our chimney.

'Oh God, Bless us and save us! Oh God, Bless us and save us! Oh God, Bless us and save us!' she shrieked. Mammy said everything in threes, in honour of the Blessed Trinity. She came racing in through the door to find the flames were leaping like demons, and Carmel and Luke were bawling with the fright. Mammy threw her precious bucket of milk in on top of the fire to put it out. She'd got back just in time: I was so close to the fire that my blankets were scorched but I just lay there, unconcerned, staring up at the flames.

Thanks to Mammy's intuition, I survived the cradle fire but I became a fretful child. Two years later, I had a terrifying nightmare that still bothers me today. I lay asleep in an iron cot in our one and only bedroom. It was so draughty, Father stuck old sacks and rags up the chimney to keep the wind and soot out. On a particularly stormy night, I woke screaming at the sight of frightening black spots in front of my eyes.

Mammy got out of bed and found me standing up in the cot, rubbing my eyes and wailing like a banshee.

'What's wrong, Maur'een?'

'Black pots, Mammy, black pots!' I screamed. She put out her hand and held mine.

'What pots, pet?

'Scary pots, Mammy.'

'Hush now, *alanna*. They'll go away in a minute. Where's your sugary rag, pet?'

There were no such things as dummies or soothers. I was given a rag of gauze filled with sugar, tied tightly into a pouch, and dipped in milk to keep me quiet. I was such a cross little weasel that Mammy was always shoving the rag in my mouth. I must have been a sight – a bald-headed child, with a short leg, sucking on a rag!

Mammy didn't see a hair on my head until I was two and a

half years old. Once it did take root, it grew wide and bushy
like a mop. With the head of hair developing admirably, Mammy
decided to tackle the problem of my short leg. She called on
Father Gibben to help it grow. The thin sandy-haired priest
steered his lovely chestnut horse into our grassy yard once a week
to bless my short leg. He'd dismount from his horse, landing
with a thud in his shiny riding boots, wearing a black wide-
brimmed hat, long military-style raincoat and cape.

Father Gibben would wrinkle his brow as he scrutinised my
leg, his gold-rimmed glasses balanced on the tip of his nose.

'Now, Little Girl, what are we going to do about this?' He'd
make the sign of the cross over my leg, close his eyes and say a
silent prayer. This ritual went on every week for a year.

There was something very soothing about the way he blessed
my leg: it made me feel secure and special and, of course, I was
convinced my leg was getting longer. Father Gibben visited
Mammy often and he never left without checking on the progress
of the leg.

One day, he stopped coming. 'Mammy, when is the priest
comin' again?'

Then she dropped the bombshell. 'Maur'een, Father Gibben
won't be comin' any more.'

'But why, Mammy?' I asked in disbelief.

'Well, pet, he's been sent to another parish.'

'Sure what'll I do now? Who'll bless my leg now, Mammy?'

'Don't worry, Maur'een, we'll say prayers and Father Gibben
will light a candle for ya.'

I was so upset. I was afraid my leg would get short again. I
tried to stretch it by putting a piece of string around my foot
and pulling hard. Then I would examine it to see if it had worked.
To my surprise, it looked as though my stretching and pulling
was paying off. The leg really did look like it was getting longer
and fatter. I raced into the kitchen to tell Mammy.

'That's grand, *alanna*,' she said, looking at me with her

beautiful smiling eyes. Mammy enjoyed supporting our childish fantasies. She had a great way of talking to us so that we didn't feel foolish.

Alanna and *acushla* were Mammy's terms of endearment but her favourite pet name for me was Maur'een. In fact, all her children were 'een's. My brother Luke was Luke'een and Peter was Peadar'een. Then there was Carm'een, Ann'een, Joe'een and Ger'een. Everyone had a pet name. She called Father the Old Sinner because he was so religious. She even had one for herself – *a body*. 'Would ya e'er make a body a sup of tae?' she'd say.

We gave each other nicknames as well. We liked to call Carmel The Miller after a famous greyhound at the time – Mick the Miller. He was the fastest dog in Ireland; Carmel was a real slow-coach. Anna was called The Cripple because she was always ill and complaining of pains. Luke was The Lamb because he was so aggressive. Ger was The Giant because he was so small. Peter was Salty because he liked lashings of salt on his spuds, Joe was The Bully because he was so quiet and I was The Little Girl.

There was a twelve-year age gap between Luke, the first born, and Ger, the youngest. Luke was an angry young fella but he was good fun to play with. Mostly we played with old wheels and sticks, bowling them up and down the road, beating the bejabers out of them. Or we'd spend hours playing with our wooden spinning tops painted up to create a kaleidoscope of colour.

I was especially close to Carmel. I couldn't go anywhere without her. I had to have her there to boost my confidence. We'd spend hours together looking for bits of broken Delph to make babby houses on the mound of turf opposite the kitchen, across the yard.

Although I was five when Anna was born, I have almost no memories of her as a baby. I do remember she was extremely pretty and had beautiful blonde curly hair. One time her head was full of ringworm and her scalp was always sore and bleeding and oozing with pus. She got very delicate after that and was

sick for years. Anna was something of a fairy. She had no resist-
ance against any illness but she had the energy to get up to every
sort of devilment, always trying to create havoc with us, inventing
some lie or other to land one of us in trouble. If Mammy was
nursing Joe or Ger, Anna would creep under the chair and scratch
at their feet. Once she had them bawling, she'd scurry back out
and make believe the cat did it.

'Cutch!' she'd yell at the cat, to shoo it away. 'Cutch!' she'd
say, breaking her heart laughing. She had a vivid imagination
and was extremely funny. Mammy used to say she was so cute
she would 'mind mice at the crossroads'.

We didn't like little Joe very much. He was so whiny. He'd
always be squealing and Mammy would order us to take it in
turns to rock his cradle for hours on end. When we thought he'd
nodded off, we'd sneak out through the window at the gable end
and play hopscotch. But Joe would just start bawling all over
again.

'Come in here one of yous and give this child a stir! Can't yis
see I'm busy?' Mammy would call to us.

'Can't anyone shut up that bawlin' brat?' we'd moan to each
other. We'd be mad that we had to give up our game again.

'You go in, Luke,' I'd say.

'No, you go in, Maura.'

'I've been in there for the last half hour. You go, Carmel.'

'Ah but, Maura, you're the one that soothes him best,' she
would say.

Mammy would get exasperated. 'Will *one* of yous come in?
Can't yis see I'm darnin' your father's socks? His auld feet'll be
freezin' out there ploughin' in this cold weather.' Of course, I
would always go in the end – anything for a bit of praise.

We were delighted when Ger arrived. That put an end to the
bawling brat. Ger never cried, only when he wanted food or a
change. I was ten when he was born. When Mammy had to go
to hospital, I practically reared him.

He had two pet goats called Captain and Raleigh. He played with them all day, every day, until they disappeared. Then he asked Joe to be his goat instead. Ger, playing at being an important farmer, would herd Joe 'The Goat' through a hole in the kitchen wall.

'G'on, up with ya!' he'd say. 'Get in there. Move on! Hup, hup.' Eventually he'd have Joe herded into the hole. One time Joe decided it would be a great *craic* to shit his pants while he was in there.

'You hafta come and clean me out now, Ger!' he yelled.

I wasn't an academic child and I thought I was too dim to learn, as did everybody else: Mammy always called me stupid and the teachers at Ballybryan National School agreed – they thought I was a right *amadán*. I knew I had a brain in there somewhere but I just couldn't express myself verbally. Whatever knowledge I acquired, I just couldn't get across. It was a terrible drawback and frustrated me greatly.

I started school a year later than other children my age because Mammy believed I was 'far too delicate' to attend. I had a miserable time struggling to catch up. I never was the least bit interested in what went on in the classroom. I was a dreamer, always scribbling on my copybooks, listening to the birds or watching the horses and carts go past.

I loved reading and writing stories but I was more practical: needlework was my best subject. That was an art with me. My teacher, Mrs Killian, said I could darn a sock and 'leave a beautiful patch'. And I could sing. I could pick up an air at the drop of a hat. When Carmel and I walked to Croghan to spend Christmas with Mammy's sister, Aunt Lizzie, I would be singing all the way there. Then Carmel would ask me to sing, and I was always happy to oblige – but only if I could stand behind Carmel with my eyes shut.

Peter, Luke and Carmel were the brightest in my family. Carmel could understand thoughts and concepts in an instant. We usually sat together at the front of the classroom with Shirley Temple staring back at us. Mrs Killian had a big picture of the child star on the wall above her head. I would sit and stare at Shirley, with her lovely curls, for hours on end. She wore the kind of frilly frock I could only dream of having. She was gorgeous.

Carmel was lovely-looking too but she was very vain. She saw herself as the beautiful one in the family; everyone remarked on her resemblance to Elizabeth Taylor with her violet eyes and jet-black hair. One time Carmel was at the mirror, taking for ever to comb her hair, and I was standing behind her struggling to rub the brush through my thick mane. I could just about see myself in the corner of the mirror. When I glanced at Carmel, I noticed her reflection looking at my reflection.

'Maura, why are you lookin' in the mirror at the same time as me?' she said. 'Sure you're not good-lookin' enough to share this reflection.' Now, she may have been codding, because she was a divil's needle like that, but that comment stayed with me for years. I wasn't a bit vain – proud, but not vain. Not at the age of ten anyway.

I lived in Carmel's shadow but I didn't mind a bit. She was a great *craic* and she would always help me with my schoolwork, especially as Master Buckley was forever making an example of me in front of the whole class. I was too anxious to learn and he humiliated me every chance he got.

I was standing at the back of the classroom next to Carmel, our cousin Josie Hickey and my best friend Biddy from the Hill the day Master Buckley taught us how to long divide. But I couldn't do it, and Carmel saw me struggling over the sums.

'I'll do them, Maura, and you copy,' she whispered.

Into my copybook the answers went.

Easy.

Piece of cake.

Then Master Buckley clocked what was going on.

'Mary McNamee,' he said sternly. 'Come up to the board and do this sum for me – exactly as you have it in your copybook.'

I went up to the board but, of course, I hadn't a clue how to do it. He banged his long pointer against the board in a temper.

'Do the sum, Mary!'

I looked down at my feet, knowing there was no way on earth I could write up the answer.

'If you won't do the sum, I'll get your brother Peter to come and do it for you.'

I continued to stare at my feet as Master Buckley marched over to the Low Infants' and pulled Peter out of his lesson. When he returned with my little brother in tow, my class started to snigger.

'Quiet!' he ordered. 'Now, Peter, can you do this sum that is puzzling your sister so?'

'I can, sir,' Peter said.

'Well, away with you.'

Peter was three years younger than me but he sailed through the sum. From then on, everyone in the school knew that Peter McNamee could long divide and his big sister, Maura, could only copy.

Perfect humiliation.

Peter was despatched to his own class and Master Buckley handed me the duster and told me to wipe the chalk from the board. He wrote up the sum again and, again, I couldn't do it. He was enraged. He lifted his hand high above my head and slapped me hard across the face, knocking me to the ground. I began to cry.

I shuffled back to my place then swivelled round on my heels. 'I'm goin' to tell,' I shouted through the tears.

The bell rang and the class was dismissed. I stood nursing my swollen cheek and bruised ego. Carmel whispered, 'Maura, are you all right? I'm tellin' Mammy, that feckin' eejit.'

Seeing us huddled together, Master Buckley came over and

moved Carmel aside. 'Now, Mary, I'm sorry I had to slap you. I want you to have this,' he said, forcing a sixpence into the palm of my hand. I thought for a second about all the sweets I could buy with it in Jim Haughton's shop but I refused it, throwing it down on the ground.

'Mary, I am *so* sorry that I hit you,' he repeated desperately. 'You won't tell anyone, will you?' I didn't answer him. I was too angry to speak.

I couldn't stand the way I was judged on my ability to long divide. I could talk and I could sing but I couldn't learn. I was always more interested in having the *craic* in the playground. Josie and Biddy made up my little gang.

On a Sunday, cousin Josie might visit with her brothers and sisters, Jimmy, Johnny and Moll; her mammy, Father's aunt Maggie, would come down with the youngest of her fourteen children. It wasn't practical to bring them all. Our favourite game was diving on Mammy's sheets, which were usually drying out on the tall grass at the back of the house. When the wind blew, the sheets would be going up and down, up and down, billowing like the sails of a ship. We'd land right in the middle of the swell. Everyone, bar Josie and me, would crawl in underneath them, and what they'd be doing in there would be anybody's business. I always threatened to tell Mammy what they were up to. I was such a telltale.

I was especially close to Josie. I missed Josie if she didn't come down on a Sunday but we always sat, or stood, next to each other in class.

During the war, a little Cockney girl came over from London to stay with a family in Ballybryan and she came to our school for a year or so. Her name was Maisie Brennan. I thought she was posh because she wore speckled, horn-rimmed glasses. Only rich girls could afford those glasses.

I decided I wanted to be Maisie's friend. She decided she didn't want to be mine. When class was over I'd hang around waiting for her to play with me but she was having none of it. She wasn't a bit interested in me. I took my courage in my hands, walked to her house one day and waited outside her door, hoping she'd come out and talk to me. I caught hold of the telegraph pole, wrapped my arm around it and swung myself round until I was dizzy. Finally, Maisie appeared.

'Why are you staring in our gate?' she shouted. 'Why don't you go home?' I couldn't believe it. How could she do that? I wanted to run home but I couldn't take my hands from around the pole. I just stood there, like an eejit, humiliation rooting me to the spot. My cheeks still burn when I think of it.

My cheeks burn a lot when I think back to my schooldays. Mammy and Father never really encouraged me to go to school. Carmel and Anna were encouraged, but not me. They made their way to the convent school on St Mary's Road in Edenderry. Anna became the only girl to study science in our family. I desperately wanted to go to the convent as well. I had a great longing to learn and I thought the nuns would be able to unlock my potential. I asked Mammy about leaving Ballybryan and following Carmel.

'Sure, Maur'een, what would you want to be goin' to the convent for? Ya can't learn anythin',' she said dismissively. 'Anyway, you'd need a bike and ya don't have one.'

Whether Mammy thought I was bright enough or not, I was damned sure I was going. My plan was to buy the bike and uniform — a blue gymslip, white jumper and a *proper* school satchel — to kit me out for the convent. Mammy had made my national school bag out of old sackcloth. It was a simple bag with a flap and safety fastener. That was all right for the national school but not for the convent. I visualised that beautiful, leather-smelling brown satchel strapped across my back and clasped across my chest. It was the symbol of success. It meant, I'm going to convent school now and I'm as good as the rest of you.

To buy the bike and satchel I needed money. Mammy felt sorry for me and went along with my plans. She told me I could rear a batch of turkeys, sell them at Christmas and keep the money from the sale.

I reared the turkeys and was getting all excited about what price I could get for them, asking Mammy where I should sell them, locally or to the higgler. He was the man who travelled round the country roads, every week, in his van looking to buy eggs and fowl. I was in the kitchen telling Mammy which bike I would have and where I would buy my new school uniform. Unfortunately, Father came home in the middle of this excited conversation and put a stop to any highfalutin notions I had of educating myself. He was strutting around the kitchen listening to snatches of our conversation.

'What are yis talkin' about?' he sniffed.

'*Musha*, Johnnie, we're just talkin',' Mammy said.

'What about?'

'Sit down and I'll make you a sup of tae.'

'Father,' I said, 'can I leave school?'

'I don't care. What will ya do then?'

'I'll go to the convent.'

There was a long pause.

'You can't go to the convent. Ya don't have a bike,' he said flatly.

'As a matter of fact, I *can* go because I'm sellin' the turkeys to buy a bike.'

'You'll not be sellin' any turkeys. They're not yours to sell.'

I looked over at Mammy. 'They are mine, aren't they, Mammy? Didn't ya say if I reared them I could sell them for to get the bike?'

'Yes, Maur'een, I did of course.'

'She's not sellin' them. They're not hers. Ya had no right to say she could keep them.'

We all got into a row but I stood my ground. Father got so

mad with me for cheeking him that he picked up a chair and threw it at me. Father always had the last word.

The Old Stone House

When Luke was twelve months old, Mammy and Father moved into a dilapidated stone house that had been condemned by the Public Health. Many of the houses round Clonmore were topped off with *scraw* and thatch to stop the rain from coming in, and the tin roofs from blowing off. Not our house: a gaping hole in the roof ensured that the kitchen was swamped with water whenever it rained. On a clear night we could look out through the hole and see the stars.

One room was permanently locked because the ceiling and walls were crumbling so badly. I never remember being in it. By the time Mammy was expecting Carmel they could only use one room and the kitchen.

The old house was just two hundred yards up the road from my father's family. They lived in a council cottage on an acre of land. Our house stood in four acres of ground and was surrounded by field after field of farmland. We lived mostly in the kitchen for the warmth off the fire and slept in an old settle-bed. It was used to hold milk buckets, pots and pans and other utensils during the day and served as a sleeping compartment at night. We didn't have much furniture but what was there was sparkling clean.

The kettle and iron pots would hang on crooks of different sizes from an iron crane across the fire. Lids always covered the pots for fear of soot falling into the food. The water and the soot often trickled down the chimney, staining Father's freshly whitewashed walls.

Outside in the yard was a draw-well, covered with a heavy cement lid, and further down was a haggard where Mammy would throw out the washing. The haggard was a combination of cow-houses, calf-houses, a fowl-house and a pigsty. Sometimes we didn't have the money to buy food at the shops so Mammy made sure the yard was nearly always full of hens, chickens, ducks and geese. Father's family kept a cow, a couple of pigs and some hens to supply their table with food for a family of twelve. It was usual to keep a couple of goats to supply milk when the cows went dry in the summer – and to bring us good luck. We also had a couple of pet lambs and a pet pig that were reared inside the house and fed with a baby's bottle and teat.

Protecting the yard was a greyhound called Rover that used to scutter and vomit all over the place. He'd take fits and froth at the mouth and scare the living daylights out of us.

'Sure he won't touch ya, Maur'een. Just keep away from him,' Mammy would say. She always took the side of the dumb animal. The house was crawling with cats kept solely for catching rats and mice.

The crumbling stone house was eventually knocked down and, between the Public Health Board, the Land Commission and the council, we got an acre of ground in Foy's field to build a cottage. We were so excited by this new cottage and would run home from school to see how far they had advanced with the building work. We were delighted with the idea of having big windows and an outside toilet. The toilet was nothing more than a board with a hole in it and a bucket underneath but it was more than we were used to. We would normally go in the ditch or behind the cowshed. There was no sewerage or piped water so we still had to carry the water from the draw-well.

We moved in there with every bit of furniture we had, which was very little as Mammy gave nearly everything away to the first tinker that came our way. She'd invite them in for a sup of tea and it wouldn't take them long to suss out that she was a soft touch. She always fell for their sob stories. The only difference between the gypsies and us was that they had money and we didn't.

We were so poor there often wasn't enough food to feed a

cock robin. Mammy worked so hard for us all. She would get up before daybreak, go to the bog for a *lock* of turf, carry it home on her back, milk the cows, bake the bread and make Father's breakfast – all before six in the morning. She broke her back to put food on the table but then she would give it away to the first passing stranger.

Mammy was good-natured to the point of ridiculousness. When I caught her giving away all the willow pattern plates from the dresser in the kitchen, I started squealing at her to stop. There would have been an infernal row. Father would be so tired from dragging and hauling from dawn to dusk, the least he could expect was a plate to eat his dinner off. Often she'd give her last shilling to a tramp. Father would be so frustrated that he couldn't control her. When the rows started, I'd sit out on the step with my fingers in my ears. I couldn't stand the constant shouting and fighting.

When the gypsies came knocking at our door, Mammy would give them three saucers of flour, three spoons of tea, three cups of sugar – again in threes in the name of the Blessed Trinity. Even if Mammy was down to her last quarter pound of butter, she'd be happy to give it away. If we protested, her stock phrase would be, 'Ah, sure God will send more tomorrow.' And we would be thinking He'd want to be sending it soon before Father comes in for his supper! As sure as God's in heaven, the Lord would send the butter the next day.

Superstition had it that if you didn't help the gypsies they would put a curse on your house for ever. One strange-looking gypsy had a habit of calling on the house when Mammy and Father were out. Carmel opened the door to him one day and screamed. There stood a huge old man in rags and a long red beard carrying a long stick, like a crosier. It was the Red Beggar Man, and his donkey. The fearsome-looking gypsy always brought that sorry little thing with him. It was as thin as a whippet and laden down with pots and pans.

Carmel got frightened when the Red Beggar Man started demanding food and money. Luckily, Mammy came around Biddy Hickey's Turn and saw the tinker on the doorstep. She wasn't afraid of him. She marched past, gathering up the children, and bolted the door. He walked across the yard and perched himself on the wall in front of the kitchen window, staring in at us for an hour or more. Then Father came home.

'What are *you* doin' here, me good man?' he asked the unwelcome visitor.

No reply.

'Did ya hear me? What are ya doin' here?'

Still no reply. Father was getting impatient. Suddenly, the Red Beggar Man made to move out of the yard, mumbling something at Father as he went.

'Say that again like a dacent man!' Father was fuming. 'Get out of here and be on with ya. Hook it now!'

Not all the gypsies would threaten you. Luby and Mary were old travellers who never gave anyone any bother. They parked up at Biddy Hickey's old house in Clonmore every year. You could set your watch by Luby and Mary: they would pitch up every spring, without fail, with their two asses, a dog and a goat. They'd park up in the ditch by the side of the road, never going into the ruin for shelter.

The better-off gypsies would have colourful Romany caravans with brass lanterns hanging each side of the door. We would hear them jingling and jangling as the horses trotted down the road. They would tether their horses to the wire or a pole and let them graze on the grass verge.

Luby and Mary didn't have a caravan; they would just tent up and go round asking for flour or milk to make bread, and often came to ask Mammy for a kettle of water. There was always a welcome in our house. Mammy would have water boiling constantly on the fire to make tea for anyone who might visit.

'God bless this house' would be the first words spoken inside the door. Then visitors would be served a sup of tea and a slice of currant bread.

Mickey Gordon was a frequent visitor. He lived with his sister, Katie, down the fields behind our house. He earned his living collecting cane from the bog to weave baskets to sell. He was a worn-out looking character with his old bit of a white beard and moustache and floppy felt hat similar to a trilby. Mickey was a character. He'd go mad every spring. Mammy always knew the signs when he came to visit.

'Can ya boil me a couple of them auld hen eggs, Mary?' he'd say. She would serve them up to him and he would go to the baker lid on the hearth and put ashes on to his egg instead of a sane man's salt.

'Ah, Mickey, what are ya doin'?' Mammy would say. 'Use the salt, Mickey. Sure you're puttin' ashes in yer egg!'

Mammy was a very sociable person, as was Father. All the men around used to go mitching to each other's houses, mostly in the wintertime, playing cards to win a turkey or a goose for Christmas. Mitching was a working-class pastime. The rich farmers had their own version of mitching. They called it whist, got all dressed up and had a posh dinner washed down with a smooth red claret. The parish priest would always be invited.

We didn't have alcohol in our house, except maybe at Christmas. Poor people didn't have alcohol at any other time of the year. Then we might have a few bottles of porter but they were kept in the parlour out of sight, not on show for all to see.

At the mitching sessions, Father would sing his favourite rebel songs. He was such a beautiful singer people would gather outside the door to listen to his patriotic ballads. He knew all the rebel songs – 'Who Fears to Speak of Easter Week', 'Wrap the Green Flag Round Me, Boys' and 'The Croppy Boy'. The singing could go on all night. Not many nights went by without my father singing to a crowd gathered outside. Old Mickey would always be there, urging him on.

'Well, that was powerful, Johnnie,' Mickey would say, wiping his white whiskers. 'Will ya sing us another? Give us a couple of bars of "Kevin Barry". I love that great old song.'

Then Father would settle himself down and sing some more. 'In Mountjoy jail, one Monday morning, high upon a gallows tree, Kevin Barry gave his young life for the cause of Liberty . . .'

Father's sweet voice was very easy on the ear. We loved listening to the old songs. Sometimes Mammy would join in. She would encourage me to get up and sing too. I had a beautiful singing voice.

I duetted with one of the Murphy boys from Toberdaly in the choir at St Peter's Church in Rhode. Once, while I was singing, I realised I could hear my own voice above everyone else's. I became terribly self-conscious and stopped immediately.

Despite my crippling shyness, I did enter a couple of singing competitions. Carmel persuaded me to enter a *feis* in Boyne Park when I was fourteen. I won a silver medal. The adjudicator, Peter's new headmaster Mr Carey, was so impressed he thought I should audition for Radio Éireann in Athlone. I often dreamt about having my voice recorded but I just wasn't brave enough to go to the audition.

I entered the Boyne Park competition again the following year and, again, I was beaten to first place – this time by my old London adversary, Maisie Brennan. Typical, I thought at the time, how dare she come over here from London with her goddamn speckledy glasses thinking she was better than me? And beating me at my own game!

Our lives back then were full of rituals. Every week we went through the pain of having senna forced down our throats, like it or not. 'It's good for yer bowels and there's lots of iron in it,' Mammy would say.

And once a week we had to have boiled nettles – those too were filled with iron and were 'good for us'. I don't know how they would do us good but whatever was in Mammy's potions, they kept us running for a week.

Mammy was well known in Clonmore for her herbal cures. She once made ointment with herbs gathered from the fields to cure a cancer on a calf's back. The vet came out to the house to put the calf down but Mammy wouldn't let him. She trusted her own cure and the calf lived. The vet was astounded.

The ointment was also good for burns and scalds but her favourite burns treatment was a cowpat. Ger got a terrible scald when he was nine after he tipped the teapot over his foot. Mammy ran outside, scooped up a cowpat and slapped it on his burn.

She made a herb soap that was good for eczema and she would roast common salt, put it in a lisle stocking and wrap it round your neck to cure sore throats. If I sang too much I would get a bad throat but the salty poultice would always do the trick.

Another ritual involved holy water and a twig. Like every Catholic house in Ireland, we had a holy water font by the back door near a picture of the Sacred Heart, which was permanently lit by a glowing red lamp. Our font was made from an old jam jar and a twig of box hedging, and Mammy would sprinkle holy water around the house with the twig every night to protect us from evil spirits.

Each McNamee child owned a Sunday prayer book and a set of rosary beads, and we would pray in front of a home-made altar in the corner of the kitchen. It had statues of the Virgin Mary, the Holy Family and the Child of Prague. We prayed most nights by this altar, our knees chafing against the concrete floor. As we got older, we couldn't wait for this nightly ritual to be over. When we got bored we would pinch each other's heels and start giggling. If we were caught, we'd get a whack around the ear for making 'a mockery of the holy prayers'.

At Mass on a Sunday, we'd often see another of my father's aunts, Biddy, strolling to Mass with her wicked dog Hitler, twelve cats and a pet goat. They would follow her everywhere, even into

Edenderry, but it was a sight to see the cats and dogs at the church door!

Ours was a very holy household. By the time I left school, I had absorbed every bit of religion the Catholic priests could teach. My First Confession was a big day in my young life. For a start, I didn't know what the word *sin* meant or what sins I would have to confess. Weekly lessons at St Peter's Church soon enlightened me. I learnt all about the three big sins: original sin, venial sin and, the most terrible of all, mortal sin.

The original sin was something we were born with from the time of Adam and Eve and didn't leave us until we were baptised. If you weren't baptised, you would go to a place called limbo. I thought limbo was up in Toberdaly where all the little stillborn children were buried. The concept of limbo was beyond my child's imagination.

A venial sin was taking something that didn't belong to you. I committed a good few of those: my friend Biddy and I used to raid Old Jim Haughton's shop at least once a week. We'd creep down to his store near The Harrow and sneak the Chester cakes out of the glass case. I couldn't get enough of those heavy-duty fruitcakes and if I couldn't get in to get one, I would make Biddy go in and take one for me.

The biggest sin of all was the mortal sin. If you committed one of those 'the Divil himself would have you'! The priests threatened us with sin. Sin was pounded into our heads. 'Walk away from temptation and keep your heads held high. The Devil's work is never done,' they'd say.

When the big day came to make my First Confession, I walked anxiously into a tiny dark box at the end of the long aisle. A disembodied hand slid open the shutter and the priest's face appeared on the other side of the wood panelling. After he settled himself down on his cushion, I blessed myself and remembered the words I'd spent hours practising. 'Bless me, Father, for I have sinned. This is my First Confession, and these are my sins.'

The priest listened intently. When my ordeal was over, he gave me three Hail Marys as my penance, made the sign of the cross and spoke to me in Latin. *'In nomine Patris, et Filii, et Spiritus Sancti. Amen. Go in peace, my child.'*

When I came out of the Confessional, I felt as though the Holy Ghost had entered my skinny little body. I glided down the aisle of the church, head bowed and my hands clasped in front of me, knelt as close to the statue of the Blessed Virgin as I could, and said my penance. The confession obliterated all memory of Jim Haughton's Chester cakes – for at least a week, anyway. Then I retreated from church as quiet as a mouse and as innocent as an angel. I felt ever so holy.

From then on, we were herded to Confession every month as though we were prize Friesians heading for market. It was the start of years of confessing, though half the time my sins were made up.

My First Holy Communion soon followed. We practised for several weeks in the classroom before a final dress rehearsal in church, the Friday before the ceremony. We were warned by the teachers not to chew the body of Christ, but a rumour went round the school that the Eucharist was so big we were liable to choke on it. I was particularly anxious because of my small swallow: I've always had to chop up my food into tiny morsels and pick at it like a bird.

At Communion Mass the following day, we all headed for the reserved seating in the long aisle, the girls on one side and the boys on the other. Like all the other girls, I was dressed in a white frock and veil, carrying my little white prayer book and rosary beads. They were a present from Mammy from the holy shop in Edenderry. A pair of white leather shoes with a button fastener completed the virginal outfit. Everything from the inside out was white. Mammy would have done an extra wash and iron for a neighbour for several weeks to get the pound to buy it all. She made sure that I had the same as the rest of the class.

When the time came to take Communion, I took my place kneeling in front of the altar. I didn't know what to expect after all the stories. I was so surprised when the Eucharist stuck to the roof of my mouth. I didn't know what all the fuss was about. It tasted like one of Nolan's wafers and melted just as quickly.

After Holy Communion I became obsessed with my little white mother-of-pearl rosary beads and white prayer book. I kept them in the shoebox that had contained my new white shoes, and tucked them under the bed. I'd take them out every so often to look at them to make sure they were still there.

I wore a white frock and veil again for my Confirmation a few years later. This time brown sandals completed the outfit: Mammy had got very delicate and the poor thing wasn't able to earn the money for the white shoes. I was the only one in sandals.

But at least the frock looked the part. Mammy asked Father's favourite sister, Bridie Glennon, to make my Confirmation frock at short notice on her Singer sewing machine. Bridie ran up a plain white dress with a pucker here and there and a row of mother-of-pearl buttons going up the front. When Aunt Bridie measured me up for this all-important frock, she commented on my peculiar shape.

'God, Maura, ya have the qu'arest shape I've ever come across,' Aunt Bridie said. 'You're shaped like a pear, and look at your arms. They're too long for your body.'

I had no idea what she was talking about, but I plucked up the courage to ask her what a pear was like. She looked at me for a second then howled with laughter.

'Have ya never eaten a pear?'

'No,' I said, bemused. Thanks to Aunt Bridie I've had a terrible complex about my size and shape ever since.

Carmel and Luke had Grandfather McNamee's pony and trap to take them to their Confirmation, but no such luxury for me: I had to fly across the fields in my brown sandals and lovely white dress, worrying that I might step straight into cow shite.

The inquisitive cattle were staring at me wondering what was the rush. Of course, they didn't know how late I was!

Mammy could turn her hand to anything. She was a dab hand with a needle and cotton and would make our dresses, knickers and petticoats – as well as the sheets we slept on – out of Odlums flour bags. They were rough on your skin but we were poor and had to make do.

She would have to boil the bags to soften them, and throw them on the hedge to bleach in the sun, hopefully removing all traces of the Odlums brand name. This didn't always work. The lads were cute and would try and lift up your skirt to see your knickers. We'd be so ashamed at the thought of them seeing 'Odlums' written across our arses!

Mammy was great with any kind of a needle. We couldn't afford shop mattresses so she made ours from the Odlums sack-cloth and filled them with straw each week. The straw, although clean and fresh, brought with it an army of prime fat fleas that devoured us while we slept. We'd get up in the morning not knowing if we had the measles or flea bites, we'd have that many red spots. I will never forget the smell of carbolic soap and Jeyes Fluid in our house. Mammy used it every week, like a sheep dip, to kill off the fleas and ticks. We were stood in a big wooden tub and the entire contents of a bucket of bath water and Jeyes Fluid would be thrown over us.

Mammy was an expert at knitting, darning and crocheting. She would sit in her chair for hours sewing and patching. She once made Peter a lovely navy blue suit out of one of her dresses. She recycled everything. Nothing went to waste. There was no such thing as running into town to buy new knickers or bodices. I only ever remember her buying me new knickers once – there were two little pockets in the sides of them – and that was when the doctor came to the school to examine us after a health scare. We didn't have the knickers long before they were loaned out to an even poorer family waiting for the visiting doctor.

Mammy was ingenious. She made our shoes too out of Father's old felt hats so that we were spared the bumbools – big festering sores – from the rough stones when we walked to school in our bare feet. In winter we wore rubber boots but often had nothing on our feet in the summer. So we thought we were the cat's whiskers in Mammy's home-made felt shoes. They became quite a novelty to the children around us.

They were jealous of our fancy footwear and would turn up at our house and ask Mammy to make some for them as well. If she was in the mood, she would be delighted and tell them to come back with the hats their fathers wore. If she wasn't in the mood, she'd say, 'Indeed'n I won't! Yous can g'on home with yourselves.' More often she'd say, 'If yous can get me a hat, come down and I'll do them for ya.'

They'd sit down, take off their shoes and let Mammy measure their feet. She'd place the shoe on to the felt and mark around it with a pencil. Then she'd get to work, cutting out the shape with her big scissors while we all sat around watching. Once cut, she'd get out her darning needle and a ball of wool and back-stitch it all together.

Mammy copied the design of our Communion shoes. She cut out the strap from the same piece of cloth and made a button-hole to fasten the shoes together. The sole was made from two pieces of felt with a piece of cardboard in between for strength. They looked just like doll's shoes. They wouldn't last pissing time. You couldn't wear them in the rain because they would go all soggy and the sole would turn to mush.

The more hats Mammy had, the more shoes she made. We'd go around collecting as many as we could. Old Mickey and my grandfather would never refuse us their old hats.

One Saturday, Father surprised Carmel and me with two beautiful new frocks. He walked in with a brown parcel and handed it to Mammy.

'There's a couple of bibs for Carmel and Maura.'

'Where'd ya get them from, Johnnie?' Mammy asked.

'Up at Fay's.'

'And where did ya get the price of them?'

'I won a few shillin's on a horse today.'

'God, that's great, Johnnie.'

Carmel's dress was powder blue and mine was lemon. Summer colours. Mammy decided to make us two flour-bag bonnets to go with them. She went through the usual long-winded process of boiling, bleaching, starching, cutting and shaping. With her dressmaking gifts she was able to turn a flat piece of sackcloth and a length of chicken wire into a beautiful bonnet.

On this occasion, we had no felt shoes or brown sandals to wear with our swanky new hats. Come Sunday, we had to attend Mass in our bare feet. We were so ashamed. Mortified, we made every excuse not to go. Mammy was having none of it.

'Yis'll go to Mass, shoes or no shoes,' she said. 'Get on with yis. Our Lord never wore shoes.'

'But Mammy, we'll get bumbools all over our feet!' we protested.

'Bumbools or no, yis'll go to Mass and that's all I want to hear about it. Your father has bought yis two lovely bibs and I've made yis two beautiful bonnets, so stop your whingein' and get off to Mass.'

Off we trotted in front of her, mumbling and moaning that we'd be made a show of and be the talk of the place. To avoid the gravel roads, we skipped over the briars and nettles on the grass verge.

We were relieved to hear the sound of a motorcar. Most families we knew used donkeys and traps but the rich would have a motorcar, and you could sometimes rely on them for a lift. There were still very few cars around at that time so we thought the driver could only have been one of the three big farmers: the Mulvins from Clonmore, Beechlawn or Roosk. When the car slowed down, we saw to our horror that it was Mr Bruntz and our snooty Aunt Nannie. Even though she was Father's sister, she looked down on the likes of us, her own nephews and nieces, because she thought she'd moved up in the world since she married Joe Bruntz, a German architect. We were banned from referring to him as Uncle Joe. We had to call him Mr Bruntz or 'The Boss'. They were very posh and full of false pride. They knew all the local gentry.

They were the last people we wanted to bump into in our flour bonnets and bare feet. Now we were even more humiliated as we climbed into the back seat.

Mr Bruntz sniffed, settled his hat, took it off again, looked at Aunt Nannie and grimaced. She sat up in the front seat wearing jewels and clothes worn only by the rich. The stench of perfume nearly knocked us out of our seat. She turned around with a jerk of her shoulders, grinning and stifling a snort.

'Have yous no shoes to wear with your pretty frocks and hats?' she asked sarcastically. We couldn't answer. We just sat in the back of her elegant car, stammering.

'The Boss' parked the car in front of the chapel and we hobbled the last fifteen feet, over the gravel road and up the gravel path, to the short aisle.

The whole congregation knew we had come to Mass in our bare feet. They were pretending to pray but we could see them nudging each other and staring at the two pretty hats perched on top of our heads. I wanted the ground to open and swallow me up. When I knelt down to pray, I tried to cover the soles of my feet with my bib, but it wasn't long enough.

We slipped out just before Mass was ended and raced home to avoid any further embarrassment.

THREE

The 'Cottage Crowd'

M ammy often said she didn't love Father and only married him out of pity. She'd tell us how she always regretted leaving her respectable family for his 'mean, scroungin', nit-pickin' cottage crowd'.

'Cottage crowd' was her name for very poor labouring people who lived in council cottages. Mammy, on the other hand, was brought up with one sister in a big thatched farmhouse that had sheds immaculately whitewashed. She lived fourteen miles away, up a *boreen*, in a place called Croghan. Coming from a small holding, she thought she was a better class of person. She often spoke of illustrious ancestors, believing her great-great-grandmother to be a titled lady who married her footman. There was never any proof: apparently, the family records went up in smoke when Republican forces destroyed Tullamore Courthouse in 1922.

Even though she proudly claimed her noble heritage, Mammy was born plain Mary Ann Hannon to Elizabeth Mooney and Peter Hannon on 30 November 1899 in Coole near Daingean – then named Philipstown as Ireland was still under British rule.

Mammy never knew her mother: she had been a delicate woman who died of kidney failure when Mammy was three years old. She was brought up on stories about her father carrying his ailing young wife halfway across Ireland searching – in vain – for a cure. Mary Ann and her baby sister, Lizzie, were sent to Croghan and reared by their Hannon grandparents.

Offaly, bordered by seven counties including Galway, Tipperary, Kildare and Meath, was 'planted' with English immigrants in the sixteenth century and renamed King's County – the name it retained until 1921. My mammy was reared in the thick of Ireland's fight for Independence and was a teenager at the time of the Easter Rising. She formed her strong Republican beliefs at a very young age. Mammy joined the *Cumann na mBan* – the Women's Auxiliaries of the IRA – and the Irish Red Cross and used her soothing and caring instincts to help those wounded souls of the Irish conflict.

Like every other county in Ireland, Offaly is steeped in stories of brave rebellions, myths and legends. St Patrick is said to have walked his horse across Croghan Hill where St Patrick's Well now stands. It is said to have sprung up on the very spot where the horse knelt down to take a drink from a stream. Dents in the stone surrounding the well are supposed to be the imprints of the horse's knees.

Mammy and Aunt Lizzie grew up in the shadow of Croghan Hill. They trudged across fields and over hills to attend school at a place called Troy's Cross. It was a long walk for the two small children. In colder weather their uncle Jim Hannon would yoke up the pony and trap and take them, in style, along the roads.

Mammy was a bright but uneducated woman; in her day only the sons – and a few daughters of lawyers, doctors and big farmers – were given the privilege of a higher education. It was a great shame for Mammy but it didn't stop her from being asked to teach occasionally while she was still at school. She loved every minute of it and was a very able tutor, even though she was only fourteen years old and had no training.

Four years later, a vacancy came up for a permanent job. The headmistress offered the post to Mammy but she turned it down flat: Mammy thought she wasn't good enough to take it. There had never been a teacher in the Hannon family and she believed she would not be accepted. She thought the job should go to the big noises, like the Egans or the Moores, because they were better than her. Despite her distinguished lineage, Mammy never liked the idea of rising above her station.

The woman who did take the job didn't live very long.

'Wasn't I lucky I didn't take it, Maur'een?' she said. 'I wouldn't be alive now if I had taken it.' She was odd like that. She could be illogical at times.

Instead of a respectable career in teaching, she settled for low-paid domestic work in the 'Big Houses' owned, in the main, by rich Protestants. The Egans, the first family she worked for, were actually Catholics and they were considered one of the richest in the county because they could afford to employ a French governess. Mammy claimed they were distant relations.

Mammy was a wild and flighty woman who didn't stay long in any one job. After the Egans she was with the Protestant Smiths of Clonin for no more than a few months. Mammy had a razor-sharp wit that would cut you dead and she would entertain us with her stories about the Smiths and the other rich people she cleaned up after.

Two of the Smith sons were famous in the area for building a car – inside their house. Of course, when it was finished they couldn't get it out! They had to take the car to pieces and reassemble it outside.

It was during her short time with the Smiths that she fell in love. Mammy was a beautifully tall, graceful woman with long brown hair framing fine feline features: she had deep-set, cat-like, almond-shaped yellow-green eyes and very high cheekbones. She had no trouble gaining the interests of men, young or old.

Tosh Jones from Toberdaly was the love of her life. They met at a dance and started spending time with each other,

cycling and going for walks. They were together for nearly two
years when Tosh left her high and dry after she refused to give
herself to him. She was far too chaste to give in to his sexual
demands.

Mammy was deeply hurt. After the break-up, she turned to
Our Blessed Lady and prayed for the strength to come to terms
with losing the man she loved. She made a promise to herself
that she would marry the first man who asked her.

Mammy decided to take up her next job as a maid, earning
half a crown a week, working for the Gills of Castlejordan. The
village was far enough away to be spared the torment of bumping
into Tosh.

The first day she hopped up on her bike to cycle to the village,
she stopped by the roadside to ask an old man of seventy for
directions. The auld one was delighted to be able to help – and
then promptly asked her to marry him! She laughed at the very
idea and promptly declined, breaking her sacred promise.

She then decided to marry the next *boy* she met. That boy
was my father, Johnnie McNamee of the cottage crowd in
Clonmore. He was born, four years after Mammy, with twink-
ling violet-blue eyes, on 6 January 1904, to Luke McNamee and
Mary Hickey. He was the eldest and brightest child and his
mother adored him. He grew into a small man with a bald head
and a quiet sense of humour.

Of course, getting involved with the McNamees didn't amuse
the folks up the hill. After all, Mary Ann Hannon of Croghan
had been left a small family legacy of twenty-one guineas. Despite
the disapproval, Mammy and Father were determined to wed.

The event took place in St Peter's Church in Rhode in 1925
with Mammy decked out in a navy blue serge suit and white
blouse. The suit was made for her by Mrs Mulligan, the local
seamstress from the gatehouse at Rathmoyle House in Dunville
near Rhode. The big house stood in over four hundred acres of
ground and was owned by an English landlord by the name of

Kerr. He shot himself on the steps of his mansion during the Civil War. The old IRA had burnt down Protestant houses at Ballyburly and Toberdaly, and when Old Kerr heard they were on their way to see him, he committed suicide. My grandfather Luke McNamee and his brother Paddy were part of the angry crowd who were going up to ambush him. Great-Uncle Paddy was fined thirty shillings for his involvement.

It was three years after this that Mammy and Father were married. After the ceremony, they went to Edenderry in a horse and trap for their wedding breakfast. No honeymoon followed: the newlyweds went back to their respective families and spent the next year living in separate houses, visiting each other at weekends. That was an unusual arrangement even for those times.

Father refused to move to Croghan; it was too far away from his mother and there was no room for Mammy in Clonmore. My aunt Nannie, who was fifteen at the time, didn't want Mammy there: Mammy was accepted by the others but Nannie was very jealous. My grandparents were dead set against giving their new daughter-in-law a roof over her head. There wasn't the room and they didn't have enough money coming in; another mouth to feed was too much for them.

Mammy used to say how she missed Johnnie during those twelve months. She would tell you, 'Sure I loved Johnnie.' Then she'd tell you in another breath, 'I married him out of pity.'

In any case, I never understood why they got married without having somewhere to live. They didn't have to get married: Mammy wasn't pregnant. That happened soon after. During their brief hours together, Mammy became pregnant with Luke and was finally allowed to move in with my father's family, in preparation for the birth.

As soon as Luke was born, my parents searched for a place of their own. The only house they could find belonged to my father's uncle, Mick Hickey. And that was the condemned stone house.

Mammy gave birth to nine children in that ramshackle house. Carmel was first. Our sister Josephine, born the year after me, only lived three months: she caught a chill that developed into pneumonia. Watt came next but he only lived for six hours.

My little brother Patrick was a happy, smiling child with the face of an angel. He had beautiful golden curly hair and huge blue eyes. I remember him so well. I recall the day that carpenter Jim Mara, from Ballybryan, arrived with a little white box, and how the neighbours came and went all day long.

Patrick was a year old when he got the fever. He was ill for three weeks or more and Mammy and Father took it in turns to stay up all night with him. They bathed him in a tub of warm water sprinkled with mustard to take away his pain. The tub was placed in front of a roaring fire and I would watch Mammy and Father, sitting each side of it, crying quietly for hours.

The morning Patrick died, Mammy crept into our bedroom and whispered to Luke, 'Luke, Luke, little Patrick's dead. He's gone to heaven.'

Luke jumped out of bed, rubbed his eyes and began to sob. I was awake and overheard the terrible news. I slid out of bed and saw Mammy and Father looking into Patrick's little crib, his tiny figure laid to rest from his pain and suffering. My little brother died of convulsions.

Father's brother, Uncle Pat, fetched the doctor and someone else called for the curate. Father Crilley arrived soon after and blessed the corpse. Mammy sprinkled holy water on Patrick's little white coffin and Uncle Pat placed it on his shoulder and carried it out of the house.

After Patrick was taken away, the house hung in heavy silence punctuated only by the painful sobs coming from Mammy's room. She didn't go to his burial: she couldn't face it. She wasn't in a fit state of mind to walk the three miles to Ballymacwilliam graveyard. She stayed with us and grieved in the rundown, damp old house.

These deaths, and many more miscarriages, took their toll on Mammy. While she was heavily pregnant with Joe, she looked so pale and ill, sitting alone in her big basket chair moving the buttons on her one and only coat to make room for her expanding belly. The coat was black, and trimmed with fur on the collar and cuffs. I remember she had a festering abscess on her hand and I watched her sewing her buttons back on, the tears running down her cheeks.

'Mammy, why are you cryin'?' I asked.

'It's all right, *acushla*.' I knew she wasn't 'all right'. How could she have been? The death of a child changes you for ever.

It was dark outside and Father wasn't back from work yet. Mammy asked Luke to fetch in the cows for milk and I helped Carmel bring in the turf for the night. We put the turf by the fire and got Anna ready for bed.

Father came home from work, eventually, cold, tired and hungry. He threw his hat on the table and took off his boots to warm his weary feet by the fire. If he'd had his Sunday hat on he would have placed it carefully on a nail on the back of the kitchen door. The everyday hat was thrown down anywhere. This particular day, it landed on the kitchen table.

Mammy looked so feeble, preparing his supper, but Father didn't notice her distress. As she reached for his plate on the dresser she began to sway and then fell heavily to the stone floor. Only then did Father see that something was wrong. He ran to help her up but caught his shin on a skillet pot and landed beside her on the floor. The dim lamp only lit up part of the kitchen and we were forever bumping into things. Father cursed the pot, hauled himself back to his feet and carried Mammy into the bedroom. Luke was despatched to find the doctor in Rhode.

Mammy spent three weeks in hospital in Tullamore and, while she was there, Father busied himself around the house, white-washing the place inside and out. He also fenced in the draw-well and all around the haggard, hoping it would make her happy when she saw how hard he'd worked.

On the day she came home, she sat in her chair by the fire rocking to and fro, the tears running once more down her face, refusing to speak. We went into the yard and played joylessly with the leaves while Father stood staring at the pigsty, his elbows resting on the wall. Nobody spoke for hours.

Life was never the same after Joe was born. The stress took its toll on all of us. I was always afraid Mammy would drown herself in the draw-well, she threatened to chuck herself into it that many times. I'd be demented with worry. I can still see Father standing at the kitchen door and Mammy threatening to throw herself in. She'd be there, kicking stones into the water and dangling one foot over the hole and looking back at Father.

'Please yourself! If that's what ya want. Work away,' he'd shout.

The thought of Mammy not being at home when I came back from school was always on my mind. Then, one day, it happened. We came back from school and found her sitting on the side of the draw-well, dangling her feet and threatening to throw herself in again. This time we knew she meant it. She told us she didn't want to live any more.

We screamed at her to stop. 'No, Mammy! Don't. Come away!' we begged. I think the shock of seeing her children hysterical with fright brought her to her senses. Eventually, she came away from the well.

Mammy gave birth to her last child, Ger, on 24 October 1938. The stirring and the rocking started all over again and things went from bad to worse. She started behaving in a very peculiar manner and would disappear for hours on end. She would leave the house before Father came home from work. At first he didn't pay much attention. He thought she might be up visiting Granny Hickey across the fields. When she came back, she would never say where she'd been.

Then one day, Father noticed she'd been gone longer than usual. He paced up and down the kitchen then went outside and paced up and down the road. There was no sign of her. Worry got the better of him and he put on his hat and coat and went searching for her.

Father was away so long we put Ger to bed and got ready ourselves. We were so relieved to hear them coming in the door. We charged out of bed desperate to see Mammy again. Father was alone. He hadn't found her.

Next morning, when she still wasn't home, Father was frantic. He got us ready for school and on the way out the door, we bumped into Mammy coming in the gate, pale and drawn-looking.

'Are yous off to school?' she asked, giving us a casual peck on the cheek. She acted as though nothing at all was wrong. That was the start of Mammy's walkabouts. Every so often she'd go missing again. Father was near demented.

Mammy would often run out of the house and Father would chase her and bring her back, if he could. More often than not she'd disappear completely, and the night vigils would start again. This went on for months. Then one day we discovered where she had been going.

The church sacristan at the Holy Trinity Church in Castlejordan found Mammy on her knees praying in the Gallery. The sacristan was walking around the church with her bunch of keys wanting to lock up. She asked Mammy to leave but she refused.

'Are you ill, Mrs McNamee?' she asked.

'No, I'm not ill. What makes ya think I'm ill?' Mammy snapped. 'Sure if I was ill, I'd be at home. I just want to stay with Our Lord and Our Blessed Lady.'

'Won't ya be afraid?'

'Of course I won't. Just go ahead and lock the church doors. I'll be fine.'

Mammy made the sacristan promise not to tell a soul that she'd been spending nights in the church. The country gossips would have made a laughing stock of Mammy. Nothing like this had ever happened in Castlejordan before, but she kept her word. Mammy finally told Father herself. He was dumbfounded.

Mammy turned to God for help and guidance after that and made a promise to Him that she would take Communion every Sunday if he made her well again. All the other churchgoers were ashamed of Mammy for this: she was the only person taking Communion every Sunday. Nowadays it's the norm to take the Host at every Mass, but not back then. It wasn't acceptable. Even the priests didn't like it. Parishioners only went to Confession and Communion once a month. Any more was seen as an embarrassment and cause for ridicule.

Old Mrs Mulvin of Clonmore was particularly affronted. She saw Mammy as this poor delicate working-class woman giving herself to the Church. And for what? The rich farmer's wife worried about the shame the 'poor woman' was bringing on the Church and took it upon herself to chide Mammy. She sent word for Mammy to go over and see her. Mammy trudged the three miles across the fields to the Mulvins' farmhouse to hear what she had to say.

'No, I won't stop goin', Mrs Mulvin,' Mammy said defiantly. 'I've made a promise to Our Lord and Our Blessed Lady.'

Mrs Mulvin even offered her plenty of good warm clothes and the scraps of cold meat, left over from her Sunday table, if she stopped making a show of herself. Mammy had to think long and hard about the offer – she thought Johnnie could do with the bits of meat – but she refused.

Looking back, I think Mammy was obviously suffering from deep postnatal depression. That wasn't recognised in those days. Women just had to get on with their lives. Through her hard work, her prayers and her beliefs she got over it.

I felt sorry for Mammy the way they all made a laughing stock of her, but she showed great strength of character and courage to go against tradition. Going to church was her salvation.

Father would rather she'd taken the scraps of cold meat. The strain was unbearable. Mammy and Father began to argue more and more.

Temper Tantrums

My father was a quiet man but he had a fierce temper when roused. I never saw him hit Mammy but I saw her attack him. If she couldn't get him to fight back she would fire stones at him. He'd set up with quite a lot from Mammy.

It would take very little for Mammy to create a row. She would always try to torment him and he would react very quickly and get all huffed up and upset. She wouldn't have the common sense to understand that there was another way of working him. Then she'd want him to get great with her but he wouldn't, and that would start another argument or they wouldn't speak for days. Neither of them cared about the effect it was having on us.

Mammy was a very highly strung woman. She'd sometimes screech and dance and hiss and spit with rage. You'd be well advised to steer clear of her ranting and raving. We'd be liable to get a thump that would land us into the middle of next week. She often pulled my hair, and she could land a good kick, but she only hit me once. It was Christmas Eve 1940 and I went along to Confession with my friend Biddy. We were supposed to come home straightaway and take care of the little ones, Joe and Ger, while Mammy took her turn at Confession. But Biddy and I went off to gather holly and ivy instead. When we got home Mammy turned on the two of us.

'Yis little bitches. Yis stayed away and yis know I have to go to Confession!' She whipped the holly off me and leathered me with it, hitting me anywhere she could get a good, clean wallop. And wasn't I bawling then? That was the only time in her ninety-seven years that she slapped me.

She never hit Peter but she walloped Luke, Carmel, Anna and

Ger. I once saw her break the handle of a broom across Ger's back because he was ill and didn't want to go to school. Poor Anna got the worst of it. She was always game for a whacking. She would stand up to Mammy and Mammy would swing her round by the hair on her head. I often felt sorry for the way Mammy treated her.

I was different. I wouldn't answer Mammy back or give her the opportunity to hit me. It was usually the tongue that gave me the lashing. The safest place away from her fiery tongue would be the middle of the *slang field*, past Foy's field and across the little *mairn*.

Of course, you'd be afraid to go home then. There she would be, in her chair by the fireside, dangling a spoon in her hand with a menacing look in her eye. She had the curious habit of squeezing her eyes closed at you if she didn't want to speak to you.

Mammy wasn't afraid of anyone. She often told me how she and the *Cumann na mBan* treated British soldiers on sports days. They wouldn't let them on to Foy's field where local people had gathered to play their games. When the patrolling soldiers tried to befriend the locals – no doubt to collect information and intelligence – Mammy, still in her teens, would stand at the gate and spit at them as they went past. Quite an admission for someone who loathed spitting so much.

Mammy and Father's endless arguments were mostly about money. Father could be classed as a bit mean with money but, sure, he never had any. Most of the time, he worked in the Sanderson's yard at Killowen. They were big Protestant farmers who owned several hundred acres of land. They had one child called Kitty. She was absolutely gorgeous-looking. She was little and walked very smart. When my father broke his arm, Miss Kitty, as we called her, came over to our stone house with a large white enamel jug full of soup for him. We couldn't wait for her to go so we could all devour the contents of the jug. Then she returned with an elbow bath to soak his sore arm.

Miss Kitty was a good few years older than me: she could have been well into her twenties. She was the first woman I ever saw driving a car. She would go to Edenderry and all over in that car of hers. I was amazed.

'Quick, come on, Miss Kitty's drivin' her car,' I'd say to the others, and we'd run out to the gate to catch a glimpse of the green car going round Biddy Hickey's Turn.

Miss Kitty wasn't a bit proud. Her family was very kind to us, and Father worked very hard for them in return. He was their yardman. He tended to the cattle and saw that the milking was done. He worked for them for years. When I was born, he was only earning fifteen shillings a week.

His day began at eight in the morning and it finished at six in the evening, with an hour off for his dinner. He quit at twelve o'clock and walked twenty acres across three fields to come home for his dinner. In better moods, he would walk in, sling his hat on the table, and ask, 'Is there e'er a bit t'ate for a poor whore?' Father sometimes referred to himself as *a whore* just as Mammy referred to herself as *a body*.

He worked with a man called Pat Walsh whose wife, the Doon Walsh, would walk over the fields with a hot dinner of vegetables and meat for him every day, all packed in bowls in a food basket. If Father didn't come home, he'd be sitting across the grass from Pat eating a bit of dried bread – if he was lucky. Mammy wasn't like the Doon Walsh. She was more scatterbrained.

The men didn't get paid till Saturday night; by Friday night, our cupboards would be bare. I remember Father walking for an hour to get home to give Mammy the money for food. She would have to go on foot to O'Toole's, in Castlejordan, three miles away, to get some dinner, walk back home and cook it. Poor old Father wouldn't get his bit to eat until nine o'clock at night.

O'Toole's had a thatched roof. It was a pub as well as a general store and always stayed opened late for the workers. Once, when I walked with her to buy the food, Mammy bought these lovely, ripe tomatoes but we had the lot eaten by the time we got home.

If Father came home from work with a scowl on his face, it would be enough to send us scurrying into the darkest corner. We'd sit quiet as mice, losing the use of tongue and limb alike. We'd know not to speak to him until he had a full stomach. We generally spoke when we were spoken to and came when called. In his opinion children should be seen and not heard. We were mere objects to do as we were bid. He never indulged in any sort of conversation with his children, except with Carmel. She went everywhere with him and shared his interest in cow shite, turf mould and haycocks. Wherever he went, she went. If he went for the cows, she went for the cows; if he went to the bog, she went to the bog; if he sowed the potatoes, she'd sow the potatoes. He never really encouraged her to go with him, she just went. Carmel had a special bond with him. I wasn't a daddy's girl in that way.

I would always stay at home when Father and Mammy, and the others, went to the bog in the summer evenings to cut the turf. I hated going to the bog. I dreaded the flies and the midges, and the turf mould going up my nose.

I might go sometimes when they'd be drawing the turf, just to get the ride on the ass and cart or to take the tea. I would rather stay at home and clean the kitchen. When they all came through the door, tired and dirty after working in the bog all evening, I'd be standing at the open hearth with the kettle hopping asking them all, in turn, if they wanted a sup of tea.

I wanted Father to praise me for keeping the kitchen tidy. I needed some kind of appreciation. Not a chance. It never came. Mammy would tell me that Father did appreciate the things I did. He'd say to her, 'The Little Girl keeps the house lovely and clean. She's great with a besom.' But he never said it directly to me. No matter how much I craved Father's affection and attention, he would never notice me busying myself around the house and doing little jobs.

Even when Mammy miscarried twins and was taken to Tullamore Hospital, and I had to run the house for her and look after five-year-old Joe and three-year-old Ger, he didn't appreciate me.

I was holding Ger in my arms and Joe was tugging at my skirt when Mammy was being taken out on a stretcher. She looked dead and I didn't think that she was coming back. We were bawling but I told myself to be strong and responsible, so I washed and cleaned and made my first cake of bread.

I'll never forget the slapping I took from Father that day. He came home for his lunch but there was no food. Carmel had gone to the shops to buy something for his lunch and hadn't come back. There was I, aged all of twelve, thinking I was the great one doing this big bath of washing with the bread cooking.

I saw Father coming in the door looking fierce cross. When he realised there was no food, he started shouting and swearing about the distance he'd had to walk. 'There isn't a scrap t'ate' he was saying and 'What's a poor whore supposed to do now?' Then he gave me such a belting across the back of the head.

I sulked and he went off in search of Carmel. He found her mitching with my grandmother. She hadn't even been to the shop. Mammy used to say I was very dependable. If I went into Edenderry, I would be twenty minutes going, twenty minutes there and twenty minutes coming back. I would never mitch or go into people's houses. Carmel was always mitching. She did what she wanted to do. Father might be angry with her but he would never hit her: she was his favourite. I was the one that got the wallop that day and I wouldn't speak to him after. And I wouldn't do anything for him.

That evening, when my bread was baked, he went to cut a slice. 'This is so hard, I'll have to get the hatchet to break it,' he joked, trying to make up for hitting me. I was still sulking. I sulked for hours.

Father was sulky too. He was never a person to forgive easily and would hold a grudge for days on end. Mammy was very obstinate. The combination of temperaments could be explosive.

A few years later, an almighty row started one day over a bike. There was always a bike upturned on the kitchen floor with someone fixing a puncture. There was never a fork or a spoon with a straight handle in our house: they were all bent from putting tubes back into the tyres. On this particular day it was Peter's turn. He was hopeless. He could never get the hang of putting the tube back in with the forks. He had his usual trouble with the inner tube, making him late for a date.

'Isn't this feckin' terrible,' he said to Luke, who was preening himself in front of the mirror. 'How can I get about without me bike?' Peter was so exasperated he threw down the tube and left the house. Luke was on his way to town, taking a battery in to be charged in time for a big match the next day. In those days radios were operated by wet and dry batteries, not electricity. We always had one in the house and one in the town on charge.

Luke finished fixing his hair and straightening his tie and, scooping up the battery, marched outside to his bike, which he'd left propped up at the gable end of the house. A few moments later, he came tearing back through the door, white with anger, turning the place blue with the cursing and swearing.

'I'll break his fuckin' neck!' he screamed. 'That fuckin' bastard has taken me whorin' bike!'

In Luke's vocabulary, everything was a whore: the hammer, the nail and the saw, the cows, the pigs and the shovel. 'Where's that whorin' fork?' he'd say. 'Give me the whorin' shovel, fuckin' whore.' Cursing was a second language to him.

'Maybe Peter didn't know ya were goin' to need your bike,' Mammy said.

'Sure he knew cursed-God-well I was goin' to the town.'

Mammy made a grab for her rosary beads. 'Will ya for God's sake stop takin' the Lord's name in vain,' she said, blessing herself. Mammy was always blessing herself. 'Sure I'll fix the puncture on Peter's bike and won't that take ya to the town?'

'Will it fuck. That crock! I wouldn't ride it to the gate. I'm tellin' ya straight, that fucker'd better not come home here tonight.'

Just then, Father walked in, lifting his hat to scratch his head. 'What's wrong?' he asked Mammy, by now on her knees fixing Peter's puncture.

'Can't ya see what's wrong?' shouted Luke. 'I was goin' to get the battery charged to listen to the match tomorrow and Peter's gone off with me fuckin' bike.'

'I'll have this ready in a minute,' Mammy said.

'Ya know what to do with it,' Luke scowled.

'Sure ya can have my bike,' said Father, settling himself into his chair. 'It'll take ya to the town. We can't miss the match.'

Luke hoisted the battery into the air and paced up and down the kitchen, seething with anger.

'Look, Luke'een, when I sell my turkeys I'll buy you a car,' said Mammy. 'Tommy Foy's sellin' his baby Ford and he only wants twenty-five pounds for it. It's a lovely little car and won't ya be able to bring your father and me to Mass?'

Father leapt up from the chair, his calm deserting him. 'You'll do nothin' of the sort! Is it a car they want under their arses now? And me an auld man who had to walk to work till I could afford me own bike.'

'I'll buy it if I like,' Mammy said defiantly.

'We'll see about that.'

'No,' said Mammy, '*you'll* see.'

'No, *you'll* see.'

Luke tried to escape the row he'd just started by standing at the garden gate but he could still hear Mammy and Father raising hell about the ownership of the turkeys. He'd had enough. He turned on his heel and stormed back into the kitchen.

'Quit shoutin' for the love and honour of Jaysus. Yous can be heard in the Castle Bog. Yous are worse than the tinkers!'

'Who are you callin' a tinker?' Mammy screeched. 'I'm not a tinker. It's you who's actin' like the tinker cursin' and swearin' and shoutin' at the top of your voice!'

With that, Luke picked up Peter's bike and hurled it as far as he could down the garden. 'I'll break it into smithereens. It's nothin' short of a heap of shite.'

Father, still smarting about the sale of his turkeys, said no more.

'Anyway, why doesn't Peter buy a new bike?' Luke continued. 'He's not short of a bob or two. Anyone'd think he hadn't two ha'pence to rub together, goin' around with the arse out of his trousers, next to nothin' on his feet and loads of cattle in the field. Here's me tryin' to earn a few shillin's and he goes and takes me fuckin' bike! How am I supposed to get to work on Monday?'

Mammy looked at Peter's bike in pieces down the garden. Her expression changed. She turned sharply to Luke. 'And you could have the same if ya weren't givin' it all to O'Toole,' she said, 'and what ya don't give him for porter goes on cards and cigarettes. Ya think bad of givin' a body a few shillin's to feed ya but ya expect plenty of food on your plate. It's easy known ya don't have to buy it or you'd soon see how far the few shillin's go!'

Mammy was raging. Father was looking out the big window, his head turned sideways, getting more and more vexed with Luke's capers.

'I suppose you'll tell Peter he didn't break his bike, will ya? You'll make up some excuse for him again. Ya forget Peter has to go to work on Monday. How do ya suppose he'll go without his bike? And there you are, promisin' Luke a car with my turkeys!'

Turkeys always seemed to be at the centre of some row or other.

FOUR

Tullamore General

We looked at the bloodied tissue in disbelief. 'Oh God, oh God,' John kept saying. 'Oh God.'

The sight of the blood shocked him and his reaction unnerved me. I was coughing up thick red blood with sickening frequency. John calmed down and phoned the doctor. He spoke hurriedly. I sat in silence on the couch, too scared to breathe for fear of bringing up blood again. I felt like a child breathing quietly to make the monsters go away.

John sat down in my chair, next to the fire, and told me not to worry.

The doctor arrived within fifteen minutes. He stood before me rubbing his hands together and asking me what had happened. I told him about the wheezing, coughing and the bleeding. He bent his long body over towards me and rubbed his chin.

'Mmm . . .' he said.

'Doctor, what is it?' John asked.

'How did it start?'

'With a wheeze,' I said, tapping my collarbone.

'Under the collarbone,' John confirmed.

'When was that, Maura?'

'About nine-thirty this evenin', Doctor.'

'Well, it could have been around half nine but it could have been goin' on to ten,' John added.

'Mmm . . . did you vomit at all?'

'No, Doctor, I didn't but I felt very sick. What do you think it is?'

'Well, Maura, you know, it could be one of three things,' he said gently. 'It could be an ulcer, it's possible it might be TB or, most likely, a rupture caused by the aspirin.'

I'd had a heart attack ten years earlier and I'd been taking an aspirin every day to thin the blood. The doctor likened it to a nose-bleed that would erupt for no reason, like the small veins bursting after a sneeze. I was reminded of the time Father spent three weeks in Tullamore General with a nosebleed. I was fourteen at the time and Mammy was putting wet towels around his face and nose, but the bleeding wouldn't stop. She was very tormented.

The doctor advised me to leave off the tablets and call him in the morning if my bleeding didn't stop. He didn't seem to think it was very serious. It wasn't a perfect diagnosis but I felt reassured.

John showed the doctor out then sat next to me on the sofa. At that moment we were two very tired old people making small talk, chatting about our children and their children. I knew John was doing his best to distract me and prevent me from being upset.

I was too scared to move. 'I hope to God this bleedin' has stopped.'

'It should be all right,' said John. 'It hasn't bled for a while now.'

'I feel a bit cold.'

'Do ya want me to light the fire? Shall I make a sup of tea?'

'No, I don't feel like tea.'

'I could get you a duvet, that will keep the heat in ya.'

'Yeh, please, get me that old pink wool blanket from the hot press. That'll do it.'

John got the blanket and brought it to me in the sitting room. I stood up and he placed it on the chair then told me to sit down.

He then, skilfully, wrapped me in the blanket. I felt all cosied-up and looked after, as if nothing had happened.

Although it was late, it was still bright outside and I could see a fierce crowd of crows flying over to nest in the trees that lined the avenue to Rathmoyle House. I looked out of the window and watched. John and I spent the next hour or so in silence – a silence interspersed by bits of tired and halting conversation.

There was still no more bleeding. John thought it had stopped for good but I didn't want to fool myself. I was thinking, I hope to God I don't have to go to hospital. I wanted to go to bed – I love my own bed.

'Shall I call one of the children?' he said.

'No, not yet.'

'But they'll want to know.'

'There's nothin' to know. They don't have to know anythin' tonight. It's too late anyway. We'll see how I am tomorrow and call them then.'

'Should we go to bed now? Perhaps it won't come back.'

'Yeh, okay, let's do that,' I said, picking up a box of tissues.

'Would ya like me to sleep in your room tonight?'

'No, it's all right. I'll be okay. Leave your door open. I'll call you if I need ya.'

It was getting on for eleven and I wanted to sleep. I wanted to fall into a deep sleep. I went to my room and prepared for bed. I put an empty margarine tub, the one I'd had on the sink for used tea bags, on the side table for fear of the coughing starting again. I propped myself up on my pillows, half lying and half sitting. Just as I was dozing off, the coughing started. Oh my God, I thought, not again. The dreaded bleeding soon followed. I called for John.

'Will I phone Ann?' he said.

'Yes, phone Ann.' I saw her earlier that day. I didn't think she would be totally surprised by the news.

Ann is the wife of my brother Ger. They live a couple of miles

up the road, in the cottage where we were brought up. She is a
true and genuine friend, even though she is much younger than
me. She is steady, brave and practical. Ann is my rock. And she's
a nurse – a good, well-informed nurse – and has been at my side
through many episodes of illness. She was always there for me
and would spend hours with me. All I would have to do was
ring her up, even when I was living in England.

I remember when I was in Birmingham, I swallowed a hair
and it was stuck in my throat. I had been eating a sandwich and
there must have been a hair in it. I phoned Ann in Ireland and
she told me what to do: get some dry white bread and chew it.
It did the trick. She's always been very professional in her deal-
ings with me, and she is a calming influence. I knew I could
count on her now. She knew me well enough to know that I
would be panicking. I can get a raised heartbeat very easily.

Ann arrived within fifteen minutes and tried to appear calm
but I could see anxiety all over her face.

'I think you ought to call the doctor again, John,' she said.
'Maura has to go to hospital.'

John saw my anxiety rising. The doctor was reluctant to send
for the ambulance; he wanted John to take me in.

'Ya know I can't drive at night,' he told the doctor. 'My eyesight
is too bad for that.'

John listened some more.

'Now, Doctor,' he said firmly. 'I think ya have to send for the
ambulance. This is now a hospital case.'

John was uptight and fidgety, rushing here and there, obviously worried.

I felt numb. I didn't understand what was happening to me. I
thought I was haemorrhaging. Is this the way I'm going to be taken?

Ann packed my hospital bag.

'Did ya put in my nightdress, Ann?'

'I did, Maura.'

'And my dressin' gown?'

'Yes, it's here.'

'Don't forget my teeth things from the bathroom – and my brush. And you'll get a towel there in the hot press.'

'All right, Maura.'

I could hear John speaking to somebody in the other room. The ambulance had arrived. A tall man appeared in my doorway pushing a wheelchair in front of him. He flicked a switch and I winced in the glare of the main light. A small, stout nurse was standing behind him.

'Hello, Mrs Murphy, how are you?' she said pleasantly, peering round the side of her male colleague. 'We've come to take you off to hospital.'

I couldn't speak. I didn't want to leave my cosy bed, I didn't want to go to hospital and I didn't want to be unwell. I sat on the side of the bed feeling very sad and upset. It was a low bed and the soles of my feet were able to touch the lush carpet. With eyes downcast, I looked at the deep red of the carpet and its tiny cream flowers. The red reminded me of the blood I'd been coughing up all evening. It was a quality carpet. I'd bought it recently from my sister Anna. There was enough in it to do two rooms and the hall. Anna had bought it to carpet her house in County Kerry, but she didn't use it and sold it to me.

It's a shame that the cottage is so damp, I thought, looking at the paper peeling off the wall under the window.

'Are you ready, Mrs Murphy?'

'I am, Nurse.'

I didn't see the need for a wheelchair but I let them help me into it. I looked about the bedroom at all the photographs of my children. One was strangely lit-up by the beams of a passing car, its occupant making his way home after a boozy evening in Doyles, no doubt.

Ellen, the first of my academic children, looked back at me in the car's light, pictured proud and austere in her cap and gown. I thought about how upset she would be to see her mammy like this, ill again, off to hospital again, and the many times she had supported me through my troubles when she was a child. Poor Ellen, I thought.

As I was being manoeuvred through the narrow door, I glimpsed the photo of Joan with her nice little smile in her cap and gown. How lovely she looked on her graduation day. I realised she was wearing lipstick. Bright red lipstick. How odd. I'd never noticed that before. Joan never wears makeup.

I coughed again and spat the thick red blood clot into the tub.

That morning I had been a reasonably healthy person, but now I was on my way to hospital. Ann and John were trying to reassure me but their voices seemed faint and far away. They seemed to be consoling each other, not me.

My mind was racing. The whole sequence of my life flashed in front of me. I wondered if John would have the presence of mind to put out food for the birds and the cats that visited our garden. I was fretting about the little robin who came to see me every day. He seemed to follow me from one room to another, popping up on every windowsill. How would he get along without me?

How disappointed my grandson Conor would be if I missed his Confirmation, and how would his brother, Declan, get on with his Irish dancing? Little Dec was only seven but he was a great little dancer. We expected him to do well in his next competition.

The ambulance driver wheeled me into the living room and there was my sister, Carmel. She was in Ireland on holiday. I was glad to see her. I wished we could be having a sup of tea and a good old natter. Instead, she was watching me being wheeled out the door. Carmel is very cool in a crisis but she showed great shock in her face that evening. Her eyes were filled with pain for me.

'Good God, John,' she said, 'what's the matter with Maura?'

John shook his head and looked over at Ann. 'Ann, will you explain?'

'I'll tell you later,' Ann said, 'Maura has to get into the ambulance.'

I looked over at Carmel. She was crying. If Carmel's crying, I thought, there must be something seriously wrong with me.

I prayed. I prayed to the Sacred Heart of Jesus and his Blessed Mother. I had so much faith in her that I carried her pendant on my key ring. I asked Our Lady of Lourdes not to take me from my children. Not yet. There was so much more I wanted to do. Just like Mammy, I believe in the power of prayer.

Ann walked out to the ambulance but John only came as far as the gate. It was obvious that he wouldn't be coming with me to Tullamore Hospital.

'Are ya comin', John?' I asked.

'No, I'm not. Ya know I can't drive in the night time—'

'Will I come with you?' Ann interrupted.

'No, Ann, you go home.'

'And I'd have to hang around all night,' John continued.

'I'll drive behind the ambulance and bring you home, John,' Ann offered.

'I'll be all right, Ann. I have the nurse with me. You go on home.'

I was very upset that John didn't come with me. I didn't expect Ann to come – it was nearly one in the morning – but I hoped John would make the effort. He knew how scared I would be. I thought it was very selfish of him. John has limits to his compassion. I couldn't believe it when I saw him going back into the house. He didn't wait for the ambulance to pull away. Maybe he wasn't able to cope with it all but when I saw the front door close my heart sank. I thought, I'll never be going back in there again. I felt like he was locking me out for good. I was convinced it would be my last journey. I was sure I was going to die.

Ann told me not to fret. That smile of hers told me to be brave. I didn't feel very brave, going out into the dark night while the rest of Rhode was tucked up into warm beds.

The ambulance doors closed with a chilling sound, like the clanging of prison gates. My body shivered with cold and dread. I was on my own, once again, making the seventeen-mile journey to Tullamore General strapped into the back of an ambulance. I felt so miserable, speeding through the villages, recalling all the years of illness I'd had to endure. The night was silent save for the ominous sound of the siren.

The nurse looked glum, sitting quietly, telling me, now and then, not to worry. Her words were wasted on me: I was terrified. She replaced the margarine tub with a steel kidney dish and I held it under my chin to catch the stinking invasive blood. It was so undignified. Her crisp white uniform was splattered with my blood by the time we got to Tullamore.

She seemed relieved to be able to deposit me at the hospital. The driver wrapped me in a blanket and wheeled me into Casualty. The perspiration was heavy on my body. I felt clammy, hot and sweaty in my light nightclothes. How lonely I felt sitting there all by myself with no one to talk to.

I was left on my own for two hours on a trolley in a cubicle before a female doctor came in to examine me. She asked me all kinds of questions designed to distract me from my predicament: 'Where do you live?' 'Do you have children?' 'What part of England were you in?' Eventually, she summoned a young nurse to get Mrs Murphy on to a chair. I was to be admitted.

The ward was dimly lit, patients were snoring and nurses were talking in loud whispers. Someone in the far corner was calling for a bedpan.

I lay in the dark, festering. I was getting angry, especially with John: I blamed him for subjecting me to so much torment and stress during my married life. I was angry with God, too, for letting me suffer. I wasn't a bad person. I never harmed anyone. Why me?

FIVE

A Domestic Life

I left school at the age of fourteen with very little knowledge and even fewer prospects. When my convent school plans came to nothing, I followed in Mammy's footsteps and settled for the life of a servant to the rich and privileged.

I'd harboured ambitions to be a nurse, but I knew I had no chance of training in Ireland. I hadn't the education or the money. I wanted to follow the steady stream of girls crossing the Irish Sea to train in England where they were more lenient because they were crying out for nurses. I needed my parents' consent. Mammy wasn't willing to give me permission and told me to ask our parish priest.

I wrote, expectantly, to Father Callery, asking him for his written consent. I waited and waited but he didn't reply. He didn't respond to me at all, but passed his response through Mammy; she had the habit of going into the vestry most Sundays to talk to the priest or give him money.

'He refuses, point blank,' she told me.

'Why, Mammy?'

'You're young, Maur'een. He says wait till you're twenty-one.'

I was desperately disappointed.

So in the first few months after leaving school, Mammy taught me how to cook, clean, sew, darn and iron in readiness for work as a maid. All this training was about to bring in my first wage: I heard that the widow Old Kate Kelly, a cripple who sat in a chair all day, was looking for a girl to do her housework and tend to her needs.

She lived quite a few fields away in the woods of Greenhill. I didn't much fancy working for her but I was in need of a bit of money to buy some vests and winter shoes, and the odd packet of Woodbines. I made the long old trek to her tin house in my winter wellies to see would she give me the job.

Old Kate took a liking to me straightaway; I thought she was ancient, though she couldn't have been more than sixty. She was a grand-looking woman and a great whistler. She whistled all day long in her fancy frocks and silky petticoats. Kate was very swanky: she had a trunk full of beautiful Irish linen, and woven and quilted bedspreads.

Kate was a well-read and knowledgeable person. She was intrepid too: she had travelled all the way across America in her more active days. She regaled me with so many stories of her great treks and intrigued me with tales about the Antarctic and the North Pole. She kept a large globe of the world and every evening when her brother, Jim, went out to tend to the livestock and fowl, she'd ask me to fetch it down from her room. She delighted in spinning the globe and stopping it at all the places she had visited. I was fascinated by this huge monstrosity and sat at her feet as she pointed out the northern and southern hemispheres. I learnt more about geography from her than I did from the teachers at school.

I was very fond of Kate. My confidence grew working for her. She opened my mind and heart to all the opportunities life had to offer. She made me feel important. I wasn't so taken with Jim. He was very gruff and had a reputation for being so mean he wouldn't give you the smell off his piss. He had a strange way of talking, a peculiar dialect I didn't understand.

I thought I was doing fine for Old Kate until three weeks into my job when I upset grumpy Jim.

'Hotten the grayse there, Maura,' he demanded one morning.

'Hotten the what?' I said, perplexed.

'Hotten the grayse. The grayse!'

I had no idea what he was talking about. He cursed me into the ground and out of it and gave me the sack for being stupid. 'You're no good to us,' he said in a fury. 'Don't bother comin' back no more.'

Kate begged him to let me stay but he wouldn't hear of it. If only I had known that *hotten the grayse* meant *heat up the grease* and fry me an egg!

I missed Kate and her stories but I missed the money more. I always liked to have a bit of money. I spent my first florin on some vests and knickers (I had an obsession for vests and knickers) and a decent pair of shoes. Mine had holes in the soles and I had to wedge pieces of cardboard in each one to keep my feet off the ground.

I was upset to leave Kate's like that. I told Mammy I'd been sacked but she remained as philosophical as ever. 'Don't mind him, Maur'een, he's a mane auld brat.'

I lay awake the night I left Kate Kelly's cottage, wondering what I would do next. Soon after, while I was in the kitchen baking a cake of bread, and Mammy was darning socks by the fire, I spied someone making his way through the yard towards the kitchen door. It was Tommy Murray of Fahy Cross.

'Mammy, here comes Tommy Murray.'

'Is it Tommy, ya say?'

We weren't really friends of his family, just acquaintances, the way you are in the country. All I knew about him was that he was a milkman and lived in Dublin with his wife and children. Mammy jumped up from her seat and ran to get the door. She loved to receive visitors.

'Do ya want a cup of tae, Tommy?' Mammy asked breathlessly, patting her hair with the palm of her hand.

'Ah, I will, missus, if you're makin' one,' he replied, settling himself down into a chair without being asked.

'Tommy, tell me, how is your mother?' Mammy enquired.

'Not a bother on her.' He sipped his tea and the two of them chatted politely.

'So, Maura, what are you doin' with yourself these days? I hear you left Old Kate Kelly's?'

I was surprised he knew so much about my affairs. 'That's right, Tommy. I've been home a while now.'

'And are ya workin'?'

Why is he so inquisitive? 'No.'

'Well, would ya like to go to Dublin?'

'Why would I want to do that, Tommy?'

'I know a nice woman in the city who's lookin' for a good girl to work in her house.'

'Oh really? And what would I be expected to do?'

'You know, cookin', cleanin', that kind of thing.'

Well, I was a girl and I suppose I was a *good* girl. I knew how to cook and clean and 'that kind of thing' – and I needed a job.

I noticed that Mammy was raking the hearth vigorously. 'What do you think, Mammy?'

'Maur'een, I'd prefer ya didn't go but, if ya want to go, sure you should go.'

Well, what should I do? I loved being at home with Mammy and the rest of them but I needed to earn my keep. They could no longer afford to feed a girl with my appetite. And I was young and I thought I ought to venture out on my own. I needed time to think about it. I always needed time to think. I could never answer on the spot like that. But then Tommy gave me a get-out.

'Ya don't have to answer straightaway. I'm goin' back to

Dublin in a few days, so ya can let me know before I go.'

'I'll think about it, Tommy. It's nice of you to ask.'

I had mixed feelings about going to the big city. I was delighted but also apprehensive. Like a greenhorn, I didn't know a bee from a bull's foot.

The morning I left, I crossed the kitchen to the hall to say my goodbyes. Mammy was the only one in the house to wish me well. I picked up the new cardboard suitcase I'd bought in the town that weekend, ready to leave.

Mammy was crying. 'Won't you take care?' was all she said. I wanted to put my arms around her but I wasn't comfortable about showing my feelings; my body shrank with tension when we hugged. I was determined to walk out the door with my head held high, and I didn't want to cry.

As I reached the gate, I turned to see Mammy standing in the doorway. Her tears upset me but I had to leave and catch my bus. When I reached the top of Wakley's Hill I stopped and turned round to see if she was still waving me off. She wasn't. I knew there was nothing left for me in Clonmore but, secretly, I hoped she would beg me not to go and give me an excuse to stay at home with her.

Ireland had little to offer the working classes in the 1940s, particularly in rural towns. And Clonmore was in the middle of Ireland's bog land. There was nothing there for a young woman like me. I resented leaving my home to work in somebody else's.

I told the bus driver this was my first time away from home and asked him to let me know when we reached the terminus. I sat and gazed out of the window as we travelled east towards Dublin. We stopped first at Edenderry, to drop off and pick up mail, then sped through numerous villages towards Prosperous and Clane.

The tall spire of the church in Prosperous pierced the sky. The church, showered with wealth, towered above the shops and houses looking splendid as the stained glass twinkled in the late evening sun.

I watched some barefoot boys playing with their wooden spinning tops, their torn trousers held up by frayed *galluses* and their woolly *ganseys* tied around their waists. One of them looked up and smiled at a young priest walking round the churchyard, his head stuck in his missal. He took no notice of the poor creature. Only the 'good evening's of the better off could persuade him to raise his head. Ireland was so class conscious. The clergy paid no heed to the poor; they visited the rich more often. Priests would have their cups of tea and their fancy dinners but they'd think hard before visiting the poor: they'd visit the sick once a month but they'd be sure to turn up for their half crown though, then shame the poor at Mass on Easter Sunday for their paltry contribution to the church funds.

Every year the whole parish had to give money for the Easter Dues for the upkeep of the church. It was the tradition for the priest to read the names, and their gifts, off the altar. Father Callery would stand up in the pulpit, holding this ledger in front of him, and read out the list of dues for the Easter period. He would always start with the rich, usually one of the Mulvins, and read out the poor man's gifts straight after.

He'd say, 'Frank Mulvin – one pound; Johnnie McNamee – two shillings and sixpence; Paddy Moore – one pound; Luke McNamee – two shillings; Matty Glennon – two shillings . . .'

It would take him an hour to read out the gifts of the entire parish. It used to anger my father but he would never complain: in those days you didn't criticise a priest, or any religious person.

I thought about Father's humiliation at the hands of the church as I clutched my rosary beads and watched the sun setting on the peaks of the Dublin Mountains. I couldn't stop thinking about Mammy's sad eyes, and I imagined Father coming in weary from work.

I tried to swallow my tears but my throat was tight with

emotion. I wished I wasn't going but I had little choice. Why don't you pull yourself together? I thought. These people don't want to listen to your snivelling and croaking.

The bus jolted.

My suitcase slid off the seat and I screeched as it fell awkwardly on to my foot. I suddenly became aware of myself again and I self-consciously hauled the case on to my lap. The other passengers stared at me.

'Barberstown!' called the driver.

Not far to Dublin now.

I stepped off the bus gripping my suitcase and looked around for a friendly face. I felt sick. I was on my own for the first time and I didn't like it one bit. I arrived in Dublin a real country yokel with no idea of city life. The stench from the River Liffey hit my nostrils and the noise of the traffic battered my ears. I was amazed to see the amount of traffic going up and down the quay. I'd never seen so many cars and coaches. Bicycles were stacked against railings like clamps of turf against a shed, and a mass of crowded heads bobbed up and down the city streets. Everyone was in such a great hurry, too busy to pass the time of day. No 'Morra, Maura!' here.

I asked the coach driver for directions to the nearest bed and breakfast. 'Is this your first time in the city?' he asked, in a thick Dublin brogue.

'Yes—' I started to say.

'Go to the end of the quay.' He pointed and then launched into complicated directions. 'Take the turn to the left, cross over the other side of the street and you'll come to a few side streets. Now the third one up is Talbot Street, turn down there, and there's a couple of cheap dives. You should get fixed up all right for the night.'

'Thank you,' I said, wondering if he said left or right off the quay.

I found a place. It looked clean but it was 7s. 6d. a night! That was as much as some people's weekly wage. I had to take it. I had nowhere else to go.

Next morning, I woke in this noisy city from a disturbed sleep. Coaches had lined the street outside my 'cheap' lodgings, cars were blowing their horns and horses' hooves clattered on their way to market.

Breakfast happened in a bay window overlooking the street. An older woman with black hair greying at the temples was standing beside a small table. I liked her kind, round, wrinkled face.

'Good morning,' she said. 'What would you like for breakfast?' She scribbled my order – toast with marmalade and a small pot of tea – into a little notepad, wedged the pencil behind her ear, and retreated quickly through a beaded doorway.

I settled my bill and met Tommy at the central bus station. We were to catch the bus out to Clontarf to meet my prospective employers. On the way, he told me everything he knew about the Cavanaghs. They were a good-natured bunch and friendly to the people who worked for them. The family was on his milk round and they were among his favourite customers.

We arrived at Clontarf on a beautiful summer's morning, the salty air catching my breath. I had a good feeling in my heart walking up the long pathway with Tommy Murray. The Cavanaghs' house wasn't far from the sea and the golf links at Dollymount. I liked the quietness and quaintness of the long tree-lined road with all its well-kept houses and splendid gardens.

The Cavanaghs owned a large three-storey house and landscaped garden with lawns and flowerbeds either side of the pathway. It was enclosed by a tall sandstone wall. Twelve stone steps led up to an imposing, glossy brown Dublin door.

My case was light. What I'd brought with me would have fitted in an oilcloth shopping bag but the case looked more respectable. I put it down on the ground, walked with jelly legs towards the front door and Tommy pushed the brass knob. I could hear the bell ringing faintly inside. I stood with Tommy, gormless and out of my depth.

The door opened and a young woman, with dark cropped hair and horn-rimmed glasses, stood before us wearing a black smock with a white frilly apron and matching hat.

Brazen as you like, Tommy swept past her and walked right in. 'Mr Cavanagh! Hello! Mr Cavanagh!' he called. 'I've brought the girl for you to have a look at.' Fancy talking about me as if I were some prize heifer.

The young woman looked me up and down and glanced at my cardboard suitcase. 'Good mornin',' she said pleasantly. 'You've come to see Mrs Cavanagh?'

'Yes,' I said timidly.

Just then Mr Cavanagh emerged from a door at the end of the hall. He was a big man: his head was big and bald and his face was crimson.

'Well, well. Hello, Tommy. And who have you with you, did you say?'

'This is Maura McNamee, Mr Cavanagh. A girl from down my way in Offaly. I told Mrs Cavanagh I'd bring her up, and indeed I have.'

I stepped into the magnificent hall. I was mesmerised. A crystal chandelier was suspended from an ornate ceiling and dusty paintings hung in every available space along the walls. The shiny tiled floor was covered with an assortment of expensive rugs. And the stairs! I'd never seen stairs so big and winding. Brass rods held a warm, thick carpet firmly in place.

Mr Cavanagh turned his beaming red head towards me and looked me up and down. 'Well, Maura, you look like a good girl. What makes you want to come all the way from home to this auld city?'

'I've always wanted to come to Dublin and when Tommy said ya needed someone to work in the—'

'Good, good,' he interrupted. 'That is good. I am sure Mrs Cavanagh will be delighted.'

'Do you employ a gardener, Mr Cavanagh?' I asked. 'It's a lovely garden ya have.'

'I do not!' he said, with mock indignation. 'That is my wee piece of paradise and no man better lay his hands on it. Have you tended other houses, young 'un?'

'I have, sir. Back home in Offaly. Will I need references?'

'Ah, no. Mrs Cavanagh lets the cook attend to all that. Tommy, have you had any luck on the horses lately?'

The two men walked off discussing form. I was to discover that Mrs Cavanagh was a gambling woman and was particularly fond of betting on the horses. Tommy also had a passion for the sport and the two of them would study the form every day, sitting opposite each other at the long pine kitchen table. Mrs Cavanagh would be chopping the vegetables while they exchanged horses and odds.

'I'm Breege, the parlour maid,' said the woman in glasses. 'Come into the kitchen and we'll have a cup of tea. Mrs Cavanagh's in town but she'll be home shortly.'

I followed her into a large square kitchen. I couldn't believe the size of it: twenty foot by twenty foot. It made Mammy's look like a broom cupboard. A fine-looking, middle-aged woman of five foot five was chopping meat. 'My name is Catherine,' she said cheerily. 'I'm the cook.'

She got up and walked down the kitchen to put the kettle on, her black head of hair bobbing with every step. She walked briskly, despite a pronounced limp.

'Most people call me Kate,' she said, in a thick Galway accent. 'It really doesn't bother me what they call me, so long as they don't call me too early in the morning!' Kate threw her head back and laughed, delighting in the sharpness of her wit. I smiled shyly. Then she set three cups, with matching plates, in the centre of the table and waddled from side to side as she disappeared into the pantry again, twice, fetching bread, ham and milk. She cut several thin slices of the home-made bread and asked me a flurry of questions. She was obviously sizing me up.

Kate had been the Cavanaghs' cook for many years. 'We're very lucky here,' she said. 'The Cavanaghs are real nice people. Don't bother us very much. They're out most of the time at dinner parties, bridge parties, all sorts of parties. They like to go to the theatre and have a late supper in town. They often have people over for a card game.'

I liked the sound of the Cavanaghs and I could see myself being quite content as their domestic. I couldn't have stepped into a cushier little number.

'So, Maura, the job's yours.'

'Shouldn't I speak to Mrs Cavanagh first?'

'Ah, no. She leaves all that to me.'

I surveyed my grand surroundings, delighted with myself. I'd landed on my feet. I noticed the big black range and funnel stove beside it. I couldn't understand what city folk would want with a range. Surely they could afford the latest electric cooker? Perhaps they are a mean bunch. Then I spotted a second cooker – electric – on the other wall. More money than sense, this lot. And a pine table. That's the latest thing. Nice. And clean. They had a beautiful red quarry-tiled floor. I hoped they wouldn't want me to scrub that too often. But all in all I was delighted to be in this beautiful house. It had a warm, welcoming atmosphere.

'Come on and I'll show you your quarters,' said Kate.

We passed the pantry, which lay back from the kitchen, and crossed the hallway to the backstairs.

'These are the servants' stairs,' she said. 'We use them to take meals up to Mr and Mrs Cavanagh. Servants mustn't use the front stairs, or the main hall.'

Kate opened the door to my tiny, musty room down in the basement. It was very basic. Apart from a single bed, which had one pillow, covered in a fancy lace pillowcase, and a wardrobe, there was no other furniture, except for a washstand and jug. It was very poky for such a big house.

I hung up my smart, new grey coat – I'd bought it with money I'd earned thinning turnips and beet – on the back of the door and noticed a bell, praying it wouldn't ring too often.

There was an identical bedroom on the other side of the small corridor. I supposed, wrongly, that this was Kate's. It wasn't. Kate was rewarded, for her years of service, with a room in the main part of the house upstairs.

We went down corridors, turned corners and strode up and down steps until we reached the nursery at the back of the house. The baby was in her cot, fast asleep. A woman, about Kate's age, was sitting in a comfortable chair reading a book.

'This is our new girl, Nanny,' said Kate. The woman smiled but carried on reading.

I was anxious to meet the lady of the house. I could get on with most people but I hoped she wouldn't spoil things and turn out to be stuck up. I needn't have worried; when Mrs Cavanagh arrived home, I liked her immediately.

'Mrs Cavanagh's ready for you now,' said Breege. I followed Breege to the drawing room. She knocked gently on the door and waited for a reply.

'Come in,' said an educated voice. I followed meekly behind Breege as she stepped noiselessly to a coffee table, picked up a tray of dirty china cups and left – closing the door skilfully with her free hand.

As soon as I saw the plump sandy-haired woman I knew that we would be more than employer and employee. She had a firm but friendly enough manner and a tiny, crooked smile that spread into a broad grin when she was particularly amused.

Mrs Cavanagh delivered a list of dos and don'ts. 'I have a place for everything, and I like everything in its place.'

'Yes, Mrs Cavanagh.'

'You'll get up at seven each morning . . .'

'Yes, Mrs Cavanagh.'

'Help Nanny with the baby's bath . . .'

'Yes, Mrs Cavanagh.'

'Tidy up the nursery day room and polish my shoes—'

'Yes—'

'. . . and then Mr Cavanagh's shoes.'

'Mrs Cavanagh.'

This was too much to take in. Well, I wasn't really taking in anything: she spoke so fast my head hurt. She told me the bell in my room would ring if they needed anything.

'The bell will be switched off tonight, Maura, to let you settle in.'

Despite the list of orders, Mrs Cavanagh would never put me under too much pressure – as long as I did what I was paid to do, and didn't upset the smooth running of the house. In return, I was to be paid a pound a week. I was made up. It was a fortune for a young girl.

'Now,' she said, with finality, bringing our first meeting to an end, 'you can go and join Kate and Breege in the kitchen for supper. I'm sure you're famished.'

'Yes, Mrs Cavanagh. Thank you, Mrs Cavanagh.'

I followed my new employer down to the kitchen. Kate and Breege were sitting on either side of the black range, Breege sewing and Kate reading.

'I've brought Maura down for some supper,' she said. 'And when you've finished, Breege, would you be kind enough to sort some bedding for Maura?'

'I will, Mrs Cavanagh.'

Mrs Cavanagh walked smartly out the door. Breege put away her sewing, took out a large white tablecloth from a drawer and covered the pine table. She crossed over to the pantry, emerged with glasses and a tin of biscuits and placed them carefully on the table. She retraced her steps and reappeared with three plates, three knives, some bread rolls, butter and cheese. Then came the biggest surprise of all: Breege handed me a glass of milk. Milk! I was expecting a hot cup of tea and a good dinner. I hadn't eaten since midday. My stomach thought my throat had been cut. Well, that's the limit. I didn't know whether to laugh or cry. I ate the meagre offerings and turned in for the night.

I decided to take a late-night soak. As I made my way to the bathroom, I heard voices. I strained to listen. The voices stopped. I tried to turn the handle but it wouldn't move. It was locked. I could hear voices again. I pressed my ear against the door. They were the voices of old people. I knocked on the door. No one answered. I knocked again.

Suddenly a deep, feeble voice said, 'Who's there? What do you want?'

'Can I use the bathroom?' I asked.

'Go away, can't you see this room is occupied!'

I ran down to the kitchen. 'What's wrong with you?' Breege asked. 'Ya look as though you've seen a ghost.'

'I think I have. Heard them, anyway. Two of them,' I said breathlessly. 'They're in the bathroom!'

Breege started to laugh. 'I should have told ya. They're Mrs Cavanagh's parents. They usually have a late-night bath together.'

An auld woman getting into a bath with an auld man! How could they? I'd never heard tell of two auld ones having a bath together!

At least they're not spirits, I thought, feeling slightly foolish. 'I was wantin' to take a bath,' I said innocently.

'Domestic staff are not allowed to have baths,' she said. 'That's what the jug and basin's for.' I was very surprised. 'It's the only rule of the house, Maura. We have to strip wash in our rooms.'

I woke next morning with a knocking on the door. 'Maura, it's Breege. I've brought you a cup of tea.' I jumped out of bed and let her in. 'Don't be expecting this every mornin',' she said, handing me a tray. 'I was makin' one for meself anyway.'

I slipped back into bed and sipped my hot cup of tea before

starting my first day's work in the city. I put on my freshly starched frock, made my way to the nursery to prepare the baby's bath and then went downstairs for breakfast.

Breakfast for the staff was at eight every morning and consisted of porridge, toast and marmalade and tea or coffee. There was an occasional boiled egg and we were treated to a cooked breakfast on Sundays.

I arranged the post and the morning papers on the breakfast tray then spent the morning polishing and vacuuming, clearing out the grates, setting the fires and replenishing the coal bucket and log box. At three o'clock, the bell rang in the kitchen. Kate jumped to her feet. 'It's time for their afternoon tea. The trolley will have to be made. We use this china,' she said, showing me the matching cups and saucers. 'Fill this silver jug with milk, but not to the top. Leave half an inch. And this is their sugar bowl.' Kate filled a matching teapot and placed a cosy over it. 'I'll take it up to them and you can do their bedtime drinks.'

That evening, I waited, nervously, for the bell to ring. I prepared the trolley, just as Kate had, and took it up the one flight of stairs to their lounge off the main hall. I placed the tea tray on the trolley outside the big oak door, and knocked gently.

'Enter!' said Mrs Cavanagh.

I winced at the china clattering on the tray as I wheeled the trolley across the highly polished wooden floor. I was terrified I would slip on the mats scattered around the room. Mrs Cavanagh pushed herself out of her seat and greeted me with a broad smile. She hoped I was settling in. 'We don't like chopping and changing staff,' she said. 'Kate is with us many years now.'

Dancing and Romancing

I soon got into a comfortable routine. Part of my job was to do the upstairs work – but not the bedrooms. That was Breege's job. I was to clean out the fires and restock the coal from the coal hole out the back, keep the sitting and dining rooms tidy, prepare meal trays and, of course, polish their shoes, which they would leave out on the landing for collection each night.

I was good at my job. I did it properly. Nobody was looking over my shoulder and I never gave anyone cause to reprimand me. I was a dab hand with a needle and would darn socks or mend frays in the tray cloths. I often helped Kate chop vegetables and, if she needed help preparing sandwiches and pastries for the dinner parties, I would help her with that. I was a great pastry maker.

Every day wasn't the same and I had plenty of spare time. It was a grand job. Some afternoons I would put on my overcoat and little black beret and take the baby Cavanagh for a walk. I felt so proud, pushing her beautiful big pram around Clontarf and comparing myself to the professional nannies from the other big houses. I liked to pretend I was the Cavanaghs' nanny with responsibilities, commanding respect, and not just a lowly skivvy.

But the Cavanaghs were a joy to clean for. I performed my duties happily and the family was delighted with me. After a month, I spent most of my wages on my first pair of leather high-heeled shoes and yet more knickers, slips and bras. And still I had some change left. I thought I was a millionaire. But that left me with a big dilemma: what to do with the remaining pound? Should I send it home to Mammy or keep it for myself? I decided to keep the spare money and hide it under the pillow in my room. Each night, before I went to bed, I would check to make sure it was still there.

Soon, I had been at the Cavanaghs' three months and was about to spend my first Christmas away from home. I helped Kate to pluck turkeys in preparation for the festive season. Christmas in Dublin was an opulent affair: so much food, drink, chocolates, and presents galore for the baby. It was a different story back home. Aunt Lizzie usually gave us a goose and home-made plum pudding and Mammy would make the cake on

Christmas Eve while we looked on, fighting with each other for the lickings of the bowl.

We'd hang our stockings at the end of our beds but we didn't get much in the way of gifts. We would get an orange or an apple and sometimes a packet of sweets and spinning tops, if we were lucky. One year Carmel and I got one doll between us. Another Christmas we were surprised to receive a silver purse each, which were dotted with mother of pearl beads. We were so delighted going off to Mass on Christmas morning.

The following year we were back to normal. I got a polish brush and Carmel got a turnip! Mother and Father just laughed when they saw our disappointed faces. We were so angry. That was the end of Christmas for us. By the time we were ten, there was no more Santie or Christmas stockings. But we always had snow and the hedges would be white with frost. It was bitterly cold but we loved it.

Mammy would place a big, red wax candle in a scooped-out turnip and sit it in the kitchen window. There were no such things as Christmas trees or decorations, except for red-berried holly and ivy that Mammy placed around all the picture frames and across the mantelpiece, along with bits of cotton wool for snow.

And, of course, Christmas in our house was a very holy occasion. Mammy would put a veil over the statue of the Blessed Virgin and white rosary beads around her neck.

I missed being around my family when I worked for the Cavanaghs but I made a few friends, mostly girls my own age who were looking after the children of the wealthy. We had a great life working in the big houses but we knew our place. They were mostly Protestants who employed Catholics to clean up after them, and that was that. It was the accepted way of things.

The Cavanaghs were not strictly classed as gentry but they were very wealthy. I was the same age as their eldest daughter Maddie. Slim and smart on her feet, Maddie had dark hair, pretty eyes and a pleasing oval-shaped face. Everything about her was pleasing. She was everything I wasn't; Maddie was a funny, clever extrovert who enjoyed the banter with her older brothers, Mick and Denny. She didn't have that much in the way of conversation with her younger brother Tim.

Mick, the eldest, was a cattle dealer like his father. He wasn't gorgeous in the good-looking sense but he had a beautiful nature. I recall that he was nothing but respectful of me. He looked out for me, always asking me how I was and did I need anything; Denny thought he was something special, that being fair-haired and handsome and a university student put him above the rest of us. In truth, he was a big spoilt brat. He seemed to go out of his way to annoy me, always trying to belittle me and harass me while I worked, especially if I was on my knees cleaning and scrubbing.

He appeared in the doorway of the kitchen one day, just as I had finished scrubbing the tiles. 'Don't go into that kitchen now, the floor's wet,' I said. Well, I may just as well have been talking to my sodden floor cloth: Denny ignored me and pushed past anyway, walking all over my clean floor. I was furious and threw my wet cloth at him. He tried to leap out of the way but it caught him on the bottom of his pristine tweed trousers, leaving a horrible damp patch. He wasn't one bit amused. He gave me a filthy superior look and marched out of the kitchen in a temper.

He would mess up his room deliberately so that I would have to go in every day and put his things back in their place. He would leave dirty cups and saucers under his bed and photographs of his girlfriend lying around. He needn't have worried about leaving his photos lying around. They would have had no effect on me. I wouldn't fancy him even if he had gold dripping from his balls! He was an over-educated, ignorant prig.

One day I'd had enough. 'If ya mess up this room again,' I said, 'you'll clean it up yourself.'

'That's what you're paid for,' he said. I never cleaned up after him again.

Despite Denny's taunts, I enjoyed my time with the Cavanaghs.

The rest of the family didn't treat me like a maid. Mrs Cavanagh made me feel almost part of the family. She was a wonderful woman. She would never look down on me and would think nothing of giving me a ride in their Jaguar. I befriended a girl in Lucan and often hitched a lift. Mr and Mrs Cavanagh would be up front and I would be perched in the back with Maddie.

I became friends with Maddie, even though I was just an employee. She would confide in me and reveal all about her friendships and loves, in glorious detail. She would be ironing her clothes and chatting to me in the kitchen as I worked. Sometimes she would even help make the family supper.

I'll never forget the night I had a date to go to the Guards Ball at the Gresham with a man I met at a dance at Kevin Street Station. I agreed to go just to get a look inside the swanky hotel. Imagine! Me, Maura McNamee from the Midland bogs, going to the Gresham! What would Carmel say to that?

I wanted to look the part so I hired a posh low-cut turquoise ball gown from a shop in D'Olier Street for ten shillings. I could never have afforded to buy a gown like that. The dress was taking me to a place where film stars and ladies of the manor went to find rich society husbands. Well, *I* was going now and I couldn't believe it.

Maddie helped me to dress and do my hair and makeup. To finish off, she lent me her precious gold chain to take the bareness off my big singer's chest. She was so excited for me. She ordered me to stand at the top of the stairs while she answered the door to my date. She wanted me to make a real impression, gliding down the stairs like Cinderella in my fancy ball gown to meet my Prince – Guard Sullivan.

I usually spent my time indoors knitting, sewing or reading but I loved to go to a dance or ball. That was something I did with Breege. She was from County Meath, thirty miles from Offaly. We were two country girls with a lot in common. We often got the bus out to Straffan and Celbridge for dances and concerts.

On one memorable night we met each other for a concert in Celbridge Village Hall. It was the night she would help me overcome my terrible shyness. I arrived first and found a couple of spare seats at the front, near the stage, and sat and waited for Breege to arrive. The hall was set out for a concert and the stage was curtained off with heavy green velvet drapes. As the hall filled and everyone puffed away at their fags, the air became heavy and full of chatter. Breege arrived, rosy-cheeked and smiling. She took off her hat and scarf and sidled between knees and chairs to plonk herself down next to me, out of breath.

'Ah, Maura, I had shockin' trouble gettin' here. I broke the heel off me shoe. I had to hop all the way home to put on these auld yokes. Aren't they a shockin' disgrace?'

'Sure who'll be lookin' at you anyway, Breege?' I laughed.

I got distracted by an old man of forty who appeared on stage apologising for the delay: the musicians were running a bit late but we were in for a treat because the band had a great reputation. I nudged Breege. 'That's more than we can say about him!' I said. She shrieked and gave me a belt on the arm. The curtains came back and there was the old man again.

'Put your hands together and give them a warm welcome . . .'

Two old ladies at the end of our row were getting very annoyed with our chatter. 'The rudeness of those young girls!' one of them tutted.

'. . . and show them we are more than a bunch of *jackeens*!' There was great applause as the musicians sat down in a semi-circle – most of them smoking and coughing – and began tuning their instruments. They started playing 'Mrs McLeod's Reel', and soon I was lost in its jauntiness.

After an hour, the bodhran player announced they were taking a break to let members of the audience have a go. It was an open invite to any brave *buachaill* or *colleen* who dared get up and sing.

'Go on, Maura, get up there and show them auld timers how to sing.'

'Ah no, Breege, I couldn't, sure I haven't practised for such a while now.'

'Don't be such a spoilsport. Get up there and give us an auld tune. Sure you know ya have a beautiful voice.'

'It's too smoky, I wouldn't be able to get my breath.'

'Ah, that's just an excuse, I'm goin' to tell them you'll sing.' Breege got up and barged past the two old ladies.

'Breege, sit down, will ya?' I whispered. Too late. She was determined to get me up on the stage.

Then the compere made his shock announcement. 'Ladies and gentlemen, we have Maura from Offaly to sing a couple of songs for us. Good girl, Maura. Come on up here.'

My heart jumped into my mouth, I could hardly breathe. The room was so full of people. I couldn't stand the thought of singing in front of them. I don't know how I got up there with my crippling shyness. I felt light-headed as I walked towards the stage. The scared part of me was saying sit down, you fool, and don't you dare think about humiliating yourself in public. But the brave part, urging me to get up there and show them, won the fight.

The old man took my hand and helped me on to the stage. He stank of whiskey and had a mouthful of filthy dirty teeth. Funny, I thought, you don't get to see the real person from the floor.

I cleared my throat and started to sing 'Kerry Long Ago' but my mind went blank when I saw a hundred and fifty pairs of eyes looking at me. I stuttered and started again with 'Mother Machree' instead. It's a beautiful old song and I got plenty of applause. I was relieved to sit back down again.

'That was great, Maura,' Breege said, grabbing my arm.

I felt fantastic. I could have sung all night, but I wasn't invited up again. Two or three boys got up after me and sang more Irish ballads. And the band played on.

*   *   *

The Cavanaghs signalled a very peaceful time in my life. It was even better when Carmel got a job in the same avenue, working for a doctor and his wife. I had two half days off a week – one weekday and always half of Sunday – and every evening to myself. I'd often go to the clubhouse at the golf links with Carmel to watch the players on the fairway. I sometimes cycled out to Dollymount in the early evenings to walk alone along the seafront. I bought a Raleigh bike in the city on tick. Tommy Murray went guarantor for me. The Metropole was another of my favourite haunts. I could be seen a couple of nights a week drooling over Bing Crosby and Gregory Peck. It was during these trips to the cinema that I began to smoke heavily. We mimicked our screen idols who always seemed to be smoking. It was the thing to do back then. We thought it made us look so grown up. I would smoke Player's, Sweet Afton, Gold Flake or anything I could get hold of.

I had had my first puff on a cigarette back home when I was thirteen. I would sneak off to meet up with Kathy Foy at her house a hundred yards down the road from us. She would give me the money for a packet of Woodbines and promise to have the kettle on when I got back from the shop. There I was with Carmel, Luke and Biddy McNamee sitting in Kathy's kitchen, each taking a puff off the one Woodbine – unable to inhale. The Woodbines were in a green carton with no top on it, five cigarettes sitting in this little pack. I would just have a couple of puffs or maybe half a cigarette. I dabbled at first and I would only smoke out of our house.

I suppose it was Kathy that got me started on the cigarettes but I didn't buy my first proper packet for another two years. I bought a packet of ten Senior Service from Jim Haughton's shop in Clonmore. They were so strong, I was as sick as a dog and nearly fainted.

When I did start smoking in earnest, I would have five or six fags a week but I would never buy them in packs of twenty, only in packs of five. A few years later, I became so addicted I would have two fags even before I got out of bed.

Although I smoked, I never acquired a taste for alcohol. Luke was the only one in the family to drink. Mammy and Father didn't drink, which I suppose had something to do with my lack of interest in liquor.

Fags were my thing. I would sit in the Metropole every week in a cloud of smoke. On one of these visits, I saw a girl, about my own age, sitting a few rows in front of me. During the interval, I decided to go and sit beside her. I made a comment about the film and we got talking. Soon we were laughing together and annoying everyone else trying to watch the film.

'Are ya long in Dublin?' I asked.

'Only a couple of months,' she said. 'I'm workin' for a family in Ballsbridge.'

'What's your name?'

'Molly. What's yours?'

'Maura.'

'I'm from County Offaly,' she said.

'County Offaly?' I shrieked with delight. 'So am I. What part?'

'Tullamore.'

'I'm just down the road. I'm from Clonmore.' We discovered we were both single and decided to meet up on our half days off. We became firm friends and Molly was someone I would turn to when my life came crashing down on top of me.

SIX

Garda Tom

November 1947 was a good month for me. True to her word Molly, my Metropole companion, phoned and asked me would I like to go with her to a dance at the Crystal Ballroom.

The half days off I spent with Molly were often on a Wednesday. Girls who worked as maids usually had to take Thursday afternoons off. All the lads knew the skivvies were let out on a Thursday. They could be seen congregating round Nelson's Pillar – a favourite meeting place for country girls and courting couples. Molly and I were smart: we negotiated our time off on a Wednesday to disguise the fact that we were servant girls.

Molly and I loved to dance. We would go to the Teachers Ballroom, which was popular with the country folk, or the Four Provinces. Sometimes we'd go to the National where all the medical students went. That was a favourite of Carmel's: she wanted to mix with the elite. She craved land, a big house and a name that mattered. Mammy didn't mind lending a hand. She was always writing to a wealthy bachelor over the fields to get him to be great with Carmel. She wanted us all to marry well.

I hadn't been to the Crystal before. Molly and I got all dressed up for the dance. She favoured figure-hugging clothes and the dress she wore that night clung like satin and swished as she walked. She was very beautiful with a well-developed figure and wasp-like waist.

I tried on my frock and stood in front of the mirror. What an ordeal! I couldn't believe what I saw. I was so overweight. I had always described myself as plump. I scrutinised my bulky frame from every angle. I looked like a sack of spuds tied in the middle. I was a peculiar, grotesque shape that I'd never paid much heed to. I decided to weigh myself. There was no denying my true weight now. The scales were clear. My five-foot three-inch frame was carrying an eleven-stone load, and an embarrassing forty-four-inch bust. What a mess! What a despicable state to be in. But what was I to do? I couldn't pass an apple pie and custard without devouring the lot. I was too embarrassed to carry on like that. I would have to start missing meals to shed a few pounds. I was so envious of Molly and her figure. She could cram as much as she liked into her mouth without putting on a pound.

As we walked along the Crystal's carpeted foyer, I noticed her slender hips and the lovely shape to her legs. How tall and slim she was. I caught sight of myself in the long mirror on the back wall. I looked like Billy Bunter in my modest long-sleeved turquoise frock. Turquoise was my colour at the time. It was as bold as I ever got.

We went down the stairs to the ladies' room to put in our coats and freshen up our makeup. I was only nineteen and so excited to be in such a grand hall. Molly told me it was usually full of nurses and guards, and anyone that thought they were something. On our way to the dance floor, Molly grabbed my arm. 'Do ya see the two fellas standin' with their backs to the mirror?'

'What fellas?' I said, scanning the room. I hadn't noticed anyone.

'Don't look now, they're starin' at us.'

Then I clocked them. 'No they're not. Who'd be lookin' at us!'

'Well they are. That's for certain.'

'Ah, don't let it bother ya. Come on and we'll find a table before the crowd gets in.'

The ballroom was beautiful, and that night it was decorated with colourful lights, streamers, balloons and lanterns. We snaked our way through a sea of backs and found a table in the carpeted bit where people sat and sipped drinks when they weren't dancing. I was curious about the fellas staring. I glanced at the mirror to sneak a look at their reflections. Molly was right: they *were* staring. One of them caught my eye. I turned away, embarrassed, and started fumbling in my handbag, pretending to be looking for something important.

We sat out the first dance and listened to Joe, the resident singer, crooning and wriggling like a slithering eel as the hall filled to bursting. He had one of those gorgeous voices; he was something of a Nat King Cole. He was black as well. The first black man I ever saw in the flesh. I had only seen black children on The Penny Prod Card at school when we were expected to sell as many of these little white cards as we could to help raise money for the African missions. The card, given to every child in the school, had a logo on the front with a beautiful black child's face in the centre. All around that logo were little dots, and for every penny you raised you prodded a hole in the card. We loved to give in our pennies. We were delighted to be able to help the little black children. Raising money with the Penny Prod Card was a custom throughout most of the schools in Ireland. Many of the priests from poor families were sent to Africa as missionaries to preach the word of God.

Joe the crooner was a small man who wore a white jacket, with a red handkerchief poking out of his breast pocket, a black silk shirt and white tie. He looked like he'd just stepped off the set of *The Philadelphia Story*. Because he was part of a band, we accepted his colour. I wondered if any of my pennies had gone to help him. We applauded and danced with the rest of the crowd returning each time to our table for a chat. Molly's tall, slim admirer strolled in our direction.

'He's makin' his way over here,' Molly whispered, kicking me under the table.

'Sure, let him. The floor's big enough,' I said boldly. I glanced over my shoulder.

'Oh my God, Maura, I hope he isn't goin' to ask us to dance.'

If ya didn't want to dance why did ya come in the first place? I thought, irritated. 'I bet he's goin' to ask you up, Molly.'

Her milky-cream freckled complexion began to change colour, first white then crimson. I noticed how the high colour only made her look more beautiful, framing her big hazel eyes. She tossed her long, wavy auburn hair over her shoulders with a flick of her wrist and then lowered her eyes. I noticed she did that when she was embarrassed.

The lad bent down and asked her if she cared to dance with him. She nodded and he took her, politely, by the elbow and glided her on to the maple floor. Molly was looking over her shoulder at me, smiling and pulling faces. She was making self-conscious gestures, raising her eyes to the ceiling and blushing. It took her a while to get into the rhythm of the dance. She looked unsteady on her feet. When the dance was over, he escorted her back to our table and rejoined his friend.

Molly sat down, reached into her bag and pulled out a delicate flowery handkerchief to wipe the perspiration from her brow. She heaved a sigh, picked up her drink and sipped it slowly. She sat staring at the glass and ran her finger in a circle around the top of it, setting my teeth on edge with a dreadful piercing noise.

'Well? What was the chat? Did he say anythin'?'

'No,' she said.

'Ya don't mean to say he acted like a dummy? Didn't he say *anythin'*?'

'No,' she repeated sharply.

The band struck up again with a quickstep. Molly looked up and said, 'Oh my God! The two of them are comin' this way. I'm goin' to the ladies' room!'

'Stay where you are,' I insisted, in a low, firm voice. 'What are ya runnin' from? Ya haven't done anythin'.'

'They think we're expectin' them to ask us out on the dance floor.'

'If they do, will ya refuse?'

'Oh no, but I don't want to feel cheap.'

'What are ya talkin' about? Why should ya feel cheap? They're only askin' ya to dance, not commit yourself.'

'I shouldn't be dancin' with other fellas when I'm engaged to somebody else.' With that, Molly pulled out a gold chain from around her neck. Hanging from the chain was a diamond ring.

'I didn't know you were engaged,' I said. 'Why don't ya wear it on your finger?'

'I do – when I go to see my fella in Tullamore.'

I got up to go to the ladies' room, and standing there in front of me was a tall, clear-skinned man with a five o'clock shadow and lively, searching eyes. He asked me to dance.

I rested my hand on the shoulder of his tweed jacket as he twisted and twirled me all around the floor. I was struck by the size of his big hands and feet. For a man with such big feet, he was a very light dancer. His handsome oval face, full lips and good strong neck fascinated me. He had perfect proportions. Roy Keane looks just like him.

'Didn't I stop you on your bike a couple of weeks ago?' he asked, in his distinct Cork accent. 'You didn't have lights on your bike.'

'I don't remember,' I said. 'I've been stopped that many times, I wouldn't know.'

Still smiling, he said, 'It was you, wasn't it? I rarely forget a face.'

'Oh, yeh, I remember now,' I said. Those eyes! How could I forget them?

We had every dance together for the rest of the evening. He told me his name was Tom Walsh and that he was a guard at College Green Station.

During one of the intervals, he asked me if I would go with him to a guards' dance at Dublin's Store Street Station. He had two tickets but no lady friend to take. I agreed.

At the end of the night, Tom gave me a peck on the forehead and we made plans for the dance at Store Street before saying goodnight.

'Somethin' has to be done about my weight, Molly.'

'Sure, Maura, you're not a bit fat. Why would ya be talkin' about losin' weight?'

'I'm eleven stone, Molly. I got such a shock on the scales. I want my clothes to fit me better in time for my date.'

Molly did her best to make me feel good about myself, and played down my ballooning weight, but the very next day I walked resolutely to the nearest chemist and bought myself some slimming tablets. One was to be taken in the morning and one again at night.

After nibbling on water biscuits and taking the slimming pills for three days, I started to feel a little lighter on my feet. My diet came to an abrupt end when I saw a maggot coming out of one of the pills. I was revolted and threw the lot in the bin.

Molly was excited about my date with Tom Walsh and helped pick out a dress, a peach-coloured gown that fitted neatly into my waist. It came from a hire shop in Westmoreland Street. My coat, the new-look calf-length overcoat, was bought and paid for. It came from Switzers where all the swanks shopped. Carmel gave me half the money for it (I had to promise to pay her back).

I felt very trendy in my new brown winter coat travelling on the bus to the Ballast Office for my date with Tom. We walked to the dance hall attached to the police station where we made up a foursome with Tom's best friends, Ned Kennelly from Kerry and Breda O'Keefe from Tipperary. The four of us sat in a row, the two fellas sandwiched between Breda and me, on chairs placed around the edge of the large room. Breda was a warm, confident woman who owned her own hairdressing salon in Inchicore. I was very impressed.

Tom and I got on great. There wasn't an awkward silence the whole evening. Then the pecking started. After a couple of dates we had our first passionate kiss on the lips. It made me tingle with excitement. I wanted more. There was feeling behind his soft, warm, plump lips. He was very good, not a slobberer like some of the boys who would splatter all over your face with horrible wet lips. I remember the dread with Sean Cooney. I only went out with him because he was Luke's friend. I used to hate every minute of it. He was forever trying to kiss me with his sloppy wet puss.

Tom was like a film star; he perfected the art of the long lingering kiss, but he wouldn't prolong the kissing bit if you didn't want him to. I felt close to Tom. My heart would ache for him and I looked forward to seeing him again and again. I felt passionately for him but I had no desire to take it further. It never came into my head. If it came into his, he didn't show it. He was always very respectful.

Some boys you'd go out with for the night would think they were on to a good thing. They'd try it on by wiggling their knee between your legs thinking you were going to lie down under them. The first boy I ever had a crush on tried that one. I was working for Old Kate Kelly at the time and I was crazy about a boy from Killowen. All the girls had a fancy for him, including Carmel. I blushed every time I saw him but he found a way of curing my liking for him: he got fresh with me in the lane outside Kate's cottage. I marched off indignantly, but not before I gave him a right slapping across the face.

'He tried to do that thing to me,' I told Carmel after. 'He's tryin' his livin' best to make me, but I won't do it.'

I wouldn't be forced into anything like that. Sure, I was only fourteen and still in white socks.

Tom never tried to 'do that thing' or wiggle his knee in. I

could have given myself willingly to Tom but sex never crossed my mind. Our love wasn't sexual; he never tried to have sex with me. The love I felt for him came from my heart, not my body. It sounds like it was a bland relationship, but it wasn't. Some girls went out and had sex but most of the girls, I knew, didn't. I'd had flings with other boys, but never sex. We weren't like that then. Courting was different in those days.

That first date with Tom was to be the start of a long and loving relationship. I thanked the Lord that I decided to cycle through the city's dimly lit streets without a rear light on my bike on that foggy November night.

I had only known him for a short time but I looked forward to our every meeting. We didn't do anything fancy like have meals. We would go to the pictures, to a dance or a football match. We might go for walks, feed ducks and drink tea. We loved to walk along the Liffey and cycle out to Dublin Airport to watch the planes taking off. We were very close and enjoyed meeting up just to be together. He was the first boyfriend I ever really cared about.

Tom was eight years older than me. He was very chatty but we talked about nothing in particular, not politics or poetry, just the ordinary things. But he was comical and a bit of a giggler. He was a lovely, generous, sincere man and he made me feel secure.

Our relationship grew more intense and I soon realised I was falling madly in love with this man. On a lovely sunny evening, a few months into our courtship, we cycled out to the airport – in those days you could cycle to the airport through beautiful country roads; there were no motorways – parked our bikes and sat on the grass verge watching the planes.

'I'm thinkin' we'll get married,' Tom said. 'Will we start savin' our money?'

'If ya like,' I said, thinking he couldn't have been serious but hoping he was.

'I've saved £3 already.'

That was all Tom ever said about marriage and I took it for granted that it would happen. I was so excited. I told Mrs Cavanagh about my news, and she squealed with delight and said we could have our wedding breakfast at her house. I believed I would spend the rest of my life with Tom.

Although I was to be his wife, I never told him the truth about being a domestic. I was too proud to say I cleaned up after rich folk. Guards didn't make dates with maids. Guards at the time were going with civil servants, not domestic servants. I let Tom believe that Mrs Cavanagh was an old woman and I was her carer. It wasn't too difficult keeping up the pretence.

As a trusted maid, Carmel had the run of the house whenever the doctor and his family went away, and she usually took full advantage of their absence. On one particular occasion, when they were away on holiday, she invited Tom and me over to 'her place' for tea.

Carmel pretended she was the lady of the house. She put on a beautiful spread, using the doctor's best cut glass and china, and laid it out on their finest white lace tablecloth. She was a great hand at making the food. We had a fresh salad with ham off the bone and home-made brown bread. My younger sister Anna came too, and she couldn't wait to devour the fairy cakes.

We sat down to our posh nosh in the family's main dining room. It was a very grand setting, and Tom went along with the pretence. It was *very* comical.

The Cavanaghs were friendly to a fault but I was never able to forget my position. I was still the housemaid, and I resented it. I had ambitions that lay beyond responding to Mr Cavanagh's calls of 'Maur'een, are my boots ready?' I was young and hopeful and this was merely a job to feed me. It wasn't my destiny. My ambition was to leave for a respectable job so I could marry Tom with my head held high.

Thanks to Tim Cavanagh's night-time antics, I left sooner than planned. It was the summer of 1948. It had been a scorcher of a day and I went to bed with my bedroom window open. I woke up, startled that someone was pulling my pyjama bottoms down. I turned over and there was Tim, the Cavanaghs' fifteen-year-old son, trying to get on top of me.

'What the hell do ya think you're doin', you little bastard?' I yelled. 'Get off me! Get off me!' I said, elbowing him in the chest. 'Get the hell out of my room.'

Tim leapt out of the bed, without a word of apology, and darted back out through the window. Just because I was the maid he must have thought I had low morals. I was disgusted.

Mrs Cavanagh was very upset when I told her what had happened in the night. Her other son Mick was outraged. He gave Tim the beating he deserved. He beat the shite out of him. I felt sorry for the boy, but he knew what he was doing. It wasn't for stirring his tea that he got it. He thought he had it made with the maid but there was no way that snivelling privileged brat was going to practise his mickey on me. I left soon after, even though Mrs Cavanagh begged me to stay.

I took a series of servant jobs in the city but I kept in touch with Mrs Cavanagh. Wherever I worked, I received a letter from her asking me to go back. Eventually I agreed. By that time, Anna was also working as a maid in Clontarf so there we were, three sisters working in the very same avenue.

Misery on O'Connell Bridge

November 1949 was not a good month for me: my handsome guard ended our relationship while he was on traffic duty in the middle of O'Connell Bridge. I had been with Tom for two ecstatic years; I didn't realise he was losing interest in me, until the day I saw him on a dirty, foggy afternoon near the Ballast Office.

Tom was taking me to a dance in Parnell Square that evening, and I had gone into the city to buy a new skirt. I crossed

O'Connell Street and then I saw him, in his smart patrol uniform, white gloves and whistle, directing traffic. I was amazed at how excited I felt just watching him.

I stood on the corner of O'Connell and Westmoreland for several minutes, admiring the man I was going to marry. But then he caught my eye and winked, gesturing me to stay where I was until the flow of traffic had eased off a little. I waited patiently. It was a bitter day but I didn't feel the cold, only a burning desire welling up inside me.

I couldn't wait for him to put his two big arms around me, hold me close to him and whisper the words I loved to hear, 'I love you.' I wanted to tell him, over and over, how much I loved him too. He crossed over to meet me, bobbing and weaving through the cars and cyclists. He greeted me with the same warmth as he always did. But then his mood changed.

'How come you're in town today?' he said sharply. 'You don't usually come in on Thursday afternoons. Is somethin' wrong?'

'I'm in to buy somethin' for tonight,' I giggled. 'A frock or a skirt.' I noticed the look of concern on his face. 'You look shocked,' I joked. 'What's wrong with ya?'

'There's nothin' wrong.' He sounded irritated.

'Ya don't look yourself, what's the matter with ya?'

'There's nothin' wrong,' he repeated. 'It's just . . . I wondered why you're in the city today.'

'Sure there's nothin' strange about my bein' here today, tomorrow or any other day for that matter.'

Tom grabbed me by the arm and led me around the corner away from the crowd.

Something was wrong.

'Where are we goin'?' I asked.

He didn't answer. Now I was irritated.

Tom pushed me into a side street and stood, just a foot away, looking at the ground, arms folded across his chest. He was in a very strange mood. Too quiet for my liking. He wasn't behaving like the Tom I'd grown to know and love over the last two years.

He raised his eyes slowly. The smile had gone from them. He was stern and still, making me feel uncomfortable. I decided to make light of the situation and tried to strike up a casual conversation, praying he would say something. He just shuffled from one regulation boot to the other. If he had something say, why wasn't he man enough to say it?

'Tom, tell me. What is the matter?'

'Ah nothin',' he said, at last, turning abruptly and marching back to the bridge. He retraced his steps to the centre of the congested road and continued directing the traffic.

I was dazed. I wanted to stay and I wanted to run away but I was too upset to move. I stood and watched him as the tears flowed down my cheeks. I had a lump in my throat and a gnawing ache in my heart. What's happened? I didn't understand. I walked away without looking back.

I didn't have the heart to buy anything for the dance. I got on the bus and went back to Clontarf. I was so troubled by my thoughts I didn't notice my stop flying past. I leapt up, rang the bell and asked the driver to stop the bus. My heart was racing with the upset. As I walked along the sea front, I couldn't get Tom's face out of my mind. I tried to figure out what had gone wrong but I couldn't come up with anything. I needed comforting. I phoned Molly.

I arranged to see her at seven o'clock at our usual meeting place, the Metropole. That gave us plenty of time to chat before I went on to the dance; I had no intention of cancelling my date with Tom. I was determined to carry on as usual and hoped he would be back to his normal, cheerful self.

I was very emotional sitting with Molly in the brightly lit ice-cream bar below the cinema. I was on the verge of tears as I watched her sipping her coffee.

'Ya sounded strange on the phone,' she said. 'Is there anythin' wrong?'

'No. Well, nothin' really. Just a slight misunderstandin' between me and Tom.'

'How so?'

'I saw him today, on duty on the bridge. He was actin' strange. Sort of shifty. He couldn't look me in the eye, Molly. That's not Tom. Somethin' is wrong. Seriously wrong.'

'What do ya mean, Maura? Was he nasty to ya?'

'No, no. Tom wouldn't harm a fly. But why did he avoid me, Molly? I don't understand. Look at me, I'm shakin'.'

'Ah, Maura, maybe ya have it wrong. Maybe he just had a grump on or somethin'.'

'No, Molly, I know Tom.'

'You're meetin' him tonight, aren't ya?'

'Well, Molly, it's like this. I may be but, then again, I may not be.'

'But you're goin' to the dance with him, aren't ya?'

'I'm supposed to be meetin' him at the Ballast Office at eight o'clock. Will ya come with me in case he doesn't turn up?'

'Oh, he'll turn up all right,' she said. 'You and Tom have been great for a long time now.'

'I'm not so sure after the mood he was in today.'

'Sure he'll turn up,' Molly said reassuringly.

I began to cry. 'If he comes, he comes, if he doesn't, he doesn't,' I said, trying to be brave. I prayed Tom would be at the Ballast Office like we'd arranged. I dreaded him not being there. I loved him with every bit of my being but now, it seemed, some terrible misunderstanding was threatening to shatter my dream. And I had no idea why. I wondered had I taken him for granted, taken our relationship for granted?

I looked at my watch. 'I'm late. It's gone eight, Molly.'

We rushed to make our way to the Ballast Office. I could see no sign of him. My heart sank. 'I've been stood up. I told ya.'

'Ah no, Maura, I don't think so. He's probably got held up.' Molly was making all sorts of excuses for him but I *knew* he wasn't turning up. 'What will ya do now?' she asked. 'Will ya go to the dance or come with me to the pictures? It's up to you.'

'I'll go to the dance; perhaps Tom's there already. I'm sure he'll explain why he didn't show.' I tried to sound convincing.

'Well, if you're not comin' to the pictures, I'm goin' home. Phone me tomorrow with the goss.'

Molly went to catch her bus and I made my way towards Parnell Square and the Teachers Ballroom. I got to the door and hesitated, took a deep breath and went inside. I felt conspicuous going in on my own. I prayed there'd be someone inside I knew and could talk to. I had a quick look around the hall to see if Tom was there. He wasn't. I handed in my coat anyway and went to freshen up. I bought myself an orange juice and stood, shyly, by the side of the dance floor, all the time looking for the one face that would mean everything to me. I searched through the dancers as they twisted and turned around the floor, but I couldn't spot him.

A boy came up and asked me to dance. I declined and he reported me to the floorwalker. The floorwalker came straight over to me. 'Why have you refused that boy?' he asked.

'I didn't want to dance with him, that's the why,' I said defiantly.

We weren't allowed to refuse a dance in those days. If someone asked you for a dance and you refused twice you would be asked to leave. Floorwalkers were a bit like bouncers. They would walk the floor and make sure everything was in order.

'Well, the way you look you ought to be privileged he asked ya.'

I was shocked by his rudeness. Well, he could think what he liked. I had paid to go in. I wouldn't have been there on my own if it hadn't been for Tom but I needed to put my mind at rest. I waited for an hour but he still didn't show. I was devastated. I had to leave. I went back to the cloakroom for my coat and bag, thinking it hadn't been worth the bother of putting them in for such a short time. As I walked briskly down the dance floor towards the door I saw him. Tom was sitting inside the door with a big grin across his face, and a tall girl in a black dress was hanging on to his every word. I could see that his sullen mood had lifted. Tom and the girl were sharing a joke and laughing.

Suddenly, it all made sense. He had found someone else! I stood back from them, hiding behind the dancers, feeling totally humiliated. When the music was over, the dancers ambled back to their seats. The crowd parted, like the Red Sea, leaving me exposed to Tom and his new girl. I stood there like a gormless dummy, holding my coat over my arm, rigid with shock.

The band struck up again and Tom looked as though he was asking the girl for a dance. It was then that he saw me. He bent forward, whispered something in her ear and walked over to me, his face flush red with embarrassment.

'Would ya like to dance?' he said, smiling. I couldn't believe it.

I couldn't speak to Tom. I was so choked. I had so many questions but I couldn't open my mouth. It was like dancing with a stranger. He could have been anyone. The dance seemed to go on for ever. I thought it would never be over. When it did finish, he simply said 'Thanks' and walked back over to the dark-haired, not-so-pretty girl he was with. That was the last time I danced with Tom Walsh.

I left, tearful and confused. I couldn't take in what had happened. I had the chance to ask for an explanation, but I didn't take it. Tom didn't say a word and I dared not ask. I was too proud to make a fool of myself.

I drifted down O'Connell Street in a sickening daze. I waited on Eden Quay for my bus to Clontarf and went over the two years we'd been together, remembering the places we'd visited, the hours we spent with each other and the fun we'd had. I'd always thought that Tom and I held each other in the highest esteem, that he loved me the way I loved him. Our love came from deep within our hearts. I'm sure it did. We were making plans to marry and putting money away for the big occasion. Who was going to stroke my head now when I was upset? Who would make me laugh the way he did? I couldn't imagine life without Tom. I took it for granted that he would always be there, but there was no marriage and no wedding breakfast, only a broken heart. Tom had found someone to take my place.

When I got back to the Cavanaghs', I lit a fire in my room and piled some extra cushions into my deep armchair. I laid my head back and thought more about Tom. I was startled by a light thud: a lump of coal had fallen on to the hearth. I crouched by the fire, placing the rogue piece of coal back on the neat, hot pile with a pair of steel tongs. I got out my box containing letters and photos Tom had sent to me, and I threw the lot into the fire. It was a relief to see them disintegrating into ashes.

The next few days were unbearable. I couldn't eat or sleep. I wanted to speak to him. I tried so many times to phone him. I picked up the phone, dialled his number and put it down again. I started wandering the city, up and down O'Connell Street, round Parnell Square, over to Westmoreland. I even stood for hours on end on O'Connell Bridge just hoping to catch a glimpse of him. I wanted him to tell me it was a silly misunderstanding; I wanted him to hold me and tell me everything was all right.

I searched my mind for a reason, any reason, for the break-up. Why did he up and leave me like that? I needed to know *why*. I sat down and wrote him a letter, my feelings pouring out of me with the ink on to the page. I wrote one letter after the other but I didn't post a single one. I threw them all into the autumn fire. I watched them go blazing up the chimney, dissolving before my eyes.

I was emotionally battered and bruised after Tom abandoned me. The pain of not ever seeing him again was too difficult to bear. I had to resolve things with him. I wrote him a note and asked him to meet me at Wynn's Hotel in Talbot Street. I didn't tell him what I wanted with him, or what I hoped to achieve, but he turned up anyway. He was sitting in the foyer reading a newspaper when I arrived. He smiled when he saw me and folded the paper.

We walked together down Talbot Street, around the quay and back up again. That was the longest walk of my life: the silence was unbearable. I couldn't think of a single question to ask him. What I really wanted was for Tom to say everything was fine between us. But he didn't.

I couldn't see a future without Tom. I never knew why he ended our relationship: I didn't have the courage to ask him.

I have always detested the month of November.

SEVEN

The Big Smoke

I tried to sleep but the continual retching into a kidney dish kept me awake most of the night. If only I could turn myself inside out, perhaps I could scrape the blood away. By morning my nightdress was soaked, blood red. I was still coughing violently when a quietly spoken nurse asked me was I all right. I shook my head in silent reply. She wiped dried blood from my mouth, drew the curtain round my bed and went about her morning's work. I wasn't happy to be curtained off: I took it as a sign that I was going to die.

In between my fits of coughing, I could hear the nurse's soft footsteps going from patient to patient, pausing at five-minute intervals. She stuck her head back inside my curtain, startling me.

'Do ya want a bowl to get a wash?' she asked sympathetically. I was too exhausted and distressed to answer. 'I'll get someone to fetch a clean nightdress.' I didn't want a change of clothes, and I didn't want a wash. I wanted nothing from them. I just wanted it to be yesterday.

The nurse slipped in through a gap in the curtain and supported my head over the dish. The screen was kept around my bed all morning. Nurses came and went every few minutes, taking my pulse and blood pressure, asking questions and making notes on a chart at the end of my bed.

I recognised one of them.

'Oh, Maura! God, what happened to you?' said Helen Killeen, the wife of our village postmaster.

A doctor appeared at midday with a nurse. They huddled together, grim faced, at the end of my bed, reading my chart. He edged closer to the nurse to peer again into the bloodied dish, and rubbed his chin. 'Mmm . . .' was all he said.

I was hoping they were sending me home, that it was just a burst vein and the bleeding would stop as soon as it started. I had a lot of faith in my GP and I prayed he'd been right.

They weren't sending me home. They were sending me to St James's in Dublin: they were better equipped to deal with 'my situation'. They had all the modern technology.

'My situation' seemed so strange and vague, as if it was happening to somebody else. I felt lost, alone and unloved. I was thinking that God couldn't punish me any more. Hadn't I been ill enough over the years? I had had nine children, three miscarriages, two heart attacks, a hysterectomy, a hiatus hernia and high blood pressure. Now this. And no one could tell me what was wrong. I was convinced I was staring death in the face. I prayed for a miracle.

I saw Peter's son Anthony in the corridor. He'd come to visit as soon as he heard the news but we barely had time to talk. He arrived as I was being wheeled towards another waiting ambulance.

'Hello, Auntie Maura. Where are you off to?' He looked shocked.

'Anthony, I'm goin' to Dublin. Would ya let John know, pet?'

The siren blared the whole way up the N4 motorway. It had been twenty-four hours since I was admitted to hospital and, still, I was being told nothing.

My travelling companion, another bored nurse, parted her lips occasionally to ask me if I was all right. What a daft question.

I was so frustrated. Sure, if I was all right I wouldn't be in an ambulance leaving one hospital for another.

The driver pulled to a stop outside St James's. Despite the warmth of the day, he laid a blanket around my shoulders and passed me, like a parcel in a child's game, to an Emergency nurse.

I shivered in the air-conditioned reception. It was crowded with people standing around, waiting, in hospital fashion. Doctors in white coats walked briskly with determined looks on their faces.

I was parcelled off again and allocated a bed, but bed was the last thing I was thinking of. If I were at home and in my health, I would only just be tucking into my afternoon cup of tea and slice of cake.

The stench of disinfectant mingled with the smell of blood in my nose. I struggled to stay awake. I felt myself drifting off to sleep . . .

The smell of disinfectant was my last clear memory for the next seven days. I slipped in and out of consciousness, catching fleeting glimpses of my children as they arrived at my bedside.

I was so pleased to see my youngest daughter, Joan. I feel secure when she's around. I knew she would be pulling out all the stops and making sure I received the right treatment. She stands by me, always. Joan's been there for me during my most difficult and traumatic times; I wasn't surprised she was the first to drop everything and book a flight to Ireland.

Joan shares my passion for diary writing. She brought her diary with her and recorded everything, anything, the doctors said or thought, taking on the role of investigator and protector. She asked the doctors to repeat and explain terms and procedures and jotted it all down in her diary. She knew I would want a blow-by-blow account and would read every word back to me when I was well enough to listen. Her diary, all my children's diaries, helped to fill in the missing pieces.

The entries were always interesting, sometimes surprising and often upsetting. I discovered, for the first time, what the children *really* felt about my 'latest' illness. The diaries also revealed small grudges and hidden hurts, and it was distressing to realise it took them all those years to say what they felt. It was devastating to read their accounts of me when I thought I was the greatest mum in the world, and to find out some of them weren't of the same opinion. Reading them forced me to reflect hard on the way John and I had brought them up, and how our volatile relationship affected them emotionally.

Joan was the first to write in her diary. I was aware of her sitting by my bed, scribbling in the dark.

Joan

Fri 18 June: It's 1.00 am and I'm sitting on the floor in Ward 3, Hospital 7, at St James's Hospital in Dublin. I'm writing in the dark. Mommy is lying in bed on her right side, a saline drip in her left arm, an oxygen feeder through her nostrils and a very sore-looking left hand waiting for the next drip. She's in her pink nightie and looking a bit more peaceful.

I arrived yesterday and walked into the ward, a very run-down and dirty place, to witness Mommy coughing up clots of blood into a blue plastic kidney tray. She didn't have her teeth in and her mouth was caked in blood. My legs weakened and my stomach cramped at the sight of her.

Mommy looks grey, as though she's dying. She was very tired and drowsy earlier, speaking in a hushed tone, and had a glazed expression on her face. Her throat was dry and sore after a bron-choscopy and two days without fluids. I stroked her back, damped her mouth, petted her and spoke softly and reassuringly to her.

On the way over I met a guy on the plane. He was trying to chat to me while I was doing my deep breathing exercises from yoga.

The guy said, 'Are you scared of flying?'

'No, it's just that my mother's really ill and I'm trying to calm myself down.'

He got it. 'Oh, God, I'm so sorry,' he said. I kept thinking, Oh God, is she still alive? I was in limbo.

'All I want is for her not to be dead when I get there,' I told him. I asked God, or whoever, just keep her alive so I could say goodbye.

The doctors don't seem to know what's wrong. It's serious anyway. They're doing an operation tomorrow to locate the trouble spot and mend it (please God).

I couldn't believe it. In her terrible state, Mommy still managed to whisper her instructions! She wants me to lock her diary in her filing cabinet and hold on to the key.

Poor Declan was the next to arrive. He's the quietest and most sensitive of my three sons. It broke my heart to see him looking so scared. It reminded me of the nine months he spent in hospital when he was a baby, suffering dreadful pain with his ears. Each time I left him in the ward, he'd cry in distress. I worried so much over that child.

Declan
The blood was horrendous. I just stared. I thought, I'm not going to lose my cool. I'm just going to make sure Mum gets the right advice off the right people.

I thought she came to, for fifteen minutes or so. She was lying on her side and having a conversation with us. She seemed like my old Mum. She was clear-headed and coherent.

Dad didn't know how to cope or know what to do. He seemed okay at first but I think it all got to him. He wasn't being much support. He's just not great at dealing with things like that. He gets a bit flustered.

Joan kept mopping blood off Mum's face. Joan and I are good with Mum and quite good for each other. We're asking lots of questions. Mum's not saying very much. She looks very poorly.

Even though I know something serious is going on, I don't believe
she is going to die. She's a very strong person. Her physical strength
got her through a hysterectomy; it will get her through this.

I was shocked the first time I read Breda's diary. She's always
been the one who made me laugh and never gave me any
trouble. I couldn't believe the negative feelings she held towards
me. But I had to admire her brutal honesty. Her words are so
powerful, I had to include them in my memoir.

Breda

I knew there was something wrong when Daddy phoned.

'I don't want ya to be upset,' he said, 'don't worry and don't
panic but I've got something to tell you.'

'Right, it's about Mummy,' I said.

'Yeh.'

He sounded very calm but I could tell he was anxious and
that he would be red-faced and jittery. He told me she'd been
coughing up blood. My nursing training told me it was serious.

I got angry because I knew I would be expected to drop every-
thing and go over. I thought it was so typical, even though I
knew she could be dying. I felt angry and resentful going over.
I'm a bit like my dad – I run away from things; I need to take
time, just to know how I feel about something, and go through
all the unreasonable things I know I'm going to go through. I
always feel like that when something difficult happens in our
family. I never know whether it's the truth, an act or attention-
seeking behaviour. My automatic reaction is that it's fake and
it's masking some other difficulty.

I don't know why this feels like such a huge burden. I've felt
burdened by Mummy's illnesses all my life. I think about the
time I was kept off school. Mummy felt she was going to throw
herself out of the bedroom window, and I had to stay there so
that I could stop her. I felt it was such a responsibility for a

ten-year-old to keep watching her all the time. I remember trying to plot my own death because, I thought, if she's not alive there's no point in me living. There was a curve down the stairs at Cuthbert Road and I thought, if I throw myself off this top step, I'm bound to smash my head against the curved bit and then I'll be dead by the time I get to the bottom. That was the plan.

Daddy knew Mummy would want all the kids round her. That's why he phoned us. He knew that he wouldn't be enough for her. I was dreading the histrionics that I knew were going to be a part of this whole thing with Mummy. I thought it would be almost like an occasion, like a birth or a wedding. Joan kept phoning and saying, 'I need to prepare you for the shock,' but I thought that was Joan's over-sensitivity.

I expected Mummy to be sitting up in bed like some queen bee and be directing it all. But she wasn't. When I walked into her ward, I thought, Oh my God! Oh my God! She's going to die. I was really, really shocked. She looked like a little alien thing, lying on her side, curled up in a foetal position. She looked teeny and thin and grey-haired, like an old lady and yet like a baby too. She totally wasn't the person that I expected her to be. She has always been strong but she looked weak and pathetic.

Mummy said my name but I knew she didn't know who I was really. I thought I had arrived just in time: I was convinced she was going to die the same day.

John needed the children around him as much as I did; he needed consoling. He got on my nerves trying to reassure me everything would be okay. I thought he was just convincing himself. I never thought he was particularly empathetic but how could he understand something he hadn't experienced himself? I was genuinely taken aback by his private thoughts. Reading his diary, I realised I hadn't given him the credit for caring for me as much as he did. It's a pity he couldn't show it in the fifty years we were married, and I had to read about it instead.

John

I went up to the hospital today with Seamus. He drove in his usual fashion, at breakneck speed. We chatted about Maura, wondering what was wrong. I remembered some of my army first aid and told Seamus that the blood was most likely coming from the lung because it was dark. I didn't tell Maura because I didn't know for certain. I think I smoked five cigarettes in that forty-five-minute journey.

Poor Declan was standing at the end of the bed with his hands on the mattress saying, 'All right, Mum?'

I said to Maura, 'Don't worry. Everything will be all right,' because you don't go in to someone and say, 'You're very sick and you look like you're goin' to die!'

The first night Maura got sick she was in the corner of the kitchen. I heard her call, 'John! John!' She was holding a tissue and there was blood on it. I thought it was just bloodstained phlegm at first. I thought maybe she was after coughing a little too hard and that she had torn her throat.

Maura said, 'No, that's thick, clotty blood. That shouldn't be.'

After the paramedics put her in the ambulance, Ann and I were sorry we didn't go with her. There looked as though there wasn't enough room, and events were happening so quickly. It was as though it was out of my control. We should have gone anyway to see what was happening – well, I should have. I rang the hospital and they told me that Mrs Murphy was settled in.

After the ambulance left, I just sat on the settee, stunned really, feeling shocking sorry that I hadn't gone with Maura. It was the wrong decision. But I was scared for her and I knew that there was nothing I could do, medically speaking. I was sorry after though. I hate the sight of blood and pain.

I woke not knowing where I was. A nurse shrieked at me for showing my bare bum to everyone going in and out of the ward. This humiliated me; I didn't want my person exposed. But I *was* exposed. 'Cover your arse, Maura!' I heard her say. I was too ill to realise the state of me. At least I was on a ward full of women.

I was bringing up blood in front of them while they were eating their breakfast. I was so embarrassed I asked the nurse to draw the curtains around my bed to shield me from them, and them from me. I wondered if I would ever stop coughing and spitting. I drifted off to sleep again with a fierce pain in my head

When I woke, it was early in the morning. My false teeth were gone. I panicked and searched feebly around the bed and under the pillow. Then I spotted them in a bowl on the locker at the side of the bed. I stretched to reach them and knocked over the kidney dish. Now blood and spittle were splattered across the floor. I tried to ring the bell over the bed to summon a nurse but I couldn't reach it.

I was offered an injection for the pain in my head, and more notes went on to a chart. A nurse told me I would be going down to X-ray to have an angiogram.

'What's that?' I asked.

'Just routine, Maura,' she assured me. 'It'll only take forty minutes.'

I wondered how on earth I would manage to lie still on my back for forty minutes with all the coughing and spluttering and, oh God, and the gasping for breath.

Three doctors came to see me. One of them was an abrupt young man who wouldn't make eye contact when he spoke. He talked about me as if I wasn't there. They studied my chart and talked some more.

My heart thumped in my breast as I waited for the porter to take me down for my angiogram. 'Mrs Murphy? My name's Peter,' said the porter. 'I'm taking you down to X-ray.'

Peter was a well-built man in his early twenties. I was taken by his good looks. He had a slim nose and sparkling brown eyes.

I trusted him immediately. He made me feel safe. He placed the kidney dish beside me and manoeuvred my bed out of the ward towards the lift. He chatted cheerily as he pushed me along the corridor. When he wheeled me into the lift, my blanket caught in the door and the kidney dish, and all its contents, went spilling across the floor. Peter wasn't a bit fazed. He stooped down, picked it up, placed it back on my lap and carried on chatting. He was a gentle soul.

The sweat was seeping out of me and I began to shiver. I was overcome with another fit of coughing. I couldn't fathom out how the sickness hit me so suddenly, without warning.

I started to think about death again. I often wondered how I would die. Now I thought I knew. I was sure I was bleeding to death even though I felt no pain, except for the insufferable headache. I had hoped I would go in my sleep. That would be the simplest, and the loveliest, way to go out of this beautiful world. I wondered if I was in a fit spiritual state to face God. But I prayed and begged him not to take me from my children. How would they cope without me? If I were to die now, they would be lost. I just couldn't leave them. They are my life.

I lay on the X-ray table waiting and listening as hospital staff shuffled around me. I heard a doctor and a nurse whispering about me. I could only pick out certain words and phrases – 'sensitive areas', 'catheter' and 'paralysis'. The panic started to rise in my chest. The doctor told me I needed to sign a consent form before he could proceed because there was a one per cent chance of paralysis. I didn't know what to do. I couldn't cope with making that decision.

'Some of your family are in the waiting room. Will I fetch them for you?' asked the nurse.

'Yes,' I said, 'yes please.'

Soon Joan and John were beside me and I wasn't so frightened any more. Joan took my hand, wiped my forehead and told me to take deep breaths. 'Try to relax, Mom,' she said.

The doctor was anxious to get on with the angiogram but Joan fired questions at him, one after the other. She was getting on his nerves, and he barely controlled his annoyance.

'A decision has to be made here,' he snapped. 'There are other procedures booked in. Mrs Murphy needs to have this angiogram. I need your consent to carry on.'

John was standing by the side of the trolley and didn't say a word. He looked helpless and confused. He seemed to be looking to Joan for guidance. She bent over me and asked me if I wanted the angiogram.

'Should I?' I asked. 'Should I, Joan?'

Joan

Mommy was so nervous about her angiogram. I took her hand and she said, 'I'm shockin' sick. I wish I could die.'

I said, 'What are you scared of, Mom?'

And she said, 'They told me I could be paralysed.'

'He says it's only a one per cent chance, Mommy,' I explained.

'Maybe I could cope,' she said. 'Sure couldn't I use a wheelchair? At least I'd be alive.'

I promised that we would all look after her.

'Will you, pet?'

Daddy was cool-headed. When it came to making the decision, he was very clear. He told the doctor to go ahead. I think it was the right decision and I'm glad he made it; I would have dithered.

John

Maura was lying on a trolley. She looked tormented and I said, 'Maura, you'll be all right.' I was never in that position myself but I knew that it was great comfort for someone to come along and say 'everything will be fine', even though I didn't know whether it would be or not. I was trying to ease her mind and give her a bit of mental comfort.

I was thinking if I say yes to the procedure and she's paralysed, I will blame myself for the rest of my life. If we said no, how would they find out what was causing the bleeding?

I feel so sorry for Maura after all the suffering she'd had to go through with childbirth and everything. I thought about the hard life and hardship we'd gone through. It all came back to me – the good times and the bad. Maybe I wasn't as sympathetic as I could have been. Maybe I wasn't that good all my life, and I regretted being the way I was when I was young. I wished I could turn the clock back and that things could have been different. Then I was saying to myself, why think about it now? Why didn't I think about it then?

I was dog-tired. I wished this wasn't happening. We were on tenterhooks. I hated to think of her in a wheelchair. The blood around her mouth kept flashing into my mind. I tried to remain strong but I'm so squeamish. I tried not to think of what they were doing to her. I just prayed quietly to myself and put on a brave face to the children. I knew it was hard for them because I felt the same myself. There were tears in my eyes but I didn't bawl out.

Seamus said we were worrying too much.

I braced myself for the incision. The nurse held my hand firmly. I grimaced and squeezed tightly. My mouth was dry: I was so scared. I was awake when they went into the artery, and it was very painful.

As I lay on my back, I wondered how I would cope with paralysis. Would it affect my whole body or just my lower limbs? If I was in a wheelchair for the rest of my life, would I still be able to do my chores? Would I be able to wash myself and look after my toilet needs? I couldn't bear the thought of my nakedness being exposed to a stranger, having to depend on someone else to wash me.

I had a great love of life, and I wasn't easily defeated. I would accept what would happen and thank God for the gift of being alive. I am a determined woman. I *would* cope.

Joan

I'm sitting in Mommy's bed in Offaly writing this diary, feeling drained and deflated. I would rather be at the hospital but I need some sleep. I don't want to talk to anyone. My heart was racing this morning, waiting for Mom to come out from her angiogram. Forty minutes they said. She was in there for four hours. I wondered whether I'd see her again. Why wouldn't the nurses come and give us an update? At last, the doctor came and said there was a lot of blood in the lungs but he still didn't know what was causing it. There is no sign of a tumour.

I suggested we should call everyone else and get them over here. Seamus thinks I'm over-reacting. He says we should wait. But he's sitting there being Seamus – all certain and in control with his right leg shaking like he's doing an Elvis impression. Daddy's with me on this one; Declan's not sure; I'll see what Olive thinks. She's flying over tomorrow. I'll be glad to see her. She's calm and considered.

Seamus is my eldest son. I heard him ask, 'How's the old lady doing?' I can't remember a time he ever called me Mammy or Mom. It's always *the old lady*. He was in his late teens when he started. That's just how he expresses himself but I've always thought it was disrespectful, as if calling me Mammy wasn't the macho thing to do.

He wasn't going to allow any of us to get too carried away or grief-stricken. He would come in regularly and his visits were uplifting. He didn't want to know the fine details, and left the caring to the others, but he always kept a watchful eye over things. He's a big softy underneath. He doesn't show his emotions but I know he feels things.

Seamus

They're all in a fucking panic. They don't know what they're doing. They're expecting the worst, I suppose. If you expect the worst and nothing happens, it's all right. But if you don't expect anything, nothing can happen.

The way I look at it, the old lady's in hospital, the doctors know what they're doing and they know how to deal with her situation. I don't need to be there pushing questions at them. I just put my trust in the doctors because, at the end of the day, if she's going to die, she's going to die. There's nothing in the world anyone can do about it.

I didn't feel anything when I saw her. The others were talking about death. If I think somebody's dying, I don't feel any compassion for them because I know we've all got to go down that road. Maybe if something happened to my son Cormac I might feel different. I don't allow myself to become emotional. I can close that side down. I shut it down because I don't want the emotions that it brings with it. I want to see clearly. I don't want anything putting me off. I don't allow myself to feel because I know death is somewhere we all have to go. It's the one thing in life that we have to do. Everybody.

I'm an odd fucker. I don't discuss things. I'm a loner. Whatever I feel, I keep to myself. I just kept cracking jokes. I'd just wait and say something smart.

As soon as I saw the old lady, I thought she would be all right. If she was going to die you'd see it coming out of her weeks before: her colour would change, she would become yellow or sallow. Her colour didn't change, so I didn't worry. She just looked fucking old. Old and tired.

Declan

Mum was put into a different ward. It looked to me like they were putting her into a ward to die – the Death Ward. The place looked like it was full of people who just hadn't got a hope in *hell; hadn't a prayer. I kept questioning 'Why are they putting her in there?'*

Olive has arrived. She looks very concerned and withdrawn. She didn't say a lot but I'm pretty sure she doesn't think Mum is going to survive.

Olive is the shyest of my children. She's quiet and dignified and keeps her feelings deep inside. She is a terrible worrier and shows her love for me by doing practical, nurturing things. She made sure that I was physically comfortable.

Her diary is a pragmatic account of her visit.

Olive

I was standing at the end of Mummy's bed looking round at the ward. I didn't know what to do with myself.

Where's Daddy? I thought.

Mummy was lying in bed on her left side. Her right arm was dangling over the side of the bed and attached to a drip. Her head was almost slumped in the pillow. She was unconscious. I don't know why but I had expected her to be sitting up awaiting my arrival and asking how the plane journey went.

The woman in the bed opposite had a visitor. It was her son, and they were watching me. Through the course of the evening, I found out that the woman – Eileen – had lung cancer and was awaiting chemotherapy. I thought, how terrible.

I sat for long periods throughout the night and watched Mummy lying in bed, hearing the odd murmur but no coughing. Compared to the other patients, she lay very still for most of the time. I kept thinking how nice and plump she was; the rest looked like stick insects.

It was coming up to midnight and still no conversation. How strange. The nurses came in checking Mummy's blood pressure. At about 1.30 a.m. she woke up and knew that she was going to be sick. Daddy told me to get the kidney bowl and hold it to her mouth. A nurse came in and gave her something to try to null the pain. Eventually she settled down again.

Still no conversation.

She coughed up some more blood but nothing in comparison to previously.

Back to watching her.

I kept thinking, how can she be so ill? I looked across at the woman with cancer and thought, what a shame.

John

Olive and I decided to stay overnight to be with Maura. We didn't want her to die on her own. I was feeling down, thinking about having to take Maura's body home and visualising the funeral. Probably being a bit selfish, I was thinking what would I do living in Maura's Rhode on my own?

I was in a state of shock; I didn't know what to think. I was putting all my energy into consoling the children, knowing that it was only a matter of a hair's breadth whether it would be all right or not.

Olive was fussing around her mammy like an old hen. I sat on the edge of the bed but she hunted me off it.

'You can't sit there,' she said, and fetched a chair for me.

That's where we stayed for the evening and into the early hours of the morning, sitting by Maura's side, watching her sleeping.

Olive kept saying, 'Poor Mummy. What are we going to do if anything happens?'

'Sure nothing will happen to her,' I said. 'She'll be all right, pet. She's in good capable hands. Some of the best doctors and surgeons are here at St James's.'

In my heart I could see that there was an 80 per cent chance that Maura was going to die. She looked like a near corpse. I thought, this is it. This time I am going to lose my wife.

*   *   *

I can see an eye. A strange-looking eye. It gives me the creeps. Reminds me of that nightmare I had as a child: I woke frightened from a bad dream, seeing big black spots in front of my eyes.

A voice now. I can hear a voice. It's a woman's voice.

'How many fingers can you see?' Is she talking to me? I don't recognise the voice. Is it Joan? Olive, perhaps?

'Maura, how many fingers am I holding up?'

Focus. Try and focus. I can see something but it doesn't look much like a finger. Is that a nurse at the end of my bed? She's talking to someone. God, I'm thirsty. I need a drink.

'Can I have a sip of water?'

Olive

I was drinking some bottled water when I noticed Daddy staring at me with glazed eyes. I offered him a drink and that's when he started tilting. He fell to the floor and I called for a nurse.

He was taken down to Casualty and then admitted to the hospital. When he came round, he was on a ventilator and drip. He looked awful.

I went back upstairs and sat beside Mummy. She came round for a short time asking who I was.

'Where's your father?' she asked. I told her what had happened and she said, 'My God,' only to fall back into unconsciousness.

Daddy was diagnosed epileptic.

How empty the house is without either Mummy or Daddy. I was left on my own not knowing what to do, trying not to panic, wondering what will happen if they both die.

Seamus

The old man was worried but tried not to show it. Then he panicked and took a fit. He can't deal with pressure. He's never had a fit before. He was never sick. Nothing was ever wrong with him. I'm sure his fit was stress related. Maybe the whole lot of them being here has added to the pressure, even though he needs them. He probably feels pushed out.

Olive was in a bit of distress about his fit because she's caught between the devil and the deep blue sea. She can't be down with him all the time and she can't be upstairs with the old lady all the time. She probably would have felt it more than anybody because she'd be closer to both of them.

Declan

Dad was lying on a trolley in the corridor. It was a bit of a shock to see him because he was almost lifeless. He had his smelly socks on. They were awful. They stank! Breda had to wash his feet. He came to, every now and then, and had another epileptic fit.

Dad's situation seems fairly secondary to what's happening to my mum. She's in quite a serious state. I don't think anything will happen to Dad. He's quite a robust person even though he's getting on in age.

A horrible thing happened. We were standing in the corridor, soothing Dad, when about six nurses came rushing towards us and they were pumping away trying to get this man's heart going. I think he died.

John

The first time I realised that something had happened to me was coming to in a ward and asking one of the children, 'What am I doin' here?' I didn't know whether I had gone mad or was after dying and coming back to life.

I had to have a brain scan. I joked to the children that they were trying to see if I had a brain, and that maybe their mammy was right when she used to say I drank so much I had no brain cells left.

I knew I was over-tired and that I wanted to sleep and rest. I had been on red alert for three days and I was physically and mentally exhausted.

* * *

Breda

Sun 20 June: When I see Mummy lying there I feel really sad. Seeing her in hospital brings everything up, like one big ball in my stomach, almost exploding; there are streams of negative thoughts and feelings and I could catch any one of them.

I'm exhausted by it all. Seeing Mummy in hospital makes me feel really tired. I don't want to face this, I don't want these feelings coming up, I don't want to feel cross, I don't want to feel angry, I don't want to feel resentful and I don't want to feel sad. I don't want to feel any of those things. I just want things to be okay.

I can hear a beautiful soothing voice. Is it Carmel? No, it's Olive talking to me. She's whispering words of comfort. She's crying and wiping the blood from around my sore mouth. I can't see her. I can't see anythin'.

'Have I gone blind, Olive?' I want to touch her and hold her hand.

'Careful, Mummy, there are tubes everywhere.' Tubes? Where am I? I can't remember. 'You've been poorly, Mummy.'

'Can I have a drink?'

I can hear more voices. A girl called Geraldine. 'That's a nice name. I've a daughter called Geraldine.'

The girl was laughing now. 'I am your daughter Geraldine, Mom. Don't you know me? You can't mistake me now, can you?'

Geraldine's very practical. She took control when others would have fussed or refused. She was good at cleaning my feet, like Mary Magdalene. Geraldine should have been a nurse: she has compassion and strength. She would bend down like an orang-utan, putting one arm around my waist and the other under my legs, and help lift me in the bed. It didn't bother Geraldine to look after my personal needs.

Geraldine

I fought hard to hold back the tears so as not to upset her. I've consciously decided to put any ill feeling towards my mother behind me.

I had mixed feelings about the situation. Selfishly, I was irritated by the news that my mother was unwell: I had just finished the final year of my degree – I had been working extremely hard – and I had planned a lovely, long relaxing summer with my children. No one was able to commit to the seriousness of Mommy's illness. In fact, the whole thing was played down because she is known for attention seeking where her health is concerned. When I saw her in hospital, I realised Mommy was, in fact, extremely poorly.

I felt numb. I tried to rationalise what was going on. Everyone seemed so dwarfed by the experience. I was fearful Mommy was going to die but I tried not to be sad. I wanted to be kind and give something back. If these were to be her last moments on earth, I wanted to make her as comfortable as possible and let her know that she is cared for.

We're doing a vigil around the hospital bed. Joan's been sleeping on a blow-up mattress. She calls it Lilo Lil. Joan's been through the worst of it. She's really exhausted. At least now we can shoulder the responsibility. I know I will do what I can within my own gifts. I'm not competing. There are pecking orders; we are a big family and each of us has a role and a position within the family.

I'm delighted that Daddy has been taken ill. I know that sounds controversial but now they're in the same hospital we can look after both of them.

Mommy's been hallucinating. She said at one point, 'Do I want to do a wee?'

Lots of bad feeling is coming out. People are having to face themselves and their own feelings. There are some underlying tensions.

We were euphoric when Mommy started coming round. We were so delighted and happy. Nobody else mattered.

Daddy was parading around in the black and white spotted pyjamas Ellen bought him. He's so proud of himself in his pyjamas, he won't wear his dressing gown.

He thinks all the other men on his ward are a bit daft. One man keeps trying to get into bed with him and Daddy keeps reporting him to the nurse.

Breda

Gen's giving Mummy lots of attention in the sweetest way. She is a very sweet person. She's neatly fussing around her and doing little things. She cuts her toenails, very quietly and efficiently. Joan's doing lots of big things, and looking after Mummy in a big way – stroking her hand and washing her face.

There's all this competition set up in our family for parental attention, for sibling attention; there are pecking orders all over the place. Some of them are striving for Mummy's attention and she gives it to the ones that don't actually seek it.

I watched Olive fluffing her pillows and Mummy got irritable and cross. Olive was patient and tearful. I got Mummy a drink. The drink was the thing that she liked. That satisfied her.

Part of me thinks I ought to do things. I ought to clean her mouth or something but I'm too repulsed by it all – not by Mummy but by the situation. I know people expect me to do something because I was a nurse. But I can't. Mummy seems like a stranger.

Olive told me when Daddy collapsed he fell like a star. The nurses rushed in and said, 'Does he have false teeth?' Olive said yes and the nurse started tugging at his bottom teeth. Olive forgot to mention that he's only got four false teeth, across the front at the top. All of a sudden she realised the nurse was trying to pull his real teeth out and shouted at her to stop.

When Dad came round he said to Olive, 'Do ya know something? I must have been grindin' me teeth in me sleep because all my bottom teeth are loose.'

* * *

John

The other morning, at about two o'clock, the clothes of the bed were being pulled back and some fella tried to get in beside me. I jumped up and ran to the night nurse.

'What sort of a ward am I in?' I asked.

'Oh,' she said, 'there are some disturbed people on this ward.'

'And do ya think I am disturbed as well? There was a buck tryin' to get in beside me.'

'He's a priest.'

'Well, ya better keep an eye on him, whoever he is!'

Carmel, my fifth child, is very calm and pragmatic. She took on the role of researcher processing all the information and passing it on to me in fine detail. She's very fair minded and loyal and would never break a confidence.

Carmel

I was horrified when I first saw Mommy. She looked so frail. When she opened her eyes, they just looked like black holes. They didn't have a pupil or an iris. And it scared me. I'd never seen that before. I thought, oh my God, she's not going to survive.

I held her hand until she didn't want me to any more. I can't do the hands-on, touchy care but I can do the practical things. That's the way I can contribute. I've never been able to do the tactile stuff. Mom's more tactile now than she ever was. Olive and I went down to see Daddy on his ward. When we arrived he was lying on the bed in his dressing gown, pyjamas and slippers. He had his hands crossed on his chest, asleep. He looked so peaceful.

Olive suddenly got this mischievous look on her face. She looked at me and then looked at the bottom of the bed. I didn't know what she was doing. Then she pointed to a pedal at the end of the bed.

'Don't you dare touch that pedal!' I said.

She started to giggle and tapped it with her foot.

'Olive, don't touch the pedal!' The next thing, she hit the pedal with full force and the bed dropped to the floor and Daddy jumped in the air, shouting and cursing.

'What are yous fuckin' doin'?' he screeched. 'You're tryin' to fuckin' kill me!'

Olive was roaring with laughter.

'If yous have come down here to fuckin' laugh at me yous can fuck off!'

Then he looked around and remembered he was in a big ward and everyone had heard him. Olive was wetting herself and Daddy looked at me.

'What did ya do that for?' he said.

'It wasn't me.'

'It was you!'

'It was Olive, actually.'

Daddy looked at Olive and said, 'Was it you, pet?' He was so annoyed he threw us out.

Paul drove like a maniac down to Rhode. He was tired and wanted to get back down to the cottage to sleep. I was putting my foot on an imaginary clutch and brake. I think I annoyed him because he said, 'If you know all the moves, why don't you take the test?'

I can see six doctors, all in white coats, at the end of my bed. Two are wearing glasses; another is leaning in over the rails.

'Hello, Mrs Murphy. You've come through a very serious illness . . . you gave us a scare – we thought we'd lost you.'

Is that Seamus? What's he doing here? He should be home in Mayo. He sounds a long way off.

Is that Paul's face I can see? I tried to touch it.

I can feel myself getting agitated. I can't see clearly. 'Why can't I open my eyes? Am I goin' blind?' I needed some reassurance.

'Try to rest, Mom,' a voice said.

'Is that you, Paul?'

'It is, Mom.'

What a relief to hear his gentle voice. He sounded tired. He was wiping the sweat from my face. I feel happy and secure when he's with me. He's my youngest child, my bab (although he hates me calling him that).

Paul's my friend who lets me be myself and listens without judging me. He sat there beside me just holding my hand.

'Hush now, try and rest,' he said. 'You've been very poorly. Just close your eyes and I'll sit here, on this chair beside the bed. You go back to sleep now and I'll be here when you wake up.'

He kissed my cheek and I started to cry.

Paul

I booked the flight and travelled alone. Alone – that is something I have never been afraid of but being alone without my mother in this world is something I'm not ready for.

My battle cry, therefore, has to be a positive approach to coach Mom into regained health, much the same as when we had to coach her in her fifties when she was on prescribed drugs which were obviously not doing her any good.

Seeing my mother in hospital, I thought she would never wake up again. Her eyes were grey and lifeless and her grip was weak. She appeared to have succumbed to the inevitable. I spoke with her but she was confused. I kissed her head, her cheeks and her hands. I relayed stories to her about her fighting spirit, her prescribed drug problem, her nine children, the time we went to my dad's work with his clothes in a suitcase. I said all this to show that this latest illness is just another one of those beginnings, middles and ends and it would be beaten like everything else.

I remember when we were kids, we used to amuse ourselves by playing hide and seek in the two-bedroom, back-to-back house. Mommy would be watching TV with my dad – seeing whether he'd won some money on the horses – with a towel draped over her knees to hide me. To me that was the sanctuary

I was looking for; every other hiding place had already been
exhausted. The cave, as I called it, was the smugglers' cove of
true and uncontested freedom from the seeker.

Joan

Ellen arrived and said, 'I've got my black clothes in my bag for
Mommy's funeral.'

I told her Mommy wasn't coughing up blood any more and,
strangely enough, I felt like a bit of a fraud. I'm the one who's
been phoning people saying you'd better get over here. It doesn't
seem as bad or as urgent now.

Mummy seems to be slowly regaining consciousness. She said,
'What's this? What is this?'

'Your ear, Mom.' I laughed.

I was awake again and on my own in the room. I could feel the
panic rising. I needed a drink. Where was Breda? I called her
name, 'Breda. Breda!' Why didn't she answer?

'Breda's in Rhode, Mom,' I heard Geraldine say. 'She stayed
with you for two days, Mom. She's gone home to rest.'

I could see long thick bones, covered in rubber. What are they?
I couldn't make them out. Are they my hands? I was afraid to
look at them. They were so scary. Someone was coming. I hid
them under the covers. When I was alone again, I took out these
strange objects and inspected them some more. What are they,
these things at the end of my arms? Seventy years of age and I
couldn't think of the word for them. Who could I ask? I didn't
want to sound stupid. I'd ask my daughter Carmel. She'd know.

'Where have you hidden the money, Mom?'

I recognised that voice: it was Ellen, my eldest. She's so witty,
just like John. Ellen the observer, the joker. She was in a happy
frame of mind. I was glad to hear her lovely voice, her received
pronunciation. She always knows how to make me laugh.

EIGHT

'A Perfect Gentleman'

I'd never heard of the Blackrock Lido until my sister Anna called and asked me to go with her to a dance there. It was the first, and last, time I ever went but that evening was to change my life for ever.

'What's the Lido?' I asked Anna.

'It's a dance hall in Blackrock. Kathy Foy goes there. Will ya come?'

'No, I'm just after lightin' a fire; I'm not dressed for goin' out.' I had settled with my cup of tea, fags and my book.

'Come on. I can't go in there on my own.'

'No, I'm not goin'. I'm stayin' in to read my book.'

'Aw come on, Maura,' she pleaded. 'Ya might have fun.'

'Oh, okay. I'll come.' Anna could be very persuasive.

It didn't take me long to get ready. I wore a skirt with a turquoise cardigan fastened at the top to hide my cleavage. Anna, as always, wore a frock.

As we walked into the Lido, Bing Crosby's latest song filled the hall. All the girls were mad about Bing. We thought he was the greatest crooner of all time. His voice was full of hope and optimism in those postwar years.

The Lido was a long, nar[row] I wasn't used to going to pl[...] getting used to mixing with the [...] Teachers Ballroom.

A few months earlier, Carmel h[...] dance at the Teachers with her a[...] Fallon, a guard at Kilmainham Stat[...] phone her one night while I was visit[...]

'Say hello to my sister Maura.'

Carmel was all excited about him a[...] phone to me. 'No, I don't want to speak to him.'

'Go on!'

'No—'

Ignoring me, Carmel pushed the phone into my hand. I didn't want to talk to her boyfriend. What would I say? I didn't know him. It was the worst thing she could have done, that and inviting me along with her to the dance with them. A friend of Dick's showed a lot of interest in Carmel at the dance, and she was flirting back, so Dick danced with me all night.

The two lads were waiting outside with their bicycles when we came out. 'Come on, Maura. I'll give you a lift home on me bike,' said Dick. I looked at Carmel and started to laugh.

'I can't believe you're offerin' me a lift on the bar of your bike in the city of Dublin.' Imagine! That was only done in the country. 'Come on then,' I said, suddenly feeling bold. I hitched up on to his crossbar and off we went.

Carmel was livid. I didn't think she was that serious about Dick but she was vexed because she thought I'd taken her boyfriend. I never tried to take boys from other girls, but men flocked around me. Perhaps I had some sex appeal. Perhaps I was a flirt, without knowing it. Perhaps it was my size forty-four chest that attracted them!

Carmel didn't speak to me for a month when I started seeing Dick. I liked him for his fun and his easy-going manner. He was

his head up in the air. He was wild and
or dancing, especially the quickstep. He was
and I was very fond of him. He had some pecu-
gs though. If we walked down the street with a crowd
eople he would say, 'Stick your leg in me arm'. And he'd say,
Why do ya bother with me?'

'Cos I like ya.'

'Say that again and I'll kiss ya.' I would die laughing.

'Do it now,' I'd say, and he would, right there in the middle
of Dame Street. I could never say no. I liked kissing Dick Fallon.
He had a beautiful mouth. It helped that he was over six foot
and very broad-shouldered. A solid-looking man. And he was
spotless. Dressed very smart; I thought Dick was gorgeous. But
not as handsome as the man who caught my eye at the Lido the
night I went with Anna.

I was sipping my orange juice when I saw him – a tall good-
looking soldier, dashing and sophisticated in his army uniform.
He had a straight-backed air of austerity about him. I was sure
he was a high-ranking officer. I couldn't keep my eyes off him.

'Anna, look at that fella at the bar,' I whispered. She wasn't
a bit interested. She had her eyes trained on the door looking at
all the other fellas walking in.

I liked the look of soldiers but I would never date them because
I didn't think they were good enough for me. But I was immediately taken with this well-groomed, dignified, soldier boy. You
would pick him out of any crowd. He looked just like the film
star Montgomery Clift. I was transfixed by his shiny jet-black
hair, pearly white teeth and brilliant smile. Very handsome! He
took my breath away.

I waited for him to ask me to dance, for I was sure he would.
No matter where I went in the dense crowd, his eyes seemed to
follow me. I was desperate to dance with him. I wanted his tall,
trim, beautiful body to whip me off my feet and spin me around
the dance floor in a wistful, romantic slow waltz. I imagined

his soft plump lips conspiring to charm me, just like in the movies. I longed for him to wrap his tender fingers around my trembling hand and guide me to the darkest corner of the hall . . . instead he stood at the bar, his tender fingers wrapped firmly around a pint of black porter. He couldn't seem to part with his beer.

I couldn't wait any longer. I heard the Ladies' Choice being announced and walked straight up to him.

'Would ya like to dance with me?' I said.

'I'll try.' He smiled.

Well, I wasn't impressed by that comment. It wasn't every man that had the privilege of holding his body close to mine. But the soldier danced wonderfully. He held me a little too close to him as he gently glided me across the floor. The singer crooned, 'Do not forsake me, oh my darling . . .' Well, I wasn't this man's darling, yet, but was sure I would be: the chemistry was there. I could feel it. He surely could feel it too. I wished the dance could go on for ever. He smiled, and my heart melted.

When the band finished playing, he surprised me with a gentle kiss on my forehead and thanked me for the dance. I was so thrilled I could have hugged myself.

I loitered in his eyeline all night but there was no sign of a return dance. How rude, I thought. The band struck up my favourite, 'The Siege of Ennis' – guaranteed to get everyone up on the dance floor. I watched as lucky girls were chosen to pair up with eager boys, all strolling towards their positions on the floor. I couldn't take the disappointment of rejection. My heart ached. Humiliation flushed through my face and neck as I made a dash for the cloakroom.

My soldier boy saved the moment. He caught me by the arm and dragged me on to the floor where dancers were beginning to form a huge figure of eight. We took up our position and waited for the music to start.

'What's your name, by the way?' he asked.

'I'll tell ya mine if you tell me yours,' I teased.

'John Murphy.'

'Maura McNamee.'

'Where are ya from?'

'Offaly.'

'I'm from Carlow.'

The music started and we were off, step dancing and twirling, linking arms and spinning. All hell broke loose. One party of dancers faced another party and met each other in the middle. A voice shouted, 'Bring her up', and another, 'and mind the dresser!' – a reference to the days when this energetic dance took place in people's cramped houses.

We spun round so fast our skirts rose above our waists, delighting boys sitting out the dance. The sweat tumbled down my glowing red face. At the end of the dance I gasped for breath and wiped the sweat off my forehead with the back of my sleeves.

'Well, Maura, will I see you again?' he asked.

'Ya might.' I kept my voice low and calm though I was sure he could sense the tremble in it.

I agreed to see John Murphy the following week. That satisfied him.

I sat on the bus home in a dream, thinking about my date with the soldier and wondering if he would turn up. John did turn up the following week, and the next and the next.

John Murphy and I dated, on and off, for a year before we got serious. He was stationed at Portobello Barracks in Rathmines and we would meet up on his evenings off. In our early courting days, he would take me with him to the army training ground in Phoenix Park and I would watch him play Gaelic football for the army team. When the game was over, we would take the bus into town and have a coffee somewhere. I would be in ecstasy, my mind filled with his conversation.

John was polite and spoke with a sweet, soft voice. He was comical and suave, and bursting with intelligent conversation. I was in awe of his knowledge and vocabulary; his command of English amazed me. He would sing to me and write romantic poems. I would read his funny words and think, you fool, you crazy fool. And he was forever quoting lines of poetry. When we left each other after a date, he would recite the first verse of Gray's 'Elegy Written in a Country Churchyard':

> *The curfew tolls the knell of parting day,*
> *The lowing herd winds slowly o'er the lea,*
> *The ploughman homeward plods his weary way,*
> *And leaves the world to darkness, and to me.*

I wondered how anyone other than a professor or university lecturer could be so full of knowledge.

We would go to the zoo or sit for hours by the bandstand in Phoenix Park. One day as we walked past the monkeys in the zoo, a flying specimen surprised me.

'Look at that monkey over there,' I said. 'He is tryin' to jump over the other one to get to his pole.'

'More like to get to his bananas.'

'What type of monkey is that, John?'

'Well now, that's an Irish monkey, Maura.'

'Don't be daft, there aren't any Irish monkeys.'

'Ah, there are loads of them. Mostly two-legged ones.'

'Get away, ya eejit.'

'Maura, I'm tellin' ya. There's one up in the White House. His name is Sean T. O'Ceallaigh. And that fella swingin' over there, that's his youngest son.'

I felt stupid and inferior in John's company, like a poor fool sitting with a genius. I didn't know enough to hold a conversation the way John did. He filled a gap in my personality. I was reserved. He did all the talking while I did the smiling. I liked it that way at the time. I never felt the need to push myself forward. Although we grew up in different parts of Ireland we had the very same education. But he had what I lacked: intellectual ability, confidence and the gift of the gab.

John knew so much about the history of 'The Irish White House'. He was often on guard duty there when dignitaries from around the world were being wined and dined. This one day, Sean T. O'Ceallaigh was inspecting the line of guards. John described him as a squat little man, a little over five foot, who smelt to high heaven of cologne and deodorant.

'He walked by us, followed by his large-framed six-foot wife,' John said, 'and we'd whisper "Jaysus, I hope she doesn't roll over on him tonight" and then stifle the giggles.'

After the inspection, all the dignitaries were introduced.

'Ambassador so and so . . .' and a soldier standing to attention to John's right whispered, 'Fuck him!'

'The distinguished Lord so and so . . .'

'And fuck him too!'

This whispered insurrection would carry on until everyone who was someone had been introduced and well fucked!

John was a fiercely patriotic soldier, despite his irreverence. He went for a pint in a hotel in New Ross one time – it was used by the upper-class Irish – and got all affronted when a group of 'golfing bucks' refused to shut up or stand up for the Irish National Anthem.

He went over and said, 'Excuse me, are you fellas Irish by any chance?'

'Yes, we all are,' the red pudding-faced one said.

'In that case, wouldn't ya show a bit of respect for your country and stand up for your National Anthem?'

Pudding man looked at John in his army uniform and said, 'Are we at war?' and they all guffawed.

'Looks like it,' John said as he hurled himself at the upstart and gave him a box.

'Will ya stand up next time, Mr Golfer?' John shouted.

The hotel manager arrived on the scene and tried to put his

hand over John's mouth to gag him. John struggled free and landed a punch on the manager.

Two burly bouncers threw John out the door and he landed on his head down the stone steps. He woke next morning in a pool of blood, and an army reprimand awaiting him at the barracks. He still has the scar as a reminder of that day.

I might not have approved of John's aggression but I had to admire him for his love of his country. And he was always very respectful of me in our courting months. When he suggested we go to the Regal Rooms cinema to see Bing Crosby and Ingrid Bergman in *The Bells of St Mary's*, I was sure he would take me to the back row, kiss me and put his arms around me. I was desperate to feel him close to me but I didn't want to give the wrong impression. I was brought up a good Catholic, and good Catholic girls didn't show those kinds of feelings. I needn't have worried – John marched me past all the other young lovers in the back row and sat down front, not a cuddle in sight. He was the perfect gentleman.

I suppose John was a bit of a catch. He was a charmer – honey to the bees, as he still keeps reminding me. He was generous too, always ready to share his cigarettes. But I couldn't believe it when he produced a packet of Player's Weights. He couldn't have got a cheaper packet if he tried; they were cheaper than the Woodbines, and tasted worse. Player's Weights were even worse than the *keeb* from the turf. When we were teenagers we used to crumble the short dry grass from the white sod of turf, roll it in newspaper and smoke it like a cigarette. It tasted like horse shite but at least it was free.

After my front row disappointments, I soon discovered that John, like all hot-blooded young men, enjoyed physical contact. He was a great kisser. He would nibble at my ear and kiss my neck. I loved him for it. And he was such a dandy. He met me in Rathmines one day sporting a soft trilby, walking stick and a beautiful grey herringbone tweed swagger coat, which I was sure he had robbed! He would never have bought it. This was the coat of a commissioned officer, not an NCO on £1 10s. a week. There was something peculiar about it.

We never had much money so we had to find entertainment to suit our pockets. We did a lot of walking. Sometimes, when we were too broke to go dancing or see a film, we would go to St Anne's Park in Raheny, sit on his jacket and laze about doing nothing but enjoying each other's company.

Eighteen months after our first date, around Christmas time, we took an evening stroll in the park. John took off his swagger coat and spread it on the grass.

'This is the ground sheet for the night,' he said.

We started with the kissing and cuddling and being happy in each other's company. I hadn't contemplated anything else happening. John was saying, 'I love you, Maura,' and his hand slid under my skirt, past the top of my stocking and towards no man's land.

'No, John, not that, not yet,' I protested. I didn't notice that he had unbuttoned himself.

'I love you, Maura. Come on. I love you.'

'John, please stop it. Come on now. Stop it. Get off me.'

Then it happened, right there in the light of a beautiful winter moon. I was aware of the stars looking down at me. I was very tense. He was groaning with pleasure and kissing my face and neck. I tried to wriggle out of it but my fighting just increased his desire. I struggled to free myself but he was too big and heavy lying on top of me. It was happening now and I knew that it was a sin.

John satisfied himself.

I leapt up afterwards, settled my clothes, and I said, 'I'm goin' home.'

'I'll come with ya,' he said, taking up his coat.

'I'll find my own way.' I stormed off, crying with anger.

John was trying to put his arm around me, and hug and kiss me, but I kept elbowing him away. 'Get off!' I said.

He apologised immediately and said everything would be all right. He planted a kiss on my mouth and told me again that he loved me. Then he marched off to catch his bus back to the barracks.

It was a painful experience for me, both physically and emotionally. I was mortified that I allowed myself to be taken. It was never my intention to be intimate before marriage. Our beautiful relationship was now stained, and I felt ugly. I was disgusted with myself. I felt dirty. I just wanted to go home, have a bath and scrub myself clean. I had lost my most valued asset – my virginity. I believed it to be sacred; it was part of the sanctity of marriage. It was the first time I had to fight for my self-respect and my virginity.

'Are you all right?' John asked, when he phoned the next day.
'No.'
'Are ya still angry?'
'Yes.'

I was so upset I could barely speak to him. John seemed regretful that I might leave him. I couldn't think straight. I didn't tell anyone about my ordeal. I was too ashamed to admit what had happened.

A few weeks after the walk in the park, John was admitted to St Brican's Military Hospital suffering from jaundice. It was there, lying in his hospital bed, all sickly yellow and his lovely green eyes the colour of egg yolk, that John Murphy proposed to me.

He handed me his money for safe keeping, in case anybody pinched it in the night, then said suddenly, 'I think me and you ought to get married.'

'Married, how are ya. Where would we live?'

'We could live in the married quarters.'

'No way. That's the fever talking. I haven't the slightest intention of getting married.'

I wasn't sure I cared enough about him to commit myself to marriage, and I didn't think anybody could take the place of

Tom Walsh. I liked John but I wasn't in love with him, but he begged me to marry him and promised to work his fingers to the bone and take care of me. I accepted.

I knew very little about the man I agreed to marry. John could be distant and guarded. He wouldn't indulge in any conversation about himself. He told me he was reared by his granny in the picturesque village of Clonegal and joined the army when she died. With her death, he lost his anchor and the army seemed like his only option. He signed a three-year contract and began his training as a private at the Curragh in Kildare. He graduated to the rank of an NCO and became a physical fitness instructor whipping troops into shape at Collins Barracks. When I met him, he had been transferred to Portobello Barracks, in Rathmines, following the National Anthem punch-up.

He was obviously a dedicated soldier, and wore his stripes with pride, but his first love was football. I wasn't interested in the game but I would go and watch him play. He was an excellent player, fast and lithe, winning numerous prizes for the army team. I was very proud of him. Despite his achievements, there was a sadness about him. He struck me as vulnerable and insecure. I didn't appreciate what a lonely person he was.

If I was going to commit myself to him, we would need somewhere to live. I wasn't about to settle for married quarters at Portobello Barracks. If that was all John could offer me, the whole marriage thing was off.

When John was well enough to be discharged from hospital, we scoured Dublin for a flat. We couldn't find anything to suit our pockets. The cheapest place cost three pounds a week and John's army salary wouldn't stretch to that. Carmel had changed jobs and was renting a bedsit in Blackrock. John and I spent time alone together there. That was a mistake: the temptation to be intimate was too strong to resist when we were alone. After the shock in the park, I didn't think it was so bad. Once it had happened the first time, the second time and third time, sex was just something we did. The taste of the grass makes a rogue of the bullock! Eventually I found it exciting and pleasurable. At least I wasn't going to die wondering what it was like.

John was a romantic, gentle and considerate lover. But perhaps we were both selfish lovers: we didn't think about the outcome. We got cavalier. Took risks. We didn't take any precautions because that wasn't the Catholic way. There was no such thing as birth control or contraception, and so the inevitable happened – I got pregnant. My period didn't arrive. I had fierce stomach pains, but no period.

I was out of my mind with worry. What was I going to do now? Who could I tell? I knew for sure I was pregnant. Mammy would be devastated. The gossips would have a field day. I couldn't bear them knowing I had done *it* so I kept it to myself.

I didn't tell anyone, except John.

He wasn't shocked or surprised. 'We're gettin' married, aren't we?' he said. 'So what's the problem?'

John was absolutely fine about it but I felt controlled and humiliated by the shame of the pregnancy. We made hasty arrangements with Father Callery, the priest in Castlejordan, and gave him the customary three weeks' notice for the calling of the banns. We had no printed invitations in those days so Father and I visited friends and family giving out personal invites. We couldn't invite everyone but we made sure each family was represented. Luke was John's best man and Biddy McNamee was my bridesmaid.

Like my mammy before, I got married in a suit, a smart grey one with a matching hat and veil bought from Arnott's of Dublin. The black suede shoes were a present from John the Christmas before. A white collarless blouse with a bow at the top and pearl buttons down the front completed my wedding outfit. Country folk didn't wear expensive white dresses with trains. We didn't bother with a photographer and I made my own three-tier wedding cake.

Unlike Mammy, I had to buy my own wedding ring. I was

excited when we walked into the jeweller's in Dublin but when the heavy security door clicked shut, I realised John wasn't with me. He decided to wait outside and leave me to choose and pay for the ring, a plain gold band that cost twenty-five shillings. How romantic! John promised to settle up with me when he got paid, but he never did.

After Father walked me up the aisle at Holy Trinity Church, he turned to me and said 'Good luck' before handing me over to my future husband. I became respectable Mrs Murphy at nine in the morning on 29 April 1953, the very same day Mammy and Father married twenty-eight years earlier.

We had the wedding breakfast at Mammy's and a reception at the Midland Hotel in Mullingar. We had a brilliant day out there. John and Biddy took the floor and entertained everybody with the jitterbug. The band played all our favourite Glenn Miller tunes.

We were supposed to go up to Dublin after the reception but we were having such a good time we stayed down in Offaly. We went back to Mammy's with a few musicians and carried on celebrating. They sat along the wall playing jigs and reels on their melodeons and tin whistles.

John and I fell exhausted into bed at five o'clock in the morning. Just as we were snuggling down, Peter appeared at the door.

'Any room in there behind you, John?' he asked. He didn't wait for an answer. Peter got in behind John and there we were, the three of us, lying in a three-quarter bed on our wedding night!

Bolting to Dublin

In those first few weeks after we married, John continued to live in his digs at the barracks in Dublin. I moved in with Mammy in the country so that I could be at home when I gave birth to my first child. John was dissatisfied with the arrangement. He wanted to quit the army and, thanks to Mammy's connections (she was a relative of the Chief of Staff) he received an invitation to leave on 'compassionate grounds'. Although his commandant begged him to stay, John left the army in June 1953 with an exemplary record. He moved in with me at Mammy's and got a job at Tong's grass factory, making grass meal for cattle, where my father, Luke and Joe worked. They would all come home with green faces (very patriotic).

Once John and I began living together, I started to think I'd made a terrible mistake. The well-mannered charmer who dazzled me at the lido suddenly changed. He became bossy and moody and tried to control my every movement. I couldn't even leave the room without being questioned. 'Where are ya goin' now?' 'What are ya goin' there for?' It used to madden me that I had to answer him.

I found it difficult being married. I wanted to feel the same freedoms I had as a single woman, to move, to cycle, to visit and to mitch without having to explain myself to John. I was expected to lose part of myself to form the union and I couldn't cope with it. I felt like a half person. I didn't want to share me with John. I didn't want to share John with anyone else either.

When he moved down to Offaly he was like a young gun. The local boys, knowing he played county football in Carlow, were desperate for him to join their teams. Ballinabrackey GAA was delighted when he said he'd play with them. John loved going out with the lads and being the centre of attention. He was a confident socialiser; he told great stories and everybody loved his fun. He couldn't see anything wrong with that, but I didn't like it. I didn't want to share him with football, his friends or the pub. He got it very easy to make friends but I didn't. I was a dog in the manger.

For John's part, he had found a ready-made family, something he hadn't experienced before. He was always very respectful towards my father and insisted on calling him Mr McNamee. It was 'yes, Mr McNamee', 'no sir, Mr McNamee'. I would be raging.

'Why can't ya call him Johnnie like everybody else?' I would say.

Some people might have been impressed with his politeness, city folk and the like, but that didn't work in the country – especially with ordinary, down-to-earth people like my father. He didn't suffer fools gladly and John's humbleness would really irritate him.

They were complete opposites. Father could be very blunt. He 'rose' from labourer to postman and on his rounds people would pester him and ask him, 'Have ya e'er a letter for me today, Johnnie?'

If he didn't like them he would say brusquely, 'Sure if I had a fuckin' letter for ya, wouldn't I stop and give it to ya?'

Father would come home from work and go feed the pigs in his postman's suit, getting all the swill on the legs of his trousers. Then he'd put them on the next day and go off to work in them. John couldn't believe it; he was very well groomed and spotless in dress and person. He was always shaving and preening and cleaning his nails. He was very clean and smart. He took a pride in his appearance. His army training, I suppose. The army also taught him how to cook and wash, and he didn't mind doing it.

John was the only one in the house that was able to tie a fashionable Windsor knot, and they would all line up for John to tie theirs for Sunday morning Mass. Father thought John was a bit of a show off but he would be there too asking Mr Humble to do his tie.

When John first came to live with us he had lots of shirts and socks. Many is the Sunday morning that you would hear one of my brothers or my father shouting, 'John, have ya e'er an auld clane pair of socks I can borra?' He would give them gladly, delighted to think that he was fitting in.

John was a great worker and full of energy. He couldn't abide lazy or idle people. He couldn't bear to see people in bed after eight o'clock in the morning. Even after a day's work he'd come home ready to help Father, Peter and anyone else who asked, to clean out the sheds, help with the milking or draw turf from the bog, without being paid. He was always trying to please and get people to like him. It worked with everyone bar Father. But Mammy played her part in that.

'Would ya e'er make me an auld sup a tae, Mary?' Father would ask, throwing his cap on to the kitchen table.

'Can't ya see I'm busy?' she would reply.

Some minutes would pass and she'd say, pointedly, 'Do ya want me to make you a sup of tae, John?'

John, knowing the friction Mammy was trying to cause, would diplomatically decline. 'No thanks, Mary Ann, I'm just off out.'

Even though I wasn't in my own house, Mammy made it clear that she wouldn't be looking after my husband. She expected me to prepare all his meals and do his washing and ironing.

My feelings towards John changed. I would never have married him if I hadn't got pregnant. Being at home with my family made little difference to his growing antagonism towards me. One morning, I was frying an egg for his breakfast and the egg broke in the pan. I was always good at doing fries but this day the egg broke and John got very upset about it.

'Ya can't even fry a fuckin' egg!' he said.

'What's wrong with ya?' I said. 'Why are you being so stupid? I've only cracked an egg, haven't I? It doesn't always happen.'

John would never have commented on the egg if Mammy had been in the house. He wouldn't have wanted her to hear him cursing.

Around the same time I saw how angry he could be in drink. I was reluctant to give him a pound out of the housekeeping to go to the match in Tullamore with my brother Joe. I knew he would spend some of it on the gate fee and the rest in the pub. I thought if I didn't give him the pound he wouldn't stay out so long.

Joe and John were in kinks laughing at me. 'Ah, go on give him the auld pound,' Joe said.

'No I won't. He has two pounds in his pocket and that's enough to waste on drink.'

'But Maura,' John laughed, 'sure ya wouldn't see me short of a few bob?'

'John, I don't have another pound to give to you. Ya have enough there. I'm savin' this for the babby's things.'

'Sure, I'll get another pound.'

How naive of me to think that he wouldn't find a way to stay in the pub. He'd drink beer off a sore leg if he had to. I relented in the end, as he knew I would, and the two of them went off up the road roaring laughing.

John got very drunk. He was so blotto when he came home that he sat on my stomach getting into bed. I was four months pregnant at the time. I let out a scream and Father called to me, 'What's wrong? Are you all right, Maura?'

'It's nothing, just a twitch of pain,' I lied.

I was hurt and angry. I rubbed my hands across my stomach to ease the hardness of my lump. I thought my unborn child was in distress, suffering all kinds of discomfort. I thought John had injured the baby on purpose. I couldn't help feeling he was trying to hurt me whatever way he could.

Next morning, when John got up out of bed, he had a hangover and was not in a talkative mood. I was rubbing my stomach, still in great discomfort.

'What's wrong?' he grunted.

'Well ya know what's wrong.'

'What?'

'Can't ya remember? Ya sat on my stomach.'

He looked surprised. 'That must have been an accident.'

'Well, it was one that hurt me very much.'

It could have been an accident but John never apologised. That was the first time he was abusive towards me in drink. Before we married, I didn't realise he was such a heavy drinker. He had always been funny and light-hearted. Now he was becoming unpredictable and the slightest comment or innocent remark would set him off. His sensitivity often came out of the blue. One day when he came in from work, I noticed his bare feet when he was changing his socks.

'God, John, you've got terrible long toes,' I said. I hadn't seen toes like them.

He shot me a look. 'Are they hurtin' ya?'

'No, they're not hurtin' me. I just think you've got very long toes.' That exchange of words put him into an angry, sulky mood for the rest of the night.

There were times when he was very good but if I'd had any idea of that nasty side of him, I wouldn't have married him, baby or no baby. His changed behaviour had an impact on our relationship. I went off him and he spent less and less time with me. He preferred the company of his new friends. His charm overwhelmed everyone. People would tell me what a wonderful man he was and how lucky I was to be with him. They didn't see the John Murphy I saw behind closed doors.

I prayed that nobody would notice the early birth of my first child in 1953, but there they were counting the months on their fingers. My daughter arrived three months premature on a Sunday morning while everyone was at early Mass.

We were all taken by surprise. I thought my pains were being caused by the return of a kidney infection I'd had the month before. Along with the crippling pain, I had a terrible urge to go to the toilet. I got up in the early hours of the morning and went outside to do a wee at the corner of the house (there was no toilet). I crawled back into bed and asked John to go call Mammy, and she sent him off on his bicycle to fetch medicine from the doctor in Edenderry. He didn't mind being asked. He was good like that. He leapt up on the bike and away with him.

I was rolling around the bed in agony. Mammy realised what was happening. 'The infection's very painful, Mammy.'

'Maur'een, it's not your kidneys at all. Isn't it the child that's goin' to be born?'

'What?' I said, surprised.

'It's labour pains ya have.'

'It's far too early.'

'Your child is goin' to be born.'

'Oh, Mammy,' I cried.

So, it wasn't wee at all. It was my waters breaking.

John arrived back from town clutching the medicine. 'I have it,' he said, catching his breath.

'You'd better cycle back into the town and get the doctor. She's havin' her child,' said Mammy.

The ambulance, the doctor and John arrived back at the house at the same time. Ellen, the first of nine children, was born just a few minutes later. I had only been in labour four hours. It was an amazing experience to think one minute you had a big lump and the next a bawling child.

She was so premature the doctor didn't think she would live. I felt weepy and frightened. I had nothing prepared, no clothes or a crib. The doctor had to wrap the baby in cotton wool and a napkin. I couldn't believe what he did next. He got hold of my good tweed coat from the back of the door, ripped it in half, as if it were tissue paper, and wrapped that around her too. He administered conditional baptism, in case the child died before she had her official Church baptism, and then he left.

Like all newborns, Ellen generated a lot of interest. My first visitor was Old Sis from the High House who came in on her way home from Mass. Old Sis, Aunt Bridie's sister-in-law, was an ignorant, nosy woman. She was born in a tin-roofed house but she thought she was above the rest of us because the Land Commission gave her a few acres of land.

Sis came into my makeshift maternity room and pulled back

the baby's covers. 'A little girl!' she said, examining the tiny little mite. 'Ah wirra, wirra, Maur'een, she's full-term.'

'Is she, Sis?' I said mockingly. 'And you should know.'

'She has eyelashes. She's full-term.'

Sis, of course, was saying my baby was conceived long before my wedding day but I wasn't about to give her the satisfaction of being right. I couldn't wait for Sis to leave.

The only indication my family gave about knowing the reason for my sudden wedding was a conversation I overheard between Mammy and Peter.

'Mammy, did Maura have to get married?' Peter boomed in a deep, accusing voice.

'No she didn't, *Musha*, who told ya that?' said Mammy.

'Everyone's talkin' sayin' she had to get married,' said Peter.

'Let them go to perjock!' she said.

The following morning the nurse came out from Tullamore to register the premature birth. She told me the child was terribly jaundiced and underweight – she only weighed three pounds – and would have to be taken into hospital. She was so under-developed that she had no eyebrows or fingernails and her skin was so wrinkled she had to be bathed in olive oil. She was the funniest looking *yoke* you ever saw in your life. You could hold her in the palm of your hand.

Ellen spent several days surviving in an incubator in Tullamore General. John cycled out there each Sunday to visit her. The twenty-mile round trip didn't bother him one bit. He'd come back and tell me how yellow she was and how well her nails were growing. He'd make me laugh by mimicking the mouths she'd be making.

I couldn't go. It was the way of the times. You couldn't go outside the door until you had been 'churched at the altar of God'. This was a blessing new mothers received in thanksgiving for the safe delivery of the child. I had a terrible desire to see Ellen but I wouldn't break the rules. I knew the child was in the best place. It was such a cold month she was better off there than at home in Mammy's cold cottage. I missed her terribly: I had only held her for one day before she was taken into hospital. Imagine these days leaving your first child in hospital for three weeks and not going to see her?

Once Ellen got to three months and started forming pretty features, she became such a gorgeous-looking baby that she took everyone's breath away. The older she got, the lovelier she became. But as a newborn, she was so frail and delicate that I was afraid to handle her. She was no bigger than a bag of sugar, her head flopping all over the place.

Mammy made all the arrangements for her christening too. Babies were usually christened within a week of being born, and sometimes within a couple of days. As Ellen was premature, she couldn't leave the house for several more weeks. There was talk of the priest christening her at home. That would have been a big thing to do. Everyone was getting very agitated, particularly Father. He was giving out about her not being christened. 'Get that pagan out of this house,' he told Mammy. Father could be very nasty. He was so ignorant he didn't know that Ellen couldn't be taken out of the house because she was premature. I think really he was annoyed that she was conceived out of wedlock. I never told him but I think he knew.

In keeping with tradition, I didn't attend the christening. Mothers didn't in those days. After a normal birth, we usually stayed in bed for seven days – the belief was that you would start haemorrhaging if you did too much – and we weren't allowed out of the house for three weeks.

I chose my brother Luke and my friend Biddy McNamee to be Ellen's godparents; it was customary to choose your best man and bridesmaid. But Luke refused to stand for her because he assumed, rightly, that she was conceived outside of marriage. I was annoyed because I believed it was an honour to be asked, just as it is an honour to be asked to sponsor a child at a Confirmation or, for that matter, to be asked to be the best man at your wedding. I was devastated that he refused. We had always been so close. That was the start of the decline of our friendship and Luke's underlying antagonism with John.

Joe agreed to take Luke's place and my aunt Bridie Glennon was Ellen's carrier, though it was not unusual for the nurse who delivered the child to perform that task. Ellen wore a borrowed christening gown, silk cap and white gloves. So off she went to church, in her borrowed cap and gown, in the back of Bridie Glennon's horse and trap.

My first expedition out of the house would be to receive the priest's blessing. That was a strange affair. This ceremony happened after a Saturday morning Mass. There would have been no special service for me. I walked up the aisle to receive my blessing, knelt down at the raised altar and waited while the priest said a prayer. He read a passage from the Bible and then he put holy oils on my forehead. It felt odd because it was like I was being cleansed after giving birth to a child. What was so wrong with giving birth? Why wouldn't you have to be cleansed after you'd had sex?

Ellen's birth knocked me for six. It was very hard accepting this little person into my life, the underdeveloped little bird with her mouth open waiting for the food. She would cry and cry and I was afraid to hold her or do anything with her for fear of letting her fall. All I could hear was this crying baby, so I handed her over to Mammy and she showed me what to do. I copied her, the way she used to lie her down in her lap making a cushion of her legs.

I think John was a little bit scared to touch her as well. He kept going out more and staying away. I felt left and alone and responsible for everything while he was enjoying the company of other people. I was weepy and fed up. Everyone would say, 'How is the child?' and 'How is John?' But nobody was asking, 'And how are you?' I felt that the baby had come between John and me. I relied on him for his strength in my weaknesses, but after Ellen was born he couldn't settle. He became even more unpredictable and unreliable, and the drinking became a fixture of his life.

I was conscious that the baby's crying was getting to everyone in the house, and John and I felt terribly uncomfortable because of the effect she was having on their lives. The cottage was too small for an extended family and Father found more reasons to resent John. He blamed John for getting seventeen-year-old Joe started on the drink and he didn't like it one bit.

One Sunday when John and Joe were out drinking, Father was pacing up and down waiting for them to come home. He found Joe outside puking his guts up, and blamed John for him getting so sick. The next morning, John couldn't get up for work. Father kept calling him but he just wouldn't get up.

'Get up outta that bed and get to work!' Father shouted. Eventually John appeared in the kitchen and Father started giving out to him. John gave him a box in the mouth and knocked him flat on his arse on the stone floor.

Father was outraged. 'You can get out of here and find somewhere else to live!' he told him.

Of course, Mammy blamed my father and took John's side in the row. She loved John and thought Father should have more sense and not be picking on him. Father turned off John completely after that.

I didn't want to leave Mammy: I was reluctant to stand on my own two feet as a wife and mother. But there was too much testosterone flying around in the Clonmore and the boxing in the kitchen made it impossible for us to stay.

We found a room at Billy and Mary Cabey's place in Ballybrittain, near the grass factory. We paid five shillings a week for the privilege of living in the Cabeys' room. It was suffocating and claustrophobic but at least we had a roof over our heads. That one room became our bedroom, living room, kitchen and bathroom. We had no furniture save for a little table, two chairs and a bed. I had no cot and no pram. We made a makeshift cot by putting two kitchen chairs together and placing a pillow on the top for a mattress.

The room was bitterly cold and I was forced to leave Ellen on her own while I searched the garden for bits of clods and sticks to light a fire. On one of my clod-searching jaunts I tripped over a stile with my bundle of wood. I felt pain in my stomach. I scooped up my wood and hobbled back across the road. I started losing blood. I thought it was my period. When John came in from work, he had to cycle to Edenderry to fetch the doctor. Dr Lennon told me that I'd had a miscarriage. I didn't even know I was pregnant. It was horrible. I had an emptiness inside. A miscarriage is twice as bad as a birth. At least with a birth you have something to hold.

After seeing to me, the doctor took John to one side and lectured him about his duties to me as my husband and warned him that I should avoid getting pregnant again for a couple of years. But he didn't tell John what we were to do to stop the pregnancies. He didn't suggest contraception – that was against the teachings of the Church – and he didn't even advise separate beds!

John and I just carried on as usual. At the time, it wasn't an issue; it was normal. You got married, you had intercourse and you created children. We both realised that these were John's natural rights according to our conditioning. And the Church's teachings seemed to suit his sexual appetite. If John wanted sex, he had sex. There was no point having your headaches in those days. They didn't work. My marriage was no different to thousands of others. Women were expected to carry out their wifely duties, come what may.

I seldom ever had the need to have sex. I didn't know anything about orgasms. I don't know to this day if I ever had one. I did have pleasurable experiences during sex. But what happened between a man and his wife was private. It took place in the bedroom and you didn't discuss it with each other or anyone else. Having children and losing children wasn't spoken of. It was taboo. There was no such thing as postnatal depression. Women were treated worse than cattle during those days. We lost the right to use our own minds and lost control of our own bodies. Nobody cared how we felt. Women, especially the poor working-class women, were brainwashed, intimidated and manipulated by the Catholic Church. We were talked down to from the pulpits. We had no rights.

After my miscarriage, I became frigid and frightened that I would get pregnant again. I didn't communicate any of this to John. If John had the urge for intimate contact, he took it. He became aggressive and threatening if I refused him his rights. I began to dread him coming home from work. I never knew what mood he would be in. If it rained it was my fault; if the sun shone it was my fault; no matter what happened, it was always my fault.

John's behaviour took a terrifying turn. One day I gave him a list of messages to pick up from the shop in Rhode on his way home from work. He had a few pints of porter and arrived home without the food.

'Did ya bring the messages, John?' I asked.

'I put them on the back of the bike.' He looked around his bike. 'They must have fallen off the carrier.'

'You're tellin' lies, John. You didn't get them, did ya?'

'I did get them, I did get them!'

It didn't help that some general stores also doubled up as pubs. Whenever John would go for messages, he would get a pint or two, and have the *craic*, and forget about me. John was hail-fella-well-met in the pub. He really needed to be liked. He used to madden me because the people he was drinking with didn't hold a candle to him intellectually; they wouldn't walk in his boots. I thought John lost his dignity and pride when he was inebriated. I would say, 'How can ya lower yourself to people ya don't know that well?' I wanted him to be strong and proud but my disappointment angered him.

Next morning, as John didn't buy the bread for his lunch, I decided to make pancakes instead. I had eggs but no milk so I had to make water pancakes. John wouldn't accept that. But I hadn't got anything else.

'I don't want fuckin' water pancakes,' he said, giving me one of his filthy looks.

'What else was I supposed to do for your lunch if I've got no bread?'

'Fuckin' pancakes.' John started shoving me and then he spat at me. I was disgusted.

'You better not be here when I come home tonight,' he said, picking up a knife off the table and pointing it at me. 'I'll kill you if you're here when I get home.'

I was confused and frightened, for myself and for my little child, but I couldn't tell a soul; no one would have believed me. John was still the perfect gentleman to the outside world. This was the person who told me he would work his fingers to the bone for me if I would only marry him. He said he would never hurt a hair on my head, and I was foolish enough to believe him. I'd had enough. I needed to get away.

I went across the fields to Tong's house where my cousin was working and asked her to ask Mr Tong's daughter, Clonagh, to give me a lift into Edenderry. She was just eighteen and I knew she had been given a car for her birthday. I thought she was my only hope of escape. I would catch the afternoon bus to Dublin to spend a few days with my sister Anna while I decided what to do next. Clonagh obliged me with a lift to Edenderry.

On the way, we met one of Tong's grass lorries in Ballymacwilliam and there was John, in the cab, chatting with the driver and grinning like a Cheshire cat. How could he attack me with a knife in the morning and then be so happy, getting on with his day, in the afternoon?

John didn't see me. I carried on to Dublin with Ellen in my arms.

NINE

Johnny and the Rat-trap Cheese

I felt guilty about leaving John but I believed my only chance of a happy, peaceful life was to create a future without him. I was determined to get away from this abusive young marriage. I felt desperate after he threatened to kill me but I had to remain optimistic for the baby's sake. I chatted to her on my way to Dublin and made a promise that she would have a better start in life.

I chose Dublin as my bolt hole because my father and brothers wouldn't have wanted me turning up on their doorstep: they would have thought I'd made my bed and I now could lie on it. And I'd have had more chance of finding a job and a flat to rent in the city. Anna living in Blackrock was also a strong incentive. At least I would have somewhere to stay for a couple of nights.

She was in a ground-floor flat in Booterstown Avenue with her husband Larry Croke and daughter Valerie. I wondered how they found it so easy to set up house. They worked together, I supposed. It maddened me that I didn't have my own home or the same kind of security. We had nothing. Everybody else was working together, trying to build a home, but not John and me.

I got a great welcome from Anna when I turned up unannounced. I didn't want to tell her the reason for my visit. I didn't want to admit my marriage wasn't working out or that John was such a bully. But she needed an explanation. She sat in her armchair, cross-legged, smoking a fag. I told her about John and the knife, and that I swore I was never going back to him. She just looked at me; I got the feeling she didn't believe me. As far as she was concerned, John could do no wrong.

Mid-morning the next day, there was a knock at the door. I knew it was John and I wasn't a bit happy to see him. If I had been in Dublin just a day longer, I could have found somewhere else to live and he wouldn't have been able to find me. He went straight into the kitchen to talk to Anna. He was laughing and joking with her. I stayed in the living room. I could hear their voices but I couldn't make out what they were saying. A few minutes later, Anna came in.

'He's real sorry, Maura. He wants to make up with ya.'

'Does he?' I said coldly.

'He says all those things won't happen again.'

I didn't believe a word. Our marriage was a farce. It was plain that we weren't suited to one another. We did care about each other, but we weren't suited.

'Will ya go and speak to him?'

'No.'

'He's had time to think things over. He's sorry. He wants ya to go back home.'

I expected Anna to take John's side. They were similar types. They were full of life and very flirtatious. Neither of them cared where the night fell on them. They were both live wires. Larry and me were similar down-to-earth types: we kept them grounded – or at least we tried.

'I won't go back there, Anna.' I wasn't ready to speak to him.

'He idolises you, Maura.'

'Well, he has a poor way of showin' it.'

John tried to win me back by saying he would sign up with

the army again and earn a regular wage to find a home for us. He squared it with Anna that he could stay while he sorted himself out. We had to share the same brown leather sofa bed but I slept with my back to him, refusing to speak. I didn't talk to him for several days.

John re-enlisted at Portobello Barracks. He left each morning and came home each night. I hoped he was changing but after his first week he didn't produce any money. He carried on working but still I didn't see a penny.

Then one evening he came home late from work with blood streaming down his face. I got such a shock when I saw him. Larry took care of him, leading him down to the kitchen to wash his face and tidy him up. Then Larry suddenly noticed that John was wearing his one and only jacket. He'd borrowed it without Larry's permission and he'd got blood all over it. Larry was so precise and very particular about the way he dressed that he was seething.

Larry marched down to me and snapped, 'He's been in a fight. Go and speak to him!' I relented and listened to John's explanation. With the drink inside him, he blurted out that he hadn't got his job back with the army at all. He'd been getting all dressed up in Larry's clothes each morning, going out at eight and coming back at teatime, pretending to be at work. The fight didn't happen at the barracks, as I'd assumed, but in a pub around the corner. He was the greatest liar that was ever born.

'I want you out of here before I get home, Murphy,' Larry said. I was surprised at his reaction because they had been friends from their early days in the army. John had been Larry's instructor and they shared the same billet. The four of us had been so close. After Larry and Anna were married, we stayed up all night to help them celebrate. They had a room in a house in Walkinstown with a live-in landlady who couldn't pronounce Larry's surname, Croke. 'Mrs Thing! Mrs Thing! There's someone here to see ya,' she hollered up the stairs when we arrived.

John and I went up to their room and drank Guinness and

Babycham until it got so late we missed our last bus home. We decided to stay but there was only one double bed. So the four of us got into it. Larry got in at the wall, Anna got in next to him, I got in next to her and John was on the outside. That's how close we were!

Some time during the night, Larry got up to puke into a basin he'd put at the bottom of the bed. John got up after him and pissed into the basin while Larry was getting sick. 'John! You're pissin' in me ear!' Larry shouted.

'You'll be all right, Larry, you'll be all right,' John said, oblivious of what he was doing.

'But you're pissin' in me ear!' We all had such a laugh at that, what with Larry being so particular.

Larry had the measure of John. When he ordered him out of his house that day in Dublin, I felt so sorry for John. He looked hounded and crestfallen. My father didn't like him in Clonmore, they beat him up in the pubs in Dublin, I wasn't welcoming to him and now his friend Larry was throwing him out.

When John left, I left with him. The bust-up brought us back together again.

We decided we needed a fresh start. We scanned the small ads for a job in England and found a titled couple looking for someone to run their sprawling Hertfordshire home. We were hired as a domestic 'firm'. I was to be their cook-cum-housekeeper and John was to be their butler.

Ray, His Lord and Ladyship's cockney chauffeur, met us at Euston Station in a shiny Rolls Royce, the likes of which I had never been in before. He took us on a grand tour of London before driving out to the country. The Rolls eventually pulled alongside the magnificent building where, it seemed, the entire extended family was waiting to greet us.

The timber-framed house was very impressive. Three steps led off a cavernous hallway to a kitchen at the back. There was a long dining room with highly polished red tiles, scattered with rugs, and a beautiful shiny mahogany table standing in the centre.

John and I were to join a small staff. A live-in nurse took care of two of the titled children and a governess looked after their education, three days a week, in a schoolroom at the front of the house. Gladys was a part-time cleaner and her husband, Ennis, was the gardener. They lived in a tied cottage in the grounds; John and I lived in the main house. We had two rooms in a large attic in our own wing on the east side. We thought we'd landed on our feet. We were glad of the chance of this new beginning.

We climbed three flights of stairs and creaked across countless darkly polished floorboards to reach our quarters. Ellen was to sleep in a doll's cot, Her Ladyship's childhood toy. It was well made, brightly painted and sat on stumpy three-inch legs. The only hint that it once occupied Her Ladyship's make-believe world was the scattering of dog-eared dolls and chewed up teddy bears.

Across the wide landing was another room, which, we were to find out, was permanently locked. During our time there, no one ever went in or out. 'Wouldn't you just know it?' John teased. 'Skeletons and ghosts locked away safely.' I was easily spooked and John knew it.

The view from our window was spectacular. We could see for miles. I opened the window and inhaled familiar country smells that mingled with a sweet floral scent wafting up from a rose garden below. The roses created an intoxicating sweet perfume in the warm breeze. Her Ladyship liked her washing to hang in the orchard next to the rose garden so the clothes would come in smelling of flowers.

I was shown to the small kitchen where I would spend some of my time cooking and baking. Our day was to begin at seven in the morning. As butler, John was expected to dress up smart in a white shirt, tie and jacket whether he was answering the door, cleaning floors or polishing silver. He would check the pantry every week and make a note of what groceries were needed in a little black book kept there for the purpose.

My job as cook was very straightforward. Her Ladyship would come into the kitchen every morning and give me her menu for the day. The menu always included fresh greens, which Ennis was responsible for cultivating. He was very protective of his vegetable patch. He took great pride in his work and only he was permitted to select the vegetables.

I often chided him about the measly bunch of vegetables he brought into the house and I would sneak down to his garden and help myself to more. It was difficult to get one over on Ennis: His Lordship's jet black Labrador and snow-white highland terrier would follow me there and back, barking and raising all kinds of commotion.

Ennis performed his duties with great precision but he did everything in such a blazing hurry. I can still see his thin, slightly stooped figure running in and out of the kitchen in his muddy boots, apron and cloth cap, swinging his little basket of veg beside him.

I got on well with Ennis and even got a smile out of him once. Although he gave the impression of being distant, he could be very helpful in a crisis. One hot summer morning, while I was chopping vegetables to accompany a pheasant lunch – His Lordship's favourite – the cold sweat of anxiety swept over me when I heard Ellen scream in her pram outside. I dropped the chopping knife and raced out to her. In my haste, I fell down the step and landed on my knees. Ennis dragged me back to my feet. When we got to Ellen, tears were plopping down her crimson face and on to her pretty pink frock. The screaming child held out her hand. She had been stung by a bee. I held her tiny swollen finger between my teeth and sucked out the sting.

'How is she, Maura?' asked Ennis.

'Okay. I think I got it.'

'You should take her to a doctor. Bee stings can be very serious.'

I brought Ellen in and sat her in a high chair in the kitchen where I could keep an eye on her.

'Ennis, would you go fetch those pheasants?' I asked. He had two hanging in the meat safe outside.

'I'll do that now for you, Maura.' Off he went, in his familiar half trot, across the yard to the small iron box on four legs. He reappeared with the pheasants hanging from a hook.

'Get them out of here now, Ennis, they stink,' I demanded.

'Be cripes you're right,' he said, holding his nose. 'They are a bit high.'

'They're not high, they're rotten!' I squealed. 'Bury them in the yard bin.' Off he trotted again just as John was coming in the door.

'John, go in and tell her the pheasant's off,' I said.

'Are ya sure they're off?'

'Course they're off. Can't ya smell them?'

'Oh, Christ. How am I goin' to face tellin' her that?'

Her Ladyship had to be consulted before anything was thrown out and, as butler, it was John's job to do the consulting.

Her Ladyship was not amused.

'Well, what's the verdict?' I asked.

'She's not happy. She'll have the ham instead.'

I opened the fridge and took out the ham. It was crawling with fine fat maggots.

'Oh, my God, John, come here and look at this.'

'What now?'

'Maggots, John!'

'Oh, Jesus! They can't have that.'

'Go and tell her the ham's off as well.'

Off he went.

'Your Ladyship, I'm afraid the ham is not suitable for the table.'

'Why not, Johnny?'

'The ham is off, Your Ladyship.'

'But, Johnny, I only bought it three weeks ago.'

'Yes, Your Ladyship. That's why it's gone over.'

She was up on her feet in a flash. 'What will we have instead, darling?' His Lordship was standing expectantly holding his carving knives. 'Shall we open a tin, darling?'

'Yes, and shall we follow that with cheese?' he said.

'That'll do nicely. Johnny, would you see if we have a tin of ham? And please bring up the cheese and the savoury biscuits.'

John scuttled down to the pantry and returned with the tinned ham. Thirty minutes later, he went back up with the cheese board. He strode into the dining room with the platter balanced on his right palm. Her Ladyship was highly amused. 'Oh darling, here comes Johnny with the rat-trap cheese!' She howled with laughter. 'That's cooking Cheddar, Johnny! We want the Stilton and Gruyère.'

'Johnny' wasn't a bit amused.

He got his own back, though. One afternoon, I was preparing luncheon and John had just finished giving the floorboards in the hall a good shine with the floor polisher when the phone rang. Her Ladyship ran across the hallway to answer it, skidded in her stockinged feet and landed flat on her back.

'Oh dear, I seem to have slipped,' she said casually.

'Are you all right, Your Ladyship?' John enquired. 'Are you hurt? Can I help you up?' He offered his outstretched hands.

'No, I am all right, Johnny,' she said, getting up off the floor, embarrassed.

John came into the kitchen laughing. 'Maura, Maura, it's for you,' he said. 'Ya should have seen her fall. Flat on her arse! And then the call was for you.'

It was usually my job to do the cleaning but John was good enough to lend a hand, especially as I had to clean and polish seven rooms upstairs, five downstairs, the main wooden hall and the back red-flagged corridor and dining room.

John knew how to make light work of it. He would use the

floor polisher to bring up a lovely shine on the mahogany dining table. He would slip out of his shoes, roll up his shirtsleeves and swish the polisher this way and that. Her Ladyship would have been horrified to see this contraption bobbing up and down on her priceless antique table.

I preferred traditional methods. I would get out my tin of Cardinal Red polish, smear a cloth in it and tie it around a broom. Then I'd get down on my knees, kneeling on a soft cloth for comfort, and buff the lot to get a good shine.

All that polishing took me a good two hours, especially if I put the television on to keep me company. That's how I found the press button bar hidden in the lounge. I was vacuuming the rug and watching Rosemary Clooney on the telly. I was singing along to 'Little Things Mean a Lot' and giving the rug a good clean when I heard a loud click. Suddenly the mat started to move and a contraption rattled and rose out of the ground. I thought I'd been chosen to witness a vision sent from God!

I was so amazed. I ran to fetch John to come and look.

'John, what the hell's happenin' here?'

'God, Maura, Lucifer's comin' to take us away!'

The two of us stood gawping at it like we'd just seen a spaceship landing. John laughed, pulling a hideous evil face and chasing me with his arms flailing.

'Stop, John! What is that contraption?' John pulled the rug off to reveal a drinks cabinet laden with bottles of spirits. 'It's the devil's brew by the looks of it,' he said.

'A goddamn drinks cabinet under the floor! What a place to store your drink.'

'Wherever they store it, is all right by me. Looks like they know I'm in need of a drink,' he whispered, grabbing hold of a bottle of brandy. 'Hey, ya know what they say about brandy?'

'Yeh, I can imagine.'

'Makes ya randy!' John tilted his head back and took a big swig.

'If ya keep drinkin' the way you're goin', Lucifer won't be long takin' ya by the hasp-o-the-arse.'

'Ah, Maura, wouldn't that be a lovely way to go?'

'Put it away before they catch ya.'

Her Ladyship wouldn't usually let you get away with anything. One Saturday, she informed me that her bedroom was being neglected.

'Maura, my bedroom wasn't polished yesterday. Make sure that it's done today.'

'I did do it yesterday,' I said defensively, realising I hadn't.

'Perhaps you could use a bit more polish,' she said sarcastically.

I wasn't allowing her to tell me off. I resented being spoken down to. I'd say I picked this high-mindedness up from my mother. She was as proud as a peacock.

I may have been finding the cleaning a bit of a chore but John adored his work. When he was off duty, he helped take care of a beautiful chestnut horse that lived in one of the outhouses. The chestnut was a powerfully built show jumper and John would often groom and gallop this wonderful animal before taking him to shows with His Lordship.

John also looked after the pig farm where his hungry new charges, a hundred pigs and a couple of sows, waited for their feed. He often took Ellen over to the sty to see the pigs and watch her get all excited, chuckling, gurgling and pointing. When one of the sows bore a litter of thirteen bonhams, His Lordship had no use for the runt and gave it to John as a present. He fed the spare in the kitchen with a baby's bottle.

Once our work was complete, the day was our own. We developed a pretty good routine that included Mass every Sunday administered in a room above a pub. It was hard to hear what the priest was saying above the noise of the drunken revellers beneath us.

Ray would sometimes take us to church in the Rolls, which made us feel very grand, and we'd hobnob with the gentry in the pub after. John would have one or two pints and I stuck to my mineral water. We didn't engage in very much conversation with the locals. We weren't familiar with that side of country life. The old gentlemen were friendly enough but they didn't chat to us.

If we didn't get a lift in the Rolls we would have to cycle the seven miles to Mass, taking it in turns to go because we had nobody to look after Ellen.

It seemed like a blissful time for us but I began to find the workload too much to cope with. I was feeling exhausted all the time, doing all that cooking and cleaning and looking after Ellen. The job was tiring me out. I wasn't coping. I had to tell Her Ladyship that I was finding it all too much. She made an appointment for me with the local GP . . .

Nightmare in the Attic

It had been a stifling summer's day, heavy and humid; a faint smell of sulphur hung in the air. By evening, a hint of thunder rumbled in the distance. Lightning threatened. It wouldn't be long now before the heavens opened, reminding me of irrational childhood fears. Tiredness gave way to a rigid fear. I sat at the kitchen table, tense and expectant. I hate storms. I never liked them, even as a child back in Clonmore. Storms always had the same debilitating effect on me. That's how I felt now: a scared little girl, alone in the storm.

The sky darkened; deafening thunder cracked above the house and sheet lightning illuminated the grounds. The heavens opened. The storm had broken. The baby was sure to wake. I heard her stirring over the intercom. I went upstairs to the attic and tiptoed to the doll's cot. But Ellen slept on peacefully. I closed the window and drew the curtains to keep out the flashes of lightning. I kicked off my shoes, climbed under the bed covers and waited for the storm to ease off. I took a cigarette from a packet on the side table. My fingers trembled as I struck the match.

I puffed nervously on the cigarette, waiting for John to come home. He had gone into town for a pint, which usually meant several pints. I snuggled down for a doze.

I was in that semi-conscious dreamy place, half awake and half asleep, when I felt hands tightening around my neck. I tried to scream but the choking grip prevented me. I thought I was having a nightmare. I was terrified. This can't be happening. Has a madman got into the house? Where's John? Is Ellen okay? I tried to call out. I groped in the dark for the switch on the table lamp to get a good look at my attacker. In my waking haze I saw John looking down at me. I could smell the drink.

I sat upright, startled and confused. 'What the hell are ya doin'?' I cried.

He straightened and laughed, and started to get undressed.

I rubbed my throat. 'What in the name of God did ya do that for?'

'Oh can ya not take a joke? You're always so serious.'

'I don't think that is too comical. What's so funny about tryin' to choke someone?'

'I wasn't tryin' to choke ya. I'm only actin' the prat.'

I didn't appreciate his type of fun. I knew that there was no point in talking to him: he was the worse for drink.

When I was sure John was asleep, I slid off the bed and lit another cigarette. I looked at the clock. Two-thirty. John was snoring. As he breathed, a stale mixture of beer and spirits filled the air around him. I stared at his thick, hairy arms and his lithe, powerful body, bronzed from the summer sun. How could he try to strangle me in the middle of the night with a house full of people below us? He was my husband; I was wearing his ring, the ring he gently slipped on the third finger of my left hand. Eighteen months ago he declared, before witnesses, his undying love for me – till death do us part.

I sat on the floor crying quietly into my knees. I pulled hard on the fag, drawing the smoke deep into my lungs, wondering why I allowed this to happen again. I felt uneasy. I was so tired but I was half afraid to go to sleep. I made sure that one eye stayed on him all night long.

Next morning, I refused to speak to him. The less said the easiest mended was the way I looked at it. I found it easier to stay silent than confront people. I didn't like to feel foolish or show that I lacked knowledge. Not speaking would be a way of punishing John without exposing myself and my weaknesses. I didn't know whether I'd brought it on myself but I had to pretend all was well. It was the 1950s; we had no therapists or government schemes to help build our self-esteem. I did my best to understand him but it was too hard, he was too guarded. There was no conversation with John. It was like pulling teeth trying to get a word out of him about who he actually was.

Breakfast for the household went ahead as usual. I was seething inside but I couldn't show it. Whatever state I was in, however angry I was with John, I couldn't let it affect my work. I was paid to do a job and I was in somebody else's house. Trouble is, when you hide your feelings to that extent the resentment just keeps on growing. There's no outlet for the anger. I lived within other people's rules; John's, the Church's, my employers' – and within my own conscience.

I made up the baby's bottle and prepared a mammoth Irish breakfast with a couple of slices of my own home-made soda bread for John and me.

'John!' I called, sharply, from the back doorstep. 'Come in for your breakfast.'

I put the warm plates on the table and made a pot of tea. John stepped in acting the prat with the horse's bridle over his head, and a big horsey grin on his face, as though nothing had happened the night before. He tried to tell me which pig was ill, which pig was well and what the chestnut was up to but I wasn't one bit interested. I felt very sulky but he was always able to make me laugh in the end, no matter how brutal he had been, no matter how angry I was with him. And as usual, I forgave him.

The following week, Her Ladyship's GP delivered the words I had been dreading. 'Mrs Murphy, the tests were positive. Congratulations. You're having a baby.'

I was very despondent to be pregnant again so soon, especially as there was still tension between John and me. I went back to the house to prepare lunch.

'Well, how did ya get on?' John asked.

'I'm pregnant again.'

'That's the will of God. What can we do about it?' he said.

I could see by the look on his face that he was thinking the same as me. We would have to tell Her Ladyship, and she would probably ask us to leave. She had accepted Ellen gladly but made it clear they couldn't accommodate any more children.

They were about to leave for a two-week summer break in Scotland; I would tell them the news when they got back. I couldn't believe we were left in that beautiful big house all on our own. We could have walked out with everything they had. Lucky for them we were a reasonably honest couple.

With our employers away, my time became my own. I wheeled Ellen into the village most days and struck up a friendship with Ann, the wife of the local bobby.

One day John borrowed a bike and went out drinking, and I asked Ann to babysit for Ellen while I went into town to buy some dungarees for her. She didn't crawl on her hands and knees like other toddlers; she swam about on her belly wearing out the front of her little frocks. I thought denim dungarees would surely last longer. I bought myself a grey pleated skirt with a red and grey jumper to match. Now that we were earning a decent bit of money, I could afford to splash out on John as well. I bought him a handsome cream-coloured Van Heusen shirt made of soft cotton and polyester. They were all the rage in the fifties. All the

Yanks were wearing them, and some of the shirts didn't even need ironing. I thought John's slim brown body would look the picture.

After my chores that evening, I dressed myself up in my grand clothes, thinking I was gorgeous, admiring myself in the mirror. They fitted perfectly. I left them on to see if John would notice. By eleven o'clock he hadn't come home. I went into the kitchen to make a cup of hot cocoa. I was sitting by the Aga waiting for the milk to boil when I heard a knock at the back door. It was the policeman husband of my new friend. He was standing there with a pushbike. I could tell it wasn't a social call.

'Good evening, Mrs Murphy. Is your husband home?' he asked.

'No, he isn't.'

'I've just followed him from the village. He must be home.'

'Well, he isn't here. What do ya want with him?'

'He's been out on that bike of his without lights.'

'Is that an offence, officer?' I asked facetiously.

'It is in this country.'

'Oh.'

'I'd like him to report to the station in the morning. Will you tell him?'

'Yes, I'll tell him.'

As soon as the policeman got on his bike and cycled away, there was another knock at the door. It was John, with drink in him.

'Did the guard come in here?' he asked.

'He did actually, why?'

'He's after me because I had no lights on my bike, but I gave him the slip.'

'Why were ya ridin' a bike with no lights?' I snapped, then flushed when I remembered that first day I met Tom Walsh.

'That's the why!'

I'd annoyed him. John couldn't take the slightest criticism. If I challenged him about anything, he would lash out.

'What did ya tell him?' he demanded.

'I told him you weren't here.'

'You're a fuckin' liar. Tell me what ya told him.'

'What could I tell him only that ya weren't here? Sure ya weren't here were you? You're just after comin' in, as per usual.'

'And when did you become a copper's nark?' John said, raising his voice.

'A what?'

'A copper's nark. Informer.'

'I didn't tell him anythin'. He asked if ya were here and I said ya weren't.'

'And what did he say to that?'

'You've to report to the station in the mornin'.'

John's temper rose. His face reddened and he started his verbals. I knew I should have kept my mouth shut. You couldn't have a civil conversation with John in that mood.

'What are ya shoutin' at me for? I didn't ask him to follow ya, did I?'

'Isn't it time you were in bed?' John said.

'I'm not ready to go to bed yet. I am drinkin' my cocoa.'

He turned all the lights off and ordered me up to bed. I got up resentfully. I was goddamn twenty-six years of age and being told to go to bed!

I sensed he was looking me up and down. I hoped he might be mellowing and admiring my new clothes.

'Where do ya think you're goin'?' he asked.

'I'm not goin' anywhere, just tryin' on some new clothes.'

'So you're all dressed up and nowhere to go, eh?'

John's tone was becoming increasingly aggressive and sarcastic. He knew how to upset and demean me.

'What are ya talkin' about, John? I bought this rig-out this afternoon. I was tryin' them on to see if they fitted properly.'

'Maybe you'll be able to wear them to Mass, that's the only outin' you will be goin' on.'

I had no ulterior motives. I may have been pregnant but I was young and still cared about my appearance. And you would never know what class of person would be calling at the house.

John made me go upstairs in front of him, punching me in the back step by step as I went. When we reached the top he herded me into the bedroom, spilling cocoa all over the floor. He looked mean. His eyes were bloodshot and bleary from drink. He had that same evil look on his face, the one I saw when he threatened me with the knife. He pinched me and pulled my hair. Then he sat there staring at me. I reached for my cigarettes to calm my nerves. He swiped them out of my hand and crumbled them to bits in front of me, like you would an Oxo cube. He knew I needed a cigarette when I was upset.

'Where were ya?' he asked again, insinuating I was dressed up smart to meet another man.

He grabbed me by the arm, swung me around and slapped me across the back of the head. 'Where were ya, I said, or am I talkin' to myself?'

'I—'

'Ya filthy bitch.'

John looked at me menacingly. His greasy, ruffled black hair hung down over his forehead, covering part of his face. He raised his hand and slapped me so hard across the face I thought he had broken my jaw. 'When I ask you a question,' he hissed, 'you answer me. Do ya hear?'

'I was down for a drink,' I said, trying to escape the blows.

I begged him to stop hitting me. I dodged past him and jumped on to the bed, my swollen throat dry from lack of saliva – the familiar sign of anxiety. John leant over me and knelt on my long hair. Ellen began to cry. I wanted to cuddle her, reassure her that everything was okay. Each time I tried to go to the cot, he stopped me by pulling on my hair and kicking me in the backside. He hit me about the head again and I blacked out. When I came to, I saw John taking Ellen into his bed. He was trying to torment me.

I went to my own room and locked the door. I couldn't get any sleep because I was so worried about her. John was drunk. I was afraid he would roll on her accidentally and suffocate her.

Some time in the early morning, I heard Ellen whimpering. I went into John's room and saw her lying on the linoleum floor beside the bed. She had fallen out as John lay in his drunken sleep. I crept into the room, so as not to wake John, and brought Ellen back into my own room.

I was afraid of John. He was only ever aggressive when he was drunk. I wished he would stop drinking. Why did I believe he was ever going to change? It was intolerable. When he was sober, he could be a funny, helpful and caring person. In drink, he was abusive but he always expected me to forgive him. He would promise never to touch me again and I always believed him, like a naive fool.

After this latest episode of abuse, I decided to confide in a Catholic priest. The next time I was at Confession, I told the priest everything.

'Father, I'm expectin' my second child but I'm not happy about bein' pregnant,' I said.

'Why aren't you happy?' said the priest.

'I don't like the way my husband is treatin' me.'

'Go on.'

'I'm not happy in my marriage, Father, not a bit happy.'

'Why aren't you happy in your marriage?'

'My husband is bullyin' me and beatin' me. He seems to want to control me and I am not allowed to be myself any more. I want to leave; I can't cope any more with bein' beaten.'

'How long have you been married?'

'Just over a year and now I am pregnant again and I am so scared, Father.' I began to cry.

'This may just be a passing phase,' he said sympathetically. 'Don't forget that all new marriages have their ups and downs and you shouldn't run away. I would ask you to give your marriage a chance to work. He must have a problem that needs your care and help. You need to work together and help each other.'

He was understanding and promised to pray for me. It was a relief to be able to talk to someone. I confided in him because I wanted to know what my options were. I realised I had no options. I had to stay with John and make the best of it. I had taken my vows and that was that. To add to my troubles, I still had to tell Her Ladyship I was pregnant. As I was mulling over the best way to broach the subject, Ennis and his wife took matters out of my hands. Within two hours of our employers arriving back home, I was called to the drawing room and invited to sit down.

'It has been reported to me that there was trouble in the house while we were away,' His Lordship said.

'What do you mean? What sort of trouble?'

'Well, Ennis has informed me that you were screaming and that police were at the house. Can you explain that? Why were the police here?'

'Well, John was out down the village and there was no light on his bike and the policeman followed him and he came round the back and asked me where John was—'

'Were they here about the screaming?'

'Sir, I don't know how to say it.'

'Maura, just tell me what has been going on.'

'John thought I'd called the police but I hadn't and he got angry and beat me.'

I started to tense up and began to cry.

'Take your time, Maura. We will sort it out. I just need to know what has been happening.'

'That's all I know.'

'Where is Johnny now?'

'He's gone to the village.'

'Drinking?'

'I think so.'

'Hmm. Tonight, Maura, when you hear Johnny coming in, I want you to come and get me and I will open the door to him.'

He wanted to shock John. He had no idea they were back from Scotland and he would be expecting me to open the door.

When John came home, he threw stones up at my window, as usual, for me to let him in. I ran along the corridor to His Lordship's bedroom, knocked on the door and went in. I went back to bed and pretended to be asleep.

John appeared moments later looking worried. 'His Lordship opened the door! Did ya not hear me?' he asked.

'No, I was asleep,' I lied.

I knew I was being disloyal, and I felt a bit mean about it, but it worked all the same. John behaved better when people were on to him.

'Jesus, I wasn't expectin' that. I thought they were in Scotland. And I'm wearin' his suit!' he said, slightly amused.

'My God,' I said. 'Why are ya wearin' his suit?'

'Ah, let him go and be fucked. He's got a whole roomful of them. He won't miss it.'

It was a nice light-worsted grey suit and it fitted John like a glove. His Lordship must have noticed but he never said a word about it. John could always see the funny side of a terrible situation.

The next morning Her Ladyship came into the kitchen to give me instructions for luncheon.

'Your Ladyship, I have somethin' to tell ya.'

'Oh.'

'I'm pregnant again.'

She paused for a moment then said, 'Maura, I am afraid that there is not sufficient room for two children.'

'I understand that, Your Ladyship.'

Soon we were boarding the *Princess Maud* for Ireland with as much as we could carry between us – and John brazenly wearing the stolen suit.

TEN

Miss Popularity 1999

I was a miracle, they said. A mystery. I had come through a very serious illness. Every scan and blood test turned up nothing. It must have been some kind of virus, they said.

My sight slowly came back and the bleeding and the sickness stopped; I was over the worst. Doctors were baffled by my bleeding but they assured me there was no sign of cancer, TB or a tumour.

'Joan, remind me again,' I said, 'what did they say is causing the blindness?'

Joan flicked backwards and forwards through her diary searching for the entry she had made.

'I've written here: "The blindness that Ma suffered was related to chemicals released from the lung".'

'What does that mean?'

'I'm not sure,' Joan said. 'That's all I've written.'

'Do you want an ice-cream, Mom?' Ellen asked.

'Yes please, pet.'

I was relieved and happy to be sitting up and chatting with my children. Things were getting back to normal. But then the blow came: 'We have to do more tests, Mrs Murphy,' a specialist told me. More prodding and poking.

John came up to my room every morning in his swanky cotton pyjamas and leather slippers to see how I was. Now instead of offering me a cup of tea and toast – his morning routine in Rhode – he would tell me what he'd had for his breakfast and complain about the hospital's paltry portions.

'A bird would eat more than they give us' was his usual summing up of the meals.

He entertained me with stories about his ward, who was snoring, puking and farting. One morning he came in flustered.

'God, I was persecuted again last night. This fella kept tryin' to get into me bed.'

'A fella tryin' to get into your bed?' I laughed. 'What fella?'

'The mad fella. He keeps walkin' up and down the corridors talking to himself, I told you about him.'

'And why didn't ya let him in? Why did ya stop him?' I said, enjoying the tease.

'How do ya know I did stop him?' he joked.

'I'd say ya did, John. You'd have your eye on somethin' a little younger and curvier!'

He laughed. 'I think they're all daft here. Have ya met the mad priest?'

'How do ya know he's mad?'

'Well, why wouldn't he be? He spends all night walkin' round blessin' our feet and makin' as much of a racket as he can.'

'Maybe he is a bit disturbed.'

'Yeh. Mad. I told ya. He shouldn't be in that ward at all.'

After our morning debriefs John would toddle back downstairs to his own ward for the doctor's rounds and reappear an hour later with a couple of newspapers tucked under his arm. We would sit in silence and do our crosswords, recreating the familiar domestic scene back in the cottage.

John liked to be back on his own ward for visiting hours so the children could see him. I think he liked the sympathy. Sometimes I resented the attention they gave to him. But I often mixed up their feelings with mine, forgetting he was their father and that they felt affection towards him. As far as I was concerned, he was an absent father when they were growing up; he didn't have the same bond with them as I did but it appeared that he was receiving just as much love.

John and I never really talked about his illness; he didn't want to accept there was anything wrong with him. I was always the ill one. He was always healthy. He put his fit down to the stress of seeing me so poorly and apparently on the verge of death. It brought on 'his turn' he said. He worried about his epilepsy in his own way, quietly and nervously. If I tried to bring the subject up it would end in a disagreement. He told outsiders, in minute detail, what was the matter with me but he never wanted to face what was the matter with him. It used to madden me that he wouldn't accept he was ill.

It seemed strange to see him sitting in his pyjamas. I almost felt sorry for him.

'Did ya ever think we'd end up here together?' I asked him.

'Ah, sure we could be worse off.'

John is philosophical about hardship, always has been, but I felt sad that here we both were, at the end of our days, in hospital and depending on the children visiting from England to look after us.

The nurses were always astounded if my room was empty. They nicknamed me *Miss Popularity 1999*. A steady stream of visitors made their way to my room every day. At times there were too many visitors; too many voices in my little side ward. I craved peace and quiet. The staff nurse was sympathetic to my needs and asked for there to be fewer visitors because I needed rest. The children agreed and began visiting two by two.

Well-wishers called me on the hour. Most of the telephone calls to John Houston Ward were for me. I was often too weak to walk the few yards down the corridor to take the call.

There was a lot going on – voices droning at the nurses' station, buzzers sounding and that telephone ringing constantly.

Hospitals are about routine, doctors' rounds, bed baths and bedpans. Food and visitors were all there was to look forward to in St James's: six o'clock – morning tea; seven-thirty – breakfast (porridge, toast and marmalade, usually); ten-thirty – Cupasoup; one o'clock – lunch (cauliflower and baked potato if I was lucky); three o'clock – tea and biscuits; five o'clock – supper (with a pudding and a glass of milk); eight o'clock – Horlicks.

The smell of disinfectant signalled the arrival of the cleaner swishing her mop under my bed. She reminded me, every single day, 'Make sure ya don't fall on that now, missus, cos it's wet.'

John Houston Ward had become my home, the doctors and nurses my second family. Everyone, from porters to radiographers, knew me by my first name. I felt like a celebrity. Several of the student nurses would pop in if they had a spare moment and tell me all about their boyfriend traumas. I became agony aunt to one particular nurse, from Tipperary, who was preoccupied with landing the boy of her dreams.

'Just be yourself, Nurse,' I would say, 'and your beauty will shine through.'

'But ya don't understand, Maura, I just can't speak when he comes into the room.'

'Well, then don't.'

'Don't what?'

'Speak. Don't speak. Let him speak to you. If he doesn't, just wait till the next time.'

'Oh but, Maura, all the nurses are after him. He's gorgeous, you'd even fancy him yourself.'

'Why? Is he dark and mysterious? Because that's how I like them.'

I offered to hook another nurse up with my nephew, Anthony.

'Who?'

'My nephew,' I said, not taking my eyes from my newspaper.

'That tall, good-lookin' fella?'

'Exactly, him.'

'Is he single?'

'I'd hardly try and hook you up with a married man!'

'No I couldn't, Maura. I wouldn't be able to face him.'

'Of course you would. Sure, he's a dote. He's an actor. He's in *Angela's Ashes* – and *Fair City*. He's lookin' for a nice girl like you.'

'God, Maura, what should I do?'

'Nothin'. I'll arrange it for ya. Next time he comes in, I'll tell him that this good-lookin' nurse from Tipp has her eye on him.'

'No, Maura, don't tell him that!'

'Well, what do ya want me to tell him? Sure aren't you a good-looker?'

Anthony was delighted that a nurse fancied him and got all dressed up for his next visit. My matchmaking went nowhere. The nurse wouldn't even come into the room. She would fly past and not even look my way. Anthony, who is not one bit bashful, got up occasionally to see if there was any sign of her on the ward.

None.

The next day she came in blushing with embarrassment. 'Ah, Maura, I couldn't do it. I was mortified. I just couldn't make myself come in.'

'He was lookin' out for ya.'

'What did he say? He must have thought I was a real eejit.'

We laughed at the good of it but that was the end of my Cupid antics in the hospital.

The nurses weren't all preoccupied by love and boyfriends. There was a tangible feeling of dread that summer while the student nurses waited for their exam results. Excitement bubbled within them. At times they could not contain their nervousness and, sensing this, I would ask an expertly casual question.

'You seem a little preoccupied today, Nurse, is everything all right?'

Well, from that small opening a gush of explanation would burst into the room.

'Maura, is it that obvious? Ah, sure I am sick with worry. I know I should have done all right with anatomy but I am useless with the lower body. I just have a block or somethin'. And if I fail one part I have to take it again in the autumn, which means that I won't be able to go to Bali with Terry and—'

'But ya won't fail, Nurse. You are a clever young woman. You're just worryin'. Everyone worries too much at exam time.'

'No, Maura, really, I'm tellin' you, I'm shite— oh sorry, I'm useless on legs and hips and feet.'

The controlled panic went on for a week. I would look out of my side ward and see some of them huddled in little groups, laughing and reassuring each other. They would sit under the two young trees in the quadrangle smoking and talking.

At last the results came out. Each in turn came into my room.

'Maura, I passed!'

'I knew you would, Nurse. Are ya pleased?'

'Oh, Maura, I'm delighted.'

I made friends with some of the other patients too. They would come in, sit on the bed and chat a while. We exchanged stories and I would share out the pounds of sweets and chocolates, gifts from my visitors. Eileen, who was in the bed opposite mine when I was first admitted, was a favourite. She was a light-hearted, jovial Dubliner in her sixties from Clontarf, a place I knew well. She was a small woman with dark hair, probably dyed. As she spoke, I noticed her slender nose and chiselled face.

Eileen came in to see me every day and she would trot out all her troubles. She told me she was terminally ill. She sat on the side of my bed, coughing her guts up.

'Ah, t'auld lung, sure it's rotten and bad,' said Eileen. 'It's cancerous.'

'I'm sorry to hear that. Maybe it will get better,' I said.

'Ah, sure it's gone too far for that. They'll soon be orderin' the coffin,' she said, her chest rattling.

Eileen still puffed away. She would tell me she was going outside for a sneaky fag.

'Eileen, should you be smokin' still?'

'Sure I'll be dead long enough. I haven't long to live anyway, I might as well enjoy myself.'

I prayed very hard for Eileen. I prayed for a miracle for her.

I tried to get my life back to normal. I remembered tasks I was doing before I got sick. Buying shares in Irish Telecom was top of my list. Only a couple of thousand punts, but I wanted them. I instructed Carmel, in the first instance, and then all the other children, one by one, to bring me in the application form for me to sign. I wanted to invest. Carmel, Olive, Joan, Geraldine and Breda were all around my bed.

'Did any of yous remember to bring in the Telecom papers?' I asked.

They all looked at each other in the way they did when they were little, silently asking each other with their eyebrows, did *you* get them?

'No,' they answered through pursed lips.

'Well isn't that fuckin' awful,' I declared.

Well, if I asked them once I asked them a thousand times to bring in the form. It was so important to me but I might as well have been talking to the wall. I was indignant. The children were all there fussing over me asking what they could do for me. When I asked them to do something practical, they didn't do it.

'To think that yous can't do the one thing I ask yous to do. One little, simple message that I ask yous to do and now it is too late! It's past the date!'

I have always been a hard taskmaster. When I want something done, I want it done there and then. I only considered later that maybe they were too traumatised to think clearly.

At the time I looked at them and I could see they were thinking, she's back and she's in one of her attacking moods.

Breda fell out with me over her daddy. She thought I was being too critical of him. I don't remember what started the row. Anyway, it was such a shock I've blanked it out. But I do remember her face glowing bright red, and her eyes all puffy and watery, as she stood there shouting at me.

'And don't come back!' I shouted after her, as she grabbed her bag and stormed out of the ward.

John went out after her.

I was astonished to think that Breda would talk to me in that way while I was sick in hospital. She'd never answered me back before, not once in her forty-four years. It wasn't Breda's form. She was always funny and pleasant.

She came back in a few minutes later, put her arms around me and started to cry. We were both bawling then. I was very happy to see her.

Breda was never one to pussyfoot around me. If she thinks I'm being unfair or misinterpreting something she says so. She helps me to see events and people clearly. She keeps my feet on the ground. I can always take Breda's advice because I know that she means well.

Breda

Tues 22 June: I had a big row with Mummy. I was challenging her on some of her attitudes towards Daddy. I said she shouldn't talk about him like that to me because I don't want to hear it. I care about him. She went really mad and told me how abusive he had been when I was little, and what he had and hadn't done.

I said, 'No, not to me he wasn't.'

She was furious and almost spat feathers, she was that angry. We had this short but very concentrated row. You can't have a long row with Mummy because she cuts you off. She really snapped at me.

'Don't talk to me like that,' I said. 'Who the hell do you think

*you're talking to? I'm forty-four years old. You might have been
able to do this to me when I was little but you're not able to do
it now.'*

*I went really mad and I couldn't believe I was doing it. Even
as I was saying it, I was thinking, she's nearly died and you're
going absolutely crazy at her. She couldn't believe it either.*

*I thought, fuck it, I'm not staying here. I'm catching the next
plane home. That's how I felt. But I was upset about saying it.
I couldn't believe I actually harboured that amount of resentment when I never believed I did. It was such a shock. I walked
out and then started to cry.*

Daddy came after me.

*'I understand what you've said, and I understand why you're
feeling the way you are,' he said, 'but you need to go back in
there and apologise to your mother.'*

'Daddy, I am not apologising to her,' I protested.

'Do you know what this'll do to her?'

'But it's always about her; everything is always about her.'

*'It has been all her life and do you think your mother is
suddenly going to change at seventy years of age?'*

'Well she should change—'

*'Should,' he interrupted, 'is a lot of things for all of us. You
need to calm down and think about it. You nearly lost your mother.
She may well have to come back again. Go back in and apologise.'*

*I went back in and said, 'Mummy, I'm really sorry . . .' She
started to cry and that upset me.*

'We've never had cross words in our lives, Breda.'

*That was the truth. I felt I had lost something. I'd lost that
place in her life where she said, 'Breda is the only one that's never
brought me any trouble.'*

Carmel

*They've ruled out TB and they've ruled out cancer. I'm starting
to feel calmer; Mommy is being herself again. She's getting her*

spirit back and retaliating again. I was in the room with Breda and Mommy when they had a difference of opinion. It was quite heated and awkward. I knew if Mom was shouting that she was in charge of her mind and her thoughts, but what a shame. How sad. We don't know what's going to happen to her and they had such a venomous row.

Seamus

The doctors have found nothing but I know there is something there. They just can't see it. It's just a matter of time. There are tensions between them all because they're all worried in their own ways. Whatever one person is saying is probably contradicting what the other is thinking. I think everybody is trying to work together but one is trying to overrule the other in certain respects. They're probably causing more confusion in the old lady than helping her. There's a lot of anxiety coming out but the wrong vibes are being passed. I'm keeping out of it. You don't need it.

The old lady got annoyed because of the state of me. I went to the hospital straight from the building site and I had my work clothes on.

She said, 'You're makin' a show of yourself comin' in like that.'

'Well that's all right,' I said, 'I won't come again.'

Then I would turn up in my working clothes all the time just to annoy her.

Paul

Another victory for the old lady is fast approaching. I wonder what the next challenge for her is going to be.

John

Wed 23 June: I knew Maura was a fighter. She is that sort of person. If that was me, I would probably lie down and die. I wouldn't be bothered to fight but Maura wouldn't give in.

She's been through a terrible lot, maybe not as acute as this, the childbirths, one year after another, the various operations, the illnesses and problems with her nerves. I knew she wanted me to be with her twenty-four hours a day to help ease her mind but I couldn't be there constantly, sitting at her bedside. I think she used to ask too much of me on purpose so that I would fail, and then she could accuse me of not caring for her. But I did care for her. And I did my best.

But Maura would say, 'He thought he would never get away so that he could go drinkin' at Doyles.'

Joan

Fri 25 June: I am sitting on a very long and pleasantly wide bench outside the arrivals entrance in Dublin Airport, waiting to board my plane. There's a carnival atmosphere on a bright, sunny morning. I am on my own smoking a tab, which seems a bizarre thing to do given that I have spent a week with people on Mommy's ward who have lung cancer and other respiratory diseases.

I'm feeling a little numb and worn out. I can't stay in Ireland any longer: I feel as though I'm not needed now. I was becoming irritated. Too much talk and conjecture. Now that Mommy's getting better, I sense old rivalries between my brothers and sisters developing and I don't want to be involved.

Nothing seems important. Even writing my diary seems meaningless. I need to remain strong, in touch with reality. But reality stinks. Reality is my mom coughing up her lungs, fretful people (myself included), worrying about jobs, boyfriends, bodies, ageing, the future, money, status, loneliness, houses and beautifying themselves – oh meaningless breathing!

Spoke to Mommy on the phone (she is able to walk slowly). She sounds profoundly tired but it raised my spirits just talking to her.

My brother Peter came to visit with his son Michael. Peter sat in the chair next to my bed in a smart dark suit contrasting starkly with his head of pure white hair.

'How are ya, Maura?'

'Not too bad, Peter,' I said. 'Ya know I haven't been very well.'

'What was wrong with ya?'

'In case ya haven't heard, Peter, I have been through a very serious illness. In fact, at one point, the doctors said that they nearly lost me. They told me I had died.'

'Sure when I had my heart attack, I died for twenty minutes,' he boasted.

Oh, here we go, I thought. He's starting on his own list of ailments. 'No you didn't nearly die.' I couldn't believe the talk and Peter sitting there in the whole of his health.

Then Michael piped up, 'And like Jesus and Lazarus you both rose from the dead.'

I'd been in hospital nearly a month. I was becoming institutionalised. I felt as though I was never going to get out of it. The routine, the hustle and the bustle became my daily life. I was feeling a little better every day and hoping that each day would be my last in hospital. I was sick of the sight of wheelchairs and X-rays. I'd been up and down the corridors like a yoyo, nearly meeting myself coming back. My ward was stuffy and claustrophobic. I longed to get outside in the warm summer sun and breathe fresh air.

Then good news came, I was being discharged. A social worker came into my ward and told me I could go to a nursing home to convalesce. I was delighted. I decided on a nursing home because I knew John wouldn't be able to look after me; he wasn't well himself, and he is nervous in a crisis. He would be there, hopping about, trying his best, but I knew he would get on my nerves and make everything about him. I needed time on my own, away from everyone. I needed time to think and reflect. To convalesce. The doctors agreed it would be good for me and I was looking forward to the respite.

Geraldine and Breda made the arrangements and packed a case for me. It was a big filthy, ugly-looking thing.

'Where the hell are yous goin' with that?' I said. There were plenty of smart bags down at the house and they brought that monstrosity. They looked disappointed. I'm sure they were thinking, after all we've done and there she is, Lady Muck, up in the bed moaning. It was inconsiderate of me to attack them like that. Maybe I was slightly angry that they were going back to England.

Later I was sent down to theatre for another bronchoscopy. Was this an oversight, I wondered? I was imagining that someone somewhere was saying, 'Jesus, we haven't done the bronchoscopy!' like a cleaner finishing her shift and suddenly remembering, 'Shite, I forgot to clean out the gents' toilet!'

Joan

Missing my mommy and feeling deep sympathy for her. Seventy and frail and in hospital on her own. How I wish she was sitting in her room writing her diary and drinking tea. She is such a strong, brave, stoical woman with so much love to give to others, even when she has been broken down.

I remember her attending my parents' evenings, advising me when I have been down and confused, hugging me in that slightly stiff and embarrassed way of hers. All that love and concern. I also remember those times when life was difficult for her, waiting at the window to see if Daddy would return on the number 11 bus from work, or the pub. How often she was disappointed, a sad and lovely woman.

Spoke to Mommy on the phone today. She seemed depressed. She sounded-off about Daddy not visiting yesterday and going to Doyles instead. Maybe she was worried about being left on her own. Anyway, this is all a process that must be gone through.

We must be vigilant and not criticise or speculate, but just be there when needed. Mommy needs that compassion right now.

Breda and Geraldine put that filthy case by the window. I couldn't leave it standing there. What if someone saw it? I checked to see what they had packed: it was too warm for heavy clothes. Would they have the sense to pack my lights? Yes. I dragged the case across the floor to see if it would fit under the bed, out of sight.

ELEVEN

Picturesque Poverty

Back in Dublin in November 1954, John and I said our emotional goodbyes on O'Connell Bridge and promised to write every week. We were going our separate ways. I had enough money to get me back to Mammy's but John had to pawn His Lordship's suit for his fare to Clonegal. All my partings seem to happen on that cursed bridge.

I needed to be home with Mammy in the last months of my pregnancy. I wanted John home with me too but things would have been a bit awkward after the box he landed on Father earlier that year. I dreaded going home without him. The *culchies* would be gossiping and having a field day. I could almost hear them talking behind my back: 'Oh, that's strange to see her home and not him'; 'I wonder what's happened?'; 'They must be split up'; 'Sure they're only a few months married.'

I would never tell them anything, especially about the beatings, because I wouldn't encourage the backbiting.

I turned up in Clonmore with Ellen without so much as a by-your-leave but Mammy didn't ask any questions. There was no resentment about me being home; John wasn't with me so there was no animosity. I just fitted back in and waited for my second child to be born. It felt like a very hopeful and prosperous time. Mammy was buying *launawaula* with money Peter was sending over from England. He was working in the kitchens of some big hotel in London. I can still remember Mammy's face light up when she received a letter from him that Christmas with eight pounds in it. That was a stack of money back then. The envelope was ripped and you could see the money. It's a wonder it landed there.

I had a grand time on this visit: I spent my days washing and cleaning and helping Mammy with whatever needed to be done. I would keep the house tidy, keep the fires down and do some cooking and baking, just as I had when I was a girl. Unless Mammy was at Mass or had gone into town, we spent most of our time together. Ellen spent her days playing with Luke's pet dog Terry. They were always together. It was Terry who taught her to walk. He would lie down on the ground and Ellen would lie beside him. When she wanted to get up, she would hang on to his coat and he would get up very slowly along with her until she was on her feet; it was lovely to see her bonding so well with that big, old grey and white sheep dog. John missed Ellen's first steps; and I missed John. Terribly. Our sense of pride and loyalty kept us together. Although he was bad to me sometimes, his absence created a void. We would never let anyone see there was any conflict between us. Nobody would have guessed that there was anything other than unity there. I still had a great fondness for him and I needed to have him with me, but I didn't hear a word from him for the next month.

I watched out for his letter from Monday to Saturday but the postman, Paddy 'The Shoe' Swords, disappointed me every day. The Shoe soon sussed my anxiety and began shouting, 'Nothin' for you today, Maura.' One morning, after weeks of waiting, The Shoe arrived with the long-awaited letter. John had some exciting news: he had applied to the council for one of the new bungalows being built in Clonegal and he thought we had a chance of getting it. In the meantime, I kept myself busy preparing for my next birth.

I wanted Mammy with me when I gave birth but I didn't expect her to *deliver* the child. But for her quick thinking, my second-born might not be in the world today.

Luke was home and cycled through thick snow to Fahy Hill to get the midwife, Nurse Geoghan. The weather was desperate. It was one of the worst snowfalls I remember. The child wasn't waiting for any midwife. I went into labour at half ten at night and my second daughter arrived forty-five minutes later.

Mammy's only light had been a candle balanced precariously on the end of the bed, stuck in its own wax. The electricity board only put in one electric light per household in the country, and that was in the kitchen. When anyone turned on their light at night, we would say, 'God Bless the electric light.' That's how religious we were. The Big Houses had their own generators so they always had light. Poor country folk had to make do with the one naked bulb. In the flickering flame, Mammy, seeing the baby was a peculiar colour, realised she was choking by her cord. Mammy very calmly unravelled it while reciting three Hail Marys. I heard Father in the adjoining room say, 'Thanks and praises be to God your child is born. Are you all right?'

'I am, Father.'

The baby was born on Wednesday 2 February, the day after the Feast of St Brigid. She was duly named Mary Brigid in her honour.

When Nurse Geoghan eventually turned up, Mammy snapped, 'You took your time gettin' here. The child's been born an hour.'

Nurse Geoghan was amazed at Mammy's skill and asked if she was a nurse. 'Indeed and I'm not a nurse,' said Mammy. 'I learnt first aid in the war. This is my first time deliverin' a child.'

'It's a good job you were here or she would have died. What time did you say she was born?'

'A quarter past eleven,' Mammy said, getting angry.

Nurse Geoghan followed her into the kitchen and asked for some water for the infant. 'It's in the kettle, Nurse.'

'Which kettle?'

'How many kettles do ya see?' Mammy said sarcastically. 'How long more are ya goin' to leave that child? It's over an hour now since she was born and she hasn't even been washed. Do ya want her to get pneumonia?'

'She's wrapped up, Mrs McNamee, she will be all right.'

'Sara-much-loss you care what happens, Nurse. What about poor Maura? Sure she should have been attended to by now.'

'I'm goin' to make Maura a cup of tea and I'll get a bottle of sugared water for the child.'

Weak from the birth and listening to the two of them bickering, I began to cry. Jesus Christ, would they ever shut their mouths? The atmosphere in the kitchen was as cold and frosty as the weather outside. Now Ellen was awake and crying and that started the baby off. And what a squealer Mary Brigid was!

Finally the midwife left and Mammy came into the room, her face white with anger. 'That auld rip,' she said. 'Wasn't I right to fight with her, Maura? The length she took gettin' here! If it wasn't for me, the child would surely have died.'

'Would she, Mammy?' I said feebly.

'Ah, sure Maur'een, don't talk foolish nonsense, don't you know very well she would. Are you a real clown?'

Mammy took Mary Brigid down to the kitchen for more sugared water to try to quieten her down and I turned over and fell straight to sleep. When I woke, it was seven in the morning and Mammy was tapping at the bedroom door.

'Are you awake, Maur'een? I brought a sup of tae.'

'Yes, Mammy.'

'Did ya have a good rest?'

'Yes, Mammy, I did. I didn't wake at all.'

'That little elk never stopped cryin' all night. But I suppose you're just glad she's here.'

'I am,' I said, easing myself up on to my elbows to take a look at my precious gift. But Mary Brigid wasn't there.

'Where is she, Mammy?' I said, feeling slightly panicked.

'Maybe the fairies took her in the night?'

'Where is she?'

'She slept all night with Father and me and now she's in the kitchen in the cradle.'

'What cradle? We haven't got a cradle.'

'We have now,' said Mammy, 'and she's fast asleep in it.'

I laughed till I cried when I saw the cradle. Mammy had taken a drawer from the bottom of the wardrobe and lined it with a soft woollen blanket. And there Mary Brigid lay, all snug and cosy, a small distance from the fire.

Mary Brigid was full of colic and didn't stop crying for the next six weeks. I was near demented from lack of sleep. Was she sick or was she dying? I fretted. 'What in the name God did I do to deserve this? I would say. 'Mammy, will you take her? I can't do anythin' with her.'

'Sure you were the same as a baby, Maur'een.'

Mary Brigid drove us all to distraction until Father came up with an idea to soothe her colic. He put a drop of brandy on a spoon. It worked a treat!

Mary Brigid was a real handful. Mammy took over the looking after of her, as she had done with Ellen. It was never a problem to me. If she felt close to my children, I was happy. As she would say to Mary Brigid years later, 'Didn't I save ya when you were born? That makes ya half mine.'

John missed the birth of his second child, sorting out the house in Clonegal, but I fully expected him to be at the christening. I wrote and told him the date, time and place but he didn't show up for it.

Mary Brigid looked so beautiful in her christening robes. She was a bonny little baby with black curly hair and legs that felt like silk. She had a big pouty mouth, high cheekbones and beautiful sea-green eyes, like John's. Her little face oozed character.

After feasting on Mammy's delicious christening spread, I saw a car pulling up and John getting out with two strangers. He introduced them as the two Dunnes, brothers Ben and JP. Their name reminded me of an old saying I often heard, 'Well done, said old Dunne, when young Dunne was born.' John arrived all smiles and not a care in the world. As soon as he walked in, he took a peek at our new arrival and he went looking for Ellen. 'Har-ushacock,' he called to her. Har-ushacock was his nickname for her. Ellen went flying over and put her two little bare arms around him. She jumped up on his lap and they had some food together. That is how they always had their dinner, Ellen on her daddy's lap at the table. He could be a very tender father.

That night, John told me about the home he had secured in Clonegal. The newly built bungalow was at number seven, St Bridget's Terrace. I was pleased as punch as that was my lucky number. It would be our first home and John had made it happen. I was very proud of him. John called on his childhood friend and distant relative Peter Murphy to collect us six weeks later.

The early morning winter sun was breaking through the clouds, highlighting the tips of the green hills. 'On the other side of that hill is Clonegal,' John said. I wondered which hill he was talking about; the village was surrounded by them.

'And that's the Slaney. When the rich English visitors came for the salmon fishing season, me and the lads would hang around them and offer to carry their gaff for two shillin's a time.'

While John reminisced, I took in the magical scene. Clonegal was the most picturesque village I had ever seen. At the top there were just three shops, three churches – Catholic, Protestant and Methodist – a pub and a school. So this is where John was reared? I thought.

'That's St Bridget's Church. I served Mass in that church for years. I was an altar boy. And behind that is the graveyard where my grandmother is buried.'

As we drove up past the shops and into the terrace I wasn't much impressed by what I saw. The terrace was built in a half-moon shape with a green patch of grass facing the houses, separating them from the main road. Most of the gardens had freshly laid lawns and borders filled with flowers. Not ours. It didn't look finished. The garden was nothing more than a mound of clay like a freshly dug grave. Where was the beautiful bungalow with the landscaped garden? I wondered.

John's cousin Lilly also had a house in the terrace, just above ours. We went straight into Lilly's that first day and she filled our stomachs with breakfast and my head with stories about John.

'We call him Nanny's John round here,' said Lilly. 'Old Nanny was always fussin' around him to make sure he was safe and out of harm's way. She wouldn't let anyone look crooked at him!'

'And she'd chase me up the field,' John added, 'wavin' a *thrawneen* high above her head shoutin', "If ya don't come home for yer dinner I'll break yer two legs."' John doubled up with the laughter.

'And his friends would be shouting, "That's it, Nanny! You break his two legs!"' added Lilly.

She told me about Peter and Willy who were part of John's teenage gang, known as The Famous Five on account of their brains. 'Maura, did John tell ya that his master nicknamed him The Professor? The Famous Five were the brightest sparks in Clonegal.'

And, as if to prove the point, John said, 'Do you know the nine parts of speech, Maura?'

'Hold on, let me think now. I'm sure I do. Noun. Verb. Pro—'

'It's simple.' He cut me off. 'Noun, verb and pronoun; adjective, adverb and preposition; conjunction, interjection and article.'

'Ya think you're so clever,' I said.

'Oh, yeh. He's very clever,' Lilly cackled. 'Very smart.'

'You'll remember this. The nine parts of a fart are thunder, wonder and report; stink, music and wind; peace, ease and satisfaction!'

'I bet it didn't take you long to learn that one,' I said.

'No, I used to do my homework walkin' up the street on the way to school because I'd have spent the previous night down the ball alley,' he laughed. 'The Master would read my copy-book and say, "Come up here, Professor Murphy, and decipher this for me."

'This one time I started to read: "Huntington Castle was built in . . . er hum, seventeen, no, fourteen fifty—" I couldn't read my own scrawl and the Master said, "Hand me that. The *puca* reads what the *puca* writes. Go and sit down."'

After breakfast we left the children with Lilly and went next door to number seven.

John was very excited. 'Go on, take the key and have a look. It's nice.'

I turned the key and it opened the door first time, which amazed me. I wasn't used to anything working properly. I walked into a decent sized square hallway and began my tour of our new house. John proudly showed off all the rooms. There was a range in the kitchen but nothing else, except a fresh hundred-weight bag of coal. At least he had the presence of mind to air the place.

'Well, what do ya think?' he asked eagerly.

'It's a roof,' I said unimpressed.

I couldn't believe what I was seeing. It was a beautiful bungalow all right but there wasn't a stick of furniture. A house with no furniture is like a pub with no beer.

'Where's the furniture you said you had from your grand-mother's house?'

'I never said that. Did I say that?'

'Well, that's what ya said in the letter.'

'I must have been drunk when I wrote it.'

Yeh, you're never any other way, I thought.

'John what are we goin' to sit on and eat off? You have no job.'

'Sure I'll get a job.' We were starting off on the wrong foot. 'So you're not pleased,' he said, marching off down the garden. 'Are you ever satisfied?' He got to the end of the garden and looked back. 'What do ya want me to do? I've only got two hands and two feet and I'm supposed to work miracles.'

'No, but you could start by tellin' the truth. You brought me down here under false pretences. You could have waited, at least, until we had a table and a couple of chairs and somewhere to sleep. Where do you propose I put the children? I can't leave them with Lilly.'

'Ah, put them where ya like!' he shouted and stormed off, leaving me standing like a fool.

I didn't know where to put myself when I arrived back at Lilly's. What would Mammy say if she could see me now? I looked out of Lilly's window and saw John striding up The Green with his hands in the pockets of his grey swagger coat. He was as straight as a lathe and the wind was blowing through his thick black hair.

'What am I goin' to do now, Lilly? He's gone and left me.'

'Where is he gone?'

'Across The Green.'

'Sit down there in that chair and I'll make you a sup of tea.'

Lilly poured me a cup of stewed tea from a blue enamel teapot that had been bubbling on the range. I looked around the room and saw the happiest-looking child sitting in his pram. Lilly went into the kitchen for a bowl of water to wash the baby's face. My stomach turned as she dragged a flannel across his nose, smearing snot all over him.

'There y'are now. That'll do ya,' she said, satisfied. She handed the bowl to the older boy who was playing on the table with a toy car. 'Take that out to the scullery and be quick about it.'

The child took no notice. 'Do ya hear me talkin' to ya? Pick up that bowl and put it in the scullery.'

Lilly took her cigarettes from the mantel, lit a fag, sat by the fire and crossed her bracketed shins. Just then, the boy dropped the bowl.

'Look what you've done now!' Lilly shouted. 'I'll break your two legs.' She lunged at him and gave him a clip across the back of the head sending the child sprawling on his arse. 'Get up, ya gobshite,' she scowled.

Lilly may have had a sharp tongue but she had a beautiful nature. She was very generous and friendly and knew how to tell a good story. I realised that John's sense of humour – and his watery sea-green eyes – ran in the family.

It was coming up to two o'clock and I'd had my fill of cute stories about John. I took Ellen by the hand, scooped up Breda (Mary Brigid, being a bit of a mouthful, had been duly shortened to Breda) and moved towards the door.

'Are ya goin'?' asked Lilly. 'Sure you've nowhere to put the child.'

'Ah, I'll be all right,' I said, 'I'll manage.'

'Well, call round if ya want anythin'.'

'I will. Thanks.'

I returned to my empty house and flicked the light switch. Nothing happened. Great. No electricity. Where in the name of God is John? Surely he can't leave us like this? If I had the price of a lift back to Clonmore I would have taken the children home to Mammy's. I had to wait for hours in the dark.

I was startled by a loud knock on the door. It was the man himself. John was standing there with a stupid grin on his face. How well I recognised that grin. It was a permanent fixture whenever he had a drink. I couldn't bring myself to utter a single greeting and gave him one of my well-practised steely stares instead.

'Look,' he said.

'Look at what? I can't see anythin'. It's dark.'

'Why are you in the dark?'

'We've no electricity.'

'Did ya not think to turn on the mains?'

John reached over my head, flicked on the mains and the whole place came alight. Every switch in the house had been left on.

'You're not as gormless as I thought,' I said, smiling.

John tapped his temple and said, 'Up there for thinkin' . . .' and pointed at his feet, 'and down there for dancin'.'

He started to tap dance, grabbed hold of me and swung me around till my head felt dizzy. I had to admit I was pleased to see him.

'Now will ya look outside?' he urged.

'Yeh, the moon's shinin'.'

'Very funny. Can't ya see the van there? I've been to get the furniture.'

'I wondered where ya were all day.'

'Yeh, I bet you thought that no-good bastard's out drinkin'.'

'You're dead right.'

'I had a couple of pints with the boys in Newtownbarry.'

'Did ya now?' Like I didn't already know.

'Do ya want to see what I bought?' He pulled a brown bag out of his pocket. 'I got these for you, me darlin'.' I took the bag. 'Go on, open it.'

I could see the bag contained cigarettes but I wanted something more useful, like a bed or a table. 'What else did ya buy?'

He went out to the van and flung open the doors. 'Come on, boys. Bring it in.'

Two fellas jumped out of the van and dashed around the back as though they hadn't five seconds to spare. Then out jumped two more.

John had kept me waiting all day and now he wanted me to play happy families in front of his friends. He was bubbling with energy and jolly remarks. Good God, I thought, he doesn't change, does he?

'Come on lads, meet the missus,' John beckoned. Oh Jesus, that was the first time I heard John refer to me as the missus and I didn't like it one bit. But there was worse to come. 'Hold it, you don't want to ruin me for life now, do ya? The missus wouldn't like that!' They all laughed. Good Jesus, if I hear that word one more time I'll scream.

I turned on my heels and went back into the kitchen, trying to curb my anger. Ellen had toddled over to the door, rubbing her eyes and whingeing. I picked her up and plonked her on my hip.

John was dishing out orders to his young helpers. 'Watch the step, Christy. Over a bit, Jack.' They brought in a bed, a table and a couple of chairs. A long wooden form followed.

'Praise be to God,' I said, 'where did you get the money for all that?'

'It was given. Friends and family. It was all promised to us. I just hadn't got round to collecting it.'

He turned to the lads and asked, 'Where's Spot? Did we lose him?'

Spot? Surely they didn't bring a dog? Haven't we got enough trouble with two children crying all night, without a dog yelping as well?

'Not a word about it,' said Jack. 'He's out for the count on the floor of the van.'

'Put the kettle on, Maura, and we'll have a sup of tea,' said John.

'It's been boilin' all evenin',' I said frostily.

'We won't be stayin' for tea,' said Christy. 'We'll go and get the last drink at Burns. Are you comin', John?'

John looked at me, sheepishly fumbling with the change in his trouser pocket. Pulling out the shillings he said, 'I've only got a few bob. I haven't got what would jingle on a tombstone! That won't buy very much.'

'No, it won't,' I said. 'You've been away all day and we'll need bread and milk tomorrow.'

'Well, you'd need more than that for the birds,' John said, being daft and doing a Irish jig in the middle of the kitchen floor. 'Aren't I fierce funny?' he said to me. Funny looking, I thought. 'Ah I won't go, lads. She's had the last word. I'll have to help get the young ones ready for bed. Make sure Spot isn't smothered. Give him a nudge when yous go out.'

'Whose is the dog?' I asked.

'What dog?'

'Spot.'

John laughed. 'Spot isn't a dog. Spot Ryan. He lives up the road.'

Next day John and I sorted out most of the belongings we had and he went off to do a bit of shopping, arranging for us to have milk delivered daily and coal and groceries weekly. I strolled up the road to fetch a bucket of water from a pump outside McCready's shop. It was a journey I would have to make several times a day. There was no piped water to our bungalow.

My daily routine rarely changed. I got the children up and washed them every morning in the basin in the kitchen for the heat off the range. Then I would take them up to the pump for more water.

John's day always began the same way too, with the newspapers. He was particularly fond of the *Carlow Nationalist*. As he had no work in Clonegal, he had ample time to swim in the Slaney with his old school friends, or go to the ball alley down in front of Purcell's Pub at the bottom of the village. He spent hours down there playing handball.

I rarely went outside the door, except for church on a Sunday. The one time I did go out, I got into terrible trouble. I went out with Carmel White, the wife of John's friend Willy. Carmel had a brilliant personality and persuaded Jack Roach, a local hackney driver, to take us to Courtown Harbour. I was flattered that she asked me to go to the seaside with her. The likes of me going round with Carmel White! She was lively and outgoing, and I hadn't two words to say to anyone!

When we got there, Carmel went off with friends, leaving me alone with Jack, a man I didn't know from Adam. We sat on a bench with our backs to the sea and waited for her to return. She was gone for hours. I told John I was going out and I would only be a couple of hours and he stayed home to mind the children. But it was midnight before I got home.

I knew John would be furious but I didn't expect to be locked out of the house. I banged on the bedroom window and Ellen toddled over and stared at me in amazement. 'Ellen, will ya open the door and let Mammy in?' She just kept looking at me. 'Open the door. Let me in, pet.'

'Mammy,' she said.

I was standing outside for half an hour before John eventually let me in. When he opened the door he hissed, 'What kept you out so late? Where were ya?'

John slapped me right across the face. 'What did ya do that for?' I cried out.

'Where were ya?'

'You know where I was. Courtown Harbour with Carmel White.'

'And how did ya get there?'

'Jack Roach took us.'

'Well, ya won't be goin' any more!' he said, giving me another swipe. 'Fuckin' around with Jack Roach!'

Going out was John's life. The socialising and the pub was what kept him going. But I was struggling. There was nothing to occupy my mind and a void crept into my life. John met up with his old school friends in Clonegal and carried on where he'd left off. Peter Murphy and Willy White were always around him. He had the security of a marriage and the freedom of a single man. He did what he liked without ever telling me what he was up to. When he left the house he could wind up anywhere.

'I'm just goin' up the street,' he would say. 'Up the street' could mean anything.

He used to spend more time mitching in Willy White's house than he spent in his own. I could see them all traipsing in and out of White's. It annoyed me that I was the little woman left at home with the kids. I could have read more, knitted or sewed more but I became obsessed with John. I let my mind wander down to whichever pub or mitching house he was in, imagining him having fun while I was sitting all alone. I couldn't wait for him to come home to share in the *craic*.

Jack Roach's mother, Nora, had the other mitching house. John painted a vivid picture of her sitting up in the corner and the men doing the dancing in their hobnail boots on the cement floor. There'd be sparks flying off the boots and Nora would be going, 'Ooh, ouch, ouch, ooh, mind me feet.'

Poor old Nora had a lot of wind in her. She used to be sitting there pumping the bellows and farting, and blaming the dog for doing it. The dog sat under the stool by her feet. When she let off a banger, she'd shout, 'Come out, Shep! Get outta there, ya dirty dog.' And she'd get up to open the door, farting as she went.

All the lads would be laughing at her. Some smart aleck shouted one night, 'Come out, Shep, before she shites on ya.'

Smarting, Nora kicked the dog out and said, 'Get out, Shep, and a lot more along with ya.'

That was the cue for the lads to leave.

The Dandy in the Swagger Coat

I was the youngest married woman in the terrace but I fitted in as best I could. The terrace women were very cliquey and they had peculiar ways. None of them bar Mrs Eddy, used to get up too early in the morning. We often saw old Paddy Dunne driving his cattle down the road and he'd be wearing his soft hat and carrying his stick. Old Paddy and his son Mickey grazed the cows down along the road in the ditch. He would refer to Mickey as 'that yella bastard' because he was as yellow as a keck. He would occasionally give the cows a wallop and shout, 'Get up ya bastards, yis yella bastards. Yis idle lazy bastards.' And you wouldn't know whether it was Mickey, the cows or the women of the terrace he was talking to.

I felt isolated. Clonegal wasn't near to anything or anyone I knew. The nearest town, Newtownbarry, was five miles away. It was no further than Clonmore to Edenderry but I knew those roads and the people on them. Here I was a complete stranger.

We didn't have too many visitors to the house. John's mother lived in Carlow and she only made the journey once. I'd been visiting my mammy in Offaly with the children and we spent the weekend with John's mother on our way back. She came home with us in a taxi and paid the fare.

She was delighted with the house, until she came inside and saw the bedroom. Beer cans and piss bottles were strewn around the room. I couldn't believe it. When John was drunk, he'd piss into any tin or bottle he could find. It was high summer, and oh the stink of the beer and piss! John had brought a drinking friend, 'The Phantom', to sleep in our bed. How dare he bring anybody home to sleep in my bed? It was bad enough him getting drunk without bringing home an old drunk and getting into my bed!

Lilly's brother Christy was a regular visitor, though. Anything for a cup of tea and a taste of my home-made bread. Every time he came in he'd say, 'Kettle's boilin', missus, it's not my business to spake.' Then I'd make the tea for him.

Christy couldn't have been much more than thirty and was prone to taking fits – the Blessed Sickness we called it. One day it happened on The Green right outside our house just after he'd had his cup of tea. I saw him swaying. The next thing he fell and started jerking.

'God, John, Christy's havin' a fit. Go out and help him.'

I was glad his fit happened outside and not in my house. It

would have scared the children. Almost immediately Lilly, Mrs Eddy, Mrs Halpin from number ten, and a couple more, gathered round Christy to see what was going on. A bit of commotion always drew a crowd.

I was slow to realise that some of the terrace women were moaning gossips. I wasn't a gossip at all – but I happened to have the misfortune of saying something about tinkers. How was I to know that one of my neighbours was related to gypsies? That comment caused a lot of trouble. The terrace women refused to speak to me after that.

And we were dirt poor. John only ever had casual work. A farmer called 'Big Martin' Redmond from across the bridge asked John to cut the corn with the combine harvester. Eager to get behind the wheel of anything that went on petrol or oil, John worked from dawn to dusk up in the fields. Ellen and I often watched him from the kitchen window. When she spotted his head bobbing into view over the brow of the hill she would screech with delight as it appeared, disappeared and reappeared.

John also managed to get a bit of work pulling sugar beet. I used to go down and pull beet with him, bringing the two children with me. I'd wrap them up in warm blankets and leave them on the headland and work right through till four in the afternoon without stopping for lunch. It was back breaking.

Everyone in Clonegal was poor, except those who worked for the forestry. We were all the same in that respect. If you didn't have it, you starved or robbed it. It was as simple as that. At one point the only food we had were potatoes, fried onions and gravy. We never had meat. We couldn't afford it. If I didn't make the bread, we would have starved. I don't know how we kept the children fed.

Then I found out I was pregnant again . . .

Seamus, our first son, was born James Francis on Thursday 12 April 1956. He was a puny child with a tiny appetite. He had eczema all over his body but he was the cutest little thing, with his blond curly hair and almond-shaped grey-blue eyes. He was the apple of his daddy's eye. John couldn't wait to pick him up and nurse him on his lap. Ellen and Breda adored him too. The girls taught their brother to take his first steps. They would stand either side of him, hold his little hands, and lead him down the concrete path to the gate. He would take a step and rest against the wall. Take another step and rest again, and so on.

We were so desperate for money that John asked me to cycle forty miles to Carlow and back to borrow money off his mother. I did everything I could not to go.

'John, I don't have a bike.'

'Can't ya borrow one?'

'I don't want to beg a bike let alone beg a pound.'

'Maura, we need the money. We have to pay the Hickeys for the coal and we haven't a bite to eat.'

'You go then. You've nothin' else to do.'

'You go and I'll keep an eye on the children. Ya know she won't give it to me; she'll just think I'll go out and drink it. She'll give it to you.'

I borrowed a bike and rode all that way to ask for a pound, but his mother wouldn't lend us a penny. She answered her door dressed to go out in her hat and coat. 'Oh hello,' she said. 'What are you doin' in the town?'

'John's asked me to come in and see if you'll give him the loan of a pound.'

'Could he not come himself?' She was cross.

'No, he asked me to come.'

'Well, I haven't got a pound for myself let alone for him! Why isn't he at work?' She walked past me, closing the door behind her, and I left without a penny. John made a right tramp out of me forcing me to beg like that.

After that, my mammy helped out by sending a food parcel down from Offaly. She used to get Mr O'Reilly, the manager of

Fay's store in Edenderry, to send out this parcel of food to me each week. He'd send a big portion of boiling bacon; a packet of porridge meal; two pounds of sugar; half a pound of tea; a pound of butter; a half a pound of margarine (Mammy knew I liked to fry eggs in margarine); two packets of Galtee cheese and sixty non-tipped Player's cigarettes. Sometimes she would include a pound note. She'd get it all on tick and pay the bill whenever she could afford it. Mammy would go without rather than see me go hungry. The parcel would arrive every Tuesday without fail, and we would share some of it with Lilly.

Ellen and Breda would get all excited when they saw the parcel because they knew that we would have food. I suppose it must have cost Mammy about two or three pounds a week but she knew we were poor and had nothing to eat. She sent that down every week until Mr O'Reilly left the store.

We looked to England again to help us out of our miserable situation. We decided that I would apply for a domestic job there and John would stay in Ireland and look after the children. My new employers sent me a five-pound loan to cover my fare. They would take it out of my first month's wages. But then I discovered I was pregnant again with my fourth child and in no position to take up my new post – but they had already sent the five pounds. What a dilemma! There was an awful lot you could buy for five pounds back then. We spent the money on food.

I got many letters asking for the money back but I just ignored them. I never dreamt they would find me in the arsehole of Carlow. Then one day, when John was out of the house, I got an unexpected visit. Two detectives from Dublin appeared at the door dressed in mufti.

'It's been reported that there was money sent to you from London and you haven't sent it back,' one said.

'That's right.' I was too honest to tell them I had never received it.

'Why didn't you send it back?' the other said.

'I didn't think they'd miss it. I've spent it and I don't have it now to give it back.'

'Well, you'll have to get it. This is a serious offence. You'll have to find the money and return it.'

I was so ashamed. I would have to borrow the money but I wouldn't go to anybody in the terrace. There would be too many questions asked. I went to Bill Sullivan, a cousin of Mrs Eddy's, because he was the only person in Clonegal who wouldn't open his beak. And I thought he was the only one who would have the money because he had no family and seemed to be fairly well off.

Well, he didn't have it but he did offer to give me the bus fare to Offaly. I knew my brother Joe would lend me the money. I met Bill Sullivan at the Protestant Church where there was no fear of the shady transaction being witnessed. I took Breda with me and we sat there in the ditch together waiting for him to come from work. We were like the Lubys sitting in the ditch, waiting to beg.

Joe gave me the five pounds willingly. Back in Clonegal, I borrowed a bicycle from Mary Anne Ryder, the curate's house-keeper, and rode into Newtownbarry Police Station with the 'borrowed' money. Cycling home, it started to get dark and I had no lights for the bike. I was pushing it along the country road when a local farmer stopped to give me a lift on his tractor. I had to stand on that tractor all the way to Clonegal. The whole experience was so belittling.

We were back to poverty, and begging and buying food on tick.

John would send me up to the shop to get food from the pretty shop girl. He told me he had 'an arrangement' so I never had to part with any money. This went on for a few weeks and I was quite happy to go along with it because we needed to eat. The day he sent me to pick up a pair of brown leather shoes, I knew there was something underhand going on. Why would she be giving John food and shoes without charging him?

One morning, when I was making my bed, I found a silver pendant under the pillow.

'Whose is this, John?' I asked.

'The shop girl's.'

'What's it doin' here?'

'She left it at Willy's. I'll give it to her when I see her.'

I thought no more about it until a couple of weeks later I found an earring under the same pillow.

'I took it from her for a joke,' he said. 'Give it to me and I'll bring it back to her.'

I felt sick. 'No, John, I'll make sure she gets it.'

That day I went up to the water pump and saw the girl standing by the shop door. I was fuming. I dropped my bucket and went to confront her.

'That's yours, isn't it?' I said, throwing the earring at her. 'I found it under my pillow! What's it doin' under my pillow?'

She said nothing. She didn't seem to know what I was talking about.

'You keep your hands off!' I was raging. 'I don't want to see any more of your belongin's under my pillow.'

I felt terrible but John was able to convince me that nothing was going on. He said I was being silly. Then I started hearing the rumours that John was sweet on the girl. I remembered seeing them leaving White's but thought nothing of it. It was a mitching house and lots of people went there. I started walking round the village with the children in the pram to catch John out. I would walk up towards the four-hundred-year-old castle fearful of what I might witness. I never saw any sign of them and began to doubt the rumours. But when the fair came to Clonegal that summer, I thought I might see John with the girl. I asked Old Gwen Halpin and her daughter Nan to come to the fair with me. Just as we got to the bridge, we met John coming home. He was alone.

He was smiling. 'Where are yous off to, ladies?' he said to Nan and Old Gwen. Then to me, 'And where do ya think you're goin'?'

'I'm goin' to the fair.'

'And who's with the kids?'

'Young Gwen.'

John ordered me to get home but I defied him and tried to walk past him. He raised his hand and gave me a good slap on the face and broke my nose.

'There's no need to do that, John!' Old Gwen pleaded. 'She's only goin' to the fair.'

I scuttled back home feeling so humiliated. John has always denied the rumours but I still felt betrayed. I was convinced he was making a fool of me.

The following Sunday, John went to Dublin for a football match with his gang. I couldn't believe it. After everything that had happened I expected him to stay home with me. I threatened that if he went, I would go out as well and leave the children on their own.

'If you go out, I'm goin' out too.'

'Please yourself. I'm goin' anyway,' he said.

John swaggered off across The Green and I ran out the door, without thinking, and headed for the Carlow Road. I imagined that when they passed me by on the road John would get out and we'd go home together. But the car whizzed past. They kept going, and so did I. I was crying along the road. I should have gone home to the children but I didn't turn back. I was confused and tried to convince myself that Young Gwen would turn up and stay with them.

I needed to be somewhere else. I walked as far as a neighbour's house up the hill. I wanted to be able to tell them I had left the children on their own but I just sat there staring into the fire not saying a word. My neighbours gave me Sunday dinner and we made polite conversation all afternoon. I must have been going out of my mind, leaving the children on their own. Ellen was three and Seamus was only six months.

Poor Breda was kneeling on the bed crying when I got home.

'Ma-mmy! Ma-mmy! Ma-mmy!' She was so upset, she thought if she kept saying my name I would turn up. I swore I would never leave them again, the poor little mites. I must have been demented. I'd never left the children on their own before. I thought I must have been a bad mother. I knew even the animal in the field wouldn't leave its young, but I had. It was a very unmotherly thing to do. I felt very guilty. I was so sad and angry and foolish.

I felt I had nothing to live for. John made me feel like a doormat, a sex object, good between the sheets and that was it. He would want sex all the time but I would have a tired head and tired body. It was all one-sided. He could be gentle and caring in our intimate moments but it wasn't like the adverts or programmes on TV today where they can't wait to get to bed and rip each other's clothes off. I wasn't mad about sex; I wasn't someone who needed sex all the time, not like John. Sex had become just like any other task. It was no more enjoyable than collecting a bucket of water from the pump or doing a load of washing. I was a slave to his sexual demands. There was no escape. I was trapped in a loveless marriage. But I couldn't leave: I was a Catholic.

TWELVE

Rats in Garr

Going to Clonegal was the worst decision of our lives. After the birth of my fourth baby, Olive, we had to survive on scallions, bread and margarine. We weren't living; we were just existing. Each year we seemed to be getting poorer and more destitute. Poverty drove me back home to Offaly. At least Mammy and Father wouldn't let us starve.

Mammy was delighted to see us; Father wasn't so pleased. Mammy responded with her familiar, quirky comment. 'Let him go to perjock!' she said. 'Sara-much-loss what he thinks.'

Ger had moved to England, Joe and Peter had moved back home and Luke was about to visit with his new wife Maudie. It was during this visit that I first met Maudie, and I liked her immediately. You could tell she was a Galway woman, she had that big, strong West of Ireland look about her. She seemed to be a very happy-go-lucky person and she was terribly funny.

Luke and his new family descended on Mammy for Christmas. I knew John wouldn't be far behind. He knew I had no intention of going back to Clonegal, and he missed his new baby daughter.

Olive had chosen to make her entrance on one of the hottest

days of 1957. She arrived after a seven-hour labour with a full head of jet-black hair and barely a wrinkle in sight.

We christened her Olive because she was born two days before the Feast of Blessed Oliver Plunkett. The children had to have a saint's name or there would have been an argy-bargy with the priests. Olive had a lovely disposition and was exceptionally quiet – unlike squealing Breda. John bonded with her more quickly than he did with any of the others. He absolutely adored her. He would refer to her as his little doll because she was astonishingly beautiful. John would sit on the chair with Olive on one side and Seamus on the other. No matter what John was doing, he would involve Seamus and Olive.

Christmas Eve was the day John chose to show up in Clonmore, in fierce bad weather with snow lying thick on the ground. He walked seventy miles from Clonegal to Clonmore to be with us. He had fairly sore feet by the time he got there. I suppose it proved he loved us. He didn't bring any gifts but his presence was present enough.

He received the usual good welcome off Mammy. She thought there was no one like him. Carmel and Anna would always have a laugh with him as well. John loved being the centre of attention. He was one of those men who had to have an audience. Mammy thought he was hilarious. He tickled her when Father went off to Mass and left his false teeth behind on the dresser. John was shaving in front of the big mirror inside the back door and he could see the reflection of Father's teeth staring back at him.

'He's not even here and he's still snarlin' at me!' he joked.

John soon picked up piecework cutting ditches and draining the bogs for Bord na Mona, the Irish peat board. He'd come home full of tales about the men who came from all over Ireland to work in the Midland bogs, holed up in makeshift homes in Lullymore. On the weekend a lorry-load of these rough, hard men would pile into Edenderry for a drink and a fight with the locals. At closing time, the lorry driver would coast up and down the streets collecting the men to take them home again. On the last run he would stick his head out of the window and shout, 'Is there any more for Lullymore before the lurry leaves?'

John didn't have the luxury of a lorry to get him to work. He had to go by bike, and pedal. We bought a woman's bike so we could both make use of it. He didn't have a problem with that – John would throw his leg over anything! He wasn't full of pride that way, and you weren't too fussy about the form of transport you used. It was either the bike or Shanks's pony.

John was well sorted with his job in the bog. He was getting £3 10s. a week. It could even be as high as four pounds if he worked overtime. After a month, he got word of a cottage going in Garr three miles west of Clonmore. It was an old herdsman's house owned by a man by the name of Taidgh Moore, a big landowner who employed yardmen, field men, ploughmen and the like. He had several men doing ditches and hedges, cleaning drains and feeding cattle out in the field.

John went over to see Moore and secured the herd's house for twelve shillings a week. It was damp and needed a good airing but we had no turf to light the fires, even though we were surrounded by bogs – the Rearon Bog, the Castle Bog, Clonmore Bog, the High Bog and the Low Bog. Bogs were part of our way of life. If you lived in a council cottage, you could apply for your Turbary Rights which gave you the right to dig for peat or turf on common land. Council tenants were given about twelve yards of bog land called a turf bank. They would cut the turf, rear it (leave it to dry in the sun and wind), save it, bring it home, dry it out and store it for the winter.

Some well-off people had log fires but the majority of them would have quite a bit of land with trees and hedges to provide the sticks to light their fires. Working-class people with cottages had barely one acre of ground and relied solely on turf. As we didn't have a turf bank or sticks, Father gave us a load of his own turf to air the cottage.

Once John had retrieved the furniture from Clonegal, the place looked homely enough but we had no electricity and, yet again, no running water. I had to walk across to the next field with my bucket to draw fresh spring water from a thirty-foot well. I felt like a pirate walking the gang plank: there was a wicked horse in that field and I wouldn't dare go in for my water until he had moved to the far end of it.

A toilet was another luxury we couldn't boast about. We used the nearest bush and the biggest dock leaf we could find. You weren't too particular about the colour and softness of tissue in those days. We dug a hole behind a blackthorn bush at the bottom of the garden. We used a bucket in the house at night and the bush was the burial ground. It was the same story for everyone. Talk about primitive.

The cottage was half as spacious as the house in Clonegal but it was twice as cosy. We were able to keep a good fire burning in the big open grate. Taidgh Moore gave us permission to take timber from his land two fields away. After John came home from work, we would put the children in one room, shut the door and go down to get the sticks. I would carry the flashlight and John would cut the sticks with a bushman's saw and carry them home on his back. We stacked the wood under the kitchen table. He always made sure we had a fire for the next day.

Often I would see a light in the distance across the bog. I thought someone had discovered our pile of wood until our neighbour, Tom Monaghan, told me it was the will o' the wisp. Legend has it that if you follow the light it will lead you astray, and probably into the nearest bog hole.

If we ever ran out of firewood or turf I would take a bucket of turf out of Tom Monaghan's clamp. And if we ever ran out of food, John would pinch potatoes and turnips from Ned Moore, another neighbour and rich cousin of Taidgh's. They were good neighbours. Ned gave us free milk in quarts and sometimes the maid would sneak in a few eggs. They'd be washed and buttered to make them presentable for the higgler.

'There's a few eggs for ya, missus,' the maid would say. 'Bring them home for the *childer*.'

Ned's wife would sometimes give us her leftovers, like the odd pound of butter, a few potatoes or a cabbage, to make a dinner. At the same time I managed to save a few shillings out of John's wage with the Bord to buy furniture on the never-never. I never ever paid it off.

We were grateful for any bit of help we could get. It was charity from the rich. They enjoyed giving it. Maybe it eased their conscience. I never had that false pride that would make people turn down charity. I was glad to receive it. We got free meat off the butcher man, Tom Ward, in appreciation for John's football skills with Rhode, the club Tom was involved with. He would come round with his van on a Saturday evening and give me the bits of meat, a few slices of sirloin steak, a couple of chops and maybe some spare ribs. That was his way of saying thank you to John for playing for Rhode.

My life in Garr was with the children and Sundays were for getting dressed and going to Mass.

Sundays for John meant football and drinking. He would have a drink with the lads in Doyles or Reddy's in Rhode. All the men, including my father, would follow the football crowd and drink in the village. Reddy's was John's favourite watering hole back then. It was one of those old-fashioned pubs that doubled as a shop. You would get a good whiff of smoke and booze coming from the bar at the back when you went in for your *messages*.

Out in the pub they thought John was a great fella. 'John's a great spree,' they'd tell me. He was especially popular with the women; they fell for his charm. I never minded that he was off playing football and going to the pub after. What I minded was how he came back from the pub. There was the usual friction when he drank. One Sunday night, I had reddened the coals under the iron baker to make a cake of bread. It was late and I had just gone for a lie down when John came home after a match in one of his irascible moods.

'I saw Peter's bike propped up against Tom Monaghan's gate,' he said.

'Did ya? Were ya talkin' to him?'

'No. I just saw his bike next door.' Then he started. 'Peter McNamee – I could beat him . . .'

John was a fighter. When he went to a match, a fella would only have to look crooked at him and he'd be threatening to beat him up. Peter's presence next door obviously wound him up, and he used my brothers to get at me.

'The McNamees, who do they think they are?' he said. Drunk people talk shite.

John followed me down to the kitchen, pushing me and pinching me. 'Just leave me alone,' I said, 'I have to make the bread.'

When we went to bed, John wouldn't move across to let me in beside him. I had to sleep on the edge of the mattress. You stupid fucking bastard, I thought, move in there and let me into the bed. I was so angry I could have cried. I wanted to get a shovel and whack him over the head with it. But I did nothing, and John treated me as if I was nothing.

John woke next morning with a nasty head on him, as he always did when he'd been out on the beer. I was so cross that I'd been harassed in the night I refused to get up.

'What about my lunch?' he said.

'Can I not get a rest? I'm tired,' I said sulkily.

'Have ya done my lunch?'

'No, I haven't. I'll get up and do it now.'

I felt so ridiculously low. I just wanted John to be normal, for our life to be normal. I only ever wanted peace. Peace, a home and enough to eat. But John was a young man of thirty, full of vitality and full of anger.

Sometimes he would come in and say nothing and the silence

was nearly as bad as the shouting. He could be very controlling. He controlled me because I let him. I wasn't a fighting spirit. If he had a good few drinks I would know to shut my mouth and say nothing, for the children's sake.

To be fair, John often came home after the pub in a very jolly mood, laughing and singing, but I wouldn't always be in a jolly mood. I wasn't such a jovial person like him. I didn't find the humour in drink and I was quietly critical of him most of the time. Just one of my disapproving looks could start something. I'd be angry at his slurping and foolish talk. I'd be imagining the smell of the beer and I'd be annoyed before he even walked in the door. I loved him when he was sober and loathed him when he was drunk; he loved me when I was good humoured but hated me when I was critical.

He would squeal, 'Why would ya want to take the bit of pleasure away from me? I've only had a few drinks!'

'Yeh, a few too many,' I'd say. 'Ya should know when to stop. Why can't ya have two pints and enjoy them, instead of twenty-two and coming home in that disgusting state?'

He was never away drinking on the days the children were born, nor on the days he was making them! At least his strong libido brought in extra cash. Our income was subsidised by 'the mickey money' – Irish Family Allowance. Men nicknamed it the mickey money after the tools of their trade. Each time they fathered a child they got money for it!

Another expression widely used was 'new house, new baby'. The old saying was right. I had no idea I was pregnant again when I moved into the cottage in Garr. It seemed that John only had to shake his pants at me and I was in the family way.

After a difficult twelve-hour labour, I gave birth to my fifth child. She weighed eight pounds six ounces and damn near killed me. I named her Carmel after my sister but she reminded me of John's mother. She looked just like a Murphy with her long features and big, watery eyes.

After the midwife had finished cleaning me up, John came in with the children. There were the usual oohs and ahs from Ellen, Breda and Seamus, but Olive viewed her baby sister with caution, saying nothing at all. She stood back from the rest as if to say, how dare another little rip come in and take over?

Carmel was fat and easy to nurse. You could get a right good old grip of her. She was a cuddly baby; Seamus was always getting in her pram and lying beside her.

For days after Carmel was born John made all the dinners, usually turnips and white sauce followed by rice or custard, cooked on the open coals of the fire. He also changed and washed the children's nappies. He was a dab hand at that. He'd had a lot of practice. Before we got married John used to look after Carmel's six-month-old baby girl, Bardis, feeding her and changing her nappies and keeping her entertained. He was ahead of the times. Other men were afraid to do 'unmasculine' chores. Not John.

Carmel's birth coincided with the arrival of some unexpected squatters. We first discovered them when I was cleaning out the grate one morning and found two of them dead in the warm ashes. John picked the rats up with the tongs, dropped them on to a shovel and pegged them as far as he could up the garden.

It wasn't the end of the rats. The house got so infested we had to close one bedroom off completely. We called it the rat room and kept it locked. The children would tell visitors, 'You can't go in there, that's the rat room.' And if I wanted to torment the children I would say, 'If yous don't be good I'll throw yous in the rat room.' It was a terrible thing to say but I didn't mean to scare them. I used the threat as a jokey deterrent and they knew I never would throw them in there. None of us would go into the rats' private quarters.

Then the rats spread to the rest of the cottage, mostly at night-time. When Carmel was two days old, a rat scurried up the bed sheets and ran right across her and over the top of my head. I screamed hysterically. John leapt out of bed and turned up the oil lamp but there was no sign of the rat. It had scarpered.

They got so brazen. They'd be sitting there at the end of the kitchen just looking at you. They were that used to being there they didn't flinch. The kids started having nightmares about them. Ellen was the worst one for that. She was terrified of everything when she was a child.

After the rats, the bats started appearing. We were even finding bats in the milk. The first time I found one drowned in the milk I ran from the house, horrified. I stayed out all morning with the children until Tom Monaghan came home for his lunch. He got rid of the thing for me. The bat and the milk went flying across the yard.

In that first summer in Garr, I had my brood along with Anna's clutch. She went to England for a few weeks and asked me to look after her children, Valerie, Vincent and Paula. I'll never forget when she left. I shut the door after her and four-year-old Vincent just threw himself down on the floor by the door, bawling, and pining for his mother. I couldn't console him. But John knew what to do. He came wheeling in with a broad smile on his face.

'Look at all my little chickens,' he said. 'Let's have a game of football; how would ya like that?'

'Yes please!' they shouted.

John made a rag football, took all the children up the garden and kicked the ball around with them. It's amazing how much fun they had with rags wrapped around newspaper and tied with twine.

The children loved John's silliness and warmth. He made them a go-cart from an old cardboard box and old pram wheels – a 'whee-doddle for shootin' crickets' he called it. They'd take it in turns to sit in the whee-doddle searching for crickets to 'shoot'. It was Seamus's favourite game. John would drag him round the garden in it and whisper, 'There's a cricket over there, Seamus, shoot it!'

'Where, Daddy? I can't see it.'

'There it is. Shoot now, bang bang!'

'I kilt it, Daddy, didn't I?' Seamus would holler, his pretend gun in his hands.

'Ya did, pet, ya shot it. Aren't you the little cowboy? We should have named you Audie.'

John was like a giant child to the children. When the meadow was cut in the summer we would all play hide and seek round the haycocks. Anna's children loved to visit.

Valerie and Ellen were right little mothers looking after their young siblings. They would help to wash them, dress them and pick out their clothes. I'd put Ellen in charge – she was five going on twenty-five – whenever I had to go shopping.

One baking hot summer's day, I locked all eight children in the garden, borrowed a bike and cycled into Rhode for some *messages*. I couldn't have been more than an hour. On the way back, I could hear them wailing. I thought, God, what's happened to them? They were all standing by the sheep wire gawping down the fields on the other side of the road. Olive, just a tiny titch, was peering through their legs. The kids were hysterical and pointing across the road.

Seamus was missing.

They thought he'd gone into Moore's field and been attacked by a cow. I never was too keen on going into a field of cattle because you never knew when there would be a wild cow, but Seamus had the habit of disappearing through the fields. I worried about him because he was as thin as a whippet. He had the skinniest little legs. John would joke that if the wind got under his trouser leg it would take him up over the fields. He was only two and a half and I couldn't find him anywhere. After I'd warned them as well. 'Don't attempt to go on to the road,' I told them. 'Do ya hear me?' They had a big acre of garden to play in. 'Don't leave the garden.' But did Seamus listen? Did Seamus ever listen? I'd even tied up the gate but he'd opened it and got out.

Seamus could have been anywhere. I searched the well first. 'Seamus! Seamus!' I called in a panic. I went back across to Moore's field searching for any sign of him. What in the name of God has happened to him? I couldn't find him anywhere. He'd disappeared. Then I thought of Mrs Groome. She'd help me look for him. I cycled down to her with my heart in my mouth.

'Mrs Groome! Would ya help me? Seamus is miss—'

I couldn't believe it. There he was, sitting in the corner of the kitchen, eating bread and jam. He went off down the road on his own at that age. It must have taken him half an hour or more. Jesus, when I think about it!

Those children of mine were so inquisitive. There was a graveyard opposite and they couldn't stay away from it. Ellen, Breda and Seamus used to spy on a young couple who did their courting among the headstones. They'd come home giggling. John thought it was hilarious and would join in the naughtiness of it.

'Did ya see them kissin'?' he would ask, encouraging them to tell all.

I had a terrible job keeping them away from the other side of the road. It was different if John was at home. He might borrow a bike and we'd all visit Mammy. He'd put Ellen on the handlebar and Seamus and Breda on the cross bar. I had the other bike and would put Olive in the carrier at the back.

On a Sunday, John would cycle off to early Mass with Ellen on the back of the bike. He'd come home and I'd use the bike to go to a later Mass. We wouldn't go together because we couldn't borrow a bike on a Sunday: they all needed their bikes for Mass. That's how we got about.

When I was on my own, I had to leave Ellen in charge. They were just the risks you had to take. It was the norm. You were lucky if you had someone to look after your children, otherwise you had to occasionally leave it to 'providence and Paddy McGinty's goat'. We had no people carriers back then and it would have taken hours to drag them all the three miles to Rhode just so I could collect a pound of butter.

Ellen became a second mother. She was always minding someone. She never really had a childhood. She was a very capable child much older than her years. But it was a very young age to leave her in charge. I don't know what I would have done without her. The others looked up to her and felt very safe with her. They knew I would be back as soon as I could and they didn't fret about it. They looked forward to helping me put away the messages. Seamus would drop the butter into the bucket of cold water (we didn't have a fridge) and Ellen would drag the stool to the cupboard to put away the sugar and tins.

Ellen was very grown up for her age but even she got spooked sometimes – especially by Nanny Daly. Nanny Daly was an old eccentric who dressed very queer. She used to walk the lanes in her strange, tatty clothes. There was always a brown hat on her head, no matter what the weather was doing, a silk scarf around her neck and a long coat that went down to her ankles. Ellen and Breda were terrified of her and would run into the house if they saw her coming. I was a little bit scared of her myself because she was liable to run across the road and shout, 'Boo!' into your face.

Another time I borrowed Mrs Groom's bike to go into Rhode, Ellen got frightened thinking Nanny Daly might come knocking at the door, so she piled all the kids into the baby's big high pram and pushed it up the road. She was only just after starting school and couldn't reach the handle, and so there she was pushing it from the body of the pram. Ellen had only got a few yards from the house and what did she do? Walk right into Nanny Daly! The old lady stuck her dry, weather-beaten face right into the pram and shouted, 'Where are you goin' with the hay poke?' frightening the fecking life out of Ellen.

Garr was full of strange characters. There was one called Jack 'The Grouse' McCabe who was very smart on his feet and wore a beret on the Kildare side – sloping to the right. He had a habit of walking into people's houses uninvited without saying a word. He gave me such a turn the day he ran into my kitchen and helped himself to a glass of water. I had my back to the door when I heard it creak open. I saw something flash across the kitchen and then flash back again. The Grouse had whipped the glass off the dresser, taken a drink and put it back again all within seconds. 'Thanks very much, good day now, ma'am,' he said, as his back disappeared out the door.

The Grouse hated his nickname but we never called him anything else. He must have warmed to it because he made up a rhyme that became well known in the area. John loved to recite it to the children. He'd put on his best sinister voice and say, very slowly, 'Lock them doors and bolt them tight: The Grouse McCabe's in Rhode tonight.'

'Stop it, Daddy, you're scarin' us. Talk properly.'

'I'm not your daddy, I'm – Jack McCabe!'

'Mammy!' they'd scream. 'Tell him to stop.'

'John, stop teasin' them,' I'd say, 'you're terrifyin' the life out of them.'

The Grouse was clever enough. He made a living doing a variety of jobs, picking potatoes and selling turf. John told me that The Grouse used to go over to Scotland every year for the potato picking. This one year he came back via Dublin on the same day a crowd from Rhode were in the city for a football match. They'd spotted The Grouse on O'Connell Bridge and shouted, 'Grouse! Grouse!'

The Grouse stopped and looked all around, but couldn't see who was shouting his name. 'I can't see ya but there's a whore from Rhode here somewhere!' he said.

Bord na Mona decided to reduce John's hours in the bog. The money he earned was now barely enough to feed us and pay the twelve shillings a week rent for the rat-infested house. And I found out I was expecting for the sixth time. With the cut in pay, it was time to cut and run. John thought he would have better prospects of work and good pay in England. This time he went on his own. I would follow with the children when he had found the work and a place for us to live.

He left for England in May 1959 and got a two-month contract with John Laing's construction firm, which was building a stretch of the new M1 motorway. He earned good money and was able to send me five pounds in a letter every week. Two months later one of John's letters not only included money but an invitation to come and join him. Mammy was unhappy that I was taking the children away again, and to England of all places. She never liked anyone going to 'that ol' pagan country' but that's where the work was. Anna and Carmel had both settled there.

The children were breathless with excitement the day they helped me pack up our things. I put my treasured bits and pieces – all my wedding presents, including a china tea set and four holy pictures, the children's winter togs and bed linen – in two tea chests. When people knew you were moving they knew you wouldn't be taking your furniture. I sold most of ours to Martin Groome.

The day we sailed for 'that ol' pagan country', I was a thirty-one-year-old mother-of-five covered in pregnancy freckles. The two tea chests went as cargo and I carried the two suitcases, and a holdall for nappies and creams for baby Carmel, and Ellen carried a smaller case, the one with the little light things in it. We wore our summery clothes for the July heat and queued with all the other passengers waiting for the barrier to open. I was carrying Carmel in my arms so Ellen took charge of the others. She was the gaffer. They all gathered around her and travelled like a little troupe, squealing with excitement to be going on their first boat trip. Every fare was paid for; in the years to come, when I wasn't able to afford the passage, I would only pay for two children and send the others ahead of me, pretending they belonged to someone else! We got away with it every time.

By the time we docked at Liverpool for the boat train on that first journey, I had washed all the children, got them out of their travelling clothes and into fresh ones. I was mortified when baby Carmel left her trademark on a bench before we disembarked. I'd been in the toilet rinsing her shitty nappy. When I went back to our seat, Ellen shouted at the top of her voice, 'She's done it again, Mammy! She's shat herself!' The scutter had smeared the bench. I wondered how quickly I could change her again and get off the boat without anybody seeing me. Ellen marshalled her brothers and sisters like a teacher out on a school trip. She was just something else. I can still see her helping me get the children on and off the train. I got down with Carmel and then she followed with Olive.

'Wait there, Seamus, I'll be comin' back for ya,' Ellen instructed. She was very businesslike. Ellen was a brilliant child.

We caught the boat train from Liverpool, changing at Crewe, and arrived in Birmingham – minus my two tea chests. They got lost somewhere along the journey and I never saw them again. I was devastated: everything I owned and cherished was in those chests.

'No Blacks, No Dogs, No Irish'

I caught up with John in Birmingham sharing a bed with a man called Christy Kenny. There was nothing funny going on. Christy was Anna and Larry's lodger, and John had hooked up with them in their one-bedroom flat in Aston (John and Larry had patched up their differences). As Christy worked nights, John would use his bed for the night and Christy would get into it in the morning after John got up. When I arrived with the children, we all shared Christy's room. But that couldn't go on for ever.

We soon found out just how hard it was going to be to find a place to live. English people didn't want us in their homes or in their neighbourhoods because we were Irish. Houses proudly displayed their offensive notices – 'No Blacks, No Dogs, No Irish'. We couldn't get past the door of any English landlord. They wouldn't all be so rude or blatant about their prejudice. 'Sorry, me luv,' they would say, in their thick Brummie accents, 'we ain't got room for all them kids.'

We pounded up and down terraced streets but the story was the same. There was no room at the inn. And finding work was no easier. Many factories displayed equally discouraging signs stating 'No Irish Need Apply'. It was so belittling. It made us feel as though we weren't worthy of a job and that we weren't human beings. We were good enough to dig their roads and rebuild their houses after the war but not good enough to work in the factories. It used to infuriate us.

We found a place to rent in the basement of a large Victorian house owned by a Mr Singh. It was advertised for 'a family of four' so we had to pretend we only had two children, and sneak the other three in after dark. We had to take the children up to breakfast in pairs, starting with the two youngest, hoping nobody would notice that the children were different each time.

Along with an army of rats, mice and cockroaches, we shared the cellar with Christy and his mother Mrs Kenny. She wasn't well and didn't speak much. John called her Mrs Forty Coats because in winter she wore three or four coats at the same time with another one over her head.

I liked having Christy Kenny around. He was my greatest ally during the rough times with John. He was always there, seeing what was going on, but he would never pass remarks or gossip to other people. 'Did ya hear that old bastard last night, Christy?' I would say. Christy would just nod. 'I never got a wink of sleep listenin' to him.' And he would nod again, in agreement.

Christy never said very much but he had a distinctive way of speaking. He used to say 'sclissors' instead of scissors and 'shlears' instead of shears. His mother spoke the very same way. She would call the Co-op the 'Cul-lop'. Christy was comical. He came with me to the Cul-lop once, a few weeks before I was due to give birth. I gave him a terrible fright at the checkout when I said, 'I've got terrible pains, Christy.'

'For Chlrist slake! Don't have it here! Wait until tomorrow,' he said, terrified that I was about to give birth on the Co-op floor. He rushed me outside to get me on the bus.

Christy shared John's passion for the pub. He wasn't abusive in drink but he was a terrible nuisance. I remember the night he won a few pounds on the horses and went to the pub for a few drinks on the winnings. John came in laughing his big thumping laugh telling me what Christy was after doing.

John said, 'He walked straight into a lamp post and he said, "Excluse me Mliss." He thought it was a lady he was after runnin' into!'

Christy was *stocious*. He stood in the kitchen with two hands in his pockets, swaying and jingling his change, still laughing about the lamp post. He noticed a joint of lean boiled bacon cooling on the table.

'Clut me a bit of mleat, Maura,' he said.

'I'm moppin' the floor, Christy.'

'Sure, then I'll clut it meshlelf.'

I carried on mopping while Christy cut the meat. I wanted to mop under the table but he wouldn't step out of the way. 'Move out thc way, Christy,' I said.

He refused to move so I gave him a skelp around the legs with the mop. 'Ouch, Jlaysus,' he shouted. 'I clut me flinger!'

'And I'll cut the bloody head off ya if you don't leave that meat alone.'

He'd got blood all over it. I had to chuck the lot in the bin.

Christy was more like a brother than a friend. He was always around me, especially when I was cooking. John never was jealous of him. They got on well together. I'd cook and he'd sit with John, doing his crossword – John with his *Daily Mail* and Christy with the *Daily Mirror*.

'I don't read that load of shlite; that's a rag,' Christy would say.

'Ah, Christy, it's not what ya read, it's what you understand that's important,' John would reply, proudly, as he threw open the tabloid with outstretched arms in front of his nose.

Christy would do anything for me. I trusted him with my life. If the children were sick, he would go to the doctor with them; if I had to go to the hospital, he would be at my side; if I needed to go the shops, he would come with me and help me with the *messages*.

Mrs Kenny was just as obliging. She'd help me take the children to the public baths on Victoria Road for their weekly dip. We didn't have use of a bathroom so the children had to trot down the road with their towels tucked under their arms. We didn't have use of the indoor toilet either. Below stairs people weren't allowed to use the bathroom on the floor above us.

Most of the other tenants were black or Asian. I hadn't seen too many black people before I moved to Birmingham. I was fascinated by the little black children walking with their parents, especially on a Sunday, with their hair parted in rows of plaits along their heads. I was transfixed by their perfectly even white teeth and the strange sucking noises they made through pursed lips. I didn't understand what the sucking meant, or why they ran away sniggering afterwards. I came over very raw from Ireland where you hardly ever saw a black person.

Years later I worked as a cleaner in Dudley Road Hospital and shared a corridor with a sweet, polite black woman called Bernice. I liked Bernice but the way she worked infuriated me. There she would be, dragging her brush behind her in no particular hurry. She'd sweep a bit here, drag it a bit further, and sweep a bit there. She was so slow! I'd be breaking my back to get the cleaning done. If she heard anybody coming she would put the brush in front of her and sweep properly.

Then one day she called me to the kitchen. 'Why do you work so hard, woman?'

'What do ya mean?'

Bernice grinned all over her soft, beautiful face and then began to chuckle until her rather large frame wobbled with laughter. 'Ah b'wana, you take these t'ings to 'eart,' she said. 'Why? You crazy or sometin'? You wanna kill yerself or sometin'?'

'I'm just tryin' to get the job done,' I said.

'White people are foolish. You know dey make busy wid work, especially dey Irish, feisty I call dem.'

Bernice walked away sucking her teeth and gurgling to herself, looking back at me standing with my mouth open. I understood her bitterness and I liked her rebellious attitude. I think the black and Irish got on well together because we were all employed in the same menial tasks; we weren't offered anything much higher than cleaning. We were all poor and working class and treated as brainless nonentities.

John and I were no different to the majority of Irish people who lived in damp, cramped conditions sharing toilets and kitchens.

We were still relying on the benevolence of others when Mammy wrote to me telling me the council was building new cottages in Clonmore. She had 'put in for one' on my behalf and got it. I didn't want the cottage anyway because it was beside a family of blacksmiths. We went to school with their children but we never liked them. As children we thought they were beneath us because they always looked sooty and black. It was a silly, childish notion but we thought they had no class. Of course, they were just ordinary people and probably better off.

After all Mammy's efforts to get the cottage, I wrote back and told her I didn't want it because we were trying to settle in England and our prospects were better. She was raging. She wrote me a letter saying, 'After I going and getting you the cottage and now you won't even come home. Wouldn't I love to have you living near me? And I would share my food with you and a bit of turf. What would you be wanting to be stay in that old pagan country for when I have you a lovely cottage here?'

Mammy never wanted her children to leave Clonmore. She wanted to keep her clutch around her for as long as she could. She would rather we stayed around her and struggled. She was the matriarch and wanted us to do as she bid. She wasn't allowing me to grow up. She would have preferred for me to follow in her footsteps and be a good strong Catholic, drudging here and there. But my stubbornness and pride gave me an inner strength to do what I thought was best, and not what Mammy thought was best.

I always had the notion that I wanted to better myself and reach the heights. It was always my intention to get a house of my own and have a key to my own front door, so I continued my habit of putting some money away each week. John was earning a good bit of money at Dunlop by now, and he wasn't going out drinking and spending it all. My first wage from him was eleven pounds a week. Ten years earlier I worked two months sweating on my hands and knees scrubbing floors for that very sort of money. I couldn't believe how well off we were. I was determined to rise up out of the gutter.

The twinges of pain began at nine in the morning and carried on all day. This can't be the day the child's arriving? I thought. It was Christmas Day. Anna was living next door by now so I was preparing our dinner and keeping an eye on her turkey as well. Anna and Larry were working in a pub off the Lichfield Road so there was I, waddling across to their flat, basting their turkey, waddling back over to our flat and basting my own.

I had everything sorted; the turkey was carved and the dinners were dished. Christy and John walked in just as I sat down. I was about to tuck in to my sprouts when the pain became unbearable. Then Anna arrived back from the pub. When she realised the state I was in, she couldn't believe I was after running up and down the fourteen steps between the two ovens.

She stayed with me until my GP, Dr Brewster, and the midwife arrived. After an agonising twelve-hour labour, my new baby boy, Declan, was born. The children were delighted by the present delivered to them on Christmas Day. Declan would be the first of my three Christmas Day babies, and the first of my children to be born outside Ireland.

Declan spent most of his young life in and out of hospital. He got a chill when he was three weeks old. When the cold cleared up, his ears started to trouble him. His poor ears were full of pus. It was like liquid corruption and stank to high heaven. The pain must have been something shocking.

When he was admitted to the children's hospital, I caught the bus out to him every day in time for his two o'clock feed. I would hold him in my arms and feed him from a bottle while his ears were raging. I felt so sorry for him, the way he was always rubbing his red ears against my arm.

Dr Brewster persuaded me to send Declan to a cottage hospital in Stratford-upon-Avon to give me a break. Poor Declan stayed there for nine months. I was traumatised going down there to see him. I would trek down to Stratford on the Midland Red bus every Sunday, often taking Ellen or Breda with me. That was tough going. I missed out on his first steps and his first words, and he missed out on a mother's love and nurturing. That upsets me even now. Declan was always upset. I can still see him, with his long curly hair, pacing the cot. He was in so much pain he would be crying and pacing, pacing and crying. I didn't know what to do with him. I used to put my arms around him and kiss him before I left but when I walked away he would cry, 'Me go, Mamma, me go?' That used to kill me. It still rips my heart. He was only a little baby.

By the time he came home I had given birth to Geraldine, my second Christmas Day baby. I always expected her to be musical: she came into the world with reggae music booming from a flat upstairs. Dr Brewster had been in attendance again. John was walking around the room smiling. 'Is everythin' all right, Doctor?' he asked.

'Yes, John, you have another fine baby. A little girl.'

'Another Christmas box,' John said.

'I think you should make sure this is the last one.'

'Ah, it's the will of God, Doctor. It's the will of God.'

'Well, it's time to cut the will of God out of you!' said Dr Brewster. John laughed.

Geraldine was the most beautiful child. I chose Christy to be her godfather and his mother was her godmother. He took on a fatherly role with her and would sit and play games with her for hours. He took her everywhere with him. If there was anything going on in the park, he made sure Geraldine was there. He was brilliant with her. Christy adored that child.

I always found Geraldine difficult, especially as a baby. I was near demented from lack of sleep listening to her continual crying. She was worse than Breda. I thought there was something wrong with her. She had a permanent sore on her forehead from constantly banging her head off the side of her cot. She was always at it. She would bang her head on anything nearby, the cot, the wall or the fireplace. I tried to stop her by lying her on her back on the floor but she would just turn over and bang her head on the floor. I thought it might have been boredom. Giving her a toy to play with seemed to distract her. Maybe with Declan being so ill Geraldine didn't get the love she needed.

The banging lasted three years and stopped as suddenly as it started. She became a playful little girl who made up stories about her fairy friends at the bottom of the garden. She was just a lovely little thing. She had two plaits and she was very petite. She was a bright child and so alert she reminded me of a meerkat. If she heard a noise she would look around her with her chin in the air and her sparkling blue eyes darting. She was particularly intrigued by the rain: if we had a heavy shower, she would watch the water seeping into the flat through the basement window.

Dr Brewster was shocked that we were living in such cramped, damp conditions and said the cellar wasn't fit for a family of nine. He wrote to the council on our behalf and asked them to consider us for a council house. He put our names down on the housing register but they decided we had insufficient points to qualify. We hadn't lived in the country long enough and were not, therefore, 'a priority case'.

I found city types standoffish. They looked down on us because we had big families. When the housing officers came round to look at the cellar, they were amazed to see so many children. It was as if they were saying, 'Does that one ever get out of the bed?' like we were having sex all the time. We weren't. We were Irish Catholics, we obeyed the Church and we had big families. Still, we were not a 'priority case'.

THIRTEEN

Don't Wake Me at Doyles

'My God, you're getting very strong, Maura!' The nurse walked in as I was trying to hide the unsightly heavy suitcase underneath the bed, pushing with my feet.

'Isn't that great, Nurse. I'm feelin' much better.'

'Here, let me give you a hand with that,' she said.

Breda and Geraldine had dropped it off on their way to the airport. They were the last to fly back to England. I was sad to say goodbye to them but at least I was leaving hospital and could look forward to a change of scenery.

I sat alone waiting for the ambulance to take me to the nursing home, thinking about what I would do when I eventually got back to Rhode and how I longed to sleep in my own bed and return to my normal life.

The door opened, interrupting my thoughts. Dr O'Connell and his team came in. They had gloomy faces. The consultant sat on my bed; the others stood around it.

'Good morning, Mrs Murphy, and how are you feeling today?' he asked politely.

'Not too bad, Doctor.'

'Well, I've some good news and some bad news.' What a

strange thing to say, I thought. Perhaps I'm not going to the nursing home after all.

'Well, let me have the bad news first.'

'The *good* news, Mrs Murphy, is that we've found the cause of your bleeding.'

I said nothing. So it's not about the nursing home.

'The bad news is, we have found a tumour on your lung.'

Still, I said nothing.

'It is operable,' he continued. 'I don't think it's cancerous but we can't rule that out. You'll be transferred into the hands of Mr Luke and his team who'll talk you through your options. He'll come and see you later this afternoon.'

Cancer? He just said cancer. Oh, good Jesus! 'So I have cancer?'

'No,' he said emphatically, 'you have a tumour with the *potential* of becoming cancerous.'

I didn't feel reassured. Cancer was the word that stuck in my mind. 'We'll do everything in our power to make you well again, Mrs Murphy.'

'Doctor, does that mean I'm not goin' to the nursin' home?'

'Well, I would still like you to get some rest. You've been through a difficult time. It would be better if you went home to be with your family. But when Mr Luke sees you everything could change: it'll be his decision.'

He wished me luck, and left the room.

I was in complete and total shock. I have cancer, I thought. Oh my God, I have cancer. He called it a tumour but I just kept thinking of cancer. That brief conversation knocked the stuffing out of me. I couldn't believe it. It was too much for me to take in. I'd given up smoking ten years earlier so why did I have a tumour? I sat in a daze, numbed by the awful news. I felt so alone, and so angry. Why me?

Cancer.

The word was all I could think about. Time just stopped. I couldn't move and I couldn't speak. I just kept thinking.

Cancer.

Cancer was the last thing I expected. I felt so isolated. How could the doctors have got it so wrong all these weeks? I had 'no cancer, TB or tumour'. That's what they told me and I believed them. I had no pain, so why wouldn't I believe them? The children were gone, I was about to be discharged, my case was packed and the ambulance was on its way to take me to the nursing home. I was even planning a holiday – when I was strong enough – to visit my grandchildren in Birmingham. Now all my plans would have to change.

I phoned John. He was speechless. He must have contacted Joan straightaway because she phoned me within twenty minutes. She wanted to fly over immediately.

'No way, don't come yet,' I said. 'Let's wait for some more news.' Discussions were going on between the doctors and surgeons about the best treatment. Joan was adamant. She was coming and that was that.

An hour later two medical students came in to see me. They wanted to ask me questions about my illness. I couldn't think of anything to say. Why did they pick on me after I've just had this terrible bad news? I didn't want to be answering any of their questions. I sat staring into space, wishing they'd go away. I just wanted to be by myself, to be left in peace to cry. But I couldn't cry. Even after they'd left my room, the tears wouldn't come.

All I could see was death staring me in the face. I didn't want to die; I wasn't ready. How could I leave my children? I needed to see my grandchildren grow up. That was my job. I was only seventy. Surely I had more years ahead of me? How could I have cancer? I hoped the doctors had made a terrible mistake, that it wasn't me but someone else.

I wished it was someone else.

Joan
Wed 7 July: 3.00 p.m. Phoned Olive at work to tell her about

Mommy. She started to cry. Met her in Rackhams for a coffee. Breda and Geraldine were at Dublin Airport on their way home. We decided to call the airport and let them know in case they wanted to stay on.

Wed 7 July: 10.00 p.m. I'm back in Ireland. Mommy was depressed, waiting for a CAT scan. But now she is chatty and thoughtful after a big meal.

Breda

Mummy's got a tumour. Thank God for that. They've said it. They've finally got there. They're saying it's a tumour with the potential to be cancerous. Don't be so stupid, the fucking thing's bleeding. It's active. Something is happening.

I feel relieved but why did it take them so long to diagnose a tumour? It's been six weeks. In that time, it could have done all sorts of things and spread in all sorts of ways. I feel really sorry for Mummy. She'll be really worried but everything's going to be okay.

Geraldine

How irresponsible of the hospital! We've been with Mommy all that time and they tell her about her tumour when she's on her own. They didn't even wait for Daddy to be there and he's her next of kin. It must have been terrifying for her.

Breda and I were making our way home. After checking in at Dublin Airport, I heard an announcement over the Tannoy. 'This is a customer announcement. Could Breda Groves or Geraldine Murphy please pick up the nearest courtesy phone.'

We were put through to Joan and Olive. They told us Mommy had, in fact, got a tumour and that she would have to be oper-ated on. Shocked, and knowing how anxious Mommy would be, I said, 'Breda, do you think we should go back to the hospital?'

Breda took control, telling me that as I had checked in I should make my way home where I had responsibilities to my

own children, who were waiting for me. We'd make separate
arrangements to go back again.

Not sure if it was the right thing to do. After all, it was only
a bus journey over to the hospital. Maybe we should have stayed?
I felt sick at the thought of Mommy lying there alone and so
helpless. I didn't know what to do for the best. I decided to
continue home with guilt, dread and fear as my companions.

Carmel

Olive rang me. She was crying and she said, 'It's cancer. It's cancer.
They told us it wasn't and it is. She's going to die, oh my God.'

She was very upset; I just went to pieces. I can't face the
prospect of Mom dying. I can't bear to think that she might die
with none of us around her.

I was spitting anger. I had to undergo a whole new set of tests.
The registrar told me I had a nasty growth on the upper left lobe
and that the top part of the lung would be removed completely.
I would 'tolerate the operation and manage'; my previous heart
attack would make surgery more dangerous.

I felt feeble. The nurses helped me to the phone whenever it
rang. I bawled to everyone who called.

I hear everyone was praying for me and having Masses said
and candles lit. There was a special Mass said for me in Rhode.
I placed my complete trust in the Sacred Heart, Our Lady of
Lourdes and the surgeons. Please God I'd be okay.

Joan

Thurs 8 July: I asked the doctor what kind of cancer it is. He
said rather firmly, 'I don't want to call it cancer at this stage. I
will call it a lung tumour with the potential to become cancerous.'
This gave us – Mommy, Daddy and me – some hope and our
spirits lifted.

The surgeon's registrar called in to talk to Mommy. He was in his late twenties and very casually dressed, like he had just popped in. He didn't sit down but leaned, nonchalantly, against the wall. We took an instant dislike to each other. I don't think he liked my questions and note-taking and I didn't like his offhand, superior attitude. Still, I wasn't there to dislike and he obviously knew his stuff.

He asked Mommy if she had had any previous surgery. When she told him about her heart attack, ten years ago, he looked surprised. We were shocked that he didn't know. What if they'd gone ahead without knowing?

My surgeon had a posh English accent and frighteningly big hands. He had the hands of a goalkeeper, not a surgeon. Surely there was no room for his huge hands poking around inside me? How on earth would those maulers perform intricate surgery? I started to have second thoughts about the operation. I considered chemotherapy or radiation, but surgery gave me the best odds.

John and Joan were with me when the surgeon stormed into my room. He explained how serious my condition was, without looking at any of us. He was like an actor gazing beyond the audience at an imaginary face at the back of the auditorium. I suppose he was performing a routine task. He'd done it all and seen it all before. But it wasn't routine for me.

He used the words 'imperative' and 'serious' and told me he needed to operate immediately. I was booked in for the following Tuesday.

'I understood that I would be goin' home for a couple of weeks.'

'No! I want you in straightaway. This needs to be done as an emergency.'

John stood at the end of my bed, with his hands on the table, looking sorrowful and concerned. 'You'll be all right, Maura. It has to be done now. It'll all work out. You're in the right hands and we'll look after ya.'

'And what would you know about it?' I snapped. 'You've never had a bit of sickness in your life.' I didn't want to hear his platitudes. The closest John came to experiencing pain was waiting for Doyles' doors to open.

John reacted in his usual hot-tempered way. 'I'm gettin' out of here. I'm only tryin' to help.' He stopped at the door, composed himself and sat back down. He didn't say another word.

I knew he would try his best to look after me but I remembered all those times he didn't support me and how he walked away whenever I was ill. He should have known I was angry and confused. For God's sake, I'd just been told I was having part of my lung removed. I was thinking, this is it. This is the way that I'm going to die – on a goddamn operating table. I wanted him to give me time to work through my feelings.

When Olive arrived she was speechless. They were all speechless. My children had no words of comfort. Olive went home to the cottage with Seamus and her daddy, and Joan slept on the floor beside my bed. She knew I would be sad and scared and she stayed to listen to my upset and fears. I told myself I must be strong and positive.

John

Fri 9 July: There is an atmosphere that something terrible is going to happen to Maura. The children can be talking about the tumour, and then suddenly someone will break down and cry. They all try to console each other. Someone has to take the lead and say everything is going to be all right. I tried to console Maura but she lashed out at me when I said, 'It will be all right.' She asked me how would I know. I had no idea. And she was right – I hadn't.

Maura is angry towards me. She always has to be angry. If there's anything wrong, the blame is cast on me. She can't accept the fact that I think so much of her. The sort Maura is, she would rather I didn't go near her at all so that she can have something to complain about. My gut feeling is that she would prefer me to walk out the door instead of going over to her to be nice. She always says, 'That smile's only from the teeth out.' Maura always passed judgement on me, telling me what was on her mind and what she thought. I didn't mind at all that she was sharp because I would be half expecting it. I understand Maura. I know her so well. She would say, 'You never knew me at all,' but you couldn't live with someone for forty-six years without knowing some of their ways.

She was bound to blame me for this illness, as she had all the others. But I didn't tell her to smoke forty Player's a day. Actually, I remember telling her to give them up because she smoked too much. But her answer was, 'Ya want to take away the only pleasure I have left!'

Joan

Mommy's surgeon is enormous: must be over 6 foot eight. Mommy didn't like him one bit. He's a rather aloof, stuffy Brit. He said that, although it was an odd thing to say, she was 'lucky' that the bleeding started because now they know she has a 'nasty tumour', and because they found it early it can be operated on.

Mommy is very depressed. Daddy was trying to console her by saying positive things but she shouted at him. Instead of taking it on the chin, and understanding her state of mind, he got hurt and got up to leave. He changed his mind and stayed in the room and sulked. I suppose he just doesn't know what to do. But being quiet and letting her do all the feeling is the only possible answer. Chivvying her certainly isn't.

I was glad when Daddy left. Mommy could speak about her fears and anger. Daddy seemed pissed off with me. Oh well, it seems part of my role in this family is to be in the firing line. I sometimes get a bit of flak from the others. I suppose I was taking executive decisions and this annoyed some people, particularly Breda and Daddy. But I thought, take your annoyance *elsewhere. Deal with it. There's no time for niceties. Mommy's the issue at hand. Doing everything by committee is very time consuming.*

Sat 10 July: Daddy didn't come to the hospital today. Mommy is really pissed off with him because he went to Doyles.

Joan and Olive sat with me on Monday not saying very much: they didn't know how to cope with my anger. Suddenly, John burst in through the door, all smiles, wearing a bright yellow jumper and grinning from ear to ear as though the world was a beautiful, happy place. Oh fuck off, you stupid bastard, I thought.

I couldn't stop thinking about that day in 1953 when I married him, and the life that followed: his regime of control and intimidation, his fondness for alcohol, and the verbal, emotional and physical abuse I endured when he had a drink in him. I was fierce angry that day, sitting on the side of the bed, swinging my skinny 'hospital legs', sobbing and feeling unloved and misunderstood. All those years of illness came flooding into my mind. And now I blamed them all on John. I thought that's it. If I survive this illness, I'm leaving you. You won't have to listen to me accusing you of not understanding me. I'll be gone.

I looked at Joan and Olive. 'When I die, I want to be cremated. I don't want to be left rottin' in the ground in a cold graveyard, fodder for the worms, where no one will visit me.'

I had a vision of being in my coffin in Rhode, with a party going full swing around me, and everyone pretending to feel sorry for my children's loss. I imagined John with a pint in his hand.

'When I die, I want to be waked at home,' I said angrily, 'in my own house, in my own bed, with all my children around me.'

I'd had the worst news of my life and all I could think of now was the crowd of people eating and drinking at Doyles.

Olive said nothing. John kept his head bowed.

'Don't wake me at Doyles,' I spat. 'I don't want anyone

pretendin' to care about me. I don't want any of those hypocrites drinkin' with my children, not after all the hardship I've had to take because of that cursed-God pub.'

Some people couldn't care if you're alive or dead but they wouldn't miss your funeral, chewing the feet off the statues in the chapel and looking for free sandwiches for their false sympathy. As soon as you die, the chapel's packed to capacity, and people saying, 'Oh, wasn't she lovely; didn't she make a beautiful corpse; what a dacent one she was.' When you're alive they don't even think about visiting.

They party at your wake whether they know you or not. The last place I wanted to be remembered was in a public house, with a few curly sandwiches washed down with oceans of porter. I didn't want the inevitable funeral fistfight because some member of the family isn't speaking to the other. I didn't want that. Oh no.

Joan said, 'You must feel terrible, Mom.'

'If yous want to have a small gatherin', with a few genuine friends, have a small party at home. There are plenty of bottles in the tin box and cut glass in the cabinet. Use them, it may be the only chance you'll have.'

'Okay. Whatever you want,' Joan said.

John

Mon 12 July: Maura said, 'If I die I don't want yous comin' up the road shedding false tears.'

I wanted to say, 'You can laugh without wanting to laugh because you can put it on but you can't cry without meaning it.' But I didn't say it. I just kept quiet.

Maura never spoke to me about what she would want if she died. She never told me where she wanted to be buried, Rhode or Castlejordan. It seems to me that she never thought she was going to die. We never talked about wills or wakes or burials. Maybe she knew that I would say, 'Maura, whatever you want

to do you do it. I don't want to make any clauses here or there.'
But she never discussed anything like that with me.

Joan

Mommy is in a very depressed mood today. Hardly surprising.
There was a very dark atmosphere in her room. She really hates
Daddy today. He isn't helping by sitting around looking all sorry
for himself. I wish he would go for a walk or ask for a lift home.

Mommy hardly spoke all morning. Then some time in the
early afternoon, after not eating her lunch, she sat on the side
of her bed, crying, her feet dangling, and she said she wanted
to be cremated when she dies. Didn't want to be left rotting in
the ground.

After a torturously long pause she said she didn't want to be
waked at Doyles. We all hung our heads. The silence lasted for
hours.

FOURTEEN

Bailiffs at Bevington Road

I was heavily pregnant when the eviction letter arrived. Bevington Road was the first home we had ever owned but we'd fallen so far behind with the mortgage payments that Birmingham City Council was ordering us to vacate.

We had moved into the house two years earlier with such optimism for our future – now it was going terribly wrong.

The morning the bailiffs came, I was alone with the children. John had gone out to buy a newspaper and hadn't returned. I tried to stop him: I didn't want to face eviction on my own.

'John, I want you here with me.'

'I'll be back,' he said. I knew he wouldn't be. It was customary for him to disappear when there was trouble.

Ellen and Breda were at school. Joan, my eighth born, was asleep in her pram and the others were in the breakfast room when the doorbell rang. Seamus, Olive, Declan and Geraldine trotted behind me with their toast in their hands when I answered the door. Olive was tugging at my skirt. When I opened the door, two muscular men forced their way in.

'There is no necessity to break in. You can walk in. You're scarin' the children,' I said.

The one with fair hair and a red face spoke. 'We're the bailiffs. We've been sent to empty this 'ouse and lock it up.'

'Well, get on with it then,' I said coldly.

We never would have owned our home if it wasn't for Dr Brewster. He was so appalled by the damp, dark cellar that he gave me money towards the deposit for a house. He did it out of pure kindness and generosity. It wasn't even a loan. It was a gift. It happened during one of his many visits to see Declan. I'd noticed Dr Brewster staring at my stomach. 'Good gracious, Mrs Murphy!' he said, in his gentle Scottish accent. 'You're not pregnant again, are you?'

'Yes I am, actually.'

'The conditions here are too damp for another baby. We'll have to do something about it.'

And do something about it, he did. Dr Brewster gave me fifty pounds towards the deposit and told me to start looking for a house immediately. I was very shocked but I didn't mind the handout. It was a way of getting out of our squalid flat. He was already giving me money to pay for my prescriptions. He spoke to me as a friend rather than a patient. I'd never had that sort of a relationship with a doctor before.

Bevington Road was perfect. It backed on to a park, had an indoor loo and bathroom, three big bedrooms, a breakfast room and a cellar. An antique wardrobe and a piano were thrown in with the price.

Before long we started taking in a string of lodgers, all Irish. The men came over from Ireland to work on the building sites. Bevington Road was a stopgap while they were looking for somewhere else to live. They would give in so much money a week for food and I would cook it for them. At one point we had eight children and eight lodgers all living under the same roof. It was a tight fit. We had to give one bedroom and the downstairs front room to our paying guests. I can't imagine where we put the children. Christy Kenny was always there too. He would come in to me for his dinner most days.

My lodgers were all very amiable lads but John was forever trying to rise rows with them when he was drunk. There were plenty of pubs for him to drink in; there were more pubs than churches. He was always propping up the bar of some sleazy hole and was seldom home before the pubs closed. Then he'd turn up with his drinking pals demanding bacon and sausages. I used to have to give them the few rashers I was after buying for the weekend. Even if I was in bed dozing, John would expect me to get up and cook. Because he wouldn't carry a door key, I never felt free to go to bed and sleep soundly. He expected me to stay awake and open the door for him whatever time he decided to roll home.

I would usually make sure I had some work to do. I was in a permanent state of tiredness. Saturday night was my busiest. Because there was no heating, I would have the tin bath in front of the coal fire in the wintertime. I'd fill it with saucepans of boiled water and all the children shared the one bath. As one got out, and before the next one got in, I'd throw in another saucepan of hot water.

The children would go to bed with scrubbed angelic faces ready for Mass the next morning. Then I'd polish their shoes and line them up under the kitchen table, in order of size, and stuff their socks inside each shoe so the children had nothing to do, only put them on. The next day we'd hoof it up to St Patrick's and pile into one pew together, my children and me. They'd usually sit together in order of age and height but if they played up I'd keep the naughty ones next to me. I'd give one of them the thruppence to put on the collection plate. I remember Declan once exchanged his thruppence for a sixpence and put it in his pocket. He took it off the plate because it was shiny!

It was hard going getting eight children ready for Sunday Mass. I could be up till two in the morning ironing their clothes and polishing their shoes; I'd be exhausted and in no mood for John when he came in making his drunken accusations about nothing. There would be a row every weekend and that would spark a panic in me, and scare the lives out of the children. I never knew where it would lead but the lodgers usually managed to calm the situation. That was more or less why I liked having them in the house, and they were good to the children.

Carmel was the lodgers' favourite and she often took advantage of them. One day Christy came home with a few drinks in him. He was telling me about a good win he had on the horses. Carmel overheard and decided to tap him for some pocket money.

'Can I have crupence, Christy?' she asked, her palm out expectantly.

'Sure I haven't got thlrupence, Carmel.'

She thought hard for a second. 'Well, can I have sispence then?'

'Sure I haven't got slixpence.'

'Well then give me a shillin',' she demanded.

'I can't give you any money, Carmel. I haven't two ha'pence to rub together.'

Carmel was only four years old and didn't understand the value of money. Christy did. He knew that if he gave money to one, he'd have to give to all.

The lodgers were always very pleasant and respectful of me. They minded their manners. But one beautiful summer's evening, after visiting Luke and Maudie with Ellen and Breda, I came back to a houseful of people all drinking and smoking and making a kip out of my home. The smell of beer and cigarettes was something shocking. All the lodgers, and Anna's husband Larry, were there drinking. The breakfast room table was full of bottles and five or six blokes I'd never seen before were sitting there, drunk.

'Mammy, who are all those people?' Ellen whispered to me.

'They're Daddy's friends,' Breda whispered back.

'Come on, we'll go upstairs and get yous ready for bed,' I said.

Then I noticed two women standing up against the wall and three more by the fireplace. I didn't know who they were but they looked like brazen hussies to me.

'What the hell's goin' on here?' I demanded.

'Please, Mammy, don't say anything,' Breda said anxiously.

'I'll say what I want in my own house,' I snapped.

'Shall I clean up the mess, Mammy?' Ellen offered.

'No, maybe your father would like to do it. It's his mess.'

Then the row started. 'Who are those women, John?'

'Friends.'

'What are they doin' here?'

'They're only havin' a drink, Maura.'

'Why are they comin' here to drink? Why didn't they stay in the pub?'

'They're just a few friends havin' a drink.'

'They might be your friends but they're not mine. I don't know these people and I don't want them here. Get rid of them!'

John made no attempt to ask them to leave so I walked up to two of them.

'Who are yous and who gave yous permission to come in here?'

'*He* did,' one said, nodding towards John.

'Well, yous can just get out. I don't want yous in my house. You've no business comin' in here, drinkin' and keepin' my children awake. Yous lot get out of here before I come back down the stairs.'

I knew I would be in for it after putting John's friends out of the house. As I took Ellen and Breda upstairs to bed, John came after me.

'Oh, God, Daddy's comin',' cried Breda.

'How dare you?' he said. 'Who do ya think you are, puttin' people out of my house?'

It was *his* house; nothing belonged to me in John's eyes. He raised his hand to hit me on the side of the head but Larry stopped him. 'Don't do that, John. Don't hit her,' he pleaded.

I remember Ellen being very frightened that night; if Breda was bothered, she didn't show it. When I got them upstairs, I noticed Ellen was trembling. I went over to her bed and put my arms around the two of them. They were scared there would be a big row. When I went to go back downstairs, Breda came over to me at the door, with her two hands clasped under her chin, and said, 'Don't say anything, will you, Mammy? Don't say anything.'

John didn't intend to frighten the children but he couldn't control himself in those tempers, and he wouldn't realise the impact he was having on them. There were times when he didn't even notice they were there. I liked to involve them in my life. If I was doing a load of washing, I'd let them wash a sock each; if we went shopping, I'd let them pay for groceries, making sure they counted their change; if I baked bread, I'd let them bake bread. They made their own miniature ones, babby loaves. It was my way of making them feel important. They'd have the shite kneaded out of them and the loaves would come out of the oven more like biscuits. But I would say, 'Aren't you the best little children in the world, able to bake bread?'

'Can I eat mine now, Mammy?' Declan would ask.

'No, pet, wait till they cool down.'

'I'm keeping mine to take to school tomorrow,' Geraldine usually announced.

Our house always smelt of baking. Scones, apple pies and soda bread – when I'd have the wheaten meal to make it – would be on the go every day. Olive always had her nose stuck in a bowl. When she got older, we became a great cake-making team, particularly at Christmas. We made cakes to sell and would charge eight pounds for each one. We could have orders for up to twenty cakes so we'd have to start baking in September. I baked the cakes and Olive helped with the marzipan, the icing and the decorations. I'd watch in amazement as she measured and rolled the marzipan perfectly, never a bit wasted.

I enjoyed the children's company; I didn't need other people's.

I never had any interests. I didn't have John's hectic hilarious life. I don't want to give the impression that I was a martyr but I took my life as a married woman, and a mother, seriously – as it was laid down by the Church.

I was cheerful enough though and I used to have great fun with the children. They were always gabbling and laughing and doing daft things that made me smile. When Norman the milkman delivered our eight daily pints, Carmel would go to the front door to bring them in, one by one.

'Give them a good auld shake, Carmel,' I'd say. 'Stir up the cream.'

Carmel, at five, hadn't quite mastered 'the shake' and proceeded to hold the bottle out in front of her and shake her body instead of the bottle.

'Not your arse, Carmel. The bottle. Shake the bottle,' I'd say, creased up.

We did everything together, my brood and me. There was only seventeen months between Ellen and Breda and they were always playing together and having fun. When Hank Marvin came on the telly with Cliff Richard, Ellen used to tease Breda something terrible.

'There's your boyfriend, Breda. He's lookin' at you again,' Ellen would say.

Wherever Breda sat, it seemed as though Hank was looking straight at her. His staring eyes freaked her out and she'd wail, 'Leave me alone.'

'He is, Breda. He's starin' at ya.'

'I don't want to see him.'

'Can't yous stop tormentin' the child,' John would intervene. 'Can't you see she's upset?'

Breda was easy to tease. She was a little angel of a child, but so forgetful. I would send her to the shop up the road for some bits of food. Off she went this one time with a shopping list and a ten-shilling note. While she was gone, Dr Brewster came to the house.

'Here, you might as well have this,' he said, passing me a ten shilling note. 'I found it at the gate.'

Breda had gone with her list tight in her fist but she'd dropped the money on the pavement. She even forgot to put her knickers on to go to school once. That was how dopey she was. But she was very comical: when she realised I was pregnant, she told the neighbour that I was 'suspecting' again.

Breda was a hoot but Olive was the one that tickled us the most. She was so reserved but she was forever cursing. If John and I weren't speaking, I'd send Olive, his pet, to tell him his dinner was ready.

'What did your daddy say, Olive?'

'He said, "Ah, tell the auld cunt to fuck off".' She was only three years old and wouldn't know what she was after repeating. I would have to smile at the sweet face relaying such a disgusting message but I found that language repulsive.

Olive was the worst one for cursing. She had the prettiest face but the foulest mouth. No wonder: she was exposed to so much bad language. She kept these milk bottles in a box and she was putting baby clothes on them, pretending they were dolls. 'Go to sleep, yous fuckin' whores,' she would say. 'Go to sleep!' Then she'd give them a whack.

If she wasn't playing with her milk bottles she was reading or making beds. I was after giving her a telling off one day and sent her upstairs as punishment. When I went up to check on her, she was walking up and down my bed crying and cursing. She was trying to make the bed but it was getting the better of her. She tucked the sheets in at the bottom and walked up to the top to settle them there, but she pulled them out from the bottom as she walked. When she realised what she'd done, she walked back down to the bottom to start all over again, pulling the sheets out from the top. The sheets just got more tangled.

'Fuckin' bastard,' she was muttering through the tears. 'Fuckin' bastard. Stay down, will ya!'

One time she peered at Carmel in the pram, pulled back the covers, looked up at me with a disgusted face and said, 'Piss and shit.'

Not surprisingly, Carmel's first word was 'shit'. When she was a toddler, she'd stand in her cot, drop her bottle and watch it fall to the floor. Then she'd look up at me and say, 'Oh shit.' I have to take the blame: back in Garr I was always saying 'piss and shit'.

Carmel and Olive became a bit of a double act, much to John's amusement. He came running into the kitchen one day, sniggering. 'Maura, I was after tellin' them to polish their shoes. Olive just said, "Carmel, why don't ya keep your shoes polished nice like mine?"'

'And what did Carmel say to that?' I asked.

'She said, "Why don't ya keep your business in your mouth and never mind mine!"'

That's one of John's top ten stories. He tells it to this day.

Dr Brewster said I wasn't strong enough to carry another baby. I'd only given birth to Geraldine five months earlier. He advised me to abort my eighth child. And my gynaecologist agreed.

'Take a few days to think it over,' they said.

A day or ten days, it wouldn't have made any difference. There was no way I was going to abort. How could I, as a staunch Roman Catholic, terminate a pregnancy? I would have been frightened to do it. Maybe the hand of God would come down and attack me for killing my child. That was my Catholic belief. I didn't agree with abortion. I still don't.

Despite the medical advice, Dr Brewster accepted my decision to go ahead with the pregnancy. He turned to the specialist and said, 'Mrs Murphy has a lovely family. This one will be more beautiful than the rest.'

And he was right. Joan was the most beautiful baby I ever saw. She was an absolutely gorgeous child. There wasn't a wrinkle about her. She arrived after a twenty-minute labour; I didn't even have time to get undressed or take my boots off. The midwife arrived just in time to deliver the child. And me lying there with my boots on!

John was working the nightshift when she arrived. When he got home from work, he came in to light the bedroom fire and take a look at the new arrival. I couldn't believe what came out of his mouth. 'Another split arse,' he said. Split arse! I was devastated. How could he have been so crude?

He could be so bad tempered and filthy minded. If anyone asked for the time, he would invariably lift the back of my skirt and say, 'I don't know but there's a lot of miles on the clock.' Pub talk, I called it. Most of his jibes would come if I refused to have sex with him, which I started to do now, especially when I was pregnant. Some women turn off tea. I turned off sex, cigarettes and John. I hated the sight of him when I was expecting. He was the prince of belittlers when he wasn't getting what he wanted.

I hated him that morning Joan was born. That was just a terrible thing to say after I carried that baby for nine months. I wanted him to be kind and supportive. I wanted to feel special. I needed to be loved.

Four months after Joan arrived, I had a miscarriage. I thought I'd peed myself in the bed one morning, but Dr Brewster confirmed I'd lost an eight-week-old foetus. He said it must have been an act of God because the baby could have been born blind: I had German measles at the time.

Six months later, I had another miscarriage. I had those familiar pains in my stomach but this time I wanted to vomit; I took out my false teeth and put them under my pillow for safety. John was working nights so I called to the lodger Paddy King to get an ambulance. I lost the baby before the ambulance arrived. There was blood everywhere. I have half a memory of being hoisted on to a stretcher and the ambulance people nearly dropping me when they slipped down the icy steps of Dudley Road Hospital. I woke up two days later thinking I was bleeding to death.

A nurse, doing the rounds with a doctor, got to my bed and said, 'This patient had an incomplete abortion. She had to have eight pints of blood.'

Incomplete abortion? What did that mean? Was I still pregnant? It bothered me because they didn't explain what they were talking about, and I was too shy to ask. I didn't want to look stupid.

John was out at a Christmas dance with Anna and Larry the day I got home. Ellen was getting ready to go to Mass, but she had no socks on her. I noticed all the children's socks hanging from the mantel drying by the heat of the fire, a row of milk bottles weighed down each one. They were filthy dirty.

'Who washed those socks,' I asked, annoyed, 'and left them on the mantel like that?'

'I did them, Mammy,' Breda said proudly.

'Aren't you the good little girl?' I said, trying to contain my anger. Could John not have made sure they had dry socks to put on their feet to go to Mass?

I was in bed, sipping a glass of hot milk, when John eventually came home. He was *stocious*, as usual, and had a horrible mean look on his face.

'Who got ya that?' he said, referring to the glass of milk.

'Paddy King.'

With that, he whipped the glass out of my hand and smashed it into the fireplace.

'What the hell did ya do that for?'

He ignored me, got undressed and climbed into bed. He was probably feeling guilty after staying out all day dancing instead of being home with the children and me where he knew he should have been. I wasn't even sulking about the drink. I was too weak and melancholic to pass comment. Maybe past experience told John that I'd be angry with him so he made the first strike.

I wasn't allowed to be sick: John wouldn't speak to me for

days. When I was sick, everything ground to a halt. The washing didn't get done, the cleaning was forgotten, bills didn't get paid. John's job was to go out and earn the money; it was my job to run the house. He was a good worker and a good provider. The only problem was he didn't only provide for us but for everyone down the pub as well, often leaving us without a penny. We were so hard up we had to buy the children's Christmas presents from the corner shop. John gave me five pounds from his drinking money and we rushed down to the shop just before it closed on Christmas Eve. The children were excited to see us arrive back with a black bag full of presents. They didn't mind that we didn't have the paper to wrap them.

We bought Ellen and Breda two china tea sets, Carmel and Olive had dolls, to replace the milk bottles, and Seamus had a bus conductor's outfit with a ticket machine. Ah, sure that was thrown to one side. He preferred to play with the girls' dolls. He was a sensitive child, though he'd hate me for saying it. We could only afford to buy Declan a game of Snakes and Ladders. Geraldine got a little teddy bear, and a Christmas dummy to keep her quiet.

We were even more hard up since I got rid of the lodgers. I couldn't cope with them in the house with all the rowing and arguing between John and me, and the lodgers were living on top of the children. That's why we started getting letters from the Birmingham City Council. We had a £1,300 mortgage with them as part of a regeneration scheme. The repayments were eight pounds a month and I was getting six pounds a week from the lodgers before I asked them to leave. By the summer of 1963, we were ninety pounds in arrears.

I always tried to pay the mortgage but there would be some reason why it never got paid. John's wages were going into the pockets of the Birmingham publicans, and food and electricity always came first with me; the mortgage was the lowest priority. I should have managed the money better but if it was a choice between paying the mortgage and feeding the children, I fed the children.

At the time I blamed John for our predicament but he didn't blame himself at all. I thought he should have looked after his family instead of going out spending our money and celebrating other people's lives. I knew it was my job to pay the mortgage but how could I put the money away when John spent it on drinking binges every weekend? He knew I was responsible for paying the bills – although I wasn't very responsible with that particular bill – and he left it to me to sort out. It was down to me to get us out of this financial mess so the three of us went to court – me, myself and I – to face the magistrates over non-payment. I was given a month to find the arrears.

I was the one who went round with the begging bowl to keep a roof over our heads. I was the beggar again. I was trying desperately to pay off the arrears but I had no hope of raising the cash. I pleaded with every bank and building society in Aston but nobody would help us. We didn't qualify for a loan.

Then the eviction letter came. We had no more chances; we had to vacate. The council was repossessing our home. We were given one month's notice to get out. I felt terrible.

'I got this today,' I said, showing John the letter.

He didn't even read it. He put it to one side. 'Well, you got us into this mess, you get us out of it,' he said.

John was very good at keeping his thoughts and feelings to himself. And his reaction was always the same: if you worry, you die, if you don't worry, you die, so why worry?

We had no choice but to wait for the bailiffs. Well, as I've said, I waited for the bailiffs. As usual, John left me to deal with the crisis. He was afraid to be around confrontation, even though he was a big ex-army guy, very manly and frightened of nothing. But he couldn't face the humiliation of eviction. That was left to me.

I thought the bailiffs were brutes for putting us out. They treated me with contempt, as if they thought I was a stupid, ignorant Irishwoman. They had no regard for my children or me when they barged past us.

I knelt down and gathered the children around me. 'Don't be scared,' I reassured them. 'Mammy's here.'

The bailiffs were so rough, banging around the house. They were breaking up our furniture and hurling it out of the back window, on to the flags below. I had collected some nice bits of furniture, including the antique wardrobe and the piano, but now the lot was being smashed into pieces. I felt sick inside.

The children were subdued that morning, flinching at all the banging and crashing going on above their heads. They sensed my fear. They were stiff with fright. Olive, in particular, was very scared. I was after smearing blue lotion over her red impetigo sores, and I felt dreadfully sorry for her.

'What are they doin', Mammy?' Olive asked anxiously.

'We have to leave here, pet,' I said, as calmly as I could.

'But why are they breakin' the chairs?'

How could I explain to a six-year-old why these two men were breaking up her home?

'Why do we have to go?' Seamus asked.

'We have to get another house to live in.'

'But we won't have any furniture for it, Mammy.' Seamus started to cry.

I was so angry. I couldn't believe the council could be so cruel and uncaring. How could they do that to us? Why couldn't they help us find some way of paying the money back?

I sat Carmel on the windowsill and she rested her foot on my bump as I changed a bandage on her foot. She'd cut it on broken glass a few days earlier. I was so pregnant I could hardly bend. The bailiffs were getting impatient with me. 'Get a move on. You're 'olding us up,' said the red-faced one. I was at the end of my tether.

'Why are you cryin', Mammy?' asked Carmel.

'Never mind, pet.'

Then the children started to cry. I cursed John for not being there.

The bailiffs finished emptying the house and herded us out into the street in front of them, as if we were cattle. Neighbours stood gawping at us as those men padlocked our front door. We were just poor Irish people being treated like dirt. We were only in England because of circumstance; we didn't want to be there. We fled Ireland because of poverty, but at least our accents fitted at home. Being poor in a hostile country was a humiliating experience. The cottage beside the sooty neighbours in Ireland suddenly seemed appealing.

'Why can't we go back in, Mammy? Can we not open the door?' Seamus asked.

'No, they've locked us out.'

'Well, I want to get my soldiers.'

'Your daddy will get them for ya later, pet.'

I was sitting on our sofa in the front garden when Ellen and Breda came home from school for their lunch. I can still remember the shock on their faces. They couldn't believe it. They just stared at me sitting there, like a tinker, with buckets and pans and basins all around me. I had eight little faces looking to me for direction but I didn't know what to say to them. I felt I had failed them.

Ellen tried the door handle. 'You can't go in, pet, it's locked,' I said.

She was shocked. 'Ah, God, did they take our clothes?'

'No, they're here in the basket.'

'They're all starin' at us,' Breda said, looking terribly embarrassed.

An old man across the road looked over and shouted, 'Get back in through the winda!' The old bastard was trying to humiliate us: the window was boarded with cardboard since it got smashed a few months before. The old man was treating us like scum. I suppose we looked a spectacle. We must have looked like tramps sitting out in the garden like that.

By the time John strolled back, with his paper tucked under his arm, I was in a rage.

'Oh, you're back!' I said. 'Thanks for helpin' me. It was nice of ya to go away, leavin' me to face everythin'.'

He must have been devastated but he didn't show it. He just sat down next to me and read his paper. What an embarrassment.

We sat and waited for something to happen. Three hours passed before a courier arrived with a letter addressed to the manager in the housing department at Bush House. We were instructed to go there and present the letter.

We had to leave everything behind. All our possessions were strewn about the place. I had packed all our belongings in boxes and trunks and filled three large wicker laundry baskets with bed linen and all the children's clothes. Of course they were stolen. Anything that was useful was taken.

We were mortified. We gave out about the banks, gave out about the council and gave out about the bailiffs. We gave out about everyone, bar the ones that were responsible – John and me. We should have made sure that situation didn't arise.

Bevington Road had such potential but it takes more than a piano and an indoor loo to make a happy home.

'Irish Scum'

Highgate Hostel was strictly for mothers and babies. John had to make his own arrangements. I was glad he wasn't coming with us: at least I could sleep freely and easily without him waking me up in the middle of the night to fry bacon. But he was still my husband and I didn't hate him. He would be permitted one visit a week – on a Friday – but he wouldn't be allowed to see the children.

We approached the hostel through two blue gates, stepping through a small door cut out of one of them. The warden seemed disgruntled as I walked under a line of washing in the courtyard surrounded by my eight children.

She took us to a room at the end of a long corridor. This was to be our home for the next two months.

'I've left the linen out for you,' she said. I took this to mean there was no maid service.

I asked Ellen and Breda to start making the beds while I went out to find them something to eat. When I got back, the warden was hopping mad. 'These beds aren't trampolines, Mrs Murphy. If you can't control your kids, you'll have to find somewhere else to stay.'

It cost us nothing to stay there but we all had to pay our way with chores. My job was to sweep and polish the corridor outside the kitchen. We had to be out of the hostel by ten o'clock every morning, and we weren't allowed back until four in the afternoon.

I had nowhere to go. I used to be perished pushing the little ones around in Joan's pram every day trying to keep them warm. Joan was smothered under the wraps but Declan and Geraldine would sit on the end of the pram, their little feet dangling over the edge and their cheeks red from the frosty air.

'Where's Daddy, Mammy?' Declan would ask.

'Your daddy's fine, pet.'

'Is he cold?'

'Ooh, no. He's as snug as a bug in a rug,' I fibbed. I didn't know where John was.

I didn't have proper warm clothes; I wore a thin green rain-coat but no stockings or gloves. If the weather was fine I would walk around the parks and sit on a bench to while away the hours. On other days I walked down to the National Assistance Board, just to shelter from the cold and rain.

The hostel was a miserable place to be but, when four o'clock came, I was nearly always the first one at the heavy double doors waiting to get back in.

I never saw John except for those Friday nights when he turned up with a bag of sweets and a couple of comics for the children, and a hot chicken for me. He told me he'd spent his first few nights sleeping rough because he was 'upset and disillusioned'.

'Have ya got a room?' I asked.

'No, I'm sleepin' in the park.'

'Surely some of your drinkin' pals would be able to give ya a room?' I said sarcastically.

'Ya have to get your digs in.'

John met up with Christy Kenny after that and slept in his spare room, a room no bigger than a closet.

Soon after we arrived at the hostel, my labour pains started and I was rushed into the Sorrento Maternity Hospital in Moseley. The warden assured me the children would be looked after. I was dismayed to find out that they had been put into care. It was John who told me, during one of his visits to the hospital.

'Who put them into care?' I asked.

'The warden contacted the council and she arranged it.'

'Why didn't you look after them?'

'But I had nowhere to put them.'

'Why didn't ya look for somewhere to put them? Ya could have found a room somewhere!'

'I don't have a home.'

'But the ones you're drinkin' with have their houses. Ya don't see their children goin' into care.'

'You're never satisfied. The children are quite happy.'

Ellen was sent into private foster care and the others were placed in care homes in Erdington. There were several homes on the one site and the children were all separated. Seamus, Olive and Carmel were kept together in one house, and Joan and Geraldine were in another. But Declan was put into a medical centre and Breda was placed into another house all on her own.

The labour pains were false but the doctors discovered I had oedema and kept me in hospital. I needed complete bed rest but how could I rest knowing my children had been scattered around

Birmingham? I felt awful but at least I knew they were being looked after, and it was only temporary.

After I got out of hospital, I packed my bags with sweets and chocolate and John and I went to see them. When we arrived, the children were all playing outside. Seamus spotted us first. He looked at us shyly and started to cry.

'Don't be cryin', pet. Mammy's home from hospital now. I'll be comin' to fetch yous in a couple of days when we get a new house.'

'Is it brand new?' he asked through snotty tears.

'It's not a brand new house but it's a new house for us, and we will all be together again.'

'And it's near the prison so you'd better behave,' John said, laughing, lightening the atmosphere. Then the questions started flying.

'Where will we get furniture, Mammy?' Olive asked.

'Where will we be goin' to school?' asked Breda.

'And Mass,' Carmel said, always the holy Mary.

I started to cry, and that started them all off. Soon everyone bar John was blubbering. I didn't realise at the time the emotional upheaval that going into care would cause. Breda, in particular, was terribly distressed and developed stomach cramps because of the upset.

I couldn't get my children out of care until the council had rehoused us. We were put into a two-up-two-down terrace in Winson Green, nestled among factories spewing pollution, with the red brick prison dominating the skyline. Cuthbert Road had no bathroom or indoor toilet and the backyard of stone flags was the size of a postage stamp. It was hardly adequate for a family of eleven but it was our chance to start again.

Except for Joan, the children came home in time for the birth of my third Christmas Day baby. Paul chose to make his entrance during the coldest winter in living memory. The winter of 1963 became known as the Big Freeze. Lads were making igloos on

Dartmoor, thousands were trapped in their homes and helicopters had to drop cattle feed from the sky. The country had come to a standstill while I was giving birth to my last child.

John visited me in hospital just after Paul was born. He was delighted that he had another son. He pulled up a chair and sat close to me.

'If you're here, who's lookin' after the children?' I asked.

'They're all right, they're fine,' he said defensively.

'But, John, who is gettin' their food? It's Christmas Day!'

'They're all right!'

'How will they be all right if there's nobody there?'

I was shocked to hear exactly how they spent their Christmas. John went to the pub as soon as he left the hospital and left Ellen in charge of her brothers and sisters. She took them to the park where they stumbled across a magician putting on a show. There was hardly anyone there apart from the poor kids from the 'backa houses' (back-to-back houses). Breda says that's the moment she realised she was one of them – the poor kids.

Seamus concentrated hard and won a cake in the magician's trick. They ran home excitedly to eat it only to find their daddy lying drunk in a pool of vomit. After Ellen cleaned up the mess, she cut the cake into slices. That was their Christmas dinner. I couldn't believe it when they told me. The coldest winter in a hundred and fifty years and that's how they spent it. I was furious with John. I knew his track record wasn't great but I didn't expect him to leave them to their own devices, not on Christmas Day.

He knew how to appease me: when I got home with Paul, he put on a great stew and created a happy, homely atmosphere. There was much excitement around Paul.

'Oh, look at his little fingers,' Carmel cooed.

'Can I hold him, Mammy?' Geraldine asked.

'Well, you sit down there on the settee and hold out your arms, but make sure that you have your back against the chair so ya don't let him fall.'

'I won't let him fall.'

'Promise?'

'I won't, Mammy, I won't. Just give him to me.'

That went on until they'd all held him for a few minutes each then I put him in the cradle by the fire and they stood by it, guarding their new baby brother.

'Mammy, he's asleep,' Carmel whispered.

'And now he's cryin,' Mammy, quick,' Olive said, as if I didn't know.

'Don't worry. He has to cry to develop his lungs.'

Ellen was in a funny little mood that day. She was looking at the baby in the cradle, with her broom in her hand and her apron on, and said to me, 'I'll never get married.'

'And why?' I asked, surprised that a nine-year-old would be thinking that way.

'I don't want to have babies like you, Mammy.'

Joan missed out on the excitement. She had to stay in care for another four months to give me a chance to recover my strength after Paul's birth. Joan was frosty when she finally returned home. She curled her lip and refused to speak to me. She wouldn't even make eye contact. I tried all my best 'mammy things' to show her that I cared: I hugged her, talked to her reassuringly and made her nice bits to eat but I couldn't win her round. She was angry that her mammy had left her with strangers for so long. Her usual gentle smiling expression had disappeared and her keen blue eyes were distant. She just sat on the chaise longue looking out the window with a 'don't come near me' look on her face.

That night, Joan refused to go to bed so Ellen volunteered to sleep with her on the chaise. She would only speak to Ellen. Ellen had a way with her, and Joan adored her.

I couldn't get a word out of Joan for days. I was the mammy that had left her and she was hurt, cut to the bone. I couldn't go out to the washing line without terrible anxiety rising in her.

I think that's when her stubborn streak was born. When she was four, I hired a photographer to take her portrait. But she refused to pose for him.

'Come on, show me your beautiful smile,' he said.

She stared back, unsmiling, with a wilful glint in her eye.

'Joan, I'll give you sixpence if ya smile for the man,' I said. The sixpence didn't work. There was no bribing or manipulating her.

When the photographer left I said, 'Joan, why wouldn't ya smile for your picture?'

'I didn't want to,' she replied airily.

'Well, pet, I suppose if ya don't want to smile, ya don't have to.' She was an anarchist even as a child.

For the first time since we moved to Birmingham, we found ourselves sandwiched between two true Brummie families. And for the first time, we experienced anti-Irish feelings from ordinary working-class people who, like us, were struggling to get by.

We were good enough to mix the cement to build their roads and hospitals but we weren't good enough to mix with their children. Mr Crabbe refused to allow his five children to play with ours. They all played together when he was at work but when he came back the Crabbe kids ran back home like ants under the door.

Their thick accents were difficult to understand but I had no trouble deciphering the insults. A galvanised fence soon separated us after a row over a pair of fur boots. John had bought a selection of boots for the children but one pair was too big to fit any of them. He never said where he got them from but the sizes were potluck. John suggested I offer the spare pair to the Crabbes. Mr Crabbe was furious. He attracted my attention from the backdoor step in his usual way. 'Oi!' He never called me by my name. 'Oi! Take these bleedin' boots back!' he shouted, hurling the boots at our back door. 'I don't want anything from you Irish scum.'

I didn't flinch. I just picked them up and brought them back into the house. I was very hurt but I wouldn't let him see that. I thought he'd welcome a free pair of boots, I would have, but he clearly didn't want to accept charity from the Murphys.

John was as philosophical as ever. 'They must be very well off to refuse a good pair of warm boots,' he said.

Mr Crabbe's wife was a totally different character. She was terrific fun. It was Mrs Crabbe who first told me what her husband thought of us. 'He thinks you're Irish bastards,' she told me. She was that sort. She would tell me everything, right to my face. She didn't care what she said but she wouldn't be trying to hurt me. It wasn't malicious. She would always add, 'He's a barmy old bleeder, don't bleedin' mind him.'

The galvanised fence went up soon after. The partition of corrugated iron stopped all contact. I thought it was a miserable thing for Mr Crabbe to do. He saw us as a threat in his country, I suppose. I didn't feel threatened by him. I would have taken the little fart up and splattered him on the ground if he ever came near me. But it wasn't just the Irish he disliked.

'Ooh, 'e don' like this one,' Mrs Crabbe would say, ''an' 'e don' like that one.' She ''ated' the sight of her ''usband'.

She was like a gossip columnist. Most mornings, after she sent ''im' off to work and the children off to school, she would come in to me for a chat and a cup of tea. John used to knock great gas out of her. She was a great one for standing by our coal fire and lifting up her skirt.

'What are ya doin'?' John would say. 'Warmin' Mr Crabbe's supper?'

'Oh blimey, you saucy thing. I'm warmin' me arse,' she would say, 'It's numb from the cold. It's bloody freezin' out there, Moira.' Birmingham women can't seem to pronounce Maura. Then she'd settle down close to the fire, with the cup in one hand and a fag in the other, telling me all her news.

Mrs Crabbe was a good sport. She would often keep an eye

on my children and make them a bite to eat. I remember the time she cooked fried eggs for them, but not to their liking: she never used to flick oil on the top of the eggs and they couldn't bear it.

'I don't want that egg, it'll make me puke,' Joan would complain.

'Yeh, looks like there's snot on them,' Geraldine would moan.

'You're rude, you're rude,' she would say. And they *were* rude to her but I always defended them when they were naughty. That could cause friction between John and me.

I came home from work one day and heard Breda bawling. 'What's Breda cryin' for?' I asked John.

'She beat up a girl in the park and tore her dress.'

'Breda? She wouldn't beat anyone for no reason.'

'Well, she did by the sound of it. The child was at the door with her dress torn, roarin'.'

'I'll go up to her,' I said, but John tried to stop me.

'Leave her where she is. She has to learn her lesson. You have them ruined.'

I was furious when Breda told me that her father had given away her favourite grey and pink silk dress to appease the other girl.

'What in the name of God were ya thinkin', givin' the child's good dress away?'

'She has to learn to control herself,' John said resolutely. 'She can't go round beatin' other children.'

He wasn't so principled or controlled when he locked me out of the house, forcing me to stand in a neighbour's outside toilet all night. It was a Sunday, Cilla Black was on the telly and John came in from the pub in a rotten mood. He walked over to the television and switched it off.

'What did ya do that for? We're watchin' it,' I protested.

'Well you're not watchin' it now,' he said grumpily.

I went outside to the loo and John locked the door behind

me, refusing to let me back in. I banged on the back door, I banged on the kitchen window and I banged on the front door but he still wouldn't let me in.

'Please let me in, John,' I shouted through the letterbox. 'Just open the door. I'm freezin' to death.' He didn't answer. He loved to see me cry. I was like a child in his hands. 'Just give me my coat and my bag and I'll go to Maudie's. Please, John!'

Through the letterbox I could see the backs of the children's heads. They were watching Cilla Black doing those daft street interviews with her big microphone. Joan kept looking round at me. She was crying anxiously. John sent the children to bed and warned them not to open the door. That's when I went into the neighbour's yard to shelter in her loo.

Joan was only seven but she stayed awake for hours to let me back in when she was sure her daddy had gone to sleep.

'Thank you, pet.'

'I hate Cilla Black.'

'Why are you sayin' things like that?'

'I bet Cilla doesn't have a life like ours.'

Cuthbert Road was a decent place to live until the council started moving even poorer families in, then it became a ghetto of poverty. Some of them had no interest in educating themselves or bettering themselves. One family ruined the house they moved into. They were filthy. They were beautiful kids but they were so dirty. I did a Mr Crabbe and wouldn't let my children play with them. I didn't want their germs coming into my house. It's not that we thought we were better, or had delusions of grandeur, but we seemed to have more pride; they seemed to be proud of being poor.

My children thought they smelt of margarine and greasy chips and nicknamed them the Margarine Kids. We thought we were better because we had butter. Another family got called the Stera People because they drank sterilised milk and we had pasteurised.

The Margarine Kids and the Stera People were no different to my own, only they were twice as poor. I encouraged my children to have ambitions to rise above the kerbstone. I was determined to see them achieve and go places. I wanted them to be able to mix with the best of them.

Ellen was the most academic of my children. She would never miss school. Even when she sprained her ankle, she hopped the whole way like a rabbit. I was so pleased when she got herself into boarding school. It was always my intention to get her a good education. That was my main objective from the day she was born.

Ellen never was an ordinary little girl. She didn't play with toys like other children. She was reading the newspaper by the time she was two years old. She was a proper bookworm. The little treasure would gather the tiny ones around her and read to them every night.

She was such a bright inquisitive child. She followed me like my shadow, asking questions and copying me. During one of Dr Brewster's visits she got up on the chair to look into his bag, asking one question after another. She wouldn't let him close it until she was satisfied.

'You have a very clever little girl there, Mrs Murphy,' he would say. 'She's going places, I can tell you.'

My ambitions for Ellen appeared to be thwarted when she failed her Eleven Plus, the test she needed to pass to win a place at grammar school. She was one of the brightest pupils in the school and was expected to pass easily. It was a great shock to everyone, to me, to the teachers and to Ellen herself, when she failed. Her head teacher told me that if she lived in a better part of Birmingham, and had a more respectable postcode, she would have passed.

Ellen was crying in the living room, soon after, talking about her disappointment. John walked in, swinging his newspaper, and asked what all the fuss was about. I told him Ellen still wanted to go to a grammar school.

'She can't go to a grammar school,' he snapped. 'She failed her Eleven Plus.' Then he turned to Ellen and hit her on the back of the head with his newspaper. 'You'll go to the secondary modern and like it!'

Ellen didn't like it. When she discovered that her cousin Bardis had passed her exam and got a place at St Francis' College in Hertfordshire, a private boarding school for Catholic girls, Ellen went down to the college to see if she could get in as well. The head nun told her she wasn't allowed in as a boarder unless she could pay the school fees, but she could be accepted as a day pupil.

Ellen came home determined to win a place as a boarder. The Tory council in Birmingham was giving grants to select pupils to go to public school and I applied to the education committee. Ellen went in to her interview on her own and impressed the panel so much they awarded her the money.

Ellen thrived in boarding school. She acquired posh friends and a refined accent thanks to elocution lessons. Suddenly it wasn't 'Mammy' any more but 'Mummy'. She gave her sisters and brothers instruction, trying to teach them all how to speak. Ellen used to teach Olive how to say 'potato' properly. Olive just couldn't master it and would fret to Breda whenever Ellen was due home from school.

'Breda, she's goin' to ask me again to say podado. How do ya say it?' Olive would ask in her thick Irish accent.

'Say *pot*,' Breda would coach.

'Pot,' Olive would repeat.

'Now say *ate*.'

'Ate.'

'Now say, *oh*.'

'Oh.'

'Right now, put them together *pot-ate-oh*.'

'Podado. I can't do it!' Olive just couldn't say it. She was so stressed out by it.

Ellen would come in with a big smile on her face. 'I'm home!' she'd say and rush over to give Paul a big bear hug. The children treated Ellen like a VIP when she came home. On her first school holiday, they sat together and stared at her as though she'd returned from some exotic holiday. Joan looked bedraggled, with her hair falling out of a ponytail and her socks gathered round her ankles, red-faced and huffing and puffing after some rough and tumble. She was always beating up boys and running away from something she shouldn't have been doing. And Paul was desperately trying to tell a new joke he was after learning.

'Ellen, knock knock,' Paul said eagerly.

'Who's there?'

'Apple.'

'Apple who?'

'Apple number two!'

Ellen feigned a laugh, knowing the joke made no sense at all. 'Here's an idea, bab,' she said, 'if you are going to tell a joke, make sure it has a punchline.'

Then she turned to Geraldine. 'And how's my little Jellybean and her little friends?'

'Oh, Mrs Millicamp is visiting her family in the country. There's trouble with the staff.'

'Trouble with the staff again?' I said fondly, encouraging the fantasy. Geraldine was a very creative child, always making up stories about her imaginary friends. She called herself Mrs Daisy and had a pen friend she called Mrs Millicamp.

Carmel was always the last to greet Ellen. She liked to make an entrance. She'd wait upstairs for the others to say their hellos then flounce in with a big toothy grin.

'Hello, Ellen,' she'd say.

Ellen would hand out presents, maybe a poster for Carmel or a book for Olive. Olive was her favourite.

'Ta!' Olive would say.

'I think that should be *thank you*, Olive,' Breda would whisper conspiratorially.

We got Breda and Olive into the same school by going through the same process but Breda wasn't quite so delighted to be going off to boarding school: she wanted to stay at home where she thought she was needed. But she soon adapted to her posh new surroundings.

I was so proud of my three girls going off with the other boarders in their brown and beige summer uniforms with their matching striped boaters perched on their heads. Boys from the local school would shout 'lesbians!' at them because they went to an all-girls' school. Ellen would shout back and the boys would fire missiles at them, crisp packets and apple cores. The boys thought my children were posh. They weren't, of course, but they did walk in an elevated way. They had a sense of status. My sister Carmel Killian said you could pick them out from a crowd because their demeanour was distinctive. They had a bit of class.

Ellen, Breda and Olive were a novelty at boarding school at first, especially with their Irish accents. 'Say it again,' their rich friends would ask. Ellen had a friend who lived in a big house with stables on the Yorkshire Moors. When she let slip that her mammy and daddy didn't have a bathroom, the friend said, 'Oh, Ellen, you're so funny. *Everybody* has a bathroom. You're not a coalminer!' The friend was always asking if she could come and see our 'lovely little cottage' and thought Winson Green sounded like such a 'cute place'.

Boarding school didn't just give the girls an accent; it gave them confidence and independence, and a view of the world that seemed accessible to them. It made them realise that there was a better life to be had.

Not all my children were interested in bettering themselves. When Seamus was eleven, I bought him a briefcase to take to school, not realising he would be too ashamed to carry it. John found the briefcase under a car on his way home from work but he hadn't clocked that it belonged to Seamus. Doing his bit as a good citizen, he handed it into the police station. He was only home a few minutes when a policeman turned up at our door.

'We've found your son's briefcase,' said the copper. John couldn't believe that it was Seamus's case he was after handed in. He didn't think to look inside for an address. He felt so foolish.

When Seamus came home from school, he walked in carrying a stick he had found outside. 'Mammy, I found a stick ya can beat them with,' he said, sniggering. He liked to think he had a role in disciplining his brothers and sisters.

'Did ya have a nice day at school today, Seamus?' I asked.

'Okay, Mom.'

'So, what did ya do? Did ya do some maths?'

'No, we did some English.'

'Did ya, pet? And what did ya write with?'

'With my biro,' he said, looking confused.

'And where was your biro?'

'In my briefcase?'

'Oh, and where was your briefcase?'

'It was in my hand.'

'Ya little liar!' I shouted. 'You wagged off school and left your briefcase out in the road.' I whipped the stick off him and gave him a thwack across the back of the legs.

Seamus wasn't interested in school but the girls knew the benefit of good schooling. It must have been hard for them coming back from their impressive high-status school to the poky, dark terrace of Winson Green – that 'little cottage' we lived in. Even harder when the funding ran out and they had to go to the comprehensive like everyone else.

'Flying in the Face of God'

I felt like a breeding machine, spewing out kids on a conveyor belt year after year. My womb was stretched to its limit. Ten years of childbirth had caused a dangerous prolapse. The pregnancies had to stop. The gynaecologist was insistent. I needed a hysterectomy – or I would die.

'But I'm a Roman Catholic, Doctor. It isn't right to defy the Church,' I told him.

'Mrs Murphy, I know you're a Catholic,' he said, 'but we are going to have to do this operation. That means removing your womb. It has collapsed. If you agree, you'll be giving yourself years to see your family grow up. Without it, you'll start to haemorrhage. You could be dead within six months.'

'Will I survive the operation?'

'You're young and you're healthy. I don't foresee any problems. If you have the hysterectomy you will be giving yourself the chance of a long life before you.'

But there was John to consider. He would find the whole idea abhorrent. 'My husband won't like it,' I said.

'You don't need permission from your husband, or the Church, Mrs Murphy.'

'And there's my children. Who'll look after them durin' those weeks I'm recoverin'?'

'Provisions will be made during your convalescence.'

Going against my Christian beliefs and the teachings of the Church troubled me greatly. A hysterectomy was seen in the same way as abortion. If I had the operation and died, would I be welcomed into heaven? I needed guidance.

I called into the vestry at St Patrick's Church to offload my concerns on to a sympathetic and understanding Irish curate. I struggled for the breath that would carry my words. The curate listened intently as I blurted out all my worries and fears.

'Is it wrong, Father? What if I go ahead and I die anyway? What will happen to me? What will happen to my children?'

'What has your doctor said, Mrs Murphy?'

'That I only have six months without the operation. Oh, Father, I am so confused. I don't know what to do for the best.'

He took my hands in his. 'Let's pray together for guidance and grace.'

We prayed in silence for several minutes before he stood up and laid his hands on my head. 'Your concern will, of course, be for your children. If the surgeon can give you more time with them, then this is surely a gift from God.'

My mind was made up. I would have the operation. I had a responsibility and a duty to the children and myself. Now all I had to do was tell John. I couldn't stomach another confrontation but I decided he could be vexed or pleased, his feelings didn't come into it.

I picked a fine time to tell him. He'd just come home from the pub, half stewed and in a sour mood. I was in bed with Paul asleep beside me.

'I have to have an operation.'

'What operation?' he asked, getting undressed for bed.

'A hysterectomy. I have to have my womb removed.'

'Ya have to have your womb removed!' he said, outraged. 'Well, that fucks it.'

'Shush, you'll wake the child.'

'What do ya think your mother will think about that?'

'Well, she doesn't have to know, does she?'

'I'll write home and tell her what you're thinkin' of doin'.'

'You needn't bother, I'll write and tell her myself.'

'You know what she'll think of that. Who do ya think you are, runnin' to Mass every Sunday and then this, huh? Flyin' in the face of God!'

I was the one who told Mammy. I cried when I read her kind letter: 'Maur'een, never mind him, you get yourself well.'

She understood my dilemma. She didn't like it one bit but she knew that it was right for me to stay with my children. She said that she would have a Mass said for me to help me get through the operation.

At least after the hysterectomy there would be no more pregnancies to stop me from having a life. I could have a life that didn't involve walking down the street with a large, swollen belly, pushing a pram full of babies, too tired to draw breath. I could do away with the outsized smocks and buy neat fitting clothes. John wouldn't be able to make fun of me in front of his friends any more, or gloat over how fit he was and how tired and old I had become.

I suppose, to quote Dorothy Parker, I had 'put all my eggs in one bastard'! The hysterectomy represented freedom. It would be a relief. If I'd taken control of my life sooner, and used some form of contraception, I could have planned my family better. The sexual revolution was all around me in 1965. I saw other women enjoying small families and personal freedom. I was astounded by what they were doing, burning bras and standing up for themselves. I was amazed at the women's libbers. I didn't totally understand what they were saying but I knew they were strong and something better was happening for women.

The hysterectomy stirred something in me. That is when the pod burst and the pea got out. It was the turning point in my Catholic belief. I started questioning my religion and doubting my faith. Why would God do such terrible things? Why would he give me nine beautiful children then take me away from them when they needed me most? I wasn't going to be controlled any more by the Church, by the State or by my husband. I wanted to be me; I was going to take control of my body, and my life.

My immediate concerns were for my children. The gynaecologist was right: provisions were made for convalescence: for the second time in eighteen months, I was putting them into care. I had promised them I would never leave them in care again but here I was, breaking that promise. And they were too young to understand why. They would be so confused. I was beside myself with upset. I had no one else to turn to: my sisters were busy and disconnected from me and my troubles, Maudie was about to give birth to her seventh child and was in no position to help. There was John but he was, well, John. He was having his own troubles. He was in and out of work, struggling with depression and, of course, dependent on alcohol – his escape.

The children needed me to be strong for them. No one else cared about them like I did. Of course John loved his children and they loved him. If he was pushed he would do his best to look after the Irish five – the eldest five – but I also knew if he had the price of a pint that he would say to them, 'I'll be back in an hour, chicks.' He would in his hat! He'd be back after the pubs closed; the children would be left to look after themselves.

I knew John cared for them but he was irresponsible. I expected more of him in a crisis, perhaps more than he was willing, or able, to give. He expected too much of the children. He wouldn't know how to wash and dress them or know what clothes to put on them. He wouldn't comb and plait their hair or tie their bows properly. He would probably use the first bit of string or twine he could lay his hands on, not bothering to find their ribbons.

He used to brush Carmel's long hair like he might a horse. And she had such a sensitive scalp.

'Ouch, that hurts, that hurts, Daddy, ouch,' she would say, leaping around.

'Stand still then and it won't hurt.'

John would pull the brush through her hair again and she'd leap back and stamp on his foot. I tried to show him how to comb long hair but he couldn't do it. He depended on me as much as the children did. He was lost when I wasn't around.

But the children still associated insecurity with me, and security with their daddy. It was an upside-down view but I understood it. Wasn't I the one that left them all the time to have babies and to flee John's violence? He might have been useless at tying bows in their hair or reluctant to watch them play football, he might have locked their mammy outside for hours on end or thumped her when he lost his temper, but they didn't feel angry with him, or at least they didn't show it. They felt secure in the knowledge that he was there. He was a large and masculine presence who may have drunk himself silly but he never left them.

And he wasn't the one associated with putting them into care either. That was left to me. When the man from the welfare came to pick up the three little ones, John was nowhere to be seen. He did his usual disappearing act on the pretext of buying a newspaper. I suppose he couldn't cope with the upset so I was the one who got them ready to be taken away. I had given them special attention: they all looked spotless and beautiful in their Sunday best. They may have been going into care but they were going with their heads held high and their shoes highly polished. At least John got a lovely shine on their shoes before he left that morning. I'd packed a little bag for them and placed it next to my suitcase in the front room; I was to be admitted to hospital that same day. Then I sat Geraldine, Joan and Paul down on the couch for a reassuring chat. 'Who's goin' for a little holiday?' I asked them.

'We are, Mammy, aren't we?'

'Yes, pets, and I'll collect you when I come back.'

'Will we go on a boat?' Geraldine asked expectantly.

'We'll all go on the boat next time, pet, but yous must behave yourselves. Do you promise?' I held back the tears as the others sat watching with sad expressions on their faces.

The welfare officer was young and gentle-natured. He arrived with three bags of sweets for the children. They clutched the sweets with one hand and had their favourite toy in the other, as they toddled off, quite happily, to the stranger's car.

They clambered on to the back seat, excitedly, thinking I was going with them. But I stood on the pavement with Breda, Seamus, Olive and Carmel gathered round me to wave them off.

Breda was crying. 'Why do they have to go away again?'

'It won't be for long.'

Just then, John arrived home in time to say goodbye to his little chicks. He popped his head in the back of the car and said something to make them laugh. When the man from the welfare thumped the door shut, their faces changed: they realised they were going alone. They jumped up on to their knees to look out through the back window as the car pulled away.

'Mammy, look at them, they're bawling,' Olive said.

Geraldine and Joan waved sadly but Paul was the worst. He stretched out his arms to me, crying and calling for me. 'Mammy, Mammy coming . . .' I could see him saying, his mouth wide open like a baby bird. It was his first time in care. My heart was in my throat; I could hardly breathe.

Carmel just stared, and Seamus ran down after the car.

'Come back, come back, come back,' he shouted.

John was careful not to say anything to me; he could see that I was vexed. It was time for me to check into the hospital. I turned back into the room to pick up my case.

'Here, let me,' he said.

I was so upset I turned my back on him and carried my own

case. We walked to Dudley Road Hospital in silence. I felt a knot in the pit of my stomach.

I thanked God I was alive and going back home to be with the children after the hysterectomy. But I was greeted with silence from John. He sat at the table eating a bowl of stew. He didn't offer me any, he just kept his head down until he'd finished. He was in a foul mood.

I had hoped he would be happy to see me but he seemed to resent me coming home. I looked to the children for comfort but they were too scared to open their mouths. Olive started to clean around the room. That was her way of dealing with anxiety. Carmel sat knitting and Seamus went outside to play.

Breda was only ten but she was sensitive enough to offer me her bowl of stew. Of course, I didn't take it. I sat on a chair waiting for some kind of welcome from John but there was none forthcoming. He finished eating and went out without saying a word.

I was in agony from the operation. I had ninety-five internal stitches and every move and stretch I made was torture. I had lost a stone in weight during my twelve days in hospital; my stockings were wrinkling around my skinny legs. I needed to sleep. I tried to walk up the stairs but my stomach muscles were so weak I was unable to lift one foot after the other. I got down on all fours and crawled instead. I heaved myself on to the mattress and Breda covered me with blankets.

'Are you warm now, Mammy?' she said.

'I'm lovely and warm now, bab.'

'Do you want a drink, Mammy?'

'Yeh, get me a cup of water.'

I felt so helpless and alone. I didn't know how I was going to cope. I was so weak that I missed Ger's wedding. He'd met his wife Ann in an Irish club not long after he moved to Birmingham a couple of years earlier. They got married on St Stephen's Day but I missed out on the big day. I felt stranded with the children. They watched me as I cried and cried, the tears bringing some relief to the tension I had felt over the operation. I couldn't do any bending, lifting or carrying for six months and I was forced to depend on my children to do the tasks I wasn't able to do. Ellen was able to help with the washing and the ironing. Breda, Olive and Carmel would help her pack the dirty clothes into pillowcases and walk the ten minutes to the bag wash. We thought only posh people could afford laundry bags. As soon as they arrived back home, Ellen would start ironing. God, sure they were great; I don't know how I would have managed without them. No chore was too much for them. So long as I was there, they were happy to help. I was saddened to see them doing for me what I should have been doing for them. They were thrown in the deep end when it came to their domestic education.

I was in a low mood following the hysterectomy. I thought a trip home to see Mammy would help, and it would give the children the opportunity to run wild in the country. But we came back home to a disgusting welcome: the familiar piss bottles and urine stains greeted me as I went into the bedroom. Piss bottles again!

I was so angry with John that I flew into a rage. 'How dare you leave such filth around the house? You filthy, dirty animal!' I screamed.

John ran off down the stairs to duck the piss bottle I threw after him; it smashed into pieces on the concrete floor. That was the first time I truly expressed my anger towards him, or had shown any aggression.

Mrs Crabbe heard the commotion and ran in.

'What's the matter? Are you all right, Moira?' she called.

'No, I'm not all right.'

'Oh, come down 'ere, you barmy bleeder! 'E's not worth it. You're bleedin' barmy. What you rowin' about?'

'I threw a bottle at him.'

'Did you 'it 'im?'

'No. Missed.'

I was so fed up. I was sick of piss. We had to keep a piss bucket at the top of the stairs at night because we had no indoor toilet, and then the children didn't always use it. They pissed in the beds instead. John and I weren't functioning very well as parents and it was obviously rubbing off on the children. They were very fretful at times and wet the bed.

Joan and Geraldine had terribly weak bladders. Their sheets always needed changing. In the end I had to resort to rubber under sheets. Joan was the pissiest of them all, which earned her the charming nickname of Pissy Legs. And she was devious too. If she was in bed before Geraldine and got the urge to wee, she would get out of her top bunk and climb down into Geraldine's to leave her deposit. Then she'd snuggle down into her own dry bed. 'Mammy! She's pissed in me bed again!' Geraldine would cry.

Joan shared her bunk bed with a teddy bear, a snake doorstop and a koala bear. Her cuddly companions got soaked in piss. It used to disgust Olive. She was forever trying to throw them out. As soon as she was old enough to lift a mop, she cleaned the house. There she was from the age of three, wiping the table, scooping the crumbs into her tiny hands and sweeping up the floor. She got very prissy. The teddies didn't stand a chance.

'My teddies have gone!' Joan would wail. 'Mom, where's my teddies gone?'

Olive tried for years to chuck those toys out. It was such a shame for Joan but John always came to the rescue.

'Olive, come here,' he would say. 'Have you thrown away that child's teddies?'

'Yeh, well, they stink.'

'Well, you get back out there and bring them in. I've told ya before, don't be throwin' the child's toys away.'

'Go and get them yourself,' Olive would mumble defiantly.

'What did ya say? What did ya say?'

John would end up retrieving the teddies himself. 'Here ya are now, pet. Take them back upstairs.' Pissy Legs would put the smelly bears back in their rightful place.

John was always an approachable dad. He had a great nature. He was kind, supportive and had an understanding of them, especially when they were teenagers. He was a good listener. He would be there for them, stand by and protect them. Although he could be nasty to me, he never hurt the children. But his treatment of me did affect them. They'd sit with their heads bowed solemnly when we rowed. Paul would cover his head with his hands or bury himself under the bedclothes, like an ostrich burying its head in the sand. When he got older, he would tell jokes to take the heat out of a situation.

I couldn't cope with John after my hysterectomy. I wanted to kill him. I felt like a trapped animal. During one nasty row, he stamped on my foot with his heavy size eight brogues, crushing my big toe. I couldn't take his persecution any longer. I had to get away. I waited for him to go to the bookies and packed my case to escape to Ireland. I hobbled up the road to get the bus to New Street Station wearing a shoe on one foot and a slipper, with the top cut out, on the other. I took Paul with me because I felt especially protective of him ever since he was a baby suffering from asthma. He had a plaintive way of crying, shedding big ploppy tears.

Breda noticed me leaving, dragging three-year-old Paul behind me, and chased after me up to Dudley Road.

'Mammy, will you come home?' she cried. 'Please, Mammy! Don't leave me.' There was fear and desperation in her voice.

'I have to go, pet.' I started to cry too.

'If you leave, Mammy, I'm goin' to kill myself.' She looked around her and saw the number eleven bus and said, 'I'll throw myself under that bus, Mammy. I will! Please don't go.'

I took her by the hand. 'Don't talk like that, pet,' I said. 'Come on, we'll go home.'

I put her in the house and went back up the road to get the bus to the station. Breda bawled when she realised I'd tricked her. Wasn't that a horrid thing to do, just go off and leave them all? I felt a terrible guilt about it, especially not being there when they came home from school. I knew I should have been there like every other mother but it wasn't possible when John was in one of his foul, disgusting tempers. I thought if I'm not here, he can't kill me. It was best to go away for a few days. The row would always blow over and I would go home when I thought it was safe.

This time I didn't go back. I was afraid to go home to Cuthbert Road. My sister Carmel Killian, who was also living in Birmingham, gave me one of her numerous houses in Handsworth. She made a business of buying and renting property and let me stay in one rent-free in exchange for looking after her lodgers. I had to clean for them, make their beds and cook their meals. I accepted the deal. It was better than going home. Actually, there was no home in Cuthbert Road. There was no warmth between John and me. It was the worst time of our lives.

Carmel didn't ask any questions. She just drove over to Cuthbert Road to pick up the children. I wanted them with me in Handsworth. They all came, except Olive. She stayed behind, sitting on the doorstep refusing to move. Olive wasn't about to leave her daddy – she was very loyal to him – and she didn't want to leave her home.

The children were hurt by my leavings, and they expressed it in different ways. When I returned, I would say to them in turn, 'Come here, pet,' and open my arms to them. Breda would come to me freely but the others were more withdrawn. Seamus found it hard to come to me. The barrier would go up and I would have to work at breaking it down. Geraldine and Declan kept their hurt hidden deep and Carmel coped by adopting other people's houses and parents. Olive and Joan were always the most reluctant; they wouldn't talk to me at all.

John turned up in Handsworth that same night.

'Ya might as well have them all,' he said, passing Olive over to me. He was very annoyed but the old familiar act of contrition started again.

'Maura, let's try and work it out . . . can we be happy for the sake of the children . . . it will never happen again . . . you know I love you and the children . . .' After endless cigarettes and several cups of tea I finally relented and went back home.

I couldn't leave John. It would have been too difficult. I had nine children, no job and no money of my own. I felt trapped. We just fell into a pattern. He would abuse me and scare me and I would run away, mostly to Mammy in Ireland. I was always running away. I left my small children in the same state as I was all those years ago when Mammy went on her walkabouts or threatened to throw herself down the draw-well.

My life was so desperate. We were just like nomads. We took it for granted that the children would do whatever we decided. We never asked them what they wanted. Olive was the only one with the courage to protest. It sounds like we were mad. We must have been the talk of the place. We argued like tinkers. Plates were thrown along with the foulest language John could muster.

The Family Service Unit would sometimes arrange for my children to go on holiday to rich people's houses in the country to give me a break. It was a welcome relief for the children too, and it gave them a chance to experience middle-class life. Joan hated being planted in rich strangers' homes. She would beg me not to send her away on those holidays. She found it a thoroughly humiliating and distressing experience. Her holiday parents' children resented Joan being there and bullied her relentlessly. But Joan didn't let on at first.

'Do I have to go, Mammy? I hate their smelly horses,' she said.

Those holidays didn't carry on much longer once I realised the effect they were having.

What a life to bring those kids into. I didn't realise how they suffered until I worked as a carer in a children's home a few years later. I saw how quiet and depressed abandoned children were. I remember thinking, how can their parents leave them to the mercy of strangers? Then I would remember my own children, and how they stayed in the same kind of homes. My actions, not being there, caused them terrible emotional problems. John's violence was another factor. When he was on nights, or away on holiday on his own, we were able to enjoy a calm and homely atmosphere. We wouldn't be waiting to see what mood he was in after work; he wouldn't be waking the children up at midnight with cold chips and he wouldn't be threatening, as he did once, 'Don't worry, children, you will have food to eat: I'll cut your mother's heart out and we can eat that!'

Lack of money was another reason for the children's emotional upsets. With the money being so scarce, we accepted second-hand clothes from the welfare. They kept a store of these clothes and we would all trundle up there to pick out the ones that fitted. Poverty meant they knew they wouldn't always get the essentials they needed, like underwear or toiletries, especially if there was a milk bill to pay. I remember Breda and Ellen going to their first dance and needing something nice to wear, so I went up to Winson Green Road and bought them their first bras and tights and two new dresses. I had to spend the meat money. That evening we dined on mashed potatoes, eggs and beans. I wouldn't let on that their dance took anything away from the table.

I did my best to juggle the money but obviously little resentments arose. Seamus still tells the sorry tale of how I was able to buy Paul a thirty-pound pair of Adidas football boots. All he got when he was the same age was a pair of five-shilling boots from the swap shop. Whoever was in most need received what little I could afford. They knew the value of money and learnt to cherish their few possessions. Most of them, anyway. When it was Declan's turn to have new shoes, he went out in the morning with his kit bag over his shoulder and his new shoes on his feet. My heart sank when I heard him coming back in, tapping across the concrete living room floor in his football boots.

'Declan, where are your shoes?' I asked.

'Shoes? Oh God, Mom. My shoes! I must've left them in the park.'

'Ya better get back there, Declan, and look for them. You know I haven't the money to replace them.'

'Don't worry, Dec,' said Paul, 'we'll help you find them.'

'Come on! It'll be an adventure,' Geraldine added enthusiastically.

They all ran to the park to find Declan's new shoes. I always encouraged the children to pull together in a crisis. They played together, laughed together and worried together. They returned triumphant with the lost shoes. 'Mom, we found them.' Geraldine was jubilant. But the celebration didn't last two minutes.

'Ah, God, Mom!' Declan exclaimed. 'I've lost my glasses.'

'Oh, Holy Jaysus,' I said, and the stampede started all over again.

Bingo on the NHS

I was agitated and confused. I looked up at the beams and had a strong urge to kill myself, to tie a rope around my neck and hang myself. I was consumed by suicidal thoughts that day in the factory kitchen.

My first paid job in fifteen years was supposed to help me out of a rut. I'd been on antidepressants and sleeping tablets since my hysterectomy. I needed to get out of the house and change my routine. For years, I felt inadequate as I watched Mrs Crabbe going to work. It was time for me to join them, get back out there and move with the world.

I got a job working shifts for a nuts and bolts factory in Winson

Green. I got a sitter for Paul, for thirty shillings a week, and set off each morning to my job as a factory swarf sweeper, feeling important to be part of the workforce again. I received nine pounds a week to sweep up the coppery shavings spewed out by the dirty, oily, noisy machines. I would move up and down the long aisles with my brush and sweep all around the legs of well-paid girls who operated the machinery. 'Mind your feet, girls!' I would shout above the noise of the relentless pumping and grinding of the machines. It was an easy job and I felt useful and free.

But then I started having panic attacks and, soon, suicidal thoughts. I just couldn't take my eyes off the beams. I imagined a rope hanging from them. I was afraid; I wanted to harm myself. I couldn't get the hanging thought out of my head. I kept visualising the rope, and my heart palpitated at the thought of getting rid of myself. I felt so insecure; I thought I was going mad. The factory nurse gave me a sedative and a cup of tea, then sent me home. I never went back. It was the start of my mental breakdown.

The nightmares were so vivid. Evil decaying faces of devils were attempting to drag me into the fires of hell while angels were pulling me back to safety. I'd sit frozen, in bed and see them all, above and below me, floating past.

'John, I can see things, floatin' in front of my eyes!' I would cry.

'What sort of things?' he'd say sleepily

'Devils and angels.'

'They'll go away. You're lettin' your mind run away with ya.'

I'd be quiet for a while and pray for the images to go away. I even sprayed holy water around the bed to keep me safe.

'John, they won't go away; they're still there.'

'Maura, just close your eyes.'

I was desperate for his reassurance but all he wanted was a good night's sleep and not to be listening to my complaints. I felt as if I was a burden. I woke up every morning wanting to die. I wished that I could just stay asleep and lose myself to a peaceful death. I would reach for a cigarette first and an antidepressant tablet next.

I couldn't cope any more. Soon, I was having daily hallucinations and had the urge to throw myself under a bus or a train, or anything that would get me out of my miserable existence. I thought about throwing myself out of the bedroom window. I would be cleaning them in my usual fashion, sitting on the sill with the sash down on my knees, thinking how easy it would be to let myself fall to the pavement below. Then I'd visualise the crunch of my skull, the splattering of blood and the children's horrified faces. That would be enough to pull me back.

The children could see there was something wrong. Suddenly the dishes wouldn't get washed, the house wouldn't be cleaned and the stone flags out the back didn't get their twice-weekly wash down with Jeyes Fluid. The children noticed their clothes weren't being ironed. Everything was in disarray. It was unsettling for them.

'Will I do that, Mammy?' Olive would ask.

'Will I go to the bag wash?' Carmel would say.

I was neglecting myself. I didn't wash, I didn't get dressed, didn't fix my hair or take any pride at all in my appearance. I let myself go. I spent hours in bed. The children would come home from school, run straight upstairs, throw their satchels on the bedroom floor and climb in bedside me.

Although I could hardly bear to go out of the house, I was afraid to stay in it. I felt the whole place was coming down on top of me. I was trapped. Trapped in the house and trapped in my own body. I wanted to get rid of this strange person taking over my mind and my life. I couldn't understand what was happening to me. I prayed and lit candles in the chapel.

I needed help. I joined the queue of scruffy, long-haired, drug-taking teenagers for my weekly appointments with Dr Owens, a psychiatrist at All Saints Psychiatric Hospital. The most valuable thing he gave me was his time. That first day I met him, I was overcome with emotion, relieved to be able to communicate my pent-up feelings without being judged. Dr Owens made me feel good and our sessions were uplifting.

The palpitations and hallucinations began to ease off and the suicidal thoughts became less frequent. I started to take an interest in my appearance again.

Dr Owens thought the root of my problems lay in my lifestyle. While I was busy giving birth to children year after year, I had been starved of human contact. His prescription surprised me.

'Have you thought about bingo, Mrs Murphy?'

In the beginning it was just a game. Soon I was hooked. Within a few months, the game I'd never heard of became an addiction. My psychiatrist had suggested it might cure my depression and anxiety.

'What's bingo?' I had asked Dr Owens.

'You know, it's a game of numbers with little books. They all play it around here. It's where people go to socialise and have a drink.'

'But I don't drink.'

'You don't have to drink to play a game of bingo. But you do need to socialise a bit more, get out and mingle.'

I hadn't been outside the door socialising in fifteen years of marriage, except to see relatives or to go church on a Sunday. I decided to give bingo a go. What harm could it do?

The first time I went was with my neighbour Lil Baker to a place called Hawleys on Dudley Road, just a hair's breadth away from the children. There wasn't big prize money at Hawleys but it was getting me out of the house. I did have a few wins there. The biggest was about twenty pounds. After a while, we graduated to a bingo hall up on the Soho Road in Handsworth. On the way home Lil taught me a fascinating Brummie pastime: eating chips out of a paper bag.

I had great fun with Lil. I loved making her laugh. John used to call us lesbians because we went to bingo together. I didn't really know what a lesbian was. If it was someone who loved the company of women he was right, but I guessed that it was something more than that if John was accusing me of it. Going to bingo with Lil made me feel alive again, like in my Dublin years before I got married.

Lil introduced me to The Gaumont on Cape Hill; the money was better there. The first time I walked in, I was overwhelmed by the size of the hall. There were rows and rows of people sitting on comfortable red-cushioned seats, their heads bent over six or seven books each and their eyes travelling up and down the pages as the numbers were called. This is serious stuff, I thought.

I started cautiously with just one book. My first attempt at marking the numbers in this vast hall was diabolical. I couldn't keep up with the caller taking each ball out of the drum. As time went by, I became brilliant at the marking and eventually moved from one book to two and from two to three. When I really felt confident, I progressed to four books.

Within a year, I was going to bingo nearly every night of the week. I would get up to The Gaumont for seven o'clock to make sure I got a seat. The bingo started at a quarter to eight and I would be home by half past nine. If I had a win, I would stay for the late-night session at ten. By the time I walked from Cape Hill, and stopped off for my chips, it would be nearly eleven when I got home.

I couldn't keep away from bingo. I went in the afternoons as well and to the morning sessions on a Saturday. Those sessions would be over in time for me to do my shopping in the market just around the corner from the bingo hall. Then I'd go in for the afternoon session, taking all the shopping bags with me. Sometimes, at weekends and in the summer holidays, the children would come too but they were never allowed in. They would sit in the foyer eating sweets and crisps, having a great time. It would only be an hour. At least I knew they were there.

While I was occupied at the bingo, I could forget about my illness and phobias. It became so I couldn't live without it. I was addicted to the idea of going out, marking numbers and hoping for a win. It was like smoking. I had to do it. I couldn't wait for seven o'clock to come. I didn't bother with Mondays or Wednesdays because they were small nights; you didn't get much money then. Tuesday, Friday and Saturdays were big nights. Saturday was the best night of all.

I was going morning, noon and night. The children had to fend for themselves. Seamus took on the role of mother and father. He was given responsibility for keeping an eye on things at home. But after one late-night session, I arrived home to a policeman opening the door to me. Another one was sitting on the couch with Geraldine perched on his lap. Paul was standing by his side wearing his helmet and the others were scattered around the floor looking startled.

'What in the name of God has happened? Where's your father?' I asked without thinking.

'You know where he is, Mammy,' Carmel revealed innocently. 'He's in the pub.'

'No he isn't, he's at work,' I said quickly.

I turned to the policeman who was getting up off the couch and explained, 'My husband works nights.'

'I see. Well, these lot were left on their own and made their way up to the station. They thought someone 'ad broken in—'

'Who's broken in?' I cut him off.

'Nobody. It all looks fine. We've 'ad a check around. No bogeymen 'ere,' he said. The children shrieked with delight as he pulled a scary face. 'But we would advise you that it's not safe to leave your children on their own at this time of night, Mrs Murphy. It can be dangerous, you know.'

'Of course. I know how to look after my children, Constable,' I said, smarting at this whippersnapper's condescending advice.

'Well, we'll be off now.'

I was seething. I shut the door on the policemen and looked at my children standing together like orphans in their nighties, pyjamas and bare feet.

'Seamus, what in the name of God made you go up to the police station in the middle of the night? Draggin' those little ones out in the freezin' cold with no coats on them or shoes on their feet!'

'But we heard some—'

'Makin' a holy show of me. Have ya no sense?'

'Someone did break in, Mammy. I heard them,' Carmel said. 'You would've heard them too, Mammy, if you were here.'

'I thought I heard them as well,' said Seamus.

'And did ya not check?'

Seamus couldn't answer. He looked humiliated. I felt sorry for him. He was just as scared as the little ones. I took him in my arms and said, 'Sure, there's nothin' to be worried about.'

Looking back, it was terrible to leave them on their own all evening. Seamus was only twelve. I took it for granted that everything would be all right. I thought the children were capable of amusing themselves, and Seamus was very sensible. He loved being left in charge and I trusted him implicitly. Sure, if I'd had the money I would have hired a nanny.

In later years, I discovered an awful lot was going on while I wasn't there. I bet I still don't know the half of it. That wouldn't have stopped the bingo addiction, though. I felt guilty about being at bingo and spending money we didn't have but I told myself, 'Well, John's been livin' a life outside his family for fifteen years, why shouldn't I?' I sometimes forced myself to sit down and calculate what money we were squandering. At the height of our addictions, we were getting through ten pounds a week each. That was half the weekly wage being wasted.

I had to feed my addiction, just like John had to feed his. I used to chide myself sometimes and say, 'Ya can't afford it, ya can't go.' I would feel self-righteous about my decision and pleased that I had the strength not to go. Then the longing would get to me and I'd go up for the second half. If I had a win, I'd think, look at what you might have lost if ya hadn't gone! That deepened the addiction.

John used to come to bingo with me sometimes. He hadn't got a clue about marking the books. He was like a jack-in-the-box, nervous and jittery, unable to concentrate. He'd be saying, 'I got that. I got that.'

'Mark them off then,' I would say.

'I got that.'

I would be trying to mark my books while keeping an eye on his. I'd see that he had missed a number and tap his book with my pen.

'What? What?' he'd say, irritated.

'John, you've missed another.' He'd have missed it again.

A voice from behind shouted one night, 'Shush, will ya, I can't hear meself think.'

'Ah fuck off,' John retaliated. 'How can he think with no brain?' he whispered to me. I sniggered. But then I looked across at John's book and noticed he had marked off all his numbers and he hadn't called.

'Ya got a full house! Why didn't ya shout?' I said. That finished it for John. He stood up and chucked the book into the air, and the pen along with it.

'That fucks it now!' he said, marching out of the hall. I was in hysterics. I couldn't see to mark my own book with the tears running down my face. He laughed about it afterwards.

John stopped coming to bingo when he realised he was running into the hall with a crowd of 'auld ones' to get a seat. You'd have to race to get a decent seat but he knew it was time to stop going when he was knocking eighty-year-olds out of the way to beat them to it!

John never tried to stop me from going to bingo, but we did bicker when money was tight. He would say, 'You spent all the money on bingo.'

'You spent all the money on drink!'

'No, you spent all the money on bingo!' It would go on like that.

I was bingo crazy but I didn't always have the thirty shillings for the price of the books. I'd make sure I got it from somewhere: I'd borrow it from anyone that would lend it to me. I would *have* to get the money; I would beg, borrow or steal for it. I often sent Seamus to the swap shop on Winson Green Road to pawn my watch. It became very valuable to me. It was often my ticket to the bingo. I'd put it into the pawnbroker's and I wouldn't be able to get it out of there until I had a win.

Finally it happened. I won The Big One. That night I was broke, as per usual. It was a Saturday and I played what they called a link game where they linked up with three other bingo halls. My books were filling up at speed – within minutes I was waiting for the elusive magical final number for a full house. I checked the prize money on the huge numbers board above me – £10,664. My heart thumped with excitement, anticipation and belief: this is my time. 'Please, God, call it. Please, God,' I whispered to myself. I waited, eyeing the numbers board for my number – forty.

'Four and one, forty-one; four and five, forty-five; four and nine, forty-nine, four and three, forty-three . . .' Every number but mine was called. Ten numbers later he called it: 'Four O, forty.'

'Hooooouse!' I yelled. Hundreds of pairs of green eyes stared at me, but I didn't care. I had said the beautiful word 'house'. Then the news came that I was sharing it with eight other lucky winners. If only he had called number forty earlier, I would have gone home with over ten thousand pounds in my pocket.

All this money! I was shivering with excitement when I got home. All the children gathered around me.

'Did you win, Mammy?' they asked.

'I did. I got the big one.'

They jumped round the house with delight. Breda and Declan were bouncing on the sofa calling, 'We're rich! We're rich!' I handed out the big fat Bluebird sweets to celebrate.

John was already in bed. He was down in the dumps that night and had gone to bed early, all depressed. I sat on the end of the bed. 'Did ya win?' he asked.

'Yeah, I won all right.'

'Ah, that's great,' he said. 'How much did ya win?'

I grinned.

'Did ya win the big one?'

'Yeah. But I had to share it. I got £1,333.'

'Jaysus, Maura, that's brilliant.'

He wasn't long staying in his dumps. John jumped up out of bed with delight and we all rejoiced.

Next morning he went flying down to Luke and Maudie's to give them some of the winnings; they were just as poor as we were and it was great to be able to help them out. I knew what I was going to do with the rest of the money. I bought a stereo, for the front room, and some bunk beds. Now everybody had their own bed. I bought beautiful red and yellow blankets, made from real good wool, sheets and pillowcases.

It was so amazing to have all that money. I took the children to the cinema to see *Doctor Doolittle,* as a special treat. I remember getting on to the bus with all these notes stuffed into my handbag and poking out of my purse but I didn't have the change for the fare. 'It's all right, luv,' said the bus conductor. He could see I had the money to pay but he didn't bother to charge me.

Not long after my big win, John was celebrating too. He was back in work, earning twenty-one pounds a week as a stoker in the boiler house at Dudley Road Hospital.

SIXTEEN

Home and Alone

I was sitting in my ward consumed by the thought of my funeral in Rhode when I heard the good news: the surgeon had a cold. My lung operation would have to be postponed. I was ecstatic to be leaving St James's, free from injections, tests and X-rays. I could push the surgery to the back of my mind, for a couple of weeks at least.

In the peace of the Sunday I was to be discharged, I sat quietly reading a book on quantum healing. Suddenly something caught my eye. I glanced up and thought I'd seen a mattress dropping past my window. A second or two later, I heard a thud. It made me jump. It sounded like someone throwing a heavy barrel from the floor above. It wasn't a barrel or a mattress. I could see the body of a woman, lying broken on the concrete.

She looked dead.

I went out into the corridor to tell someone. Four nurses followed me back into my room and looked down at the quadrangle.

'Oh my God!' said one.

'She's thrown herself out of that window,' said another.

I wondered who the woman was; did she have a family? Why

was she so tormented that she'd want to harm herself? It reminded me of my preoccupation with suicide thirty years earlier.

Moments later, the quadrangle filled up with panicked nurses, running in all directions. I was transfixed. I looked across the hospital grounds and noticed other curious patients craning out of their windows, unable to take their eyes off the commotion below. A stretcher arrived and took the woman inside. The onlookers dispersed.

I asked after her. She had a couple of broken limbs, but, miraculously, she wasn't too badly damaged – yet I couldn't get the woman off my mind.

'Are you ready, Mom?' Joan said suddenly.

'Yes. Take me home, pet.'

I felt old and feeble as Joan guided me to the lift to take me back to Rhode. I had a sudden pang of anxiety to be leaving the security of the hospital. I had been in bed for a month. If I needed help, I just pressed a bell and someone came. I'd been waited on, washed and fed. What would I do now? How would I cope?

It was another beautiful day. The sun was splitting the trees, and the cloudless sky was a magnificent shade of petrol blue. Oh, what a lovely sight. I was so happy to be travelling out of the city and into the open spaces. I wound down the window and took gulps of fresh air deep into my lungs. The feeling of freedom was awesome.

I was excited to be getting back to my beautiful garden. I'd spent every spare minute sowing and planting when I first retired. The wild overgrown acre, with its multitude of weeds and nettles and rusty palings, was now a perfect mature cottage garden stuffed with roses and honeysuckle, their fragrance intoxicating at this time of year. The conifer hedge – the perfect windbreaker – the smoky poplars, the apple, plum and cherry trees, the Virginia creeper and variegated ivy were all my own handiwork. I longed to sit out in the sun and absorb their loveliness.

I arrived home at four o'clock and surprised John. He was pleased to see me. The grin that irritated me a few days earlier now seemed friendly and welcoming. He offered me his arm and walked me, gingerly, to the back door. I didn't think I'd be walking back into that house again. There was an atmosphere of subdued delight, as though I'd just returned from a long trip abroad.

John had thrown open the windows and doors, releasing the smell of turf, polish and cabbage and reminding me that I was back in Rhode. I could tell the molly maid had been at work: Olive had the place looking pristine clean. John was cooking his favourite dinner. He was crestfallen when I refused a meal. I went straight to bed and slept for the rest of the day.

Eight o'clock next morning, John knocked tentatively on the door. 'Maura, are you awake?' he whispered. 'Do ya want a sup of tea?' I welcomed his knock every morning.

Joan had rearranged my bedroom and took out the clutter. She removed boxes of books, stuffed my collection of teddy bears into a black plastic bag, hung up my clothes and stored piles of old newspapers in the garage. She squeezed a single bed in next to mine, so the children could watch over me throughout the night, and placed a vase of lilies on the windowsill.

John did his bit, cooking and cleaning. Despite his efforts, I was still feeling antagonistic towards him, still blaming him for my illnesses and berating him for not understanding what I was going through. No one could understand the isolation that comes with being told you have a tumour. Nobody could really know what I was feeling, and nobody could help. I had to come to terms with it on my own – and I felt alone.

John
When I saw Maura coming through the door, I was pleased to see her home again. I brought her tea and looked after her the best I could. She can be nasty to me and say that I don't do

anything for her. Well, all she has to do is ask and I do it. She
has all the children helping. I do my best.

Being home was an anticlimax. I was back to reality. I felt like
a leper, low and weak and in need a bit of companionship. I
wanted the attention I got in hospital to continue. Having a
tumour made me feel contagious. But I was still the same person.
I hadn't changed. My hair was thinner and I'd lost a bit of weight,
but I was still Maura Murphy.

I spent my days sitting in my basket chair in the front garden,
wrapped in a blanket with my straw hat planted firmly on my
head, soaking up the afternoon sun and mulling over the past
few weeks. During Geraldine's visit, my sister Carmel rang.

'Do ya know, Maura, I was talkin' to a friend about this man
Jim Murrin in Edenderry who had cancer,' she said. 'He got a
cure from Aloe Vera. Have ya ever heard tell of it?'

'No I haven't. What is it?'

'They call it the medicine plant. I think Jim Murrin went to
some faith healer in Edenderry and she gave it to him. He's cured
of cancer now. Why don't ya go and see him?'

'I'll give him a call,' I said.

Jim was away in Europe but his mother was happy to speak
to me. Geraldine drove me into town to see Jim's parents. We
sat around their kitchen and talked. Mrs Murrin spoke openly
about her fears for her son's life. The cancer had affected all his
organs; he hadn't long to live.

'We were so worried when we were told that Jim only had
three weeks to live,' she said. 'He had three lots of Aloe Vera.
When he went back up to the hospital they found no trace of
the cancer.'

Doctors were baffled, she said. Something miraculous had
happened. Mrs Murrin was convinced the combination of Aloe
Vera, relics from the holy shrine at Medjugorje and a lump of clay
from the grave of a local curate had all helped to shrink his cancer.

The Murrins led us into their sitting room where we knelt and prayed in front of a grotto made up of a statue of the Virgin Mary, a small font of holy water and a candle. After, they wished me luck and promised to light a candle and pray for me in their prayer group.

I had gone to see them because I was looking for hope; something to hold on to, something that would enable me to be strong and positive about what was going to happen to me. I felt less anxious after my visit. Our conversation relaxed me and made me determined to develop an attitude of positive thinking. I couldn't wait to tell Paul. He would approve.

I knew there was a lot of talk about Aloe Vera being a healing plant. Perhaps it really could shrink my tumour.

Geraldine

Fri 23 July: Mommy's coping amazingly well. She's being quite pragmatic about the whole issue of her illness and she's keen to get on with the operation. She's working towards it, mentally, and even looking for alternative remedies.

We went to see a family in Edenderry whose son was diagnosed with cancer. They showed Mommy their altar and gave us some clay from the grave of a priest who had recently died. They have a lot of faith in him. Mommy's been uplifted by the experience. It's making her feel better about herself.

Mommy enjoys having her hands, arms and feet massaged. I'm just happy that I'm doing something for her. She's eating well and healthily and maintains the diet she had in the hospital. Daddy's making the meals most of the time, and he's doing most of the cleaning. I brought Mommy Granny's Mass card and the holy water Seamus's son Cormac gave me. I put them on the altar that Declan set up by her bed. He put the priest's clay on it, a piece of lace that Olive bought, Mommy's rosary beads and a crucifix. The priest comes in every Friday to say prayers.

Ellen found some Miraculous Medals on the ground in London that were exactly the same as Granny would have worn. One of them was inscribed with a prayer – the very same prayer that Granny used to recite. Ellen picked up the medals and brought them to Mommy.

I began to wonder if the doctors had forgotten about me: I'd been at home nearly two weeks and hadn't heard anything about my operation. Maybe they had made a mistake? They could have. I didn't feel like I had a tumour. But then the phone rang. John looked agitated. 'Maura, it's the hospital.'

It was the inevitable phone call. I started to tremble but I had a sudden burst of adrenaline. I was ready to face anything.

'Hello, Mrs Murphy? I'm phoning from St James's Hospital in Dublin. Your operation is going to be postponed.'

'Again?'

'Yes, the surgeon still has a cold.'

I was happy it was postponed because it would give the Aloe Vera time to do its job. But then I didn't know what to do with myself. I moped about the cottage, picking up ornaments and putting them down again, moving picture frames from one surface to another, sitting down and standing up. I couldn't relax. The anxiety brought on stomach cramps. I decided to make an appointment with the spiritual healer for the following week.

Again, Geraldine was my chauffeur. We took a left outside Edenderry just before a sign that read *Sheridan's Cement Factory*. The road was covered with a light dusting of pure white cement. It looked like snow. The car crunched over a gravel driveway to a house that looked as though it had been plonked on the top of the hill. A lazy-looking mutt was guarding the front door and a big smiling woman, in open-toed sandals, was waiting to welcome us into her home. 'Mrs Murphy, isn't it?'

'Yes, and this is my daughter Geraldine.'

'I'm Mrs Sheridan. Come in,' she said, 'come in,' gesturing with her arms as if she was backing a car into a parking space.

She opened a panelled door to the left of the hallway. 'This is the treatment room.'

We were left on our own staring at a sparse room. It had a large brown treatment couch in the middle, laminated posters of the human body and framed certificates, confirming her credentials, on the wall, and stacks of miniature bottles, identically labelled, along a shelf.

Mrs Sheridan walked back in clutching a pouch. 'Slip off your shoes, I'd like you to lie on the couch, please.'

I felt apprehensive as I lay on the bed. 'I'm a little nervous in these situations,' I said. 'I suffer with palpitations.'

'I have a rescue remedy that will help you with that. If you want me to stop at any time, just say so. Now try and relax.'

She then introduced me to her world of spiritual healing. She spoke calmly in a low soothing voice, waving a crystal over my body to 'unblock my energies' and rested her hands on my head. I felt different when it was over. My head was light. It seemed to work well for me. I felt totally calm and relaxed on the journey back to Rhode.

I saw Mrs Sheridan once a week for three weeks to have my 'energies balanced' and I took the potion four times a day. The results were remarkable. I convinced myself that it was doing me good. I started to look and feel better and my energy was beginning to return; I even managed short afternoon walks round the cottage. I began to wonder if I actually had a tumour.

Joan

Sat 31 July: Somehow the horror of Mommy's surgery has subsided but it comes back in flashes of worry and sadness. Had a tiny weep this afternoon sitting in the garden – I felt a pang of sadness about all the sayings that Mommy has and I can hardly recall them, or not properly anyway. I feel sad about the thought of her not being here saying all her stuff that sometimes irritates and annoys me.

Spoke to Mommy yesterday. She was distracted by company and seemed in great spirits. The hospital still hasn't confirmed her operation. She's still hoping for a miracle to happen. She wants more time for her positive thinking and alternative treatment to 'work'.

Spoke to her again later and she sounded distressed. I thought it might be about Daddy, and it was. A very brief feeling of 'oh no' came over me and then quickly dissipated as I thought, ah your lovely Mommy is alive and kicking and still getting vexed with Daddy!

Mommy said, 'He is so stupid and immature, I think he still fancies himself, dressed up like a lord and spending his weekend in Doyles.' I get her annoyance. He could show a little restraint especially when she is in her horrible predicament.

I was getting stronger and enjoying being at home again chatting with the children on the phone. John was getting on with his routine, which meant spending too much time and money in Doyles. He went every Saturday and Sunday, and sometimes Monday.

He's one of the cleanest people ever to walk into a pub in Rhode. He was always spotless. He thought he was God's gift, always wearing different suits and colours and ties and highly polished shoes. I'd watch him getting dressed up to the nines, feeling full of his own importance. I knew people in the pub would comment, 'God, he's got another suit on him today.'

John had so many clothes. That was a far cry from the days when he stole His Lordship's suit. Now he swaggers round thinking he's Lord Dunville. He'd put on his new trousers and say, 'Does that fit on my bum properly?'

'Who the hell do ya think will be lookin' at you, at seventy years of age? Ya silly old fool!' I'd say. He'd laugh and preen even more.

How he got rid of sixty pounds in the pub in a weekend I don't know. I was annoyed with him for neglecting his rightful duty, stopping home with me and caring for me, knowing I had a tumour and might be dead within a couple of months. All he could think about was going to the pub and spending his pension. Doyles always came first.

John
Sun 1 Aug: Maura berated me again for going to Doyles. Sometimes she's fine about it. I can spend the morning doing my bits of chores, around the house and in the garden, and then get ready for a couple of pints, listen to the boys and have a laugh. You would think that I was the only one going to Doyles but there are ten or fifteen in it. Maura was always against drink right from the time we were married. And she was right.

She can exaggerate things that happened and just say that I was drunk. And she can dismiss my worries and my aches and pains because of the drink. Say I had been off the drink for a couple of weeks. I might chance a pint and get a stomach upset. She would say, 'Well, what do you expect? It's the drink.'

Years ago when I used to go for a pint she would accuse me of wasting money and try to get me to stop. I gave her the full running of the money and the banks. I let her make all the decisions about buying and selling houses or moving here or there and still she used to try to stop me from taking a drink. I had no control over her going to bingo. She just got ready, got her bag and went. I never stopped her. But she would try to stop me from going to the pub. Sometimes, to avoid a row, I wouldn't go or I would do some tasks to put her in a good mood for when I came back. I think if Maura could have just accepted that I took a drink it would have made all our lives a lot easier. She hates drink.

Breda
Mommy's illness reminds me of our lives being so out of control as children – the eviction, being in care, the head lice and the hostel. Oh the hostel!

We were stuck in the hostel, and Daddy was sleeping in the park. I was desperately worried about him. In my child's eye, I pictured him sleeping under newspapers and having to go into public toilets to keep himself looking the way he wanted to look and carrying around all his belongings in a plastic bag.

I remember my older sister Ellen deciding that she had to be kind to all the tramps because somebody might think our Dad was a tramp. She used to go up to all the people lying on benches and ask them if they wanted her to find a cup of tea for them, and asked them if they were all right. She was very, very kind.

I had a constant pain in my stomach when I was a child. I got used to things just happening to us and seeing that my parents had no right to challenge anything. When your parents can't control what is happening, the world is a very frightening place.

I felt a burning shame the day the bailiffs evicted us from Bevington Road. I remember coming home from school and seeing them throwing our furniture out into the street and it smashing into smithereens. They were just brutes. I stood on the corner for ages; I didn't want to walk past the neighbours who were standing on their doorsteps, laughing and jeering at us. I knew we were better than them.

This is bringing it all back   having nowhere to live when we first came to England and standing on the doorways of houses, where there were vacancies, and seeing the notice 'No Blacks, No Dogs and No Irish'. I thought, they think we're not as good as animals. But I've got a brown coat with a velvet collar! Why don't they think I am good enough to live in their houses?

Ellen was home, drinking tea and making us laugh. I enjoyed her visits. She is a very interesting person, one of those people you enjoy listening to. She has such great command of the English language. When Ellen and her daddy got together they had endless intelligent conversations. They were always discussing some important issue of the day and I would listen intently.

That's how I did my learning, by listening to other people's conversations, picking up words but not letting on I had no idea what they meant. I would just nod in agreement then run to the dictionary. I'd memorise the new word and use it later in other conversations, pretending I knew something. What I learned from Ellen and John I never forgot.

We were so proud of Ellen when she got her degree. But I'll never forget Mammy's reaction: 'What would Ellen want to be takin' a degree for?' she'd say. 'Sure aren't there plenty of people born to do that. What sort of talk is that?'

Mammy thought Ellen wasn't from the right sort of background to be educating herself. Mammy rubbed me up the wrong way. She was always belittling of my family and my children. She thought I boasted too much about them.

She would say, 'You're always braggin', Maur'een.'

'Sure, I like braggin' about them,' I'd say. 'If I don't, who will?' I think Mammy was jealous of how they got on. They were able and intelligent and I didn't run them down. I liked to build them up. They each had a good brain and I encouraged them to use it.

Mammy was crippled with social shyness and a lack of self-belief. Not Ellen. We knew she'd go far.

The Friday Ellen was home, Friday 6 August, the phone rang. She took the call. I was in the kitchen about to tuck into my dinner. I pulled myself out of my chair and reached for the rescue drops. 'Oh no. Not this weekend, please!' I said. I knew it was the hospital. Ellen looked at me with tears in her beautiful eyes. I couldn't understand why they would call me in on the verge of the weekend; they usually tried to empty wards, not fill them up. Ellen looked brittle. I tried to put on a brave face, for her sake.

She passed me the phone. 'I'm calling you in for your operation on Tuesday. Ring the admissions department on Sunday to arrange a bed,' said a male voice. Very brusque and formal. Not how I imagined the conversation would go – 'How are you, Mrs

Murphy? I have good news for you; I'm calling you in for the operation on Tuesday next. I hope you will be well enough to come in.' No such thing. He wasn't at all supportive.

I thought I was going to pass out. 'You are first on the operating list. There's no time for delay,' he continued.

My hands trembled. My mouth was dry from nerves. 'What's the hurry?' I squeaked. 'I'm feelin' so well. Could it not wait for a couple of weeks?'

I'd made him cross. 'Mrs Murphy! 'You have a cancerous tumour. It is important to have this surgery as soon as possible . . .' What is he saying? I don't have cancer! I have a tumour *with the potential to be cancerous*. That's what they told me. '. . . so call the hospital on Sunday . . . bed available . . .'

I couldn't take it in. He talked so fast. 'Fine,' I heard myself say. I felt sick. I *do* have cancer. I was sure they knew all along. Ellen put her arms around me. She was crying but she stayed calm. John was at the door, trying to get rid of someone who was selling turf. 'We have trouble in this house tonight,' he said. 'Come back next week.'

John looked very worried.

Dinner went uneaten.

SEVENTEEN

Sick with Delight

We thought we were really posh getting such a beautiful house. The children shrieked with delight; they couldn't believe it. Ellen, Olive and Carmel walked the whole mile of City Road with mops, buckets and cloths to spring-clean our new home. Geraldine, Joan and Paul trailed behind with basins full of crockery, blankets and pillows. I took the delicate china on the number eleven bus with Breda.

I'd spent nine years trying to get us out of Cuthbert Road. Finally, in the summer of 1972, the council agreed to rehouse us. A housing office from the council came out to 'assess our needs'. We got off to a great start. She loved the Irish.

She checked all the rooms and went out into the yard. 'How do you cope with all the children and that little bit of a yard?'

'They play in the park.'

After a long conversation, she paused and said, 'I will find you a nice house in a good area, Mrs Murphy,' she said. 'You deserve it.'

We couldn't believe our eyes when we saw the house they were offering. It was in an area of the city called Edgbaston, a posh postcode for the likes of us. There was nothing 'councilly' about it. It was a big, well-maintained pebble-dashed semi with a wide Tarmac drive – big enough for two cars if we had them – and a garage. There would be no more hopping on to the road from our doorstep. The hallway had a polished wooden floor with a coat cupboard and pantry leading off it. There was even a servants' bell system over the kitchen door from the days when the likes of Neville Chamberlain lived in Edgbaston.

'Wow, someone important must have lived here,' I said to Ellen. The bells didn't work but they looked impressive. The back room had french windows overlooking a garden the size of a football pitch. 'Oh my God!' I gasped with delight.

Ellen was awestruck. 'Mummy, it's perfect,' she said.

We explored every tree and shrub in the garden. There was a conservatory attached to the garage, an outside loo and a side entrance. Upstairs there were three big bedrooms, a bathroom and a separate toilet. We didn't know what to do with ourselves. Had they made a mistake and given me the wrong keys? What were we going to do with all this space?

I was sick with delight. 'We're takin' this.' I would find the rent somehow. The council was asking three times more than we were already paying for Cuthbert Road. 'John will never pay that,' I said to Ellen. John was more cautious than me with money. We called him at work from a phone box and raved on about it.

'John, oh God, John, it's beautiful. Absolutely gorgeous.'

'What, Maura? What's beautiful?'

'The house is beautiful, John. You have to come and see it.'

'Oh, Daddy, it's brilliant . . .' Ellen shouted through the open door of the red telephone box.

'Listen, I can't talk now. We'll talk about it when I get home, okay?'

'But I don't want to lose it. We have to sign for it. You won't believe it, John, it is beau—'

'Okay, calm yourself, I said we'll talk when—'

'It has a huge garden—'

'Maura, we'll talk later.'

I wasn't waiting for any later. I got back into town as quick as lightning to sign for it. Whatever John said, City Road was ours.

The day before we moved was absolutely glorious. It was July, the kids were about to break up from school and Winson Green was humming with the heat – and swarming with lice. There was an epidemic of lice in the city and my children didn't escape the juicy black bloodsuckers. No matter how much I washed their hair, cleaned it and steel-combed it, I couldn't get rid of them. They were like vampire lice. In the end, the nit nurse at Declan's school recommended some special bug-busting lotion. I doused every head in the stuff the night before we moved house. I was determined that those lice weren't moving into our beautiful new house with us. The girls helped me wash all the bedding and lay the mattresses in a row out on the lawn to air.

The children put all their summer energy into setting up home in our swanky new house. Ellen, Breda, Olive and Carmel took charge of the cleaning and organising and Seamus had the task of taming the overgrown garden; his daddy gave him instructions to mow the lawn, cut back the ivy and clear the 'orchard' – well, we did have *five* apple trees.

Seamus enjoyed the authority but he was no gardener. He tried to rope in the four little ones. 'Declan, mow that lawn,' he shouted.

'No, Daddy told you to do it.'

'Well I'm tellin' you.'

'I'm goin' to the park,' Declan said, storming off with his football under his arm.

Seamus had to reconsider his strategy. 'Gen, will you mow the lawn?'

'No.'

'I'll give ya twenty-five pence.'

'Okay.'

'And us!' Joan and Paul piped up.

Once I realised we had elderly neighbours, I sent the four little ones up to do their gardens. One, Mrs Badger, was in her seventies and I thought she could do with the help. 'Sure she's just an old lady,' I said. 'Get up there and give her a bit of a hand.' They'd go off begrudgingly but I was satisfied we were making a good impression as helpful neighbours.

The children would come back with bright-red faces, from the summer sun and the exertion, telling me that 'Biddy Badger' had given them ginger ale in return for their help. They thought she'd give them money.

'Ah, never mind. You'll get your reward in heaven,' I'd say.

The children were getting fierce fond of the money. Paul and Joan had the bright idea of setting up a sweet shop in the garage, with the doors open, hoping to catch passing trade. They bought a bag of halfpenny sweets and tried to sell them for a penny each. They laid them out in a neat row on top of the decorating table and waited all day for a sale. Nobody came so they ate the sweets between them.

We all tried very hard to fit in with our neighbours. Even John. He cut their hedges every week in the summer in exchange for two bottles of Guinness. He planted vegetables at the bottom of our garden too and grew tomatoes in the glass-roofed conservatory. Everything he sowed, grew. All summer long we had radishes, lettuce, scallions, potatoes and rhubarb, and there were always green tomatoes ripening on the windowsill. That's what I remember most about the early years in City Road: laughter, sun and salads.

We all agreed that moving to City Road was the best day of our lives. So long, Winson Green! John and I went through a happy patch, and the house was always full of children, Declan's friends mostly. They'd be in the front room dancing to Sparks or Queen on the stereo. If Ellen was home she might turf them out and

close the door so she could study. Though how she concentrated
I don't know. Paul, the joker in the family, was always dancing
about making us laugh. One time, he was in the kitchen polishing
his football boots while Olive and I were making Christmas cakes.

'When you've finished those boots ya can polish the hall,' John
called to him, as he went upstairs to get ready for work.

'All right, Dad,' Paul said reluctantly.

John was in a jolly mood, singing 'Rudolph the Red-Nosed
Reindeer', unaware that Paul was downstairs taking the rise out
of him. Paul was prancing around like Ken Dodd waving his
duster in the air, like a tickling stick, to the beat of the tune.

John sang, 'Rudolph the red-nosed reindeer had a very
shiny—'

'Cock!' Paul said, with a swipe of his polishing cloth.

'And if you ever—'

'Touched it.'

'You would—'

'Get an electric shock!'

Paul loved to entertain, particularly if the house was full to
bursting with friends. We ran an open-door policy. It was like
New Street Station. It was even worse when I decided to become
a registered child minder and looked after three or four children
at a time.

John was very good with the children: he talked stupid and
played up to them. They became very attached to us. I looked
after a doctor's son whose parents lived in an upmarket part of
Birmingham. He didn't last long with us – not after the council
arrived and repainted our front door. We had a beautiful, wide
white door with black studs all over it. Then the council arrived
to repaint it municipal green. What a giveaway. All the council
houses were painted green back then.

'That'll be repainted tomorrow,' I told the workman.

'You can do what you like tomorrow. I 'av to paint it green
today.'

The little boy's parents saw what a good paint job they were doing and asked me for the name of their firm. When I said Birmingham City Council they were appalled to discover we were council tenants, and took their child away.

We didn't care that we were council tenants. John and I were delighted with our surroundings and the children we looked after loved being with us. They wished we were their parents, probably because we were so free and easy and there was so much chatter, excitement and singing going on.

Breda had inherited my gift for singing so I found the money for her to have singing lessons with a local tutor. He was very impressed by the range of Breda's velvety voice. I hoped she would hit the big time when she was asked to appear on *Opportunity Knocks*, the talent show that launched the careers of people like Mary Hopkin and Lena Zavaroni. Breda's potential excited me and I suppose I tried to live my dream through her. I wanted the reflected glory.

We all went into overdrive when she passed her two auditions and was called back to appear live on the show. I organised extra singing lessons and arranged for her to sing in the bingo hall in Cape Hill so she could practise with a microphone in a big setting. She was as nervous as a kitten but we'd go down there twice a week, in between the afternoon and evening bingo sessions, and Breda would belt out her favourite song, 'Both Sides Now' by Joni Mitchell, unaccompanied. She sang it beautifully and I cried every time I heard her sing it.

I thought she was good enough to win *Opportunity Knocks*. I imagined her singing like a star and at the end of the show I pictured Hughie Green announcing his famous catchphrase, 'It's make-your-mind-up time.' The clapometer would register the votes as the audience clapped furiously, and Hughie would announce, 'Breda Murphy is this week's lucky winner.' But after all the weeks of training and practising in the bingo hall, Breda pulled out. Like me, she couldn't get over her stage fright. I believe a good singing voice is handed down to each generation. My father had it, I had it and Breda had it but she wasn't able to combine ability with confidence. I was bitterly disappointed for her – and for me. Another waste of a talent, I thought.

My ambition for the children didn't stop at singing. I paid for Declan and Joan to have guitar lessons and I had ideas of Joan and Geraldine doing a bit of modelling. They were such beautiful children, Geraldine in particular with her mass of freckles and perfect features. She was the picture of neatness; Joan was striking too but she was a scruffy little tomboy. I got them all dressed up and took them to a modelling agency in Birmingham. But, again, my plans didn't come to anything: the girls were too shy. Maybe I wanted them to model more than they wanted it for themselves.

If the garden at City Road was crying out for vegetables, the garage was crying out for a car. I couldn't drive but I bought a car anyway. And the fuss it caused you wouldn't believe. I had to have it parked around the corner because John would have blown a gasket if he'd known.

It wasn't any old car. It was a beautiful year-old ruby red Vauxhall Viva. I bought it on tick for six hundred pounds. I had to sell two gold rings that I'd bought with my bingo winnings to pay the first two instalments. The salesman drove it round the corner and parked it just below the telephone box. And there it stayed. The children and I would go out every day and just sit in it to admire it. After a few weeks, my brother Ger drove it into the garage for me. John was oblivious. That's the way we worked things out. I would get a notion to buy something, act on it without discussing it with him and then wait for the right moment to tell him. I rode roughshod over him because he was an extremely cautious man. I figured that it was the only way to improve our lives. And I knew he would eventually see it my way.

It was another month before he spotted the car in the garage.

And the proverbial hit the fan. He went outside to the toilet and there it was, in front of him. And he wanted to know who owned it. At first, I told him it belonged to Ger but I had to confess in the end. He wasn't amused.

'Who the fuck do ya think is goin' to pay for that?' he shouted.

'I'd hardly be askin' *you* to pay for it. You've never paid for anythin' I've bought.'

'What the fuck do ya want a car for? Ya can't even drive.'

He had a point there. 'I can drive,' I said defiantly.

'You can't drive, Maura, ya haven't passed your test.'

'I'm takin' lessons. It's my car but I wouldn't tell you that ya can't drive it.'

'No, but I *can* drive.'

'And I *can* learn.'

John refused to have anything to do with the car. It sat in that garage for twelve whole months before it was used, but I kept on about wanting to drive. John said I would be a danger to everyone on the road, and I probably would have been. I thought I was great, but I wasn't.

I would say to John, 'If you were to back that car out of the garage and on to the road, and point it in the right direction, I'd be well able to drive it.'

And he would make a laugh of me. 'And how would ya get back? You'd go all the way until ya hit the sea.'

I was determined to master this driving lark and took numerous lessons. I thought that driving equalled freedom. It didn't come easy, though. I had a psychological block about turning right. I could turn left, I could drive straight on and I could reverse but I couldn't turn right. I used to think to myself, now, if I can get a route where I can just go left all the time, I'll be able to do it.

'Turn right here,' the driving instructor would say.

I would turn the steering wheel but I couldn't get the clutch and accelerator to operate together. 'I can't do it.'

'Just go into first gear, give it a little bit of acceleration and turn slowly.'

'I can't do it. I can't turn this thing.'

Meanwhile, about fifteen infuriated drivers would be stacked up behind me all hooting their horns. The more they beeped, the more I stalled.

'Take your time, turn the key and give it a bit more juice.'

'But I've done that.'

'Try again.'

'You'll have to drive it yourself.' I slipped across the gear stick and into the passenger seat and made him take over. What a block. I couldn't turn right for years.

A couple of weeks later, John left the Viva out on the drive facing the garage. I thought, I'm sure I can drive that car in the garage and back it out again. So I got into the car, with Paul in the passenger seat, and I managed to get it in and out. No problem. But at the fourth attempt, I drove in at an angle and Paul started shouting, 'Put your foot on the brake, Mom. Put your foot on the brake!' In the heat of the moment, I hit the accelerator by mistake and smacked into the garage wall, crunching the wing. I couldn't believe I'd crashed my beautiful car without even taking it on the road. And I hadn't even finished paying for it. I got out of the car and put an old grey blanket over the bonnet to hide the damage from John.

He knew straightaway of course – the blanket trick wasn't going to fool him – but he pretended that he didn't. He played this big game, saying he needed to go into the garage to get something and I would say, 'No, John, you stay where you are. I'll get that for ya.' He kept it up all evening; I was beside myself. He was all right about it in the end.

Although I'd bought the car for myself, I also got it for Seamus to keep him out of trouble. He was seventeen and it was at the time when Olive and Carmel were wearing crombies and skinheads were all over the place. Seamus palled around with his cousin

Johnny McNamee, Maudie's lad, and they used to drink together every weekend. On one of these drinking nights, Seamus was kicked from the top of a hill right down to the bottom by a rival gang.

'But how come ya didn't get any bruises?' I asked.

'Because I rolled myself up and I let them kick me like a ball,' he said. His theory was sound enough: if he rolled down in front of them, they would think he was a lunatic and leave him alone.

A row erupted some other night in the pub and the skinheads were running in all directions. Seamus was chased all the way home. This time he hid behind someone's hedge. As he crouched on the ground he could hear his heart thumping in his chest, afraid the lads chasing him would hear it as they ran past. At least if he had use of a car he could get in and shoot off if he got into trouble.

Seamus was my biggest challenge; he was an easy child but a difficult adolescent. I spent more time worrying about him than any of my children, especially when he started taking a drink. He thought he had to be tough because that's what he grew up with: men had to be macho and strong. Seamus grew up in a time when sensitivity in men was not seen as a positive characteristic. His male role models were big men who worked hard, drank hard and played hard – just like his daddy. Seamus had such a great relationship with John. They adored each other. Seamus liked to be tough, like his daddy, but he was too trusting of people and he was easily led.

I was terribly tormented by his association with skinhead gangs. I thought gang culture was based on ignorance. It seemed odd to me that an Irish lad like Seamus would be part of a fashion that hated immigrants. Sure weren't we immigrants ourselves? I was surprised about the fights.

I wasn't always proud of the things he got up to. He was expelled from school when he was fifteen for being the 'ringleader' of a fighting gang. He was a bright creative boy but his teachers didn't pick it up. As far as they were concerned, he was an Irish working-class boy, attending a comprehensive school with twelve hundred others, destined for the life of a labourer. It frustrated me because I knew Seamus had a good brain but he wouldn't use it. I tried to get him into boarding school in Luton but he wouldn't go. He thought boarding schools were for sissies. He preferred having the shillings in his pocket. He regrets it now though. He said of his own son, Cormac, years later, 'He's never goin' to pick up a shovel. He'll learn from my mistakes.'

I was cooking John's favourite dinner, bacon and cabbage, and Joan was washing the potatoes. Something caught my eye and I turned round, sharp. I couldn't believe what was standing behind me: a policeman with the tit hat on.

'What the hell are you doin' there?' I asked.

'I've had a report that your son has shot somebody.'

'What? He did what? What are ya talkin' about?'

'What I'm talking about is that we've had a report that your son has shot somebody with a pellet gun from the upstairs window. Where is your son?'

'What do ya want him for?'

'Your son has injured someone. He needs to come with me to the station.' He was recording everything I said in a notebook.

'Hold on a second – who invited you in here?'

'The door was open.'

'And it's still open, so go back out to where you came from. When I invite you in, ya can come in.' He didn't record that. 'You heard what I said. When I invite you into my house, ya can come in. Now go back out.' The bobby didn't move so I gestured towards the door and walked him back out.

'Paul?' I called up the stairs. 'Come down here.' Paul appeared on the landing. 'There's someone here accusin' you of shootin' someone.'

I didn't believe Paul had done anything wrong because I didn't hear any gun going off.

The copper stepped back into the hall and made to go up the stairs. 'You're coming to the station with me,' he said.

'Over my dead body are you takin' him. Now get out.' I stood on the bottom step of the stairs with one hand on the windowsill and the other on the banister. The officer went outside, strolled over to his car and called for backup.

'Paul, come here. Have ya shot at somebody?'

'No, Mom. I shot at a traffic cone.' I'd seen the air rifle in the bedroom earlier that day. I knew I should have confiscated it.

A second officer arrived and the two strong policemen frog-marched a tearful Paul to the Panda car. 'You're not takin' him down the station. I've got to contact his father first.'

'It doesn't matter who you contact, he's coming with us.'

'If you're takin' him, you're takin' me as well.'

I grabbed my coat and climbed into the back of the police car with Paul, leaving Joan to watch over the boiling bacon. It was so embarrassing. The neighbours were there gawping at us.

Paul was locked in a cell at Ladywood Police Station, looking like a scared cat. He was terrified out of his young life. 'What is he locked in there for?' I asked the bobby behind the desk. 'Can't ya see he's scared to death? Let him out. He hasn't killed anyone.'

'We have to take him down to take his fingerprints and photograph him.'

'No way are ya doin' that. He's under age. He's neither goin' to be fingerprinted nor photographed. He's not sixteen yet. I don't want him with a criminal record.'

I wouldn't let them do anything to him until his father arrived. They were very angry with me. I phoned John. He arrived at the police station refusing to put up the bail so we could take Paul home. I was raging. He was prepared to leave him there overnight.

'Maura, let the police do their job,' he said.

'So you're goin' to let him stay here, are ya – with these thugs?'

'If he did somethin' wrong, he ought to be punished.'

And he *was* punished. Paul was found guilty and fined sixty pounds. The lesson was learnt: don't rise the gun. That was Paul's only brush with the law.

Not long after the shooting incident, I got a phone call from Steelhouse Lane Police Station informing me that they had arrested Joan for shoplifting. 'Oh, Jaysus, here we go again,' I said. 'Another one in trouble.'

John was at the hospital club celebrating his fifty-first birthday. He wasn't one bit happy when I asked him to leave the celebrations to bail out another child.

'What have ya done, Joan?' he demanded. 'What's this all about?'

'They've said I've stolen fish fingers—'

'Well, have ya or haven't ya?'

'Yes and no.'

'That's enough of that nonsense.'

I gave Joan such a lecture when she came home.

'Joan! Fish fingers! How low can ya stoop?'

She was very upset.

'Wouldn't a bit of salmon have been better?' I joked. 'But seriously, pet. Let this be a lesson learnt. You've been caught once. Ya don't want it to happen again. Nobody will employ ya with a criminal record.' Her life of crime began and ended with fish fingers but the nickname Fingers Murphy stuck for years.

Joan was always in trouble, usually for fighting her brothers. She objected to being singled out to do what she saw as women's work. On a Saturday morning, she'd sit with the boys watching Chris Tarrant on *Tiswas* while the girls vacuumed, dusted and polished. If I dared ask her to help with the housework, her stock answer would be, 'You don't ask them,' nodding at Paul and Declan, 'but you ask me. Just because I haven't got a dangler.'

Dangler or no dangler, she could be pretty hot-headed. But not as hot-tempered as Declan. I never knew when he was going to get into trouble. He was full of anger. He didn't cope well with his adolescence. In a way it was learnt behaviour. Declan was very much like his father: he couldn't manage his frustration.

I was always waiting for the knock on the door. He was up at Piddock Road police station after he got caught joy riding. A friend's father owned a used car garage and they stole a Rolls-Royce off the forecourt. Declan was the only one who got caught. John and Seamus called me out of the bingo hall to tell me.

Declan got up to all sorts of devilment and he was prone to frequent fits of bad temper. At seventeen, he broke the post office window when he tried to collect his dole money. He flew into a rage because they wouldn't cash his Giro. Then he took his temper with him to Bournville College and turned the tables over when he went to enrol for his A levels. I think his intolerance was caused by the pain he suffered with his ears.

I wished he'd had more self-control. I lectured him and lectured him. 'Just count to ten and walk away,' I would say. But I always stood by my children, no matter what they were accused of. And I encouraged them to stand up for themselves, even against their schoolteachers. 'If ya don't understand a question,' I would say, 'never be afraid to put your hand up and ask, because that's what teachers are there for. They are there to teach.'

Declan never was scared to express his opinion. During one religious instruction lesson, the teacher was preaching about parables and Declan stood up and asked, 'Sir, if the meek are supposed to inherit the earth, why does the Pope live in such splendour and his people live in such poverty?' The teacher thought Declan was being facetious and marched him off to the head.

Joan was forever challenging the teachers' authority. And they challenged her insubordination. She'd come home from school with a sulky puss on her that would curdle the milk, a sure sign that there was something wrong. I'd wait for the curled lip to dissolve then ask her how her day had been. She'd fiddle with her fingers and play with her hair, giving me the excruciating details of her latest tale of woe.

I listened to her for years complaining about the teachers' accusations of impertinence. It was one thing after another with Joan. I was always being summoned to the school because of that one. During PE once, she refused to jump the hurdles and got up a group of friends to sit out the lesson.

'What are you doing? Trying to lead a revolt?' asked her PE teacher. Joan sat on the gym windowsill, refusing to answer. 'Who do you think you are? My equal?'

'But, Miss, doesn't God say we're all equal?'

Joan's quick wit made her a star with her classmates but even I was shocked by one of her quips. She was late for school one morning and her form teacher demanded an apology. 'What's wrong with you, Miss?' Joan enquired. 'Didn't you get your oats last night?' The whole class thought it was a humdinger. Unfortunately, the teacher couldn't see the humour in it.

I like to think I bred a sense of healthy disrespect for authority in my children. I was anti-authority. I used to say to them, at the top of my voice, 'Don't let them speak to you like that. They have no right!' I had to question my anti-authority stance, though, when I discovered Joan had been thrown out of *all* her classes and had to do her exam revision sitting in the corridor outside the headmistress's office. I think perhaps always taking their side wasn't such a good thing. I should have been more strict.

As you rear your pup you have your dog, as I always say. The youngest four were the ones that got into most of the trouble. I can see now that not being there for them – John in the pub and me at the bingo – may have had a serious effect on them. Had we been more together and supportive, and not indulged our own needs, the children would have felt more loved and secure. Maybe they were getting into trouble to get our attention. They kept their fears and secrets to themselves. Maybe like me they felt that there was no one to confide in. Things seem so much clearer in hindsight.

But I was always very protective of them when it came to their education. I was always up at the school looking out for them. When Geraldine failed her Eleven Plus I was up there in a flash demanding to know what had happened. I knew Geraldine was bright enough to pass. Her teacher had thirty-odd children going for the test but only one pupil got through, and she had been given extra tuition. I was raging like a lioness at the end-of-term Parent–Teacher evening when I had to listen to the teacher pointing out all of Geraldine's failures and low marks.

'Don't you take a bit of the blame for that?' I asked.

'No, I don't.'

'Well, perhaps you should. Maybe if ya paid a little bit of attention to the rest of the class, and not just your star pupil, Geraldine would have got through.'

She was cross. 'How dare you speak to me like that? Who do you think you are to speak to a teacher like that?'

'You call yourself a teacher? You wouldn't teach kittens.'

I got her that vexed she ran out of the classroom crying and protesting. I took no notice and moved on to Paul's teacher. The headmaster appeared a few moments later and tried to escort me off the premises.

'You will have to leave the school, Mrs Murphy. You've upset one of my staff.'

'And I'm very upset for my child.'

'Well, you'll have to leave the school now.'

'I will not leave,' I said. 'Carmel, go and get your father.' I sent Carmel because she was the fastest runner.

By the time John arrived, I was in the foyer downstairs. The head was still trying to put me out. John had been at work and came racing into the school with his sleeves rolled up and his big arms bursting out of them.

'What's wrong? What's goin' on?'

'They're puttin' me out,' I said.

The head put up his hand. 'Mr Murphy, we don't want any trouble here. Your wife has been asked to leave because she's causing trouble with one of my staff.'

John turned to me and said, 'What's the problem?'

'I questioned one of the teachers about why Geraldine didn't pass her Eleven Plus.'

The head did his best to usher us out of the foyer but he made the mistake of touching John on the arm. 'Get your hands off me!' John snapped.

The head lost his courage and called on Mr Bond, a tall, slim, Canadian teacher with glasses. 'Mr Bond, Mr Bond!' called the head. 'Come here quickly.'

'Yeh, come on down here, fuckin' 007. Come on down here and see if ya can sort me out.'

John ripped up the school reports and threw them on the ground. The children thought it was great to see their father taking on the teachers. He was very quick with his words; you wouldn't know what he would come out with. We might have been poor but we had spirit. I thought my children had suffered enough in their young lives and I didn't want them to experience any more hardships at the hands of people who didn't know, or care, what life they'd had.

The next day, the head called all my children into his office to tell them what a terrible father they had. He gave them back their ripped reports and said, 'I hope you're all proud of yourselves.'

He wrote to me to tell me not to bother sending them for the final three weeks of the term. They were all summarily expelled.

Paul and Joan were transferred to another junior school and Geraldine moved up to senior school as originally planned. The children didn't care: they had an extra three weeks tagged on to their summer holidays.

Love, Sex – and My Holy Candle!

As I see it, there's a right way to leave home, and a wrong way. Ellen left at nineteen to go to university and Breda left to get married. But I was angry with Olive for the way she left. She moved in with her boyfriend's family. I couldn't understand why. It was such a backhander.

I felt it was an insult to my moral standards, sleeping with her boyfriend in his family's house. His parents were obviously more liberated. She left thinking her life was her own, which, of course, it was, but I thought she could have done it in a different way.

Olive had always been there. She was like my right-hand woman. I missed her for all her graciousness, serenity, style and class, and all that she did to help me. She was brilliant with flowers, at organising and cooking. Her confectionery skills are out of this world. She made City Road feel like a real home. When she moved out, she left a void. She took the fun and light-heartedness with her. I couldn't cope with it. I felt at a loss.

I didn't know the boyfriend's parents; I never met them in all the thirteen years she was going out with him. I stayed away from them out of bloody-mindedness. It was very mean of me, especially as Olive still came back home and helped me with the shopping and cleaning. She may have left me but she didn't neglect me. Even if I wasn't speaking to her she would come. I remember stubbornly refusing to speak to her one morning while I was making breakfast for Seamus and John. Olive just sat there. Eventually I felt sorry for her.

'Would ya like some bacon, Olive?' I asked.

'Yes please, Mummy,' she whispered, breaking down in tears. I went out into the kitchen and had a little quiet weep myself.

We never fell out again after that. I suppose I was a little bit jealous of her. She was shown so much love and I had none. Her boyfriend used to buy her these little gifts for Christmas or for her birthday and she wouldn't just have one present, she would have a hundred and one all wrapped up in a box and tied nicely. It was one of those lovely things that you saw in films but it never happened to you. He was very gentle with her. That's when I realised how much love meant to people.

Carmel thought her life would end when she couldn't marry a boy she was crazy about. She met him in Ireland on a visit to her granny's. When her holiday was over, she wouldn't come home. I had to go there myself and bring her back. She cried all the way to Dublin.

It was always an effort to persuade Carmel to come back home. She loved Ireland, and she was a great favourite of her granny's. She wanted to be anywhere bar home. She got it into her head that the middle child didn't get as much attention as the others, and she played on it very well. She thought she could spend all her time in somebody else's house without being missed. Of course, it wasn't true. She was a big flower of a presence with a huge personality, always entertaining us. But when she had a boyfriend, he took priority.

I remember the day I realised Paul was sweet on a girl. I was waving goodbye to him as he crossed the road to go back to school after his lunch. Some girls blushed furiously when they walked up to him. Oh, oh, there goes the last of my children, I thought.

Shortly after he said, 'Mom?'

'What, bab?'

'Will you not call me bab any more.'

'Why, bab?'

'Don't call me bab in front of my friends any more.'

'Okay, Paul, if you don't want me to call you bab any more, I won't.'

'Thanks.'

'But you still are my bab.' He smiled.

I have to laugh when I think of Paul. For someone with such a foul mouth he was very coy about his own sexuality. When he was in his teens, he told me he had a pain in his 'lower abdomen'. I thought he was talking about his stomach and called the doctor out to see him. I went upstairs with Dr Jairaj.

'So what's the matter with you, Paul?' asked Dr Jairaj.

'I have a pain in my scrotum.'

I knew Paul would be embarrassed so I stood outside and listened on the other side of the bedroom door.

'No, no, Paul. Not your scrotum,' said the doctor. 'It's your balls, Paul!' I had to stifle the giggles.

I went back into the bedroom after the doctor left and said, 'Oh, so it's your balls, Paul! Can you believe he said that?'

Paul cried laughing.

Geraldine was still only seventeen when I noticed a change in her. She was standing by the fireplace with her arms folded across her stomach. The zip of her skirt was open. She looks odd, I thought. I took her into the front room so we could be on our own.

I asked her outright. 'Geraldine, are you pregnant?'

'No I'm not,' she said indignantly.

'Well, I think you are.'

'Well, I know I'm not.'

'I know you are. Go down to the doctor in the mornin' and get yourself tested,' I insisted.

John was shocked into silence when I told him.

Geraldine came back from the doctor and went straight upstairs. She was terribly upset by the news. She must have known something was wrong: her skirt wouldn't meet on her. She just thought she had put on weight, but you can always tell by the sight of a person if she's pregnant or just fat: there's always a little rise in the stomach.

'Well, what's the news?' John asked. 'Has she been to the doctor?'

'Yes,' I said. 'She's pregnant.'

'Where is she?'

'She's upstairs in bed. She's very upset so don't say anythin' to her.'

The two of us marched up the stairs together and gave Geraldine a hug. 'Don't worry,' I said.

'We'll look after ya,' John said.

'Everything will be okay. We will look after you and your child. Ya can stop here as long as ya like.'

'Come on down now,' said John, 'and we'll have a sup of tea.'

There was never any aspersion cast on Geraldine when she got pregnant so young, or on her little baby Jonathan, but I didn't want to see all the girls going out and getting pregnant. I'd say to my boys, when they got girlfriends, 'Respect them and you leave them as ya find them.'

John was very good with the children when they reached adolescence. He took on the role of explaining the facts of life to them when they reached fourteen. Ellen and Breda were just after coming home from a dance and John sat them down.

'Don't let anybody, any boy, make ya feel bad,' he said. They looked shyly at each other and listened. 'If they touch ya, ya tell them to feck off with themselves. If ya get into any kind of bother, come home and tell me or your mother and we will sort it out.'

Once the children were over eighteen and eligible to take the vote they were eligible to do what they wanted, so long as they didn't bring boys or girls home and sleep with them in my house.

I always taught them that sex isn't dirty but an expression of love between two people. But I would not allow my children to have a sex life in my house. 'While you're livin' here, you will respect me and my house,' I would tell them. 'You will live under my rules. If ya don't agree to those rules, then ya can leave and get your own flat.'

They could have sex if they liked as long as I knew nothing about it. Unfortunately, with some of them, I knew all about it. Late one night, one of my daughters brought a boy to the house while John was on nights and I was in bed. I got up, for some reason, and heard strange noises coming from downstairs. I walked into the living room, turned on the light and squinted. I didn't have my glasses on but there was no mistaking what was going on. There they were, the two of them, both naked, with my little holy candle burning beside them! I was shocked. She jumped to her feet, startled.

'Would anyone like a coffee?' she asked.

I ignored her. 'Isn't it time you went home?' I said to the boyfriend, in a manner that wasn't so much a question as an order.

I thought, if a man wants to have sex with a girl why doesn't he take her to his own mother's house and disrespect her there? The boyfriend came down to the house the next evening to apologise and I gave him a right talking to.

'How dare you? Don't you ever let me see that happen again in my house! Ya can go where ya like if ya want to do things like that but you're not goin' to do it here.'

He was very apologetic and blamed it on the drink.

I was impressed by Joan's boyfriends. She always went for wealthy handsome Middle Eastern students. The lads were drawn to her pretty features, lovely figure and long hair. It was like silk threads, going all the way down her back.

All of a sudden the beautiful hair was cropped short. Then some girl with a posh gravelly voice kept phoning the house asking for Joan. They would talk for hours, holding up my line. The girl kept phoning and phoning and she would insist that I tell her where Joan was. It began to annoy me. She was the most persistent, insistent person I ever came across. I never could have the use of my own phone. It was bad enough with Paul and his girlfriends. But I couldn't understand how two young women could be on the phone for that length of time. I decided I'd had enough.

'Joan, who's that girl that keeps phonin' ya all the time?'

'That's my friend,' she said.

'What friend? Do I know her?'

'No, you wouldn't know her, Mom. Her name's Heather. She's just my friend.'

'Well, would ya mind tellin' Heather to stop phonin' here. My phone's occupied all the time and I can't use it.'

Joan raised her eyes to heaven and walked away. But I started putting two and two together. Years earlier, Joan had been standing by the fire wearing a tie, a waistcoat, a leather belt and her daddy's flat cap. John looked up from his newspaper and declared, 'God, that one's butch.'

'What do ya mean, butch?' I asked him.

'What I say – butch.'

Joan walked out of the room muttering, 'Yeh, Butch Cassidy.'

I decided to tackle Joan about this Heather friend. I waited for her to come in one evening and thought, this is it, I'll ask her outright. She was standing on the chair in the kitchen, as she often did, leaning on the fridge and Paul was frying fish fingers.

'Joan, I've somethin' to ask you,' I said. 'I want ya to answer me truthfully. Are you a lesbian?'

Well, Paul was so startled he dropped his fish fingers on the floor. His mouth nearly dropped with them. 'Mom!' he said.

'Paul, when I have a question for you, ya can answer me.' I turned back to Joan. 'Are you a lesbian?'

'Yeh,' she said defensively.

'And so who's that girl who keeps phonin'?'

'My girlfriend.'

I half expected the answer but I was still shocked when she confirmed it. 'Well, we'll have to discuss this then,' I said, as calmly as I could. For a split second, I felt sick. I was dumbfounded. I didn't know where to put myself. I was absolutely devastated. I gripped my hair with my two hands with the shock. I couldn't comprehend what it meant. If she hadn't had boyfriends, I wouldn't have been so confused. I was silent for a long time, hoping she was playing about. Just acting the prat. I felt burdened by her sexuality. I didn't want to believe it was true. I didn't know how John would react to the news but he was the first person I told.

'Do ya remember the day ya said Joan was butch and I didn't know what ya were talkin' about?'

'Yeh.'

'I know now, and you were right. She's confided in me. She's a lesbian.'

'Has she told ya that?' he said.

'Yeh.'

'Oh, well. There's nothin' we can do about it.'

I didn't think it was normal in a healthy family. Surely it was an illness? I wanted Joan to get some help so I made an appointment for her to see a psychoanalyst, one Breda recommended. Joan agreed to go, even though she was twenty-six years old and could have told me to mind my own business.

'Well, how did it go?' I asked her when she came home.

'Fine.'

'What did she say?'

'She asked me what I was doing there.'

'And what did ya tell her?'

'I told her my mom sent me.'

'And what did she say to that?'

'She said, "Joan, I am afraid I can't see you if you've been *sent*. There's nothing wrong with you. Come back when *you* want to be here."'

I didn't accept Joan's sexuality for years but I had to tolerate it: I couldn't lose her. She meant a lot to me whether she was a lesbian or not. Although I did wonder what it was all about.

What was lesbianism? How could two women be intimate with each other?

'Joan, I understand friendships between women,' I said, 'I've had friendships myself, and I understand men and women expressing their love for each other, but what I don't understand is, how can lesbians be intimate?'

'You don't have to have a dangler to be intimate,' she said with typical bluntness.

'But what do lesbians do?'

'Mom, have you ever heard of oral s—'

'That's enough!' I shrieked. 'I don't want to hear any more!' Good Jesus, I couldn't listen to her.

I learnt over time to put Joan's sexuality into perspective. Anyway, it was her business, not mine. She didn't force it on me. She allowed me time to get my head around it. She was very intelligent in that respect. I never saw her as an inadequate or a filthy person. I don't feel disgusted by it now. I realise that you mustn't see gay people as peculiar, or as if there is something wrong with them. There is nothing wrong with them. People should follow their own paths. Heterosexual relationships in my day were no recommendation for young people to get married.

Joan was my daughter who was damn near being taken away from me before she came into the world. She is still my lovely child and I accept her for the way she is. I'm not ashamed of her and I wouldn't try to change her.

EIGHTEEN

'Poor Auld Johnnie'

I had never hugged my father before; I only ever shook his hand. Embracing wasn't the done thing in our family; the welcome lay in the handshake. That was the first time I ever hugged him, when he was lying in hospital unable to talk.

He was delighted to see me, and he *was* lucid, but it was odd to see him looking so thin and frail. He looked like a little old man, pathetic, a shadow of himself. It was a terrible shock to see how much he had changed since his illness. He got all upset so I gave him a hug. I had never seen my father cry before that day.

Mammy was after falling down the stairs and hurting her back but she insisted on coming with me to see Father in hospital. I'd padded her out in the car with pillows for the journey. My nephew Dessie drove.

Father started to cry when he saw Mammy. She just sat by the bed holding his hand and repeating the same words, 'Poor auld Johnnie. Poor auld Johnnie.' I had to walk out. I couldn't stand seeing him like that.

'Poor old devil,' I said to Dessie.

'God help him. Workin' all his life and now look at him.'

'It's hard on Mammy to sit there.'

'She's strong. She's able to take it,' he said.

Seeing Mammy and Father together in Jervis Street Hospital reminded me of the last summer I was home. I'd walked into the house and found the two of them asleep on the two-seater couch with their arms around each other holding hands, and the two old grey heads together. They had pulled the couch up close to the range letting the door swing open to see the red hot turf inside. Shep was lying at their feet. That was the first time I had ever seen them in that warm and loving situation. It was the most wonderful sight I ever saw. They used to fight like tinkers but they obviously loved each other. Those little thoughts made me feel so sad. They were coming to the end of their days but I wanted to remember them when they were strong and healthy, when there was no need for emotion. Now Father was sick and in terrible pain.

When he got really poorly, Mammy nursed him at the house. The hospital diagnosed inoperable prostate cancer and wanted to transfer him to St Luke's, the cancer hospital. 'No way am I lettin' Johnnie go to St Luke's,' Mammy declared. 'He's comin' home with me. I'll look after him.' They had been together a long time; she couldn't let him die in hospital. She was determined to nurse him herself, even though she was eighty.

At home, Father began to feel a little better and even managed to walk in and out to Dessie's every day. Mammy walked along with him too but she'd get impatient because he wasn't able to keep up with her. 'Hurry up, Johnnie!' she would shout to him. 'Hurry up, ya slowcoach. Stop dillydallyin'.'

'Sure, Mary, I'm not able to go any faster.' Mammy was so sprightly and healthy that she refused to believe he was too sick to keep up.

Father was home for months before he got bad again. Mammy made a bed up for him in the parlour, and one for herself across the other side of the room so someone could be with him day and night. Of course, Mammy knew he had cancer but she didn't realise how advanced it was.

The following autumn, we were sent for. Father's health had deteriorated so badly that Mammy wanted us all around him. I arrived in the early hours of the morning and went straight in to see him. He was too sick to know any of us but he was calling for everybody. Mammy was in the room with him, praying. 'I'm delighted you were able to get home,' she said. 'Your father's very sick.'

'Oh, poor thing.'

The nurses were going in to him every day. Mammy said he didn't have long to live but she still hoped her prayers would save him. He was just so little and frail. He was the image of his own mother lying there, in that room. There wasn't a sign of him in it. I flung my arms around Declan and burst into sobs.

Everyone was sombre and quiet. We took it in turns to watch over him. I sat with him that first night. The room was very dark, save for a bulb that wouldn't show tuppence worth of light. In the shadowy darkness, Father spooked me when he suddenly reached out with his arms and made odd noises like he was gasping for breath. I took it to be the death rattles. Oh my God, I thought, he's not going to die with me here on my own? I didn't know what he wanted. I felt a little afraid of him. He didn't look right.

I shot up to Mammy's room to tell her what had happened. 'Ah, Maur'een, he's askin' ya for a drink. Your father only wants a drink,' she said, hopping out of the bed to fetch a glass of water. I felt so bad. I can't believe I let my mother get up out of bed at her age to tend to him. She must have thought I was a foolish person but she was used to looking after him; I wasn't. I froze.

I went back in to Father and helped him on to the commode. I had no bother lifting him out of the bed and holding him because he'd got so light. Then I put a cushion in a chair and put a blanket around him to give him a rest from the bed. As he sat there he seemed to be brighter.

I stayed up for hours chatting with Luke and Peter about Father. Luke went home every April to help Father cut the turf in the Castle Bog, and he was reminiscing about those times and about how hard Father had worked to earn his living, what a great man he was, how he loved Gaelic football and admired de Valera. We went over every aspect of his life.

'He's gone very frail since I came here last,' I said.

'He's sick, Maura,' Peter said. 'We'll kneel down and say the rosary.'

Peter didn't make it home until four in the morning. Mammy was up an hour later, putting the kettle on. We were sitting drinking tea when there was a thud against the door.

'That'll be Billy, lookin' for his breakfast,' Mammy said.

Billy the ass came looking for his oats every morning at half five. He'd bang the door with his head. If she didn't get up and answer it quick enough, he would go round the house and knock at the window.

They'd had Billy for years. He was a working donkey. If Father had to fertilise the land, Billy would pull the cart of dung. If Mammy went for her messages, Billy would pull the cart of food. She talked to Billy like a friend. He had become more of an old pet ass since a sore breast from his collar put him into early retirement. The two of them were always fighting over that ass. Even if Billy was in pain Father would insist on taking him on errands.

'That poor ass with the sore breast?' Mammy would say, alarmed. 'Ya won't take him.'

'I will take him.' Father tried to be firm.

'Ya won't take him!'

'I will take him if I like.'

'You will not.'

'Well, you'll see,' Father would say, tugging at Billy.

'No, you'll see.'

'No *you'll* see.'

'No – *you'll* see!' Mammy could be defiant.

They'd be having a fit over the ass. That could go on for another half an hour but Mammy would always have the last word. And she'd always win. She'd unyoke Billy and walk him back round the house.

Mammy loved Billy. She fed that donkey every morning at half past five, even on the morning Father died.

We were all in bed when Ger popped his head around my bedroom door. 'Maura,' he whispered. 'Are you awake? Father's dead.'

'Oh my God,' I said, and blessed myself. 'Go down and put the kettle on. I'll be down in a minute.'

We'd only been back in Birmingham a week.

I got up quietly and told the children, 'Johnnie's dead.' I felt so terribly sad. Then I noticed the old chiming mantel clock had stopped dead on three o'clock – the exact time he passed away.

Father was already laid out on his bed when I arrived home in Clonmore. I walked past a crowd crammed into the room saying the rosary, and bent down and kissed him on the forehead. I didn't know if that was the right thing to do but that's what I did. I felt numb, as if a cloud was coming down on top of me. It was a peculiar feeling. It's an odd thing to say but Father looked gorgeous in his white funeral robe and blue sash with his rosary beads wrapped round his fingers. He looked at peace. He could have been sleeping. 'Oh, doesn't he make a lovely corpse,' I heard someone say.

I usually avoided wakes and funerals because of a bad experience I had when I was a child of six. Mammy took me to her uncle's wake in Croghan. I didn't know him at all. We went into the room where he was being waked and someone, I don't who, suddenly lifted me up and held me over the huge, cold, clammy corpse.

'Kiss the corpse,' instructed the stranger. 'Kiss the corpse.' My God, I got such a fright!

I often had to represent the family at funerals. Years ago, when someone died, every household was represented by somebody. You would go with an offering for the dead and leave it on the table next to the coffin. It would be for the church really. My father would send me off to funerals with two shillings and I'd tear along the lanes on my bicycle, riding off the saddle all the way to the church. I would stride up to the altar, leave my shillings and disappear smartish.

Wakes always attracted the men, or rather the porter did. There was always beer and food at wakes. Women would go as well but they wouldn't stay through the night drinking like their men. I'd heard that there were parts of Dublin where the Dubs used to look up the death notices to see who was dead then gate-crash the wake, just to get a free drink.

Father drew a big crowd when he was waked. His death made me sad but I knew I had nothing to reproach myself about. I didn't think, if only I wasn't nasty to him or if only I hadn't done this, if only I hadn't that. I never gave my parents any hassle. I'm sounding like the goody goody but I never did anything wrong – except allowing myself to get pregnant before I was married. Apart from that, I had a clear conscience.

It was lashing rain when Larkins' hearse came. Mourners were huddled in the kitchen when they brought in the oak coffin. Luke, Peter, Joe and Ger tried to take Father out through the front door but common sense would have told them the coffin was too long to make the turn in the tiny hallway. They shouldered the coffin this way and that but they had to give up in the end and take him out through the back door. The crowd in the kitchen stood out in the rain to make room for them. Happy is the corpse that the rain falls on.

Cars were backed up for a mile or more outside The Holy Trinity Church; they'd never seen a funeral like it in Castlejordan.

Mourners came from all over the county to pay their respects. Father was very well known and terribly well liked. He was a sociable man who never stopped yapping.

I sat next to Mammy in the women's long aisle and the lads were in the men's aisle. Men and women didn't share the same seats back then. Father Flynn said Mass. He was a very great friend of Mammy's. He was her mentor. She used to confide everything in him, no matter what had happened. She used to refer to him as 'the lovely priest'. He went up to the house nearly every day to visit 'the old sinner' when he was sick. Mammy and Father had been going to that church for more than fifty years. It's where I was christened, and married.

After the service, the congregation shuffled across to the long aisles to shake our hands and offer their condolences. 'Sorry for your trouble,' they would say. Funerals are sad occasions but this seemed especially sombre.

Father's coffin was draped with the Tricolour and taken to a graveyard a quarter of a mile away. Six soldiers from the Curragh walked each side of his coffin and honoured him with a twenty-one-gun salute in recognition of his days as a Freedom Fighter. Father had medals for bravery for his part in the Republican movement.

I stooped down and picked up a spent cartridge to keep as a souvenir. Mammy stood straight and proud during the salute, with all seven children standing side by side. She remained placid and controlled. She didn't show her upset then. Mammy never would show her emotions in public.

After the funeral, she went straight up to the room where Father was waked, and sobbed. I remember Luke going up to the room telling her not to be crying. I never understood why he couldn't just let her cry.

'Mammy, why do you allow him to tell ya what to do?' I said. 'You're eighty years of age, for God's sake.'

'*Musha*, Maur'een, Luke'een thinks he knows best.'

'Well he doesn't know best. If you want to cry, then cry.' I felt sorry for her because I think she desperately needed to release her emotions. Why should she have to put on a front?

When I went back into the room a bit later, I found Mammy under the covers. Oh my God, I thought, what is she doing in the bed where my Father has just been waked? I thought that was very odd.

'Mammy, what are ya doin' in Father's bed?'

'Sure, Maur'een, your Father won't touch me.'

I suppose she wanted to be close to him. A part of her was gone. Even on his deathbed he said he wouldn't have made it through life without her support. She was everything to him. He thought she was a wonderful woman.

The next night, Mammy was reminiscing about Father and his land. He'd got the house from the old Land Commission and by 1972 he had enough cattle to qualify for a bit of land to go with it. I was pleased for him because I knew what it meant to him. Poor people like my father would rent their grazing land on an eleven-month contract. By the time he died he owned fifty acres.

There was a good deal of talk about Father's land after the funeral but I didn't know about the will until years later.

'Who made the will?' I asked Mammy.

'Your father.'

'I didn't know he made a will.'

'How would ya know he made a will? Ya know nothin'.'

'I know enough to know that I'm not interested in his will, or anythin' to do with money or anythin' to do with land. Mammy, I don't want to know.'

'Oh, you're not interested in anythin'. You're just a foolish person.'

Mammy went to the turf box and pulled out a jam jar. Tucked inside was Father's will. 'Here, read it yourself,' she said. It was in the solicitor's handwriting and signed by my father. He left everything to Joe because he was the one who stayed at home to look after them in their old age. And that's as it should have been. There had never been a reading. It was Joe's idea to keep it in a jam jar in the turf box. That was typical of Joe. He didn't like authority or anything official. He was anti-everything.

The Don Juan of City Road

It was a relief to be home after the funeral, away from the smells of the country, the muck and the silage and the noise of the pigs, donkeys, calves and geese. John was playing the Dr Hook record 'When You're in Love with a Beautiful Woman'. He seemed irritated when I walked in the door.

I came back to the grind of housework, changing sheets and washing clothes. I was sorting out John's clothes for the cleaners when I came across a scrap of paper in his jacket pocket. It was a note to John from a woman saying how much she loved him. I laughed. It must have been someone's idea of a joke.

I took the letter downstairs to show the children.

'I think your daddy's got a girlfriend,' I said.

They read the letter and fell about roaring laughing. The very idea of John with a girlfriend! He was fifty-one years old. It would never dawn on me that someone his age could be going around with women. Who would be interested in a bald old man with false teeth wearing a cap and glasses?

'Well, it's not his money she's after,' I said, unconcerned. The laughing continued as we tried to figure out who she was, this mystery letter writer. I nicknamed John The Don Juan of City Road. I didn't take it particularly seriously but I had to ask him about the note.

'Sure that's just a load of rubbish,' John said, dismissing it. He told me it was someone having a joke. I believed him. That was the end of the conversation. But then I noticed John's behaviour and routine changing. I could depend on him coming in for his dinner on the dot of six-thirty. As soon as I lifted his plate to put it on the table, he would walk in. Suddenly the whole pattern of his life changed. He started coming in later and later, sometimes not eating his dinner at all and I would have to throw it in the bin. That used to anger me more than anything, throwing out good holy food.

'Why aren't ya havin' your dinner?' I would ask.

'I'm not hungry, Maura.'

'But ya always love your dinner.'

'But I told ya, I'm not hungry. I don't want it.'

'If ya didn't want it surely ya could have lifted the phone and told me?'

'Can't ya just leave me alone? You're always on about some-thin',' John would complain.

Then he would be sprucing himself up to go straight out again. I hardly ever saw him. He started wearing better clothes and nice aftershave, and he wanted everything perfectly pressed and ironed, and I used to do that for him. He was always polishing his nails, and his shoes would be glittering. I started thinking; something's not right here. Something *is* going on.

Christmas was the big giveaway. He received loads of presents, one of those very good silver cigarette cases and all sorts of different coloured underpants. I knew I hadn't bought them for him and I knew he wasn't the sort of person to wear red nylon briefs! He always wore traditional white or blue Y-fronts.

'Where did ya get the red knickers?' I asked him. 'I've never seen those before.'

'Can I not choose the colour of me own clothes now?' was all he said.

His attitude towards me didn't change – at first. That didn't change until I became a detective. I searched the car looking for evidence. I found little things that shouldn't have been there, like an electric razor under the driver's seat.

When John came home late one night, he parked the car on

the road, under a street lamp. I could see him foostering about and then I watched him empty the ashtray out on to the side of the road. I went out early next morning to search the car and found fag ends with lipstick on them. I waited for the ashtray to fill up again.

'By the way,' I said casually, 'when did ya start wearin' lipstick?'

'What are ya talkin' about?'

'What I say, when did ya start wearin' lipstick?'

'What do ya mean, wearin' lipstick?'

'Well, I found a lot of cigarette ends in the car with lipstick on them. It's obvious that someone is sittin' in that car along with ya that's wearin' lipstick.'

'It must have been you.'

'It's definitely not me; I'm hardly ever in the car. I never see it.'

He was annoyed.

'Who's been in the car with ya, John?'

'Nobody.'

I began to think he was planting the cigarette ends, because I got the impression he was enjoying annoying me. I wouldn't go in the car after that – I refused to sit in the seat that somebody else was sitting in.

I would say, 'If ya have somebody else, just tell me. Go with her. I don't care if you're with her or without her. I couldn't care less. All I want to know is the truth.'

But he would never ever tell me the truth. 'You're paranoid. You're makin' it up,' he would say.

'I can live with you, I can live without you, but I'm not sharin' you,' I said.

I knew there was something more to it but he was telling me lies. That went on for nearly a year, well into the next summer. It became something I had to prove. I would walk for miles, pushing my grandson Jonathan in his pram, hoping to catch John out. It was just like Clonegal all over again. My whole mind was taken up with *her*; I couldn't relax; I couldn't even go to bingo I was so upset. I got desperate. I would watch him all the time and sneak around the boiler house, where he worked, looking for evidence. One afternoon I opened the door and saw him sitting next to some woman. He leapt up.

'Is that the one you're goin' out with?' I asked.

'Don't be talkin' shite and go home,' he spat.

I knew John would be angry with me for turning up at his work. I was like a stalker. He tried to push me out of the room. 'Go home, you've no business bein' here. Get out before I call security to have ya removed.'

'Go on then, call them.' When I wouldn't leave, he got a broom and he hit me on top of the head.

Joan would follow him too. I had everyone spying on him. It was a lot to ask of her. But Joan would always offer her help. In hindsight it wasn't right to involve the children. I was asking them to be disloyal to their father, and putting them in a diffi-cult position.

That August, John raised a terrible row when I said I was going with him to the club to help celebrate his birthday. He said I couldn't go to the club. He didn't want to see me going in there. He was so vexed he picked up Joan's guitar and made to hit me with it. Joan screamed at him to stop.

'Don't you fucking hit her!'

John raced up the stairs and grabbed Joan around the throat.

'I don't want to hurt ya,' he shouted. 'Leave me fuckin' well alone.'

He knew we were only going to the club to spy on him, to see if we could catch him out. I was winding him up. I thought if I got him to a certain pitch, he would become feverish and blurt everything out in an explosion of words. It was a calcu-lated risk, but he was more elusive than I gave him credit for. He never admitted a thing.

It was the club's barmaid who confirmed the affair in the end.

I felt that I was being treated like a bit of shit. John had humiliated me with his lies. The year had been torture. It was my *annus horribilis*.

I pulled myself together and gathered my spies around me to find out where the woman lived. I needed to confront her. I asked for Anna's help. She drove me around Solihull looking for John's car parked outside the woman's house. We drove around aimlessly, in and out of every side street, but we never found it. I walked the shoe leather off my feet to see if I could catch him. It was Joan who found her in the end.

One Sunday, instead of going to bingo, we drove across Birmingham to the woman's house. I would ask her outright. When I rang the bell, a woman, years younger than my own children, came to the door. She was dark-haired and extremely good-looking. I thought, she's too young; she can't be having an affair with my husband. She couldn't have been much more than twenty and he was over fifty. As soon as I saw her, I made up my mind that she wasn't the one John was sleeping with. He was probably just fantasising about her.

'I'm Maura Murphy,' I said, 'John's wife.' I asked her plain and straight, 'Are you havin' an affair with my husband?'

She said she knew him from the club but, no, she wasn't having an affair with him. I believed her. I left satisfied that she was telling me the truth. I thought she's a woman, she wouldn't be telling me lies. She must have thought I was a stupid old woman going up and asking her silly questions. I said I was sorry for bothering her, and left.

The next morning, when John came in from work, he said, 'Did ya go out last night?'

'I did.'

'Where did ya go?'

'I went to bingo. Why?'

'I just wondered. Did ya see anyone?'

'No. I didn't.'

'You're a fuckin' liar, aren't ya?'

'Oh? Why?' I kept my cool.

'Ya went to that woman's house, didn't ya?'

'What woman would that be?'

'You know what fuckin' woman. The one you're accusin' me of havin' an affair with.'

'Well, aren't ya havin' an affair with her?' I said.

'No, I'm not.'

John sat down to do his crossword and I made up my mind to pay the woman another visit. She must have phoned John as soon as I left her house. The mere fact they were in contact with each other was the proof I needed. I marched up to her house again. She opened the door. 'You lyin' bitch!' I yelled on her doorstep. 'You *are* havin' an affair with my husband. Why did you lie to me?' The woman shut the door very smartly.

A couple of days after that, John came home from work in a very odd mood. He wasn't angry but I could tell he was simmering. He looked superior. 'I hope you're happy now,' he said.

'Why?'

'Ya told me lies the other day. Ya went up to that woman's house.'

'What woman are ya talkin' about?'

'Ya know fuckin' well what woman I'm talkin' about. Ya went up there to that woman's house and got her into trouble.'

'Oh, did I? What sort of trouble?'

'Her husband's put her out.'

'Well, maybe there was a reason why he put her out.'

'And you'd know all about that, wouldn't ya?'

John refused to eat his dinner, just went upstairs to bed and stayed there for the rest of the day. He spent a lot of his time in bed after that. It was obvious that he didn't want to be with me in the house any longer. 'Get off my back,' he would say if I questioned him about anything.

He started spitting venom at me day and night. He seemed to hate me. He woke up once in the middle of the night to go to the toilet and started muttering at me, thinking I was asleep.

'You're nothin' but an old cunt and an old whore,' he said. 'You've fucked my life up, you ugly-lookin' bitch. You squinty-eyed old cunt.'

When he got back into bed, he started to goad me again. 'Oh, you're awake, are ya?' he said.

'Yes. How could I sleep listenin' to you and your filthy tongue?'

Here we go, I thought. Why am I lying in this bed with him? I got up and climbed into the spare single bed in Declan's room. Declan was twenty. I was glad he was still at home for moments like that. Next morning, John came into the room without a thought for anybody and started cursing me all over again with the cunts and the whores. He was hopping on the floor with simmering rage demanding to know why I'd got out of the bed, making a show of him. He said I was belittling him by leaving his bed.

'Dad, why are you talking to Mum like that?' Declan asked. 'Why are you calling her those filthy names? You know she's none of those things.'

John wasn't used to being confronted. I remember well the time he gave me a thump on the back, and my false teeth went flying into the sink. Olive shouted, 'You leave my fuckin' Mom alone.' John was so shocked. Olive was about to hit him and she was only sixteen. The children didn't challenge him very often. Joan and Olive stood up to him but it was unusual for Declan. I was very surprised. John was surprised too and said nothing in his own defence, just closed the door and went off to work.

No gardening was done that summer, no grass was cut, no tomatoes ripened on the windowsills. Everything was knocked on the head: John was depressed and angry. His behaviour became intolerable. He needed to talk about the other woman. He needed to keep me informed about her movements.

'I don't know why you're tellin' me. I couldn't care less what happened to her. Why don't ya fuck off out of my life and just leave me alone?' I said.

John lost control. He picked up a kitchen chair and threw it at me. I ducked down behind the couch. 'You fuckin' old cunt, you've ruined my life,' he shouted.

He packed his clothes, took a blanket out of the airing cupboard and stormed off out the door, saying he wasn't coming back. Of course, he turned up again at six-thirty next morning, raging that I'd put the lock and chain on the door. He burst it open just like Bodie and Doyle.

'What are ya doin' here?' I said.

'I live here, don't I?'

'Did she not want ya?'

'Ah, fuck off, you old cunt.'

John's affair was a terrible slap in the face. I felt foolish, let down and used. I never trusted him again. I never had any sort of feelings for him after that; I wouldn't let him come near me. He had killed everything.

When John finally admitted the affair, I felt a real sadness for him. He looked like a broken man the day he poured out his heart to me in the sitting room at City Road. I listened without interrupting. There were no raised voices, just the language of a broken heart that told of deep emotion and regret. He told me how much he loved this woman and how she loved him, and how it was breaking his heart. I realised that Dr Hook hadn't been for my benefit. He played it loud over and over, drinking whiskey and getting maudlin.

As John cried, I felt sadness and pity for the man I'd known for over thirty years. No words can describe the heartache I saw in his beautiful misted green eyes. I'd have been a block of ice not to have sympathy for such a proud, independent man who'd let his guard down. I had only seen him cry once before. That was when Seamus was knocked down by a car when he was four.

John was late home for his dinner and I'd said absent-mindedly, 'Where in the name of God is your father?' Seamus and Olive took it upon themselves to get him out of the pub. Seamus was hit by the car just outside the pub where John was drinking. I think he blamed himself. When he came home from the hospital he just threw himself on the bed and started to cry.

Here he was crying again because he had lost the person he loved. But that person wasn't me, and he told me so. My heart bled for him, all his aggression faded away. I wanted to reach out to him, put my arms around him and hold him. I couldn't. But I was willing to listen to his outpouring of love for a woman who wasn't even born when we were married. I was reliving my own heartache in that room. I was thinking of Tom Walsh and how the man I loved had jilted me so unexpectedly. I understood John because I had been through the very same.

When he finished talking, he was subdued and sad. 'Well, why are you here then?' I asked at last. 'If you care that much for her, why don't ya go with her?'

And his answer was, 'If she was able to do that to somebody else before me she can do it to me.' He was as logical as ever.

After his tearful confession, John expected our lives to slip back into the same old routine, me cooking and going to bingo, him gardening and going to the pub. I tried to reignite some togetherness and have a family life again but we were like two goats tied together in a field, one going one way and one going the other. The strain was unbearable.

I found out a lot more once the affair was out in the open and my resentment and bitterness grew. Ellen told me about the Valentine's flowers. I was married all those years and John never gave me a gift on Valentine's Day. But the year of his affair he borrowed ten pounds from me to buy me flowers. I couldn't believe it. I was over the moon until I found out he'd bought his bit on the side flowers as well – with my money!

John never was one for splashing out on me. While he was

buying *her* expensive bottles of French perfume, he was bringing me home half bottles of Smitty he'd found in the skip. That wasn't long being hurled down the garden.

Some of the children knew about the affair and I felt let down by them for not telling me. I was used to the children being on my side and defending me. I wanted the same support over the affair.

Declan saw John and the woman together one day and John cursed him for being ignorant when he refused to speak to her. They had a terrible row after that. He came in from work and Declan was coming in the gate at the same time.

John parked up the car and said, 'Declan, shut the garage doors.'

'No,' said Declan.

'When I tell ya to shut those doors, you shut the doors,' John said.

'Oh, why don't you go and fuck an old whore.'

'Don't be such an ignorant little bastard.'

John was furious. And I was shocked by what Declan said to his father. I'd never heard him talk like that about women before. He'd become quiet and self-contained, listening to music or playing his guitar. I think John felt threatened by him, by all the lads: they were young and handsome and dating young women.

'Come on then, come on,' said Declan. 'Why don't you beat me like you've always done?'

With that, John lunged at him and gave him such a wallop. The two of them were hitting and pushing each other but John ended the fierce row by banging Declan's head on the side of the television, bursting his eardrum. The blood was all up the wall. It was vicious.

Geraldine appeared, holding Jonathan, and shouted at John to leave her brother alone. I ran upstairs and woke Seamus: I knew he'd be able to calm the situation down. Even as a small boy, he had that ability. He rushed downstairs in his underpants. They were all trying to placate John. Paul joined in as well. I sandwiched myself between the five of them, trying to push John away. I left the room in the end and let Seamus deal with it. When I walked back in, John had disappeared, Seamus had fainted and Paul and Geraldine were sitting on top of Declan. Geraldine still had Jonathan in her arms!

'What the hell are yous doin'?' I shouted. 'Get up off him and leave him alone. What are yous turnin' on Declan for? Turn on your father; he's the culprit.'

Declan fled through the french windows and sat down the bottom of the garden crying in that silent way of his. My heart was thumping. I was so angry with John for that. It was such a carry on.

I still tried to make our marriage work. I convinced myself that I'd fallen back in love with John and wanted to be everywhere that he was. Even though we'd taken each other for granted for years, I thought I wanted him back in my life. I suppose I was cramping his style. He wanted space to lick his wounds.

One Sunday, after I made a lovely roast, John ate his dinner and went straight to bed without speaking. I marched upstairs to have a chat with him but he wasn't having any of it. I got angry and pulled a suitcase down from the top of the wardrobe.

'It didn't take long for her to destroy everything that I tried to build up – my family and my life,' I said while I packed.

'There was nothin' there to destroy!' he shouted, and banged the suitcase lid down on top of my hand.

I felt rejected. Worthless. After all those years of marriage and child-bearing, I felt like a used-up dishcloth. I felt lost, as if nobody cared what happened to me. After the affair, things were never the same. Once most of the children had left home, I wandered in and out of their empty rooms thinking, my God, what's here for me now? I was no good to myself or anybody else. If I didn't get out of this marriage, I thought, I would go crazy. I was teetering on the edge of another breakdown. I needed help.

I left home, packing nothing, telling no one and moved into

a women's refuge in Alum Rock. The refuge, run by the Catholic Housing Association, was a bleak Victorian building made up of several terraced houses knocked into one. We all had our own bedrooms but we shared a kitchen, which had a row of cookers back to back down the middle. The other residents were mostly elderly Irish women.

I resented being in there but Paul would visit and say, 'Think positive. You have a strong mind. Don't let these things destroy your own power. You don't have to run away. Face it and sort it out.'

After ten weeks, I was mugged in a phone box. A couple of young Asian kids stole my handbag as I was making a phone call to John asking him for a divorce. All my lovely bingo pens were in that bag – and my wedding ring. I had all my rings on a chain. I took it as a sign that divorce was the only solution to my problems, even though I was more upset about the bingo pens. I served divorce papers on John, citing him as an adulterer. Suddenly he wanted to be in touch with me. He sent a message asking me to meet him at the house the next day.

The house felt neglected, it wasn't a bit clean, and John had an odd, dismissive attitude. There wasn't a bit of warmth between us. We were like complete strangers.

'Ah, so ya came,' he said.

'Yes, I came.'

'Would ya not put on a bit of dinner?'

'Ya surely don't expect me to put on your dinner?' I was flabbergasted.

'So, ya want a divorce?' he said.

'Yes, I want a divorce.'

John complained about how we took each other for granted and accused me of not helping him or being there for him. I said it was a shame that it had to come to this, feeling that I had no choice but to go away. 'What did you expect me to do?' I said. 'Stay here and set up with you and that woman day after day?'

'We're gettin' old now. We shouldn't be splittin' up at our age.'

'Well, ya should have thought about that before ya started goin' around with that woman.'

We talked all afternoon, just the two of us in the front room. He told me he would buy the house – councils were selling off their housing stock – and we would start again. I realised I'd made a mistake, leaving John. I had nothing, no home, no one. I didn't think I was clever enough to take on a job and survive on my own. I wasn't strong or confident enough to go and set myself up independently. I was a broken woman. It was easier to go back to John. I didn't care about him any more but I thought if we bought the house and sold it in a few years for a profit, I could buy my independence. It was time for me to take control of my own destiny, which meant going back to John.

I stayed that night and carried on as John's wife, although I never let him come near me again. I shared the same bed but I kept to my side, and he kept to his. I have never been intimate with him since the affair. I couldn't cope with it. Even today, I can be in the same room as him but I haven't got that need for close contact.

I thought our lives would settle back down when I moved back in but everything came in on top of me. I'd gone back to a loveless marriage. I doubted and mistrusted John and he hated me for not being *her*. The affair knocked me for six. I couldn't cope with everyday life. I suffered debilitating panic attacks, took sleeping pills and became addicted to Ativan, a sedative prescribed to relieve my anxiety. But the tablets had severe side effects – they brought on hallucinations, dizziness and depression. And I would have fits of anger, which was totally out of character. I became agoraphobic and didn't put my foot outside the door for four years. I went no further than the doorstep; I would spend hours standing in the window, watching people going about their business. My routine never altered. I would light a cigarette, even before I got out of bed. I would have two or three then get up, drowsy from the sleeping pills, and pop an antidepressant into my mouth. I would do my chores, watch a bit of TV and have another fag.

The hallucinations were terrifying. I would see blood coming out of the taps when I ran my bath, and my breakfast looked like a plate of worms. I thought I was losing my mind. Cats turned into lions and our poplar trees moved like triffids, threatening to attack me. I should have been certified insane and locked up. Anything would have been better than continuing with my miserable little friendless life.

I would see snakes sliding onto the bed and over my body. If Jonathan was in the bed beside me, he turned into a snake right before my eyes. I leapt out of bed and ran down the stairs. Seamus was there. 'God, I'm so scared, Seamus. I think I'm goin' mad,' I said.

'You're not goin', aren't you already gone?' he said, trying to be funny. I opened the door, ran out into the front garden and prayed for the snakes to go away.

Paul came out. 'Come on, Mom, come back in. You'll be all right,' he said.

I trusted nobody. I became paranoid. I thought people were talking about me and sniggering behind my back. I imagined they were whispering, 'Can't go and see her. What's she goin' to be moanin' about today?' Nobody understood me. John most certainly didn't. His cure for agoraphobia was, 'Put on your coat and go for a walk.' I was too ill to see the funny side. He was in denial, too scared to admit there was something wrong with me. My illness was brushed aside as paranoia or hypochondria and I was told I over-analysed my problems. I was shocked by the lack of sympathy. Nobody, except for Joan and Paul, had the strength or understanding to help me. Joan would come in and I would feel better. I always seemed to be able to cope with things more when Joan came. My other children were angry, as if they couldn't come to terms with my illness. I was demanding so much attention. My personality had changed, and my children couldn't cope with it. I started to think there was a conspiracy going on between John and the children. I saw a psychiatrist and tried group therapy. Nothing helped. I got so desperate, I called the Samaritans in the middle of the night to help me through some of the hardest times.

My daily fix of Ativan was at the root of my problems. It nearly destroyed my mind. Nobody told me about the side effects. Nobody told me I should have taken it for no more than four months. I had been taking them every day for four years. I caught a television documentary about addictive pills and I suddenly realised I wasn't alone. It wasn't just me; others had experienced similar traumatic side effects. I began a slow, painful eighteen-month journey to wean myself off the tablets.

Those tablets blew my mind: they had negative side effects but they also unlocked a stronger, more expressive Maura Murphy. I woke up and saw myself as a human being again. Suddenly I had words in me; for the first time in my life I had something to say. I began to keep a diary. My mind came alive with the memories of my childhood. Something was unlocked in me. Everything came flooding back and words began to flow. My lack of composition, punctuation and command of the English language had prevented me from expressing myself – until that moment. I wanted to communicate what I really felt. I started to write everything down, all that had been trapped in my subconscious all those years. The writing absorbed me. No more would I be 'the illiterate fool' as John called me.

In November 1987, John fired his last barrage of insults at me. I was writing my diary when he accused me again of destroying his life. He sat down with that look on his face.

'We have to talk,' he said.

'Do we?'

'Shut that book, we have to talk.'

'Talk? What have we got to talk about?'

'You've destroyed my life, ya cunt. Why did I ever marry you?' John's face began to contort with nastiness; my heart began to palpitate.

'Close the book!' he demanded.

'No, I'm writin'.'

'What are you writin'?' John was getting tightly wound.

'I'm writin' my diary. Ya know I keep a diary.'

'A diary! What would you want to be keepin' a diary for?' he said. 'Who do ya think you are, some authoress?'

I think John felt threatened by what I was recording, thinking I must be writing things about him. And of course I was: *he's bothering me again. Why doesn't he go to hell?*

'If I want to write in my diary,' I said, 'I will write in my diary. It's none of your business what I do. Ya lost control over me when ya started fuckin' around.'

'Ya needn't tell me that you were the goody goody. Why don't ya just fuckin' admit that you slept with Tom Walsh and Dick Fallon?'

'I am not goin' to admit to something I haven't done. I know the things I did and I know *that* isn't one of them. I never did. They both respected me. I don't want to be listenin' to any more of this crap talk,' I said, 'I'm goin' to bed.'

John was obsessed with sex. For an intelligent man sex was all he could think of. He had a bad, filthy mind. I was sick of listening to his insults. I never usually swore. I didn't think I could ever express myself in such vulgar terms. But I started thinking, if he can talk to me like that, then I can talk to him in the same way. No more would I see myself as a *thing* to be used and abused. I was nearly sixty. I had a mind and a will of my own and I would exercise my freedom of speech.

Joan helped me to rehearse my revenge. I had looked up the word *cunt* in the dictionary. I was surprised by the definition. I always thought it meant prostitute. I thought, it's in the dictionary so it's a legitimate word and I can use it.

My opportunity came soon enough. John was reading his newspaper. Paul was sitting on the sofa. John was agitated and he called me that word again. Here goes . . .

I got up off the chair, walked across the room and started to scratch myself. 'Oh, I've got an itchy cunt,' I said. 'I have to scratch my cunt.'

John was flabbergasted. He jiggled his feet and shook his newspaper in disgust. Then I faced him, like I'd rehearsed. 'John, I'm *not* a cunt, I *have* a cunt,' I said. 'If I *was* a cunt I would have a clitoris from my neck to my navel, and I'd be hairy all over—'

'That's filthy talk!' He screeched like a girl and jumped to his feet. He couldn't believe what he was hearing. Paul was dying laughing.

John never ever called me a cunt again. That finished the cunt.

NINETEEN

Will I Survive?

'Mrs Murphy! Go into the side ward there, please,' the nurse hollered down the corridor. How harsh, I thought. I felt like a number on a rota for that day's business. She was so indifferent; I was extremely anxious. The least she could have done was walk up to me and greet me in a calm, reassuring manner. I was checking into a hospital, not being thrown into a prison. I had cancer, for God's sake.

'Do you know why you're here?' a chubby blonde nurse asked at last.

'Don't *you* know?' I was dumbfounded. After the trauma I'd already been through! I was about to face the biggest operation of my life and they didn't even know. I felt weepy.

'We haven't had your notes yet.'

'I was told Friday night that I have a malignant cancer that needs an operation – after I had previously been informed that I had a tumour with *the potential* of becoming cancerous.'

The nurse was shocked and defensive. 'We are only the nursing team . . .'

I couldn't speak. I felt too choked.

'My mom's a bit concerned and feeling upset,' Joan said. 'It might be helpful if you could explain what's going on. She was told to come here today but it seems like nobody's ready for her.'

The nurse got there eventually and managed to put a smile on my face.

Since my phone call from the surgeon, two days before, I'd felt shaken and despondent. Ellen was being the court jester, cracking jokes, in an attempt to keep my spirits up. It was all lost on me. I wanted to be on my own, to be quiet with my thoughts. I didn't want to have to focus on my cancer. I didn't want to think about anything. I was too panicked. I had received the greatest shock of my life.

I had felt reassured when Joan arrived to drive me to the hospital. She's calm and cool-headed in a crisis. I protested about the length of time I had to wait to be seen. If getting to St James's that weekend was so important, why was I kept waiting so long?

'Mrs Murphy, you'll be meeting Mr Young and his team tomorrow. They'll come round and talk you through it. The best thing you can do is slip into bed and have a rest.'

'I thought Mr Luke was my surgeon?'

'He's still off with a cold.'

Breda
Sun 8 Aug: Dad phoned and said Mummy's having her operation. Thank God for that. She could survive on one lung, as long as the cancer's not in the other lung as well. Dad said there's little point in all of us being here. She'll need our support afterwards. He and Joan are managing it together.

Joan
It seems Mommy has a good chance of surviving the operation. She apologised for being a 'coward' and said that she was terrified. She doesn't realise how strong she really is. The next few days are going to be very difficult for her. Please God let her waiting and suffering be over soon.

She became aware of a tightness in her chest. She is a little worried about that. For the rest of the day she was on good form doing her crossword, reading a book from CancerBACUP and chatting about stuff. She talked about her feelings towards Daddy, about her fears and her courage. She seems calmer about the operation and more certain that she will survive it and live those extra years. This is good. I am very happy that I spent the day sitting with her and listening and chatting, looking into her lovely sparkly eyes, instead of running around doing things. It was calm, friendly and honest. She hopes that this calmness lasts until tomorrow and on to Tuesday.

All we – I – can do now is hope, and be strong for her. Being back at St James's makes me feel sick, the thought of them cutting Mommy open, knowing how ill she's going to be after surgery and how scary it will be. Will she survive the operation and will they discover more cancer? What happens after? Completely horrible time.

The nurses had never heard of Aloe Vera curing cancer but I took a few drops anyway. They didn't seem to mind. The thought of going under an anaesthetic terrified me.

My surgeon Mr Young looked pristine in his lovely grey suit and white shirt. He strode into my room with a big smile on his face and shook my hand. I introduced John, Ellen and Joan.

He sat on my bed and put his two hands around mine. He put me at my ease straightaway. 'I suppose you'll be wanting to know what's going on?' he said in a soft Northern Irish accent.

'Yes, Doctor.'

He took out his notebook and drew a diagram of a lung pinpointing where my tumour was and what part of the lung they were planning to remove.

'I think you'll be better off without it,' he said.

'What caused the tumour?'

'Well, Mrs Murphy, it's quite possible that it's been growing for two to three years. It's now got to the stage where we need to remove it.'

'I am absolutely terrified of havin' that operation, Doctor.'

'Well, let me tell you this, you will be walking around the ward the day after with the physiotherapist getting your lungs working.'

'Will I, Doctor?'

'Yes, you will.'

'What about pain?'

'It'll be nearly a pain-free procedure.' I just looked at him. 'I know you don't believe me but we've got a good team here and we will look after you before, during and after the operation. You will be out of the hospital after seven days.'

'But will I survive the anaesthetic?' I asked. 'Will my heart stand up to it? What about my diabetes?' I was seventy years of age, after all. Mr Young was sympathetic to my fears and answered all my questions. He told me about the possible complications but said there was only a 2 to 3 per cent chance of not surviving the operation: my age and heart condition were significant factors.

'Doctor, after the operation, what about convalescence?'

'Well, Mrs Murphy, I'd rather see you at home hanging out your washing and doing your cooking and your bits and pieces. I don't want to see you stuck in hospital because that's where you pick up infections. There's no point in us doing this operation unless you're going to have a normal life afterwards.'

I felt comfortable with Mr Young. He had no airs or graces – what a relief – and he displayed great kindness with his mild manner and relaxed attitude. I was pleased that he was performing my lung operation, and that his hands were chubby and small.

Ellen was sniffling and crying – she had a heavy cold – taking everything in and contemplating what was happening to her mammy. John was listening intently, looking concerned.

The hospital chaplain came by shortly after and asked me if I would like his blessing.

'Yes, I would, Father.'

He gave me the Sacrament of the Sick, blessed me with his stole, and made the sign of the cross with holy oils on my forehead, hands and feet. He said he would remember me at Mass the following day. This gave me inner strength and I felt peaceful and positive.

John

Ellen is a mixture of emotions, calm and witty at times and then tearful and worried at others. We went up to Dublin on the bus, which we hailed down from right outside the cottage, and talked about her mammy for the whole journey, remembering good times and bad. Ellen has a great memory for little things that happened.

'Poor Mummy,' she said, 'she doesn't look well. I hope she will be all right.' We went into the ward and the minute she saw her mammy in the bed the tears rolled down her face. And the roars of her! She was terrible tormented. I tried to console her. Sometimes it felt as though I had two patients: one in hospital and the other beside me on the bus.

I had many phone calls that evening. Geraldine, Carmel and Declan phoned wishing me luck. Declan said he was really upset and worried about me and hoped I would be all right. The children were praying and lighting candles for my safe surgery. Again, almost every phone call was for me. Prayers were being offered in the chapel in Rhode. Their concern helped me to release my own tears.

Ellen said she missed me out of the house. 'You never miss the water till the well runs dry,' I said.

Ellen and John promised to have a Mass said for me in Rhode

on the morning of the operation. You can't beat the power of prayer.

Later that evening, while Joan was gone for a break, I had a visit from a stranger. She wore a blue dress and cardigan and had a huge cross around her neck. She didn't say what religion she was from and I didn't ask her. I was glad of the company. The woman sat talking with me for over an hour. I was lonely and weepy but I had a feeling of great strength after she had gone. The lady in blue left a little book of prayers with me and I read it until I dozed off to sleep.

Joan was asleep on the floor next to my bed when I saw an apparition of Mammy and Our Blessed Lady sitting near my left shoulder – on the side of the bad lung. They were both smiling at me and praying. Our Blessed Lady was holding a single red rose in her hand. Mammy was wearing a white frock with a high collar. She was the mammy in the photograph I have above my mantel at home, aged fifty-eight and at her most beautiful. She was holding white rosary beads between her two hands as she used to when she prayed.

A tired young doctor, in a theatre cap and gown, broke the illusion. He came to inject something into the vein in my neck. 'This will hurt,' he said. He asked if I'd had an injection in my neck before but I couldn't answer him: I was so scared. I'd had that many injections, one was the same as another. He smiled and inserted the needle into the vein.

I had a restless night after that, waking with the drouth of death on me; I was gasping for a drink. I stayed awake for hours tossing and turning until daylight.

At six o'clock a nurse gave me a blue gown and white theatre socks. She walked around the bed and let out a scream. 'What's that?' she asked horrified.

'That's my daughter Joan.'

'Oh my God, I thought a dog was after gettin' in through the night!'

'Charming,' Joan said.

The nurse gave me instructions about the morning's procedures and told me I was the first in the queue.

Joan

*Tues 10 Aug: 6.00 a.m. Spent last night sleeping next to Mommy.
I first slept on the chair beside her with my head on her pillow,
as close as I could get I suppose, but as the night wore on I ended
up on the floor, all the time aware that this was operation eve,
listening to Mommy breathing through her stuffed nose and even
praying to Mary for her.*

*The nursing team came in and asked Mommy to take a shower
and get ready for surgery. She had to shave under her left arm,
put on surgical stockings and a gown. I shaved Mommy's armpit:
she was hardly able to lift her arm up straight. All the time a
sad worry hung over the actions. She looked so small and lovely
and worried, but she was fighting the worry.*

*She was due to have her operation first thing this morning
but it's been postponed – yet again! Initially she was relieved at
the reprieve but she became agitated when she realised she was
in limbo, waiting to hear. Then she was told that she would be
second on the list, 9.30 a.m. Again we waited. I was glad of the
extra time with her. What if I was never to see her again?*

*Then Mommy was told there weren't enough high depend-
ency beds for surgery to go ahead. Poor Mommy. What the fuck
are they playing at? We sat angry and sad and bemused for hours.
What next? She wants to skedaddle. I'm feeling the pressure now.
It is so hard to watch her worrying and feeling angry and
regretful. It is pain personified. What a complete organisational
mess this is and poor Mommy stuck in the middle of it. If we
had money would it be different?*

I wrapped my rosary beads tightly around my fingers and prayed
earnestly to God, asking him to protect me and keep me safe.

I dipped my hand into a drop of Lourdes water and blessed myself. I had been ready for my operation for eight hours. By the time the porter came to take me down, it was two in the afternoon.

'They're ready for you now, Maura,' said the nurse. 'Hop up on this trolley.'

I wasn't prepared for my reaction. The sight of the trolley made me feel sick. I was petrified. Clammy and cold.

'But they said I could have a Valium. They said I could have a Valium because I'm so nervous.'

'Okay, Maura, don't worry. I'll go and see if sister has written up a prescription.'

My heart was thumping. I could feel tears running down my face, although I didn't realise I had started to cry. I tried to be brave. Joan walked beside the trolley as the porter pushed me towards theatre. I had a strong impulse to jump off that trolley. I wanted to shout and curse and tell the whole bloody lot of them to get the fuck out of my sight and leave me alone. I was angry with everyone. I was sick of pain but I offered it up to God for my sins. I thought about having half my lung taken away; how would I breathe? I felt like a cornered rabbit.

Joan waited with me.

'Nurse, Nurse, I'm very scared,' I whispered.

'You'll be all right, Maura, they're a great team and he's a great surgeon. They know what they're doing.' I was still petrified.

But then I felt a spiritual calmness coming over me as they put a needle in my hand. A jolly woman, dressed in a cap and gown, busied herself around me, talking the whole time. The more she talked, the more relaxed I felt. I watched her fiddling with tubes and hoisting a drip above my head. Mr Young came in and gave me a big reassuring smile.

'You have nothing to worry about, Mrs Murphy,' he said. 'You are in good hands.'

'Our Lady of Lourdes, protect me and keep me safe,' I whispered. I felt myself getting drowsy. I wasn't afraid any more.

Joan

Tues 10 Aug: 3.00 p.m. Oh God, oh God, oh God! Mommy has gone in for her operation. Oh, please survive, Mommy. Oh shit, I feel so fearful and panicky. I don't know what to write. Words are crap, shit, pathetic. I must stay strong. Mommy's eyes, oh God – she was so scared, her mouth was so dry. She looked like a very old little girl. Please treat her well, Mr Young. Please be good to her because she is so lovely and she deserves the utmost perfect, wonderful treatment. My lovely Mommy. Stay strong, Mommy. Stay here with me. Don't go away. This is all too horrible.

Mommy went up to the high dependency at 6.45 p.m. I phoned minutes after her arrival. She was 'stable' but the nurse told me I could visit to 'settle myself'. Mommy was thrashing her head from side to side and her eyes were rolling around. I must have looked shocked because the nurse came up to me and told me not to worry: it was normal. She said it was a bit like being completely drunk. She said the next three days are critical but should she survive she has a great chance of living a good long life.

I held Mommy's hand and stroked her arm. She was looking for comfort. Her arm felt cool. I told her that she had done well to survive the operation and that she was loved and should continue her fight for life. I whispered that the others were making their way over to see her.

I gave the nurse my number so that she could get in touch if there was an emergency. Oh please, phone, do not ring. I am worried about Mommy's survival.

That fucking phone did ring, at 3.00 a.m. I grabbed it and shouted, 'What!'

'Are you a beautiful woman?' said a male voice.

'What? I'm Joan. Is that the hospital?'

'Are you a beautiful woman?'

'Oh.' I'd twigged. A nuisance call. 'Please go away,' I said, putting down the phone.

How bizarre to get a weird phone call on that particular night. I didn't care. At least it wasn't the hospital.

John

When I went into the ward with Seamus. Maura looked like death lying on the bed. She had all these tubes and masks. She couldn't speak, she just flickered her eyes. I was glad that she had survived.

Joan

Wed 11 Aug: It is now 10.30 a.m. (nearly the eclipse). Visiting Mommy and she is in much pain. She is sitting up in the chair beside the bed. I can't believe it. I watched Seamus feeding her a drink through a straw. She had a mask on (a nebuliser). She was trying to sip water up a straw through a hole in the mask. She hasn't got the energy to place the straw through the hole.

She said, 'I am shockin' sick' and 'my back is shockin' sore'. I bet it is, Mommy. BUT she looks extraordinarily well, better than I had dared imagine she might look a day after major surgery.

I was telling Mommy that Daddy and Seamus were on their way up to see her. A nurse overheard me. 'Maura!' she shouted, 'Do you hear that? Your husband is comin' up to see you. Isn't that lovely?'

Mommy just moved her head slowly, from side to side, with a little knowing grin. 'No,' she was saying, 'it isn't.' The nurse was so shocked; I laughed. I thought it was hilarious.

I phoned Auntie Carmel to update her. She sounded very concerned and I was able to calm her down with that story. She cried with happiness that Mommy's sense of humour was still *with her. I feel at peace now and know that Mommy will recover.*

After seeing Mommy in so much pain, I thought smoking was a stupid thing to do. In a big gesture, I threw my brand new packet of tobacco and cigarette papers in a bin outside the hospital.

I sat on a wall and waited for the eclipse. Staff poured out of the hospital to see it. An eerie silence descended the closer we got to the eclipse. It was broken by peals of laughter as some radiographers came out carrying X-rays of bones and teeth to use as eye shields as they looked up at the sky.

I turned to Seamus. 'Seamus, will you do me a favour?'

'What?'

'Would you get my tobacco for me?'

'Where is it?' he said.

'In that bin.'

'Fuck off!'

'Oh, please!'

He did.

Geraldine

I walked through the woods by the house thinking about Mommy. It was the day of the eclipse. Bloody eclipse. I couldn't see anything.

Joan

Thurs 12 Aug: 6.00 p.m. I went off to Dublin and picked up Geraldine. I had to pull over to the side of the motorway on the way and throw up. Need some sleep. Geraldine and I went to see Mommy briefly.

Breda

Mummy looked quite healthy for somebody recovering from an operation. She looks like she's going to survive.

Daddy's coped really well. I could see he was anxious and

thinking how could he live without her. His colour was high. He's also calm and organised. He's keeping everything on track. He's allowed everyone to do what they have to do to make them feel that they are a worthwhile presence.

Mummy would have you believe that Dad is a flibbertigibbet who can't sit still or hold an emotion or a thought. That's not the truth. When the chips are really down, he is quite solid.

Geraldine

Thurs 12 Aug: Mommy was still very drugged up and unaware of what was going on when I saw her, but she was able to chat in and out of consciousness.

On the wall was her X-ray. It showed one lung and the shadow of the heart. I said to Joan, 'She's had the whole lung removed. She was only supposed to have part of it removed. I hope she doesn't see that.'

It's done now and there's the evidence, I thought. I felt such a sense of sadness. I wasn't bawling, in fact, I was smiling. I was concerned and anxious but I didn't cry. I'm really going to try to make an effort to make this woman as well as possible but how do you live with just one lung? I don't know what I can do for her but I'm trying to be as upbeat as possible.

We got a fright last night. Joan had a cold and didn't want to infect Mommy so we sat in the corridor. I was on a chair and Joan sat in a wheelchair. All the lights were off and just behind us there was a very long, dark corridor. We wondered if the hospital was haunted. We thought it would be a brilliant setting for a ghost story. We were a bit hyper, chatting away. Suddenly there were footsteps, walking very slowly, very purposefully, up the corridor. The footsteps were drawing closer and closer, and getting louder and louder, and heavier and heavier. Suddenly a man stepped out of the darkness and into the light. I shrieked and he shrieked. Then the three of us started to laugh. It was a priest.

Joan and I should never sit together late at night because we are always hearing footsteps.

Joan

God I am exhausted. It's 9.00 p.m. Picked up Carmel from the airport. She was very morose. She was going through a load of 'what if's . . . and I was getting exasperated because I thought, we have just spent the fucking week trying to keep positive and here comes Mrs fucking doom and gloom, 'Oh, what if she dies?' They were thoughts that we were all thinking but it takes Carmel to come out with them.

There are tensions and rows in Rhode. Olive called me, saying, 'Well, Mummy might as well not have survived, if this is all that she's got to face.'

Carmel

We were sent out of the room so the nurses could dress Mom's wound. Everyone was sent out, including Dad. I just happened to look round at one point and I saw the wound. It was about twelve inches long and went from her shoulder blade to her waist. I was heartbroken. The scar was very red and angry. It made me feel really sad for her. I felt so sick I cried.

'Did you see it? Did you see it?' I said to the others. It made me retch. It gave me a sensation of pins and needles in my stomach – the same sensation I had when, as babies, each of my lads fell over for the first time and I saw them bleed. It made me realise how vulnerable they were. When I saw that scar, it made me feel exactly the same. I thought, isn't life fragile?

Dad looks very frail. He looks distracted and concerned but he can't display it. He's going to the hospital every opportunity he can, even if it means going on the bus. He goes no matter how many times Mom criticises him, or tells him to go away or says, 'What are you doin' here?'

I sometimes think they're always in competition to be the most

ill and that frustrates me because their illnesses are poles apart.
Hers is life-threatening and devastating. His epilepsy is not so
life-threatening but it could threaten him at any point in his life.
Mom doesn't seem to acknowledge that he has got a serious
illness. We can't take Daddy's illness seriously.

I was back on Robert Adams Ward and happy to see familiar
smiling faces. Joan was beside my bed. My back was sore and
my neck ached. The staff looked pleased to see me and told me
how well I was doing. I had made it.

Mr Young came striding towards me with a great smile on his
face. 'How are you, Mrs Murphy?'

'I'm all right, Doctor.' He held my hand and took my pulse.

'I'm sorry to have to tell you I had to take the whole lung.'

'Did you, Doctor?'

'Your right lung is very healthy. It should be all right.'

'That's good to know.'

I felt very uneasy and worried about how I would breathe with
just one lung. But he said I had nothing to worry about: the
remaining lung was very healthy and the lymph glands were clear
of cancerous nodes. The lung would expand in time to take over
the work of two lungs.

Mr Young said the wound was healing nicely. It had only been
four days since the operation and I was to be allowed home the
following Tuesday. Hospital was no place to be after surgery of
this magnitude, he said. I would be sensitive to all types of germs
and infection. I would heal much better in my own house, so
long as it was damp-dusted each day.

My joints and heels were so tender; I was having ointment
rubbed into them every night. Someone suggested that I might
wear bed socks to protect them; I was still wearing my white
theatre socks and the nurses weren't impressed. I kept them as
a souvenir.

Geraldine

Tues 17 Aug: I enjoy the hospital visits. We're allowed to stay there all day and all night. Mommy and me have perfected our technique to help lift her up in the bed. She calls me an orangutan – legs out, legs apart, bum out and using my whole body to lift her. It's all about the position, and putting as little strain on my back as possible. Unfortunately, poor Daddy couldn't get it right.

Mommy's coming home from the hospital today. It's important that she has as germ-free a place to stay as possible. Today I'm going to clean her bedroom. I'm taking everything up and giving it a really good clean from top to bottom – washing the curtains, washing the blinds, cleaning the windows, vacuuming the mattress and headboard, changing all the sheets and making sure it's as dust-free as possible.

A Dr Chang brought me the good news: I was going home. He was on call that morning and it fell upon him to tell me that I was well enough to be discharged. It was a glorious day.

I would miss the young girls who spent time sitting on my bed, chatting to me when I was scared and lonely, and holding my hand reassuringly. They had become my extended family and I might never see them again.

It was going to be sad to leave the team that had carried me through such a horrible illness. God bless their hands.

TWENTY

The Easter Rowing

I heaved the car door shut and began my final journey to Ireland on a drizzly, foggy night. Summer was all but over; the days were still warm but the nights were becoming chilly. My last day in England was hectic. John helped with the packing and all the children were home for my big send off. I was leaving England for good.

I'd had enough of City Road life, the hassle, the affair, the drinking and my disappointment in John. It was time to look after myself. Time to shove off. I'd done my job rearing my children. They were grown up now, with children of their own. I'd watched my youngest child, Paul, marrying his childhood sweetheart just two days earlier. I could leave in the knowledge that they were all happy and settled. I was ready to live my own life. I was looking forward to retirement in a cottage in Offaly. I decided to retire to the roads I knew well.

John had been true to his word. When I moved back home after the affair, we bought our council house under the Tories' right-to-buy scheme. The children were horrified when I voted Conservative, and I haven't voted for them since, but they were offering us the chance to buy our house. I saw the potential for property values to rise, and we could use any profit to put down a deposit on a house in a better area. We had bought City Road for seventeen thousand pounds; six years later it was worth eighty thousand, and property in Ireland was going for half nothing.

We sold the house to Seamus and his wife Laura. I was to retire to Ireland and John was to join me three years later, when he officially retired from the boiler house. Secretly I hoped he would stay where he was.

Initially he accepted my plan and we both agreed to sell up; I couldn't make that decision on my own because my name wasn't on the deeds. But I handled everything. John had to do nothing, only sign the contract. He liked the idea of being left with a bit of money, his share of the profit, having a bit of freedom himself and not having to account to me. But I never knew for sure how he felt about it because he wasn't open enough to tell me, and I didn't give him much of a chance to say anything. I was moving back to Ireland and that was that.

'If that's what ya want to do,' he would say.

'Yes,' I told him, 'that's what I want to do.'

'Maura, do whatever ya want.'

But when it came to finalising the sale, John had second thoughts and refused to sign the deeds over to Seamus. He was upset because he was seeing his home going from underneath him, even though it was agreed that he would continue to live in the house, with Seamus and Laura, until he joined me in Ireland.

I told him he had to stick to the agreement. He relented in the end but he wasn't happy. None of this he expressed clearly while sober. John's true feelings would all come out when he was drunk, in a rant.

I was wrapped up in the excitement I felt: I was buying my freedom, albeit temporarily. I'd been plotting my retirement for twenty years. I was sixty-one years old now, and it was finally happening.

Monday 11 September 1989, the removal men came on the dot of nine. It had taken me a week to pack but I had my helpers, Ellen, Breda, Olive, Carmel, Geraldine and Joan. The cottage wasn't big enough to take all my furniture; I had to leave some of it behind, including a mahogany dining room table, a 1930s kidney-shaped dressing table and my light-oak writing bureau, which I had bought for fourteen pounds. I saw the exact same one on the *Antiques Roadshow* that went for thousands of pounds.

The remaining furniture was going off on its eight hundred pound journey across the Irish Sea. I followed behind the removal men with Seamus and Joan. John came along as well, just to see me settle in. He was next to me on the back seat lepping and jumping like a hen on a hot griddle, announcing that he had changed his mind about coming. He was making us all nervous. 'Do ya want to get out?' asked Seamus. John didn't give him a straight answer, so Seamus revved the engine and we were off.

We picked up the keys to the cottage from Moore, the solicitor in Edenderry, then drove out to Dunville in Rhode.

The cottage smelt damp and unlived in even though Gerry Hickey, a distant relative and the previous owner, had been down to light the fires for me. Peter's son Paul had left two bags of logs and two bags of turf outside the back door. We shuffled from one room to the other. I didn't like the wallpaper. It was ancient, patterned and had gone so mouldy it was slipping off the walls. 'That'll have to go,' I said. I opened the door to the bathroom. 'This is goin' to be changed.'

'God, Mommy,' said Joan, 'that toilet's disgusting. Did we bring any bleach?'

'No, and we've left the box of cleanin' stuff behind.'

It was a dotey little place, though, and I could see the potential.

When I was a child, the cottage belonged to the sailor Hickey and his wife, distant relatives of my grandmother's. The original cottage only had three rooms: two bedrooms and a kitchen in the middle. That kitchen is now the sitting room, and a bathroom, extra bedroom and new kitchen have been built on to the back. It wasn't a castle or a mansion but it was a place I could live on my own, where I would be free to open and close the door, get up or stay in bed, without any questions being asked.

The furniture arrived at five-thirty and Breda and Olive turned up a while later. The removal men were down-to-earth, hardworking helpful Brummies. It was a terrible shock when one of them got a message that his wife had died. It was very upsetting, for everyone. There was a collection in Doyles pub to get him a flight back to England that night. News of the death put a little bit of a dampener on the whole thing. Joan, Breda and Olive worked like Trojans helping me to unpack. There was no sign of John or Seamus. Neither of them did a hand's turn. They went up to Doyles for a pint (or three).

John was glad to be back in the pub, having a great time, meeting all his old friends. The drinks were flying in his favour all night. The women were left to get on with the hard work but we had fun. We enjoyed the *craic* and being foolish. We took rolls of photographs. I brought all my houseplants from Birmingham – a spider plant, several geraniums and a spectacular yucca – and Olive found the right positions for them. It made up for the bleak view out the windows: there wasn't a shrub or a flower to be seen in the garden.

I was happy to be back in Ireland, and so was Mammy. She would never welcome you with a handshake, let alone a hug, but she visited me every day smiling and acting delighted. 'Thanks be to God you're home, outta that ol' pagan country,' she said.

'Well, I'm here now, aren't I?' I said. I felt secure to be near Mammy again. She understood me.

The following day, John went back up to Doyles and Breda and Joan drove into Tullamore for a sweeping brush, two doormats and the cleaning stuff – and promptly left them behind in the shop. Olive went with them to buy bread and raspberry jam. She didn't forget those. It was like her to concentrate on the food and the flowers.

John came home and tucked into a dinner of bacon, cabbage and spuds, while Breda got stuck into the kitchen, pulling the paper off the wall. Then she drove back into Tullamore with Joan to rescue the sweeping brush and mats. We had nearly everything now except a mop and bucket, a dustpan and brush and a toilet brush. It's funny how you forget those boring essentials when you move house.

That evening we all took a break from decorating and cleaning and went up to Doyles with John. I was over sixty years old and that was the first time I had ever been inside a pub in Offaly. We had a great laugh. John was trying his best to get Breda up to sing.

'Breda, give us a song.'

'No, Dad.'

'But ya have a beautiful voice, pet. Just one song.' After much cajoling, she got up and sang a beautiful Irish song in Gaelic. You could have heard a pin drop. They were mesmerised by the 'Brit' singing in the mother tongue. She was very popular in Doyles. Not as popular as John, though. The drinks were still 'flying in his favour' and he was *stocious* by the time we got home.

I was very lonely when the girls went back home but I knew I had made the right decision to retire to Ireland. John was sad to be going back to Birmingham but he promised to visit me again soon. I hoped he would stay away. I needed to clear my head. I had been off the tablets for six months and decided to take regular walks up Fahy Hill. It was hard going but you could see all that was beautiful about Rhode, all the things you never think about when you're living there and struggling to get by: the big oak trees, the patchwork of fields with its assortment of colours and textures, the Big House at Rathmoyle, and the line of small cottages, nestling side by side, all the way up to the village.

It was difficult to settle in on my own. I was accustomed to the noisy, brightly lit city, but now I was plunged into the darkness of the countryside. And the winds are something desperate in the country, especially in the winter. They unnerved me. I mistook the cracklings of bushes for footsteps, thinking strangers up to no good were walking around the cottage. An owl would hoot. That was eerie.

The days were no problem. I was busy in the week, sorting things out, rearranging furniture, putting out my books and cuddly toys, Delph and ornaments. Sundays were peaceful. I would get up early, have my tea and smoke two or three cigarettes before my wash. Then I would toddle off to Mass after breakfast, stopping off at Flynn's butchers on the way back to buy myself a hot chicken for dinner. The afternoons would often be spent at Mammy's. It was very relaxing walking the three miles to Mammy's in Clonmore. This time I stuck to the tar roads.

The weekdays couldn't have been more different. My neighbour Kitty came to me every morning on the dot of the clock and put her head around the door. 'Are you dead or alive, Maura?' she'd shout.

'I think I'm alive, Kitty. I'm not sure,' I joked from my bed.

After my smokes and breakfast, I would get to work in the acre clearing the multitude of weeds, nettles and rusty palings. Every spare minute was spent in the garden, sowing and planting. The first thing I did was plant a row of conifers as a windbreak, then smoky poplars, flowering weeping shrubs, roses and honeysuckle. The apple, plum and cherry trees I planted would produce home-grown fruit, and the Virginia creeper and variegated ivies would cover the gable ends.

After gardening I would sit down at my writing desk – an old school desk I took with me that Joan and Geraldine rescued from a skip – to write up my diary. By late afternoon I was usually inundated with visitors, mostly teenagers from around the area. The lads used to help me with little bits of outside work and I would pay them and feed them. I made a good friend of a girl called Noleen and organised a surprise sixteenth birthday party for her – the first birthday party she'd ever had.

I was like the Pied Piper. Kitty's daughter Caroline often stayed. The girls were always walking up to the shops for me and helping around the house. I liked the company and banter of teenagers. They were full of stories and fun; they brought the place alive.

It was lovely to have so much activity in the cottage but I needed to get out more. One beautiful sunny Sunday the cars were flying past on their way to a fair in Rhode football field. They all waved but no one offered to take me with them. I needed a car.

Building work on the garage started on St Patrick's Day 1990. My neighbours thought it was a terrible disgrace to build on a holy day – and John thought it was wholly disgraceful to be building at all.

'What would ya want a garage for when you've no car to put in it?' he asked one day when he phoned.

'Sure I'll get a car.'

'And what is that costin'?'

'Nine hundred pounds,' I fibbed. He would have a hairy fit if he knew I'd spent fifteen hundred pounds. 'It's a little less than what you'll spend on drink in the next year.'

'And whose money are ya goin' to use?'

'I'll use my own money.'

'And where would you get money? It's my money you're usin'.'

'No, it isn't.'

'Well, where did ya get the money?'

'You know I made a few thousand on the exchange rate.'

'And where did that money come from in the first place?'

'John, what are ya goin' on about?'

'It's me that worked twelve-hour shifts to pay the mortgage that made that money.'

'I'm not askin' you for the money. I'm just tellin' you that I'm buildin' a garage and a turf shed *and* I'm puttin' in central heatin', *and* I'm buyin' a new range, *and* I'm gettin' new units for the kitchen *and* I'm buyin' a car.'

'Don't I have any say in it?'

'I'm only tryin' to make a nice home for us. Why is it that every time I want to do somethin' when money's involved it has to constitute an almighty row?'

I thought John was probably jealous because everyone was pointing out how well I had done since I retired and what a difference I was making to the house. He wasn't getting the same kind of attention. But the garage stood empty for the next two years.

John came to visit that Easter, and we had a nasty row. The day he was due to go back to England there was no sign of a mood on him. He'd gone to Mass, and then went drinking in Doyles. I had ironed and packed his clothes so that he could have a couple of hours' kip before catching the overnight coach home. I'd made a special bit of dinner, T-bone steak, lots of vegetables, gravy and a trifle to follow. Afterwards, I made a cup of tea and moved to the sitting room to watch Offaly versus The Lily Whites. John joined me five minutes later with his mug of tea. He seemed a little off balance. He made it to the armchair and sat down.

'Did ya enjoy your dinner?' I asked.

'I did.'

'Why don't ya go and lie down for an hour? I'll call you at five o'clock.'

Well, I surely wasn't prepared for the lambasting I got after that. His face was beetroot red and screwed up in anger. Out of the blue he shouted, 'You've fucked my life up good and proper, you auld bitch. Ya don't want me here. Ya want to get rid of me.'

'What are ya talkin' about? How have I fucked your life?'

'You've even packed my case. You've ruined my fuckin' life.'

'Why have ya come home here with that nasty expression on your face?' I said. 'I've cooked the dinner, I've ironed all your clothes and I got your case packed and ready.'

'You're nothin' but an old whore.'

'It's a shame the people in Doyles can't see the real John Murphy. I don't have to listen to this crap. Keep it for pubs and don't be bringin' it home to me.'

I got up with my cup of tea and left the room. John hurled his mug at me, splattering the freshly papered walls, threatening to punch me, and chased me out of the sitting room. Then he grabbed me around the throat, just as Noleen showed up in the hallway.

'Get out quick, Noleen,' I shouted. She refused to leave without me, dragging me by the arm. I was stuck between the back door and the hall door with Noleen pulling me out and John dragging me back by my hair. He caught my heel and shoulder in the glass door and burst the pane with his fist.

'Get out!' he said to me and, turning to Noleen, 'and you can fuck off as well.'

'Come on, Maura. John's mad, he's mad,' she said. 'He looks mad.'

I flew like the wheels of hell out the gate, my cup of tea still in my hand. 'John looked shockin' vexed,' she said.

Noleen got an awful fright and I was as grey as a badger. I couldn't speak. 'Noleen,' I gasped. 'I think I'm goin' to have a heart attack.'

I went back home five hours later and walked gingerly around the house. There was no sign of John. I thought he had left but then I spotted the case tucked in behind the couch. I couldn't believe it. He must have gone back to the pub. I tipped it back to Dessie's that night. I didn't want to stay in the cottage with John in that frame of mind.

John apologised the next morning while Dessie fixed the door. He used one of his old tricks to win me over. He stood outside the open door and threw his cap into the kitchen. It landed right in front of me; he knew if the cap got the welcome he'd been forgiven and it was safe to enter. The cap trick didn't work this time.

'It shouldn't have happened, Maura,' he said, 'but ya drove me to it.'

'I didn't drive ya to anythin'. Ya did it yourself.' I was raging with him. 'I'd rather ya left and didn't come back if that's how you're goin' to behave, makin' a show of yourself.'

My peace had been disturbed. I sat in silence in my empty cottage. There was a queerness about the house. I phoned a guard and we talked about police protection or a barring order but John would have needed to be residing in Ireland. I could have gone through a costly legal process but I couldn't afford to pursue an action against him.

John rang me that same night after he got back to Birmingham. I was very cool with him. 'How can ya come home creatin' that kind of a racket, pretendin' to be such a nice person to the outside world?' I said. 'I don't want ya to come here again unless ya change your ways.'

I was nasty to the point of being cruel. In his lighter moments John would joke that he never promised to be my lawful wedded husband 'from this day forward' only 'from this day *fortnight*'. How could a man who behaved like that be so jovial and say he had any fondness for me? I was angry for a very long time.

Dear John . . .

I had a disturbed night's sleep, waking intermittently with a sick stomach, feeling tired and anxious. Ellen was home. She had bought two steaks from town that day and we had a gorgeous dinner together. I'd opened a pack of twenty, had a smoke and watched a late film starring Burt Lancaster and Kirk Douglas. I had a final cigarette in bed before turning over and going to sleep.

I woke at three o'clock with crushing, stabbing chest pains radiating down my left arm. My arm felt dead and heavy. Ellen phoned the doctor.

Dr Fahy listened to my heartbeat and took my blood pressure. 'You've had a heart attack,' he said.

Pain has been the story of my life. Sometimes I think I was born to suffer. I was in and out of hospital all through the mid-seventies. I'd had another heart attack fifteen years earlier, on the night of the Birmingham pub bombings. That attack kept me in hospital for ten days and I was warned to stop smoking. I sneaked out to the hospital toilet for a crafty fag. The doctor came looking for me, and didn't he appear in the toilet and I was after promising I wouldn't smoke any more?

'Oh, we are smoking, are we?' he said. He looked very annoyed. 'Out you come now. You can put that cigarette out and get back into bed.'

I felt I'd let myself down, but I was a heavy smoker at that time, puffing though twenty cigarettes a day; that was always my quota.

A second heart attack didn't surprise me, not after the Easter upset with John. Dr Fahy called the ambulance from the bedside phone.

'Would ya put a few things in a bag for me, Ellen. Make sure ya don't forget me cigarettes,' I said.

The ambulance took me to intensive care at Tullamore General Hospital. I was put through test after test. Enquiries from England flowed all day. One after the other, the children made contact to see how I was doing. You'd think your children had the right to enquire after their mother's wellbeing but the staff nurse complained. 'You'll have to stop your children from callin',' she said, 'or I'll have to employ a secretary.'

It wasn't what you would call a massive heart attack but it gave me a fright nevertheless. I took it as a warning to give up smoking. I'm sure the children were delighted. They wouldn't have to be told to 'avail of the duty free' on their trips abroad any more. I never lit another cigarette. I stopped smoking on 3 June 1990. I kept my last packet of fags for three months as a souvenir.

John arrived at the hospital with Olive and Paul. It was the first time I had seen him since our terrible row. He was doing his best to be caring, bringing in apples and pears – and any other hard fruit he knew I wouldn't be able to eat. It was famine or feast with John.

Back home, I was weak and exhausted but recovering in my own bed. John tripped over himself to be helpful, doing chores and cooking, fetching and carrying, getting all my tablets and making sure I had everything I wanted. But he wouldn't miss his nights down the pub. He was still 'hail fella well met'. He came home from Doyles with some friend or other and knocked on my bedroom door. 'Maura, Maura, I brought someone to see ya,' he whispered.

I opened my eyes and saw his silhouette, with that fecking grin, standing in the bedroom doorway. 'What, what are ya talkin' about? What time is it?'

'Itsch juss one o'clock,' he slurred, trying to keep his false teeth in place. I looked at my watch.

'It's half past two for fuck's sake. Tell whoever it is there are plenty of daylight hours if they want to come and see me.'

John went back to the kitchen with his tail between his legs. 'Sssch! Shee's ashleep,' John said, in a loud whisper. 'Will ya have a drop of whiskey?'

'Ah no, John. It's time to go now if the woman's asleep,' I heard an anonymous voice say.

'Ah, sit down there in that old chair and have one.'

John often brought someone home with him after we'd rowed. He did it to pave the way for an easy welcome. It was a relation of throwing the cap in the door. I resented everyone seeing John as this great, charming, generous, lively character because I knew different. I knew he was a street angel and a house devil.

I suppose there were many reasons for my heart attack but I believe the Easter rowing was the trigger. His nastiness had paid off, I thought.

During his next Easter visit, John rose yet another row about money, the work I'd done on the cottage, the improvements I had made and the praise I received from everyone.

'Ya think you're fuckin' wonderful,' he said. 'Ya think you're great, doin' all this.'

'No, I don't. I'm just buildin' a home for us. My name is on the deeds as well.'

'Ya seem to forget it's my money payin' for it.'

'No, it isn't. It's my money,' I said.

'What fuckin' money are ya talkin' about? You never worked a day in your life.'

'What do ya think I was doin' when I was lookin' after our nine children? Was that doin' nothin'?'

I had used up all my surplus cash and I was existing on the fifty pounds John sent over to me every week and a small pension. When I asked him again for money to buy the car to put in the empty garage he just snorted.

'What are ya laughin' at?' I said. All I'm askin' ya for is two thousand pounds out of the twelve I left ya with.'

It was then that I discovered John had managed to spend seven thousand pounds of the house profit within seven months. I was fuming. It was supposed to be our retirement nest egg but it disappeared into thin air. The children defended him, saying it was up to him to spend his money as he wanted.

'You had your share and you used it the way you wanted to use it and now ya want mine, as usual,' he complained. 'Ya don't want to see me with anythin'. It's just money, money, money with you. Ya can't talk about anythin' but money!'

'I'm strugglin' here to make ends meet and you deny me the price of a car.'

'You're never satisfied. You're always lookin' for somethin' else. Haven't I helped you enough? Ya don't want me over here. Ya just want my money. If ya don't want me to move over here, just say so. I'm quite happy where I am.'

'That's your decision,' I said. 'You must decide what you want to do. I'm quite happy where I am as well. I don't want ya comin' here with your filthy bad temper. I'm not able to cope with that any more. I've come here to relax and have a bit of peace in the last years of my life.'

I yearned for peace. I would have been happy if we could be this idyllic couple, relaxed in our old age, supporting each other, shopping and gardening, going for walks down the country lanes or taking trips to the lakes in Mullingar. But our lives always revolved around John and the pub.

I didn't want to see him any more. I didn't want him to retire to Ireland. I didn't want any more stress. I wanted to put my foot down and tell John never to visit me again. But I didn't do that. I took the coward's way out and wrote to him instead.

Mon 21 May 1993:

Dear John

I've just spoken to you on the phone. It's five-thirty a.m. and I'm really angry at being treated like a fool. Any time I ask you for money, it's like a red rag to a bull. I don't know why that's a problem to you. Anything I've spent since coming here was to make a comfortable home for both of us . . . well, let's get one thing straight here. Right here and now. You are retiring in four weeks' time and it's obvious you're not a happy person. There is no one pointing a gun to your head. You have to make some positive decisions about your life – what's left of it . . . I am no longer able to cope with that intimidation and stress, and I feel sure you have a little consideration for my state of health. You didn't show me much kindness throughout my young life. All I ask now is that we try to live in peace and quiet.

I can live easily on the dole here; at least I'll be free from
another heart attack. So think very carefully about your deci-
sion. It may be best for you to get a separation or divorce from
me. It's obvious that you feel obliged to come here but I don't
want you to feel that I am a liability to you. If you want your
freedom from me, you can have it. You won't have to account
to me any more for your actions or what money you spend. I'll
put the house on the market and we'll split. I'll move out of your
life. I can't come to terms with your selfish and irrational behav-
iour. I can do without a car, John. I never did have many luxu-
ries. I wonder why?

  Good luck
  Maura.

I wanted to separate from John, and from my whole family. I
just wanted to be relaxed and free. I had given my life to everyone
else and I wanted to take a little back for me, but he needed my
emotional support and I needed his financial support. And I felt
internal and external pressures to stay with John. I knew that
some of the children didn't want me to leave their father. They
would have been very upset, even though they were all over
twenty-five. They thought he was vulnerable and that his temper
would dissolve and all would be well again. But the pattern was
established: row and make up; row and make up.

  We made up, and he moved in.

I couldn't bear to look at John's retirement photos. I was too mad
with him. The children had arranged a big party for him at an
Irish hotel in Edgbaston adorned with huge home-made retirement and good luck banners – *Slán agus Beannacht*, they said.

  Joan had treated her daddy like a star, following him around,
like the paparazzi, with her camera all day long. She had the job
of keeping him sober for as long as possible before his party. But
he gave her the slip and headed for his local. All the party guests

were waiting at the hotel for his appearance but there was no sign of him. Jack Murphy, his cousin from Clonegal, was the only one with the nose to sniff him out. John turned up anaesthetised an hour and a half late. That drunken grin of his was prominent in every photo.

The children were disappointed that I didn't make it over for their daddy's retirement but I was in one of my best selfish moods. I didn't want to know anything about it. There was no party for me when I was sixty. I couldn't understand their loyalty to him. They were behaving like he was God's gift to them and I resented it because he never went to any of their parties. He didn't go to their school sports days, or parents' evenings, and he even thought hard about going to their weddings. I didn't think that he was worthy enough to have a party.

It shocked me to find out it was Joan's idea. She explained that they wanted to show their appreciation for all the twelve-hour days he had worked in the boiler house to clothe and feed them. They also felt sad for him: he was lonely and drinking heavily.

It was unfair of me to be critical; he was their father, not mine. I didn't have such a great connection with my own father and found it strange that my children should love their daddy so much.

But we settled into as happy a retirement as was possible, for two people continually at loggerheads, but I was determined to gain my independence in whatever way I could. I eventually scored a victory over the car kerfuffle and bought a Nissan Micra. I still hadn't passed my driving test so I would have to drive on a provisional licence – or use my pensioner bus pass. Even having a bus pass was some kind of achievement, I suppose. I'd applied for it at the same time John applied. His pass arrived a few weeks later but nothing came for me. It must be lost in the post, I thought. I called the Department of Social Welfare in Sligo.

'Where's my bus pass?' I asked the woman on the other end

of the phone. 'You've given one to my husband but not to me.'

'A bus pass has been issued to your husband. You can use it as a passenger so long as you travel together,' she said.

I was outraged. 'I don't want to be a passenger. I want my own pass. I want to be independent.' John was standing in the corner of the kitchen listening to this conversation, squirming.

'There's nothing I can do about that, Mrs Murphy.'

'It's my right to have my own bus pass. I don't want to always travel with him. I want my own signature on my own bus pass.'

'But Mrs Murphy, we don't issue separate passes to married couples. You'd have to be accompanied by your husband.'

'I don't want to travel with him.'

'And I don't want to travel with you!' John screeched in the background. He was incensed.

'Have yous not heard tell of equal rights?' I shouted down the phone. 'I want my equal rights.'

'We'll be in touch with you,' she said, exasperated.

My bus pass arrived two weeks later. It was a small but significant victory. I progressed to a wheelie bin after that. John sulked for a whole day because I dared to express the will to make a decision for myself.

'John, I was thinkin' of gettin' a wheelie bin,' I said innocently.

'What do ya want with a wheelie bin? Can't we put the rubbish out in bags?'

'I'm not always able to carry out the bags, sure I'm still recoverin' from the heart attack.'

John raised his eyes to heaven. 'I'll carry them out.'

'Yeh, but you're not always here. I'm gettin' a wheelie bin and that's that. And stop tryin' to think for me and tellin' me what to do. I am long past that stage now.' John shook his head and walked away. It was an outrageous waste of good money, he said. I won't even tell you what I said to him about pissing money down the toilet in the pub. He carried on drinking; I carried on moaning about it. After he retired to Rhode, I was receiving regular calls from Doyles asking me to pick up my inebriated husband.

John would get so drunk one of the barmen would often deposit him outside the cottage on his way home. But he wasn't always chauffeured around Rhode. He would usually stagger the half-mile home grinning and singing the Petula Clark song 'Sailor' all the way.

One time he was so pissed he fell in the ditch and lost his false teeth and glasses. My teenage grandsons, Carmel's son Kieran and Jonathan, were visiting that time. They carried their granddad into the sitting room and put a packet of frozen peas on his head, showing great concern. But they were dying laughing inside. Each time the giggles possessed them they rushed into the kitchen to laugh, as silently as they could. Then they'd go back in to John all sombre and caring.

Mammy loved it when John retired to Rhode. Even at the age of ninety, she was able to have good sport with him. He would entertain her, come in wearing one of my hats or even one of my dresses. One time after we'd had a disagreement, and he was trying to get around me, he came in wearing my big old grey gardening dress over his trousers. He looked just like his grandmother, especially with the green checked tablecloth on his head. Mammy died laughing. 'You're shockin' funny, John,' she said. You wouldn't know what John would appear in next.

If John said, 'Ah, fuck it,' Mammy would reply, 'Double fuck it!' She wouldn't say anything too dirty but she'd say *fuck*. That wasn't a swear word as far as she was concerned because of the German Fokker warplane.

She was always codding the children. A favourite trick was to sit in the chair like the little old lady she appeared to be and ask Geraldine for help. 'Geraldine, would ya help me out of this chair, I need to go to the toilet.'

'Okay, Granny, take my arm. That's it.'

As Geraldine tried to lift her granny up, Mammy would yank her by both arms and land her granddaughter on the couch beside her. 'Ya think I'm auld, don't ya?' Mammy would say, cackling.

Mammy was so well loved. She was the oldest woman round Rhode. She became the village matriarch. Everyone called her Granny, on her insistence, whether they were related or not. 'Call me Granny or Mary Ann,' she'd tell people, 'but don't call me Mrs McNamee.'

Everyone was really impressed by the way she rode a moped well into her late eighties. The red and white moped belonged to my father. The engine had long ceased to work, so there she would be pedalling this lump of heavy metal up and down the hills.

Mammy loved being out and about. 'I'm comin' too,' she would say. If John ever got the car out she'd say, 'You're not leavin' me behind!' She loved to be driven all round Offaly, like in *Driving Miss Daisy*, but she seldom got out of the car. She was like a child. She would accompany her carer, Mary-Jo, on her rounds visiting all the other sick people.

She lived with Joe up at the house in Clonmore. It looked like the two of them got on well together but I remember how cross he was when Mammy had her hair permed; when she got a blue rinse in her beautiful hair, he wouldn't speak to her for days. 'They weren't born with makeup,' he would say, 'and they weren't born with permed hair.' Mammy still had a terrible temper on her. She hit Joe with the fire tongs and he thumped her back. It wouldn't have made a difference if Mammy was a hundred and five, she would still attack. They were always thumping each other.

Physically Mammy was still very strong for a woman in her nineties. John always remarked on the size of her wrists: she had massive arms and wrists. No wonder, carrying a large sack of turf home on her back every morning when she was younger.

Mammy wasn't frail but as she got older she started to feel

real sick with her stomach. I would bring her up to the cottage, put on the hot blanket and prepare a tea for her. I'd give her a wash and lovely clean nightclothes and let her sleep for hours. She lived with me for almost three months at a time, leaving Joe to fend for himself up at the house.

I always knew when she wanted to go back home because she'd create some kind of a row. I wised up to her eventually. 'Mammy, if ya want to go home just say so and I'll take ya down.'

'How do ya know I want to go, Maur'een?'

'I know perfectly well. You're risin' a row and there's no need for it. Ya don't have to rise a row with me to take ya home.'

Then she'd laugh heartily and clap her hands. 'Aren't you shockin' good?'

John never minded Mammy coming to stay with us. She was very good to us when we were young and he never forgot that. He would make Mammy her Sunday dinners and take Joe his dinner on a plate covered with a tea towel. John has a warm heart, a kindness and caring for other people, no matter how ungrateful they are.

He used to tell Mammy how good she'd been and she liked to hear him say it. She loved a bit of praise. She would sit in the car wearing some funny old hat and say, 'Don't I look lovely today, John?' and then repeat, 'Do ya think I look nice today, Maur'een? Do I look lovely in this hat?'

Carmel came home one time with an Alice band on her head. Next time I saw Mammy she had one of Joe's ties wrapped round her head in a great big bow, copying her granddaughter. She never lost her vanity, or her sense of humour; she was quite comical in old age. She didn't smoke or swear when I was growing up but by the time she hit seventy she was doing both. She smoked Goldflake. I was so surprised.

'When did ya start to smoke, Mammy?'

'Last year.'

'What did ya start smokin' for?'

'Well if yous can smoke, I can smoke.'

Mammy never inhaled. She would be smothered in a cloud of smoke, often drinking Bailey's. She didn't use a glass. She would get down her mug of tea off the mantel, chuck the dregs into the fire and fill the mug to the top. 'That's a lovely drink, Maur'een. Shall we have another?' she'd say. Then she'd get the staggers and would be likely to fall anywhere. When she became an invalid, she would drink the Bailey's out of a Tommy Tippee cup.

Maura

Monday 18 Nov 1996: Today has got to be the saddest day of my life. I feel a loss, loneliness and emptiness that cannot ever be filled . . .

Carmel's daughter Bardis opened the door and threw her arms around me. 'Auntie Maura, she's gone.' I had just returned from a trip to Birmingham when I got the call about Mammy's death. I had a little weep but I didn't bawl; I tried to be dignified.

Doyles undertakers handled Mammy's funeral. Tommy kept his hearse and coffins at the back of his pub. John and I drove down to Peter's to see Mammy's coffin being wheeled from the kitchen to the little sitting room where she would be waked and mourned overnight. I had missed her by one hour. She died at six-thirty.

I always wondered how would I ever cope without Mammy. Whenever she was sick I thought she was about to die, ever since I was a little girl. Yet when the time came and she did die, I didn't cry. I just felt numb. I wasn't bothered by it. I got through it very well. I was able to go over and kiss her on the forehead and say, 'God bless you, Mammy.' It felt weird to think last time I was there she was alive.

John and I went home to the cottage, banked the fires and made a cup of tea. I went back down to see Mammy at midnight and spent two hours in silence in the wake room. I wouldn't go in to her on my own. John, Peter, Ann and Margaret Hickey were in there saying the rosary. I prayed for Mammy to rest in peace. She looked at peace in her blue suit and white blouse and her marble rosary beads entwined around her fingers.

Tuesday 19 November we gathered for the funeral service at The Holy Trinity, the church Mammy had trudged to several times a week for nearly seventy years. Four parish priests offici-ated. It was a beautiful service. Father Flynn said what a great woman Mammy had been and what a lovely family she had reared through all the trouble and strife, and what an asset she was to the community, always at Mass and Communion. She inspired many who worshipped there.

I felt a panic rise when the priests were talking, even though I accepted that she was old and that she was gone. We were nearly as old as her. I could imagine her dying laughing at us, 'Look at them!' I could hear her say. 'They're nearly all as auld as meself.'

We all walked behind Tommy Doyle who helped wheel the coffin to the cemetery gates. Luke, Peter, Joe and Ger took over and carried Mammy to her burial ground. They went at such a lick we couldn't keep up with them. The steep graveyard looked pretty in the brightness of that bitterly cold day. We all stood in a line to the side of the grave while the priests said the funeral prayers.

Nobody cried.

John wouldn't have missed Mammy's funeral for the world. She was like a mother to him. We were getting on better at this time; there was a little more togetherness. I was glad that he walked with the children and me to the grave. I was grateful for his support. He was trying to understand how I felt about losing my mother.

Mammy was put into the same grave as Father, up from his own father and mother, and his Aunt Biddy. The hardest part was seeing the pallbearers lower Mammy into the ground. Luke threw the first shovel of dirt. It was so sad to see both parents down under the clay. What a terrible, isolated cold place to be for two people who were so full of life and so fond of laughter. I couldn't bear the thought of Mammy and Father just lying down there in icy cold graves with nobody visiting them. I will never be buried, I promised myself. I want to be cremated. I don't want to be fodder for the maggots.

We all went back to the lounge in Doyles for drinks and food. Not just a cold buffet; we had a proper sit-down meal with soup and a hot dinner. Seamus and John moved out of our circle and went looking for more comical company, mixing with the regulars in the bar. Joan and I went to Carmel's and we reminisced about Mammy. John came home blind drunk. No respect for the dead.

I didn't stir outside all day, I was too sad, but Breda and Declan went to visit Anna who had a bungalow in Castlejordan with a petrol station attached. Mammy was delighted when she bought it. It was always her wish to have her children around her. She liked to pop in to Anna's for a cup of tea after Mass.

I was sensible enough to know Mammy wasn't going to live for ever but I do miss her terribly. She got so ill she was better off going to God, where she wanted to be, and meet up with my father again. I knew she died a happy death and a holy death. Mammy lived a great life, a simple, humble, religious life. She was very beautiful, loving, good-natured and generous. But she was the devil's needle too – dictatorial, self-centred and condescending at times. She had all the qualities to be a great woman. She taught us everything we knew. I knew she loved me, but then I never gave her much cause not to care about me.

I have her beautiful picture on the mantelpiece at home. It was taken at Peter's wedding when she was fifty-eight. Mammy was sitting next to my father and having a laugh, as usual. That picture keeps her in my memory.

TWENTY-ONE

Rhode to Recovery

I stared at the twelve-inch scar on my back. It went from my shoulder blade, round to my side and underneath my rib cage. It repulsed me. I was horrified to think someone had cut me open and taken away my lung.

Joan was with me in the bathroom in Rhode, holding up the hall mirror.

'My God, that's very long,' I said.

'It's amazing how it's healed so quickly.'

'That doesn't look healed to me, Joan. It's very blue. Do ya think I should get it checked out with the doctor before we go?'

'No, Mommy, we don't have time. We'll miss the ferry. I'll make you an appointment with my doctor in Birmingham.'

It was the first time I had seen the evidence of the surgeon's incision. I looked like a delicate bloodless creature; Maudie gave me six months to live. 'Help me with my bra, Joan, and don't forget the cotton wool. Ease it in gently under the strap.'

I didn't tell John I was leaving him. I couldn't face any more rows, and he wouldn't have understood why I had to go. I'd been plotting my escape from the moment I left St James's three months earlier. I'd fought, and won, a life-threatening battle against lung cancer. It gave me the courage to walk away from my oppressive marriage.

I had been delighted to be discharged from hospital. I'd thought about being home, my comfortable bed, the smell of roses outside the bedroom window, the robin hopping on the sill and the jack-daws pecking at the glass. I was looking forward to the ordinary things – cars racing past, tractors chugging heavily laden with turf, even John marching off to Doyles.

I was still a little apprehensive about leaving the security of the hospital. I was about to lose the nursing care I'd come to rely on. They looked after me so well on Robert Adams Ward, just like a mother would care for her baby, washing me and feeding me, turning and positioning me in whatever way was most comfortable. Those nurses oozed kindness.

Tuesday 17 August 1999 was a good day to be going home. There wasn't a cloud in the beautiful blue sky. I was weak from the heat. Even on my healthiest days, I could never take the sun. My light summer dress clung to me from the perspiration. As I waited for Breda and Geraldine to collect me, I picked up the *Daily Mail* to do my crossword. My right arm was so weak I could barely hold the pen between my fingers.

A male nurse walked into the ward. 'I see you're readin' an English paper,' he said sharply.

'Yeh, what's wrong with that? I lived over there for thirty years. Anyway, I only buy it for the crossword.'

He seemed properly put out. 'Well, you can put that away or I won't be doin' anythin' for you.'

'That's all right by me,' I said defensively.

He made me feel unpatriotic, and me the daughter of those who fought to free our country! I couldn't say much, breathing was difficult with one lung doing the work of two. The nurse left the room.

'How dare he tell me what paper to read?' I mumbled to Joan.

'It takes more than reading the right paper to liberate your country,' she said.

I put down the paper and asked her to help wrap my get well flowers.

Breda and Geraldine arrived full of smiles. I dragged myself from the bed, hampered by a great heaviness on my left side where my lung used to be. I felt as though I would tumble at any minute.

'Oh, look at Mummy all ready to come home,' gushed Breda, as she rushed over to give me a big hug.

'Are you looking forward to coming home, Mom?' asked Geraldine.

'You can be sure I am.'

'All right then,' Joan said, 'I'm off. I'll give you a call later.'

I arrived home in Rhode feeling sure I would never be strong again. Breda and Geraldine walked each side of me and took me straight to my bedroom. Geraldine sat me on the bed, took off my shoes and lifted my feet up on to the hot mattress; the electric blanket had been set to number two since morning. It was eighty degrees outside and my bed was cooking.

She laid me back on the pillows and crouched, like an orangutan again, lifting me up in the bed, as if I weighed no more than a child.

'Is that comfortable, Mom?' she asked. She was so gentle and kind and didn't hurt me at all. 'Would you like a bowl of soup?'

'Yes, please. And I'll have a crispy cob as well.'

I slept sitting up, like the superstitious Victorians who thought their spirits could float off to heaven through the tops of their heads, should they have the misfortune of dying in the night! I was propped up by a mountain of pillows to help my breathing and coughing. A kettle was kept boiling by my bedside at all times. I breathed the soothing vapours of eucalyptus oils to help soften the cough. The turf dust was a problem: the cottage had to be damp-dusted every day. I was well spoilt.

Geraldine became my nurse for the next three weeks, lifting

me and turning me, washing me and feeding me. My ugly scar didn't worry her. 'It's shrinking by the day, Mommy,' she reassured me. She did all the practical things, leaving Breda to do the talking and nurturing and the titivating of my hair.

The children rallied round again, careful to continue my hospital regime. The staff had prepared a special diabetic menu of baked fish, salads, beans, pulses and home-made soups. Carmel made batches of delicious chicken soup, ladled into several plastic containers. It looked like Tupperware tubs were breeding in the fridge. She took her eight-year-old son Declan out of school for three weeks to make sure she could take her turn with the caring. She was brilliant. She was too squeamish to wash the wound but she was very practical and great company. She kept the chat going. I never felt I had to say a word, unless she was filling in my diary for me. I was too poorly to hold a pen so I would talk and she would write it up.

'Mom, shall we do your diary now?'

'Yeh. You're the night nurse tonight, so write that.'

'Okay.'

'*Geraldine gave me a bed bath last night. My back has been very sore. I have a hard cough. Carmel had to switch on the kettle to bring some steam into the room to act as a nebuliser—*'

'Take your time, missus. I've only got one pair of hands,' Carmel said.

'And I've only got one lung.'

'Carry on.'

'*Joan arrived at five o'clock. I'm looking forward to arrival of Paul et al. Paul, and the Irish flag and the tiger turned up at ten past ten; Dominic and Naimh had their faces painted on the way over on the boat . . .* Am I goin' too fast for you, Carmel?'

'No, carry on.'

'*Very busy day today. I was jiggered and confused. Too much talking. Ten talking, one listening. John at Doyles . . .* Is he ever anywhere else?'

I never dreamt I would ever have to depend on my children again to take care of me and help me through my private daily rituals. They walked me to and from the toilet, gave me bed baths, brushed my hair and creamed my flaking old legs. All the children – even Declan and Paul – took turns to come from England to nurse me back to health. As one left, another arrived. I felt loved and cosseted as I slept and rested. Sometimes I couldn't readily accept the care I received. I thought I didn't deserve it: I'd never had it before. Wasn't I the one that did the caring?

Salad sandwiches and cups of tea were being made from dawn till dusk to feed the stream of visitors – Tommy Doyle popped his head round my door at one point. I had morning visits from my GP and the district nurse. She would come every day to clean my scar. She was surprised to see I was making such good progress. 'Sure I don't think you were sick at all, Maura,' she would joke. That always gave cause for a laugh.

She wasn't amused when Father Cribben walked in and announced, 'I've come to give the last rites.'

'I don't think so, Father! Well, ya won't be givin' it here today.' The nurse was taken aback.

'Oh I'm only jokin',' he said.

I was in surprisingly good spirits but I could be cranky at times – mostly with John, although that didn't surprise anyone. He couldn't do anything right as far as I was concerned. He was so clumsy. One day I swung my legs gingerly over the side of the bed to go to the toilet. John came in with a tray of breakfast, just as I was standing up. I head-butted the tray right out of his hands. Of course, I accused him of bouncing the tray off my head on purpose! I was extremely antagonistic towards him.

One morning, when the nurse didn't show up, I asked him to tend to the scar. He was reluctant. He couldn't believe it was right across my whole back; he thought it would be a discreet little scar. 'Oh, my God! That's worse than I thought it would be. It looks angry. It must be very sore.'

'Yes it is. If you had half your back taken away, how would you feel?'

His hands trembled as he applied the antiseptic cream.

'Did ya wash your hands, John?'

'Of course I've washed my hands.'

Six weeks after I was discharged, I went back to St James's for a check-up. My surgeon was happy with my progress and said I had done much better than many half my age. I saw my chest X-ray. I could see the heart and one lung very clearly. But there was just a grey shadow where my other lung used to be. That's another organ gone, I thought. I wonder how many more I'm going to lose?

'What happened to the lung?' I asked.

'Oh, that. That's long gone into the bucket,' he said, slapping me on the back.

'Your remaining lung is very healthy,' he said. 'It'll move across and do the work of the two lungs. It should give you many more years of life.'

'That's great, Doctor. I'm very happy to hear that. Thank you so much.'

I was absolutely delighted. But the next day I couldn't stop thinking about my lung lying in a bucket. It really disturbed me. It made me feel the same way as I did when I miscarried a four-and-a-half-month foetus. I felt bereaved. There was a void. And I was upset that the surgeon had been so jolly about it all. I struggled hard to put the lung and the bucket out of my mind. I concentrated on getting better – and finalising my secret arrangements to leave John.

It's amazing what you can stuff into the back of a Saab. But it was still a struggle closing the boot with my duvet and pillows crammed on top of my suitcases. Joan and her dear friend Jackie Dietrich packed all my clothes and shoes, twenty years' worth of diaries, my favourite books, my precious collection of Lilliput Cottages and my £135 Steiff Bear. I had packed as many of my belongings as possible without rousing John's suspicions.

It was fitting that Joan was with me on that final journey. She understood my desire for freedom. She has an inner loveliness, an unselfish quality and a willingness to help. I was blessed to have her. She understood why I kept the full truth from John.

I did drop heavy hints, though. 'I've got to get out of here,' I told him after his dinner one day. I always made sure he'd had his dinner before I told him anything that might rise a row. He was more accommodating on a full stomach.

'Why do you?' he asked.

'I need to spend time in England, John. I need time to recuperate.'

That was my story. I gave the reason that there wasn't enough medical help for me in Ireland, no carers were coming in to me any more, no district nurse was taking care of my wound, and the children had gone back to their lives in Birmingham. The truth was I couldn't cope with being alone with John. I needed the kind of care he couldn't provide. He wasn't about to wash me and change my underwear – and I wasn't about to ask him.

The forecast that November day was bleak; the crossing was expected to be rough. 'Mom, I think we need to get going now. Shall we say goodbye to Daddy?'

'Okay, pet. Would you put that mirror back up on the wall?'

'I'll do that,' said John.

'All right then, John. I'm off now.'

'Well, don't forget to call me when ya get there,' he said, planting a kiss on my cheek. 'I'll be waitin' to hear that you arrived safely.' He stood at the cottage gate waving me off.

As we got to Dún Laoghaire the sun broke through the blanket of autumn clouds. We were in for a beautiful calm crossing after all. The sun glistened on the waves, creating a spectacular

Catherine wheel effect. It was as though the stars were falling out of the heavens and saying, 'Good luck, Maura Murphy.'

I suppose I was a bit gullible and naïve when I first married John. As a young woman, I never looked for the nasty side of a person and was prepared to accept people at face value. But like the plot of a good novel, events revealed themselves slowly. Life dealt me some hard blows and I was forced to look deeper into people's characters and motivations. Being with John Murphy taught me that.

I had fantasised for years about leaving him and having a life outside of being a wife and a mother. I craved independence and freedom. I just wanted to be me. I tried to leave John many times but Catholic marriages were sacrosanct. You made a commitment and took the oath 'Till death do us part'. I don't believe in that any more.

Postscript

My anger is dead and buried in the bogs of Offaly. John and I have remained friends, despite everything. I've written all the resentment out of my life.

Last year would have been our fiftieth wedding anniversary. We haven't lived together for five years but we talk on the phone every day. We are not divorced, merely separated by the Irish Sea. We seem to have a better relationship living two hundred miles apart!

Although we had a turbulent life together we still hold a great fondness for each other, even at this late age of our lives. John and I overcame poverty and worked our own salvation. We did it together, and we're still doing it – in our own way. We are mostly at peace with each other, although we still manage to find reasons to visit the museum of our marriage.

When I found out I had cancer, I thought here is the end of a worthless life. But I knew I wasn't ready to die. My inner strengths got me through. I am looking forward to my sixth cancer-free year. I feel there are plenty more days ahead.

Acknowledgements

Grateful thanks are offered to the many who made this book possible.

Deepest gratitude to Val Hudson, my UK publisher, to Jo Roberts-Miller, Georgina Moore, Barbara Ronan and the team at Headline UK, and to Ciara Considine, Breda Purdue and the team at Hodder Headline Ireland.

A special thank you goes to Jackie Dietrich and my daughter Joan Murphy for their hard work and continued support.

To my agent Mary Pachnos from Gillon Aitken Associates, I greatly appreciate your endeavours.

Also thank you to Mr Young and his medical team at St James's Hospital in Dublin; to Peter Acunda who sat with me and helped me to relax; to the nurses and the ancillary staff of John Houston and Robert Adams wards who showed me the utmost care and attention, their kindness and tolerance was unsurpassable. Thank you all for saving my life.

My heartfelt gratitude goes to Father Cribben of Rhode Parochial House who lifted my spirits with his prayers and humour.

Thanks also to my GP, Dr Hoffman, my Consultant, Mrs

Morrison of University Hospital Selly Oak, Birmingham, and all the other medical staff who continue to look after me. And a special thank you to Steph Roberts, my carer.

I would particularly like to acknowledge and pay tribute to my nine children who sat with me throughout my most critical moments, willing me on with kindness and loving care. They aren't just my children. They are my real friends.